Curbing the Court

What motivates political actors with diverging interests to respect the Supreme Court's authority? A popular answer is that the public serves as the guardian of judicial independence by punishing elected officials who undermine the justices. *Curbing the Court* challenges this claim, presenting a new theory of how people perceive the Supreme Court. Bartels and Johnston argue that, contrary to conventional wisdom, citizens are not principled defenders of the judiciary. Instead, they seek to limit the Court's power when it suits their political aims, and this inclination is heightened during times of sharp partisan polarization. Backed by a wealth of observational and experimental data, Bartels and Johnston push the conceptual, theoretical, and empirical boundaries of the study of public opinion of the courts. By connecting citizens to the strategic behavior of elites, this book offers fresh insights into the vulnerability of judicial institutions in an increasingly contentious era of American politics.

Brandon L. Bartels is Associate Professor of Political Science at George Washington University and a coeditor of *Making Law and Courts Research Relevant*, published by Routledge (2014). His research has appeared in journals such as the *American Political Science Review* and *American Journal of Political Science*.

Christopher D. Johnston is Associate Professor of Political Science at Duke University. He is a coauthor of *The Ambivalent Partisan: How Critical Loyalty Promotes Democracy*, published by Oxford University Press (2012), and *Open Versus Closed: Personality, Identity, and the Politics of Redistribution*, published by Cambridge University Press (2017), both of which won the David O. Sears Book Award.

Curbing the Court

Why the Public Constrains Judicial Independence

BRANDON L. BARTELS
George Washington University

CHRISTOPHER D. JOHNSTON
Duke University

CAMBRIDGE
UNIVERSITY PRESS

CAMBRIDGE
UNIVERSITY PRESS

University Printing House, Cambridge CB2 8BS, United Kingdom

One Liberty Plaza, 20th Floor, New York, NY 10006, USA

477 Williamstown Road, Port Melbourne, VIC 3207, Australia

314–321, 3rd Floor, Plot 3, Splendor Forum, Jasola District Centre, New Delhi – 110025, India

79 Anson Road, #06–04/06, Singapore 079906

Cambridge University Press is part of the University of Cambridge.

It furthers the University's mission by disseminating knowledge in the pursuit of education, learning, and research at the highest international levels of excellence.

www.cambridge.org
Information on this title: www.cambridge.org/9781107188419
DOI: 10.1017/9781316979754

First published 2020

Printed in the United Kingdom by TJ International Ltd. Padstow Cornwall

A catalogue record for this publication is available from the British Library.

Library of Congress Cataloging-in-Publication Data
NAMES: Bartels, Brandon L., 1975– author. | Johnston, Christopher D., author.
TITLE: Curbing the court : why the public constrains judicial independence / Brandon L. Bartels, George Washington University; Christopher D. Johnston, Duke University
DESCRIPTION: Cambridge, United Kingdom ; New York, NY, USA : Cambridge University Press, 2020. | Includes bibliographical references and index.
IDENTIFIERS: LCCN 2019058311 (print) | LCCN 2019058312 (ebook) | ISBN 9781107188419 (hardback) | ISBN 9781316979754 (ebook)
SUBJECTS: LCSH: Political questions and judicial power – United States. | Judicial independence – United States. | Justice, Administration of – United States – Citizen participation.
CLASSIFICATION: LCC KF5130 .B37 2020 (print) | LCC KF5130 (ebook) | DDC 347.73–dc23
LC record available at https://lccn.loc.gov/2019058311
LC ebook record available at https://lccn.loc.gov/2019058312

ISBN 978-1-107-18841-9 Hardback

BLB: For Nicole, Addison, and Bentley
CDJ: For Amy, Hannah, and Connor

Contents

Figures

Tables

Acknowledgments

This book is the culmination of a collaboration that began in 2007 at Stony Brook University, where Brandon was an assistant professor and Chris a PhD student. While those early conversations laid the foundation for the current project, our thinking about public support for the Supreme Court, and why it matters, has evolved quite a bit over the last decade. In the end, we knew that a book was the only way to accommodate the ideas and empirical results we had accumulated. We expected to be done much sooner (*said every other author we have ever talked to*), but we think the extra effort has made for a much better final product. Our first thanks, then, go to Cambridge University Press, and particularly Robert Dreesen, for being so patient and for giving us the latitude to "write the best book we possibly can." We have tried our best.

Research on the foundations of Supreme Court support seemed to expand greatly around the time we began collaborating. The community of scholars in this area has been very helpful to our project and pushed our work to new levels. We would like to give special thanks to Dino Christenson, James Gibson, David Glick, and Michael Nelson for stimulating ideas and feedback along the way. We presented our work at past conferences and received helpful feedback from Deborah Beim, Michael Nelson, Benjamin Woodson, and Michael Zilis. We have also received useful comments at seminars and workshops at George Washington University, MIT, University of Maryland, Indiana University, University of North Carolina, and the DC-Area American Politics Workshop. Three anonymous reviewers also provided helpful comments at early stages of the project. We would also like to thank Diana Mutz and the Time-Sharing Experiments for the Social Sciences for funding the 2009 TESS experiment (via NSF grant 0094964). All errors and omissions, of course, remain ours alone.

Bartels wishes to thank his colleagues at George Washington University who (perhaps even unbeknownst to some of those colleagues!) helped clarify his thinking about this book project (both substantively and logistically). These include Celeste Arrington, Sarah Binder, Eric Grynaviski, Danny Hayes, Eric Kramon, Eric Lawrence, John Sides, and Paul Wahlbeck. Bartels also gives a special thanks to Eric Kramon, a collaborator on multiple emerging projects, for helping him think about conceptualizations and theories about judicial power and independence within a broader comparative context. He also thanks George Washington University for research money that helped fund two of the studies reported in this book. Last but not least, Bartels is grateful to his extraordinary wife and partner, Nicole, and his two awesome kids, Addison and Bentley, for being great sources of support throughout the project and particularly for all the laughs, fun, and quality time together.

Johnston wishes to thank his colleagues at Duke who have provided support in various ways over the years and whose work inspires him to be a better scholar. A special thanks goes to Sunshine Hillygus, who coauthored an earlier paper related to this project, provided guidance at various stages of writing this book, and collaborated on the 2017 Qualtrics Panels study. A special thank you also goes to Rose Graves for data collection help in Chapter 3. Johnston is grateful for research funds provided by Duke that helped make this book possible. Most of all, Johnston would like to thank Amy, Hannah, and Connor for their love and support from the beginning of this project to the end, for their tolerance of extended deadlines and weekends at the office, and for being the best people he knows.

1

The Guardians of Judicial Independence

The US Supreme Court rules on some of the most important issues in American politics. Naturally, these decisions strike a nerve with many Americans. In the wake of the 2015 landmark ruling *Obergefell* v. *Hodges*, in which the Supreme Court ruled that the Constitution guarantees a right to marry for same-sex couples, Republican Governor Bobby Jindal of Louisiana argued that "The Supreme Court is completely out of control, making laws on their own .... If we want to save some money, let's just get rid of the Court."[1] Senate Majority Leader Mitch McConnell (R-KY) stated that the "American people, through the democratic process, should be able to determine the meaning of this bedrock institution [marriage] in our society."[2] And Republican Senator Ted Cruz of Texas, nearly the 2016 Republican nominee for president, proposed constitutional amendments to overturn federal court rulings legalizing gay marriage and to strip the federal courts of their ability to hear same-sex marriage cases.[3]

Citizens United v. *FEC* has engendered the same level of vitriol from Democrats and liberals. In this 2010 case, the Court ruled that corporations

1 Hensch, Mark (June 26, 2015). "Jindal: 'Let's just get rid of the Court.'" *The Hill*. https://thehill.com/blogs/ballot-box/presidential-races/246301-jindal-lets-just-get-rid-of-the-court.

2 Mitch McConnell Senate Website (June 26, 2015). "McConnell on the Supreme Court's Marriage Ruling." www.mcconnell.senate.gov/public/index.cfm/pressreleases?ID=2A454FAD-3CEE-41BD-A824-87BA6C64805F.

3 Senator Cruz proposed these amendments before the Supreme Court's landmark *Obergefell* ruling but after several Courts of Appeals had ruled that the Constitution guarantees the right to marry by same-sex couples. Senator Cruz perhaps saw the writing on the wall that the US Supreme Court would follow suit.

have constitutional free speech rights to spend unlimited amounts of money in elections to help candidates win.[4] Senator Russ Feingold of Wisconsin did not mince words in describing it as "one of the most lawless decisions in the history of the country" that will "set a dangerous new precedent for our democracy."[5] Democratic senator and 2016 presidential hopeful Bernie Sanders stated that he would "not nominate any man or woman to the Supreme Court unless that individual is loud and clear in saying he or she will vote to overturn *Citizens United* and do that as quickly as possible."[6] Former senator, secretary of state, and 2016 Democratic nominee for president Hillary Clinton also called for a litmus test on choosing a nominee who would overturn the ruling and pledged to "fight for a constitutional amendment that overturns it."[7] And former president Barack Obama, in an unprecedented move, criticized the Court's ruling in his 2010 State of the Union speech while five out of the nine justices sat in the front row. "With all due deference to separation of powers, last week the Supreme Court reversed a century of law that I believe will open the floodgates for special interests .... And I urge Democrats and Republicans to pass a bill that helps to correct some of these problems."[8] Senate Democrats eventually proposed a constitutional amendment to overturn the ruling.

In both cases, politicians are discussing measures to subvert the Court's authority, often accompanied by harshly critical language that calls the legitimacy of the Court's decision-making into question. Importantly, however, politicians in these examples are motivated primarily by *policy*

[4] The ruling also applied to unions, but liberals are most upset with the aspect of the ruling related to corporations.

[5] Prupis, Nadia (February 22, 2011). "Russ Feingold's PAC, Progressives United, working for campaign reform." *Truthout*. https://truthout.org/articles/russ-feingolds-pac-progressives-united-working-for-campaign-reform-2/.

[6] Sutherland, Paige (December 4, 2015). "If elected, here's how Bernie Sanders would choose his Supreme Court nominees." *New Hampshire Public Radio*. www.nhpr.org/post/if-elected-heres-how-bernie-sanders-would-choose-his-supreme-court-nominees#stream/0.

[7] Levinthal, Dave (April 7, 2016). "How 'Citizens United' is helping Hillary Clinton's White House bid." *NBC News*. www.nbcnews.com/news/us-news/how-citizens-united-helping-clinton-win-white-house-551226.

[8] CNN State of the Union Coverage (January 28, 2010). "Transcript: Obama's first State of the Union speech." *CNN Politics*. www.cnn.com/2010/POLITICS/01/27/sotu.transcript/index.html. Also notable in this event was the response by Justice Alito, who was among the justices present at the address. In response to President Obama's remarks, Justice Alito shook his head and appeared to say, "Not true."Kady II, Martin (January 27, 2010). "Justice Alito mouths 'not true.'" *Politico Now Blog*. www.politico.com/blogs/politico-now/2010/01/justice-alito-mouths-not-true-024608.

disagreement with the Court's decisions. These are not principled objections to the Court's institutional role in American politics or style of decision-making as a general matter. Rather, such attacks on the Court emerge in response to rulings that conflict with preferences over policy or narrow partisan and electoral interests. Indeed, note how these same politicians react when they *agree* with a Supreme Court ruling. In a one-eighty from his *Obergefell* criticism, Governor Bobby Jindal praised the Court's *Citizens United* ruling, saying that "any kind of attempts to limit our First Amendment speech rights doesn't work and isn't effective."[9] Claiming that "some in this country have been deprived of full participation in the political process," Senator Mitch McConnell argued that in the ruling "the Supreme Court took an important step in the direction of restoring the First Amendment rights of these groups by ruling that the Constitution protects their right to express themselves about political candidates and issues up until Election Day."[10] Senator Ted Cruz has both praised the ruling and heavily criticized Democrats for proposing amendments to overturn *Citizens United* and "repeal the free speech protections of the First Amendment."[11]

We see a similar about-face in reactions toward the Court among Democrats in light of pleasing decisions. In praise of the Court's *Obergefell* ruling, Senator Sanders stated, "Today the Supreme Court fulfilled the words engraved upon its building: 'Equal justice under law.'"[12] Secretary Clinton followed suit, arguing that the "U.S. Supreme Court's ruling on marriage equality represents America at its best: just, fair and moving toward equality."[13] Like his fellow Democrats, President Obama invoked values of equality, stating that "the Supreme Court recognized that the Constitution guarantees marriage equality. In doing so, they've reaffirmed that all Americans are entitled to the equal protection of the law."[14]

[9] Ta, Linh (October 12, 2015). "Jindal: I support Citizens United ruling." *Des Moines Register*. www.desmoinesregister.com/story/news/elections/presidential/candidates/2015/10/12/jindal-support-citizens-united-ruling/73840666/.

[10] Politico Staff (January 21, 2010). "Pols weigh in on Citizens United decision." *Politico*. www.politico.com/story/2010/01/pols-weigh-in-on-citizens-united-decision-031798.

[11] Ted Cruz Senate Website (accessed March 31, 2018). "United Liberty: Ted Cruz blasts Senate Democrats for trying to repeal the free speech protections of the First Amendment." www.cruz.senate.gov/?p=news&id=1351.

[12] Bernie Sanders Twitter Page. https://twitter.com/sensanders/status/614439399238057984.

[13] Hillary Clinton for President Twitter Page. https://twitter.com/ImwithHer2016/status/747052188715868160.

[14] Washington Post Staff (June 26, 2015). "Transcript: Obama's remarks on Supreme Court ruling on same-sex marriage." *Washington Post*. www.washingtonpost.com/news/post-nat

These examples seem to suggest that the *process* by which a ruling is reached matters little to attitudes toward the Court. Rather, concerns about the justices being politically or ideologically motivated (e.g., "activist" or ignoring precedent) are not consistently applied across decisions. Such concerns seem to (conveniently) arise in cases where decisions are disagreeable, and then only as a way of justifying attacks on the Court. As Peter Irons explains, "Cynics, including myself, know that a so-called judicial activist is any judge or justice who votes to strike down a law we support, or uphold one we oppose."[15] *Citizens United* and *Obergefell* were arguably similar in terms of the degree to which they were decided in a political or ideological manner, but politicians only emphasize these characteristics of rulings when they disagree with them. When they agree with a ruling, they invoke positive procedural aspects, such as the Court properly interpreting the Constitution and adhering to precedent, and core American values of fairness, justice, and equality. It seems that policy agreement with the Court is the key driver of attacks on the Court's authority. Procedural aspects of a decision enter only as a way of *rationalizing* ideologically driven assessments.

In these examples, politicians are reacting to single disliked decisions and mostly call for measures to limit the Court's power within a narrow issue area, for example, through a constitutional amendment that would overturn the decision. Sometimes, however, the Court threatens partisan and ideological interests in a more general and enduring way. In such cases, partisan actors may seek to reduce the Court's independence in an equally enduring fashion. The most famous example occurred during President Franklin D. Roosevelt's second term in office. The Supreme Court had recently struck down several pieces of legislation in the president's New Deal program and seemed, as a general matter, hostile to the emerging liberalism of the Democratic Party. In response, the president proposed a bill that would add a justice to the Court for every sitting justice who failed to retire at the age of seventy – thus, its historical legacy as FDR's "Court-packing plan."

We need only look to the last few years to find similar examples of broad attacks on the Court's institutional integrity and independence from partisan politics. In February 2016, Justice Antonin Scalia passed away unexpectedly, giving President Obama the opportunity to create the first liberal majority on

ion/wp/2015/06/26/transcript-obamas-remarks-on-supreme-court-ruling-on-same-sex-marriage/?utm_term=.09e075902cf9.

[15] Irons, Peter (February 4, 2019). "Has the Supreme Court lost its legitimacy?" *NBC News*. www.nbcnews.com/think/opinion/has-supreme-court-lost-its-legitimacy-ncna966211.

the Supreme Court since the Warren era of the 1960s. Just an hour after Justice Scalia's death was announced, Republican Majority Leader Mitch McConnell vowed to block any Obama nomination until after the 2016 presidential election, arguing that Americans should have a say in who fills the empty seat.[16] In spite of this, President Obama nominated Judge Merrick Garland to fill Scalia's seat. Norms against politicizing the Supreme Court suggest that Garland would be given a fair hearing in the Senate and a timely vote, but his qualifications, experience, and purported penchant for moderation were not enough to offset Senate Republicans' determination to prevent a liberal, Democratic majority on the Court. In the end, McConnell's gamble paid off handsomely for conservative interests: Donald Trump won the presidency, and the Republican-controlled Senate confirmed a reliable conservative in Neil Gorsuch in April 2017.

As if such drama and conflict were not enough, Justice Anthony Kennedy retired in 2018, leaving another seat to be filled by President Trump and a Republican Senate. Like the Garland saga, the ideological stakes could not have been higher, but this time President Trump, via his nomination of Judge Brett Kavanaugh, would have a chance to create the first reliable *conservative majority* on the Court in the modern era. Justice Kennedy, a center-right justice during his career, had been a crucial swing vote who frequently bolstered liberal interests, especially on hot-button culture war issues like gay rights in which he authored the majority opinion in *Obergefell* v. *Hodges* legalizing same-sex marriage in every state. Democrats, in turn, tried to use McConnell's 2016 reasoning to argue for a hiatus on determining Justice Kennedy's replacement until after the 2018 midterms: Americans should have a say in the composition of the Senate that ultimately confirms the next justice. Republicans, in control of the Senate, rejected such delay tactics as inappropriate, and the ultimate appointment of Kavanaugh – after perhaps the most contentious nomination battle in memory – now leaves the Court poised to move legal policy in the conservative direction for the foreseeable future. Indeed, there is worry on the left that abortion rights – and other issues important to liberal causes – are directly threatened by Kavanaugh's replacement of Kennedy.[17]

[16] Everett, Burgess, and Glenn Thrush (February 13, 2016). "McConnell throws down the gauntlet: No Scalia replacement under Obama." *Politico*. www.politico.com/story/2016/02/mitch-mcconnell-antonin-scalia-supreme-court-nomination-219248.

[17] However, Kavanaugh's appointment also permits the possibility that Chief Justice John Roberts may assume a "swing vote" role, akin to that of Kennedy, in order to moderate the Court (e.g., Mark and Zilis 2018).

In response to this process, prominent liberal commentators have publicly called for attacks on the Court's institutional integrity to mitigate the expected consequences of a conservative majority on the Court. Major left-leaning media outlets have published editorials supporting fundamental institutional changes to the Court – such as Court-packing and ending life tenure – that would have the effect of diluting the power of the sitting conservative justices and redirecting the long-term ideological path of the Court.[18] For example, writing in the context of the heated Kavanaugh hearings, liberal commentator David Leonhardt endorsed a constitutional amendment that would limit justices' terms to eighteen years and give each four-year presidential term two guaranteed appointments to the Court.[19] Leonhardt argues that the current system is too contentious and heated and "does not respect the will of the people" but that his favored proposal would make the Court "more consistent with democratic principles."[20] Like attacks on single decisions, calls for fundamental institutional changes seem to arise primarily in response to (long-term) policy disagreement with the Court, but they are *rationalized* in terms of widely accepted democratic values.

Thus, for both the left and the right, actions that threaten the Court's power have become fair game. It is not our place to evaluate each proposal for its desirability – perhaps there are changes in this vein that would indeed improve the functioning of the American government and move us closer to our shared ideals. We take no positions on these normative issues. But our book's theory and empirical findings – focusing on when and why the public supports such attacks on the Court – have important implications for the extent of the Court's legitimacy and ultimately its independence and power in the political system. In this sense, our work can inform debates over possible changes to the Court and its role in American politics.

[18] For links and useful discussions of these proposals, see Matthews, Dylan (October 5, 2018). "Court-packing, Democrats' nuclear option for the Supreme Court, explained." *Vox*. www.vox.com/2018/7/2/17513520/court-packing-explained-fdr-roosevelt-new-deal-democrats-supreme-court; Segall, Eric (December 4, 2018). "Yes, it's time to reform the Supreme Court – but not for the wrong reasons." *Salon*. www.salon.com/2018/12/04/its-time-to-reform-the-supreme-court-but-not-for-the-wrong-reasons/.

[19] Leonhardt, David (September 18, 2018). "The Supreme Court needs term limits." *The New York Times*. www.nytimes.com/2018/09/18/opinion/columnists/brett-kavanaugh-supreme-court-term-limits.html.

[20] And indeed, this proposal would likely bind the Court's decision-making more tightly to the ebbs and flows of public opinion (McGuire and Stimson 2004; Stimson, Mackuen, and Erikson 1995).

CURBING THE COURT

In the examples of the last several pages, politicians are talking about *curbing the Court*: reducing its power and independence in the US system of government and attacking its authority to render final judgments on law and constitutional meaning. We adapt Staton's (2010, 8–9) conceptualization of *independence* and *power* and the subtle distinction between them (see also Hall 2011; Nagel 1975). Judicial independence means that a court can rule free from coercion by other political actors – the decision reached reflects its sincere policy preferences. Judicial power means that a court "can cause by its actions the outcome that it prefers" (Staton 2010, 9). That is, a causal relationship exists between a court's sincere policy preferences and the policy that it ultimately obtains. Independence and power mean that the Court does what it wants and gets what it wants, respectively, even when other important actors have conflicting preferences. For courts in democratic systems, we can thus distinguish between the ruling and implementation stages of policymaking. At the ruling stage, a court that is free from external political influence (i.e., independent) decides the case according to its sincere preferences. But while independence is a necessary condition for judicial power – to get what it wants a court must rule how it wants – it is not a sufficient condition. Power is only realized when a court *induces compliance* and the decision is followed as the court prefers (e.g., Hall 2011; Staton 2010). A powerful Court is both "autonomous and it is obeyed" (Staton 2010, 9).

Public support for Court-curbing forms the core outcome of interest throughout our book. We think of curbing actions as falling into one of two categories.[21] *Narrowly targeted* (or *narrow*) Court-curbing seeks to mitigate the consequences of a small number of (perhaps only one) disliked decisions within a circumscribed issue area – marriage or campaign finance, for example. This includes the types of actions highlighted in the first few pages of this chapter, such as reducing a ruling's impact through legislative means, imposing "litmus tests" on the issue for new nominees, overturning the ruling through a constitutional amendment, failing to comply with the ruling's prescriptions, or removing the Court's jurisdiction in the specific policy area. *Broadly targeted* (or *broad*) Court-curbing, by contrast, seeks to alter the institution in a more enduring way. This

[21] Court-curbing also has a rich history of inquiry in the institutions and judicial decision-making literature, particularly related to conflicts between Congress and the Court (e.g., Clark 2011; Murphy 1962; Nagel 1965; Pritchett 1961; Rogers 2001; Rosenberg 1992; Stumpf 1965). The discussions in that literature connect to the Court's legitimacy as well.

includes the kinds of proposals discussed in the previous section, such as sharply restricting the tenure of justices, making it easier to overturn rulings through the imposition of congressional or public veto points, or removing the Court's power of judicial review altogether.

Court-curbing is a clear, direct threat to judicial power as it reduces the ability of the justices to get the policies they want, for example, by removing judicial review or overturning or refusing to comply with a ruling. Consistent with formal work in political science (e.g., Carrubba and Zorn 2010; Vanberg 2001), we argue that Court-curbing is also an *indirect* threat to judicial power through its effect on judicial independence. This is because threats of Court-curbing alter the behavior of strategic justices who wish to avoid confrontations with other branches and with the public. That is, the Court may choose a policy other than its sincere preference – say, one closer to the legislature's ideal point – to ensure compliance, avoid legislative overrides, or to defuse an attack on its broader powers.[22] In this way, judicial constraint is often unseen because it manifests as a reduction in autonomy rather than a reduction in formal powers. This can lead to erroneous perceptions of the Court's independence and power; while the justices rule and those rulings are obeyed, their decisions are at least partly endogenous to the preferences of other actors.

Given this conceptual framework, public support for both forms of Court-curbing implies low support for judicial power and independence. It indicates a preference for making the Court more accountable to the preferences of the public and elected officials, whereas opposition to curbing implies a preference for a robust, independent role for the Court as a powerful policymaker whose rulings should be faithfully implemented. Throughout the book, we will use both terms – *judicial power* and *independence* – with the aforementioned definitions in mind.

Both broad and narrow Court-curbing also have important implications for our understanding of the Supreme Court's *institutional legitimacy*, which we define as perceived rightful authority to render rulings for the nation (see Caldeira and Gibson 1992; Gibson and Nelson 2014; Tyler 2006a) and a belief that the Court is "appropriate, proper, and just" (Tyler 2006a, 375). Legitimacy implies principled (sometimes called "diffuse") support for the Court, as opposed to instrumental support in which

[22] Some have argued that Chief Justice John Roberts did just this when he "flipped" his position on the Affordable Care Act in *National Federation of Independent Business* v. *Sebelius*.

judicial power is simply a means to a policy or partisan end. We discuss these implications in greater detail in this chapter and throughout the book. At this point, we make it clear that we treat "support for Court-curbing" and "institutional legitimacy" as related, but distinct, concepts.

THE RECEIVED WISDOM

How are politicians, journalists, and activists able to get away with shattering norms involving the judiciary and attacking the Court's power? How, for example, was Mitch McConnell able to successfully block the legitimate nomination of a Supreme Court justice in 2016? How are calls for Court-packing now acceptable lines of discussion in mainstream political outlets?

All of this is surprising considering prominent theories in political science and the legal academy. Indeed, a conventional wisdom argues that citizens are guardians of judicial independence: elites who are dependent on public support refrain from curbing the Court because they fear reprisal from their constituents (e.g., Carrubba 2009; Friedman 2009; Nelson and Uribe-McGuire 2017; Staton 2010; Stephenson 2004; Vanberg 2005). This strong public support for the Court is thought to be rooted in core democratic values (e.g., Gibson 2007; Gibson and Nelson 2015b), perceptions of procedural fairness (e.g., Tyler and Rasinski 1991), and long-term socialization to the deliberative, principled, and symbolic aspects of the Court (e.g., Gibson and Caldeira 2009a, 2011; Gibson, Lodge, and Woodson 2014). Citizens are willing to punish elite actors for attacks on the Court – even favored ones, such as co-partisans – because they care about the institution for its own sake, not simply for the policies it produces. In this way, the public serves as a key veto point or "pivotal player" (Krehbiel 1998; Tsebelis 2002) that makes Court-curbing a costly endeavor. So long as elected politicians are aware of the public's orientation toward the Court, they will resist pushing too hard to implement curbing measures.

We think an emerging literature on public support for Court-curbing – as well as casual observation – calls the received wisdom into question. The purpose of this book is to present an alternative view. We argue that citizens are willing to curb the Court in response to discontent with its decision-making. In our view, citizens are often an important force *constraining* the discretion of the Court and binding it more closely to the majoritarian institutions of American political life. We argue that this is especially true in times of high partisan polarization at both the elite and mass levels (e.g., Armaly 2018; Clark and Kastellec 2015). While some (e.g., Gibson 2007) have argued that the Court has escaped the problems seen in other institutions due to polarization (e.g., Congress, see Hetherington and Rudolph 2015), we believe there are both theoretical and empirical reasons to think otherwise – that intense partisanship directly threatens the power of the Court relative to other actors in the political system.

We will develop our claims in greater depth throughout the book. In the remainder of this chapter, we expand our summary of the received wisdom on public opinion and judicial independence. We then summarize our own contributions and provide an outline of what is to come. Finally, we provide a brief discussion of what is at stake in this debate.

The Electoral Connection and Judicial Independence

It is often claimed that the Court is weak relative to the executive and legislative branches of American government. While Article III of the Constitution vests the broad "judicial power of the United States" in the US Supreme Court, it does not confer specific powers to the Court like Articles I and II do for the other branches. Even if one subscribes to the scholarly view that the Court's power of judicial review is implied in Article III (e.g., Friedman 2005; Kramer 2004; Treanor 2005),[23] the Constitution does not specify parameters for using or enforcing that power.

Moreover, the debate over implied powers masks the more important question of whether the Supreme Court's rulings vis-à-vis the invocation of judicial review are afforded *judicial supremacy* – authority as the final and binding word on constitutional meaning for everyone in the country (see Friedman 1998, 2005). And that logic applies to the Court's other rulings as well, including statutory interpretation. Indeed, the Supreme Court faces a rather unique situation as it seeks to make policy. In *Federalist 78*, Hamilton famously argued that the judiciary is the "least dangerous" branch. While the Court has the power to pass judgment on the law and the Constitution, it has only weak powers of *enforcement* –

[23] This argument by legal scholars largely supplants a more traditional story that Chief Justice John Marshall, in the Court's famous *Marbury* v. *Madison* (1803) ruling, "created" judicial review (e.g., Friedman 2005). After all, seven years prior to *Marbury*, the Court, in *Hylton* v. *U.S.* (1796), employed judicial review to uphold a federal law. *Marbury* was the first case in which the Court struck down a federal law as unconstitutional.

neither the "purse" nor the "sword" as the saying goes. In practice, this means that the justices rely on other actors in the legislative and executive branches to respect and implement their decisions.

The efficacy of the Court thus rests on the willingness of political actors to affirm, abide, and enforce decisions that may conflict with their own interests, and it relies on their hesitance to use their own powers to coerce the Court into agreement via threats to its institutional integrity. In the absence of such compliance and forbearance, the Court may strategically alter its decision-making to avoid overt conflict – it will back down and live to fight another day (Carrubba 2009; Carrubba and Zorn 2010; Choper 1980; Clark 2009, 2011; Epstein and Knight 1998; Epstein, Knight, and Martin 2001; Rosenberg 1992; Staton 2010; Stephenson 2004; Vanberg 2005; see also Segal, Westerland, and Lindquist 2011). In this sense, the mere possibility of Court-curbing truncates the Court's feasible decision space. The Court anticipates possible responses from other political actors and adjusts its own behavior accordingly to achieve an outcome that balances concerns with independence, policy outcomes, and institutional integrity.

If the Court is so weak when it comes to enforcement and so vulnerable to attacks, why would political actors with much to gain from subverting Court decisions respect judicial supremacy? In fact, historically speaking, judicial supremacy was *not* embraced during early America, but subscription to it increased throughout the nineteenth and twentieth centuries (Friedman 1998, 2005; Friedman and Delaney 2011; Kramer 2001, 2004; Whittington 2007). History contains illuminating examples surrounding the ebb and flow of the Court's power in the political system. Some argue that Chief Justice Marshall sought to establish judicial supremacy in *Marbury*, but it was not widely embraced in those early years of the new constitutional order. In fact, Chief Justice Marshall arguably strategically retreated from his preferred outcome (granting commissions to the "midnight judges") because he anticipated noncompliance from President Jefferson. There is also President Jackson's famous quip in response to the Court's 1832 *Worcester* v. *Georgia* ruling that gave Native Americans a semblance of sovereignty in their interactions with state and federal government: "John Marshall has made his decision; now let him enforce it." The Court's infamous *Dred Scott* decision, which ruled that slaves were not US citizens and the federal government could not regulate slavery in the new territories, arguably led to the Civil War due to the ruling's activation of antislavery forces. And, of course, the Court's ruling in *Brown* v. *Board of Education*, which ruled that the "separate but equal" doctrine of racial segregation was inherently unequal, met fierce resistance in the Southern states even after the Court announced its most full-throated assertion of judicial supremacy in *Cooper* v. *Aaron* (1958). Thus, respect for judicial supremacy is not guaranteed even in the United States.

Yet many argue that the twentieth century is generally characterized by widespread subscription to the principle (e.g., Friedman 2009; Kramer 2001, 2004). How is it that the Court sidesteps the implementation problem (to the extent that it does)? One explanation is the electoral connection. In this view, if the *public* affords the Supreme Court a high level of legitimacy – again, "rightful authority" to render final rulings for the polity – then political actors in the elected branches will hesitate to directly attack the Court because they fear reprisals at the voting booth (Friedman 2009; Nelson and Uribe-McGuire 2017; Stephenson 2004; Vanberg 2001, 2005). Put another way, citizens who see the Court as a legitimate institution will support the Court for its own sake – they will pursue preservation of the Court's power as an end in itself. In this sense, though the Court's power is not fully codified, it emerges because of widespread perceptions of legitimacy in the public and, in turn, the strategic behavior of elected officials. This presents the Supreme Court with a dilemma that other institutions do not face (or face to a lesser degree). Because its power and authority are not codified into law, its efficacy is intimately tied to whether the American people believe that it is appropriate and justified for the Court to maintain this authority.

Public Support for the Supreme Court

Theories of judicial independence and power thus place citizens front and center. Accordingly, there is a long-standing literature which seeks to document the public's "institutional loyalty" or "diffuse support" for the Supreme Court (e.g., Bartels and Johnston 2013; Caldeira and Gibson 1992; Casey 1974; Gibson and Caldeira 2009a; Mondak 1994). To what extent do citizens see the Court as special, unique, and worthy of defense in the face of brazen political attacks, even when – *especially when* – they disagree with its decisions? A robust conventional wisdom exists that the Supreme Court enjoys an exceptional degree of institutional support that is largely unaffected by partisan concerns and polarization. For example, Gibson and Nelson (2015b, 173) argue that the legitimacy of the Supreme Court is not much dependent upon the Court making decisions that are pleasing to the American people. Nor is the Court's legitimacy connected to the ideological and partisan cross-currents that so wrack contemporary American politics. Whether desirable or undesirable, it seems that the current Court has a sufficiently deep reservoir of goodwill that allows it to rise above the contemporary divisions in the American polity.

The conventional wisdom on public support is strong enough that some have argued the Court has *too much* legitimacy and thus too much power to render final judgments on constitutional meaning. Take arguments for "popular constitutionalism." This line of thought challenges judicial supremacy and seeks a stronger popular role in decisions about constitutional meaning (Kramer 2001, 2004; Tushnet 1999). According to Kramer (2001), our country's founding was premised on "the people" having the final say on constitutional meaning, but they – along with the elected branches – gradually delegated this authority to the Court via an organic process of "political supports" that emerged as the norm of judicial supremacy in the twentieth century (e.g., Friedman 1998, 2005, 2009; Kramer 2001, 2004; Whittington 2007). Gibson and Nelson (2015a) also explore the possibility that the Court has too much legitimacy in the public and examine the implications of seeking greater democratic accountability. In the popular media, Matthew Yglesias argues that delegitimization of the Court in the wake of the Kavanaugh hearings would be a desirable outcome.[24] Indeed, he argues for more democratic accountability in constitutional interpretation and a rediscovery of popular constitutionalism. These and similar arguments take as a starting premise the received wisdom that the Court has exceptionally strong levels of institutional loyalty in the mass public.

Strong public loyalty to the Court is thought to be rooted in perceptions that the Court makes decisions in a fair and just manner and that it is fulfilling its unique role as the primary institution defending the Constitution and the rule of law (Gibson and Caldeira 2009a; Tyler and Rasinski 1991). In this view, citizens withdraw their support from the Court only if they see its decision-making as corrupted by politics and partisan interests (see Gibson and Caldeira 2009a, 2011). The Court should be "above the political fray" and deserves deference so long as it faithfully executes its role as a dispassionate interpreter of the Constitution. Former

[24] Yglesias, Matthew (October 5, 2018). "Brett Kavanaugh's confirmation will delegitimize the Supreme Court – and that's good." *Vox*. www.vox.com/2018/10/5/17941312/brett-kavanaugh-supreme-court-legitimacy.

New Jersey Supreme Court judge Peter G. Verniero, in his response to President Obama's State of the Union remarks on *Citizens United*, typifies this idea: "The court's legitimacy is derived from the persuasiveness of its opinions and the expectation that those opinions are rendered free of partisan, political influences. The more that individual justices are drawn into public debates, the more the court as an institution will be seen in political terms, which was not the intent of the founders."[25] Since the foundations of loyalty, in this view, revolve around perceptions of the *way* in which the Court makes its decisions – rather than the ultimate *outcome* of those decisions – we refer to this as the *process-based* approach to understanding support for Court-curbing.

There are three related strands of the process-based view. The first, rooted in procedural justice theory (Tyler 1994, 2006a, 2006b; Tyler and Rasinski 1991), argues that Supreme Court legitimacy is dependent on perceptions that the Court makes its decisions in a fair and just manner based on legalistic principles (e.g., Farganis 2012; Nicholson and Howard 2003; Ramirez 2008; Tyler and Rasinski 1991). Conversely, perceptions that the Court is too mixed up in politics or that it favors some groups rather than others lead to a withdrawal of support and a willingness to consider major institutional changes.

The second argues that the foundation of the Court's power is the widespread affirmation within the mass public of the rule of law and other democratic values, including liberty, support for minority rights, and political tolerance (Caldeira and Gibson 1992; Gibson and Nelson 2014, 2015b). The Court is the primary "minoritarian institution" in American government and citizens are socialized early on to respect the unique role it plays in "checking" the elected branches and facilitating rule-of-law maintenance in the political system. In this view, support for Court-curbing is found primarily among the small minority of citizens who reject these core values as guiding principles for American politics. Among those who affirm these values – which is the clear majority – even politically inconvenient rulings are legitimate because they reflect the Court's role as protector of the rule of law and democratic rights.

The third perspective, labeled "positivity theory" (Gibson and Caldeira 2009a), argues that institutional loyalty is fostered by exposure to the Court's legitimizing symbols and other positive elements that emanate

[25] Liptak, Adam (January 28, 2010). "Supreme Court gets a rare rebuke, in front of a nation." *The New York Times*. www.nytimes.com/2010/01/29/us/politics/29scotus.html.

from the Court's unique style of doing business. In this view, the "sausage-making process" of judicial decision-making is largely hidden from the public eye (see Hibbing and Theiss-Morse 1995, 2002). Instead, what the public sees is a carefully curated image full of legalistic elements that serve to differentiate the Court from the more overtly political branches, such as judicial robes, the scales of justice, and the use of legal jargon justifying decisions (e.g., Gibson, Lodge, and Woodson 2014). Thus, even in the context of disagreeable decisions, citizens are exposed to symbols that counteract negative feelings about the outcome of the case and promote deference to and respect for the institution and its rulings. This mechanism serves as a foundation for the "to know the Court is to love it" effect (e.g., Casey 1974; Gibson and Caldeira 2009a, 2009c; Gibson, Caldeira, and Baird 1998). As we will discuss further in Chapter 2, these three "flavors" of the process-based approach are complementary, rather than competing, theories.

In sum, the Supreme Court's independence and efficacy derive in part from the willingness of average citizens to defend the Court from attacks by the elected branches, even when doing so implies forgone policy and partisan benefits. The received wisdom is that the Supreme Court indeed possesses a high degree of legitimacy in the public mind, because people see the Court as properly executing a unique and important role in American government. At a macro level, this suggests that Court-curbing is typically outside the feasible space of policy options for elected officials. Put another way, the public serves as a "veto player" (a la Tsebelis 2002) or "pivot" (a la Krehbiel 1998) in the context of strategic interactions among the branches of American government. The public remains loyal to the Court in the face of disagreeable decisions, their elected representatives are held in check, and the Court's authority is robust and consistently maintained.

CHALLENGES TO THE PROCESS-BASED APPROACH

We began this chapter with several anecdotes that seem to challenge the received wisdom. Here are elected officials aggressively attacking the Court's decisions and, in some cases, even threatening the Court's long-term institutional integrity. Savvy politicians use rhetoric they believe will be welcomed and endorsed by their respective bases. But are those perceptions accurate? Do *ordinary Americans* really support or oppose curbing the Court based on whether they agree or disagree with its rulings and ideological direction? Moving beyond anecdote, recent research suggests that the Court is less protected by public opinion than the received wisdom suggests. Indeed, citizens show increased support for Court-curbing in the face of decision outcomes that conflict with their policy wishes. We consider this emerging literature to fall within a broad *policy-based* approach to understanding Court-curbing: what citizens really care about is the *outcome* of the decision – that is, whether the ruling furthers their political goals. Procedural aspects and core democratic values, by contrast, are largely an afterthought.

In *The Limits of Judicial Independence*, Tom Clark (2011) demonstrates that Court-curbing legislation aimed at subverting the Court's power is introduced in Congress with surprising frequency – by his count, nearly 900 distinct proposals from Reconstruction through 2008. About two-thirds of these proposals are statutes and about one-third are Constitutional amendments, and they include (among other things) attempts to limit tenure on the Court, jurisdiction stripping, and removing judicial review entirely. Clark argues that the introduction of Court-curbing proposals in Congress is primarily a position-taking endeavor in that representatives do not typically view their proposals as likely to be enacted. Nonetheless, Court-curbing proposals may serve two important functions.

First, they serve as a signal that representatives are fighting back on issues of concern to their constituency. The introduction of (say) a bill to strip the Court's jurisdiction on marriage cases is a costly signal of commitment to the conservative position on this issue. Yet the very fact that representatives use this tactic to drum up support suggests that Court-curbing is welcomed by average citizens when they disagree with a decision – exactly opposite to what the received wisdom suggests. Indeed, Clark argues that the second function of Court-curbing proposals is that they serve as a credible signal to the *Court* that its decision-making is out of step with public opinion. In Clark's model, the Court monitors the volume of such proposals in Congress and adjusts its decision-making when the "chatter" gets sufficiently loud. In this way, the Court preserves its institutional integrity by bending to the public will at least some of the time (see also Choper 1980). This of course implies that the Court has less independence from majoritarian institutions than would be the case if the public cared only about process. Clark demonstrates as much in the empirical side of his work where he shows that the introduction of Court-curbing legislation tracks public mood and confidence in the Court and that the Court's decision-making responds to shifts in the introduction of Court-curbing legislation. As an anonymous justice remarked in an interview (Clark 2011, 236), "We know if there is a lot of public interest. We have to be careful not to reach too far."

While important, this work does not directly demonstrate that the public responds to disliked decisions with support for Court-curbing. Recent work in the public opinion literature has begun to fill this gap. Hetherington and Smith (2007) highlighted meaningful ideological divides in general Supreme Court evaluations, but they attributed most of those divisions – liberals being more supportive of the Court than conservatives – to retrospective evaluations tied to the liberal Warren Court legacy; only the most aware and motivated citizens perceived the right turn made by the Court since that period. Subsequent work, however, has highlighted the role of left–right divisions in response to contemporaneous judicial policymaking.

In an earlier study, we showed that perceived ideological distance from the Court ("subjective ideological disagreement") is associated with lower institutional loyalty in the mass public (Bartels and Johnston 2013). Previous work had found null effects of policy or ideological preferences on diffuse support and legitimacy, but those works did not operationalize preferences in relation to the Court's policymaking (e.g., Caldeira and Gibson 1992; Gibson 2007; Gibson, Caldeira, and Spence 2003b). Capturing policy or ideological disagreement entails assessing an individual's preference in relation to the Court's policy signal – either one's perception of the Court's general ideological tenor or the direction of a specific ruling. Using an experimental design, we also demonstrate that exposure to a single disliked decision reduces citizens' support for the Court. The various strains of the process-based approach suggest that citizens will resist attacks on the Court even when they see it as producing uncongenial policy outcomes, but our work suggests substantial public responsiveness rooted in policy disagreement.

And other recent research concurs (though see Malhotra and Jessee 2014 for a conflicting perspective). Christenson and Glick (2015a), for example, demonstrate that institutional loyalty fell among citizens opposed to the Court's blockbuster ruling on the Affordable Care Act. Nicholson and Hansford (2014) find that the public's willingness to accept a Court decision is conditional on both their own partisanship and the perceived partisanship of the Court's majority carrying the ruling. Sen (2017) reports that citizens care primarily about partisanship when considering nominees to the bench. Zilis (2018) finds that dislike toward groups benefiting from a Supreme Court ruling, as well as general ideological disagreement with the Court, negatively influences the Court's legitimacy. Additional work by Zilis (2015) shows a limited capacity for the Court to legitimize its rulings with the public (see also Franklin and Kosaki 1989; Marshall 2008, 1989; Clawson, Kegler, and Waltenburg 2003; Woodson 2019).[26] And Mondak (1994) anticipated this literature over twenty years ago in work demonstrating that public acceptance of decisions ("policy legitimacy") flows, to a substantial extent, from agreement with the decision outcome.

AN ALTERNATIVE FRAMEWORK

The upshot is that there is reason to question the received, process-based wisdom. At the same time, there are at least three reasons to consider these recent policy-based results as only tentative. First, advocates of the process-based approach have responded to these challenges and do not consider them strong enough to warrant a significant change in perspective (Gibson and Nelson 2014, 2015b). Second, the empirical evidence in favor of the policy-based approach remains thin when compared to decades of work on the process-based approach. And finally, the policy-based approach lacks a strong conceptual and theoretical foundation and thus stands, at present, as a series of loosely connected empirical results. The purpose of this book is to meet these challenges by providing a set of robust theoretical, conceptual, and empirical foundations for the policy-based approach to understanding Court-curbing in the mass public and its implications for legitimacy and judicial power.

Theoretical Foundations

In Chapter 2, we extract three lessons from the field of political psychology which form the basis for our theoretical understanding of mass support for Court-curbing. First, we argue that citizens are only *weakly principled*. While most people endorse a set of core democratic values related to Court legitimacy – such as the rule of law and the rights of political minorities – these values are not strongly binding on their attitudes and behavior (e.g., Prothro and Grigg 1960). Rather, citizens give in under the

[26] Additional work by Hoekstra and Segal (1996), Clawson et al. (2001), Stoutenborough et al. (2006), Bartels and Mutz (2009), and Christenson and Glick (2015b) shows a generally robust legitimizing function of the Court, but there are typically important moderators of this function, e.g., awareness, interest, or salience of the issue (see also Woodson 2019).

pressure of policy and partisan demands. Put another way, while support for these values is not empty, citizens care more about winning salient political battles than they do about protecting the Court for its own sake.

Second, we argue that *political reasoning is motivated*. Many citizens – politically engaged people especially – recognize that their support for Court-curbing conflicts with their commitment to democratic values, and they find this disconcerting (Festinger 1957). As argued by Kunda (1990), people do not generally feel at will to believe whatever they want without good reason. Responding to demands both psychological and social, people want to hold beliefs and attitudes that are consistent with their own values and that are justifiable to a dispassionate observer in these terms. Drawing on this idea and studies that apply it to the Supreme Court (e.g., Badas 2016; Gibson, Lodge, and Woodson 2014; Simon and Scurich 2011), we argue that support for Court-curbing initiates a process aimed at justifying this support through appeal to process-based considerations and core democratic values. As we have suggested, people do not justify Court-curbing in naked partisan terms. Rather, they cloak their support in the language of widely shared norms regarding the Court's purpose and how it ought to function and argue that the Court has failed to meet these standards in practice. Disliked decisions are argued to be "lawless," an affront to the Constitution, and rooted in partisan considerations and special interest influence. Fundamental changes to the Court are justified because the *other* party has corrupted the process or because such changes would make the Court more democratic and fair.

Such process-based concerns with Supreme Court decision-making arise primarily when decisions are inconsistent with policy, ideological, and partisan preferences but are conveniently forgotten or ignored when the Court is making congenial decisions. Thus, people justify *policy-motivated* Court-curbing attempts in *process-based* terms. Liked decisions, it seems, are faithful to principles of objectivity and fairness and are rooted in the dispassionate interpretation of the Constitution. And when the Court is moving in a congenial direction, fundamental institutional changes are rarely topics of discussion. We thus turn the process-based approach on its head: perceptions of procedural fairness serve as only a weak constraint on Court-curbing because they are, to a large extent, derivative of citizen desire to either curb or protect the Court.

Third, we argue that *partisan polarization shapes political cognition*. One of the most striking features of contemporary American politics – compared to past decades – is the degree of elite and mass polarization (e.g., Iyengar, Sood, and Lelkes 2012; McCarty, Poole, and Rosenthal

2006). Republicans and Democrats in Congress are more homogenous within party, and divided between parties, than at any time since before the Great Depression (and probably even further back than that). At the mass level, dislike of one's partisan opponents is more intense than at any other time point for which we have data. Research suggests that both elite and mass polarization have important implications for how citizens make political judgments and decisions (e.g., Druckman, Peterson, and Slothuus 2013; Mason 2018). As we discuss in Chapter 2, sharp partisan divisions lead to greater reliance on partisanship and related dimensions of political conflict and reduce reliance on other considerations, such as democratic values. Applying these results to the Court, we argue that partisan polarization poses a direct threat to judicial independence because citizens are less likely to defend the Court in the face of strong pressure from in-partisans. While citizens may be willing to forego partisan benefits to defend the Court under some conditions, polarization raises the stakes dramatically. Indeed, for weakly principled citizens, the stakes are simply too high, and the long-term institutional integrity of the Court is sacrificed at the altar of short-term partisan gain. In this way, we derive a set of expectations for how *political context* matters for the Court's power relative to the other branches of government, and we contribute to an emerging literature on the implications of political polarization for democratic norms and institutions.

Conceptual Foundations

We also challenge the conceptual foundations of classic work on public opinion toward the Supreme Court. Most of this literature begins with Easton's (1965) distinction between "diffuse" and "specific" support. Specific support is short-term *approval* of the Court's outputs: does the current policy output of the institution match my desires? Diffuse support, by contrast, has been reconceptualized as legitimacy and long-term institutional loyalty (Bartels and Johnston 2013; Caldeira and Gibson 1992; Cann and Yates 2016; Christenson and Glick 2015a; Gibson and Caldeira 2009a; Gibson, Caldeira, and Spence 2003a, 2003b; Gibson and Nelson 2014, 2015b; Zilis 2018).[27] Based on this framing, the literature has revolved around the question of whether diffuse support responds to

[27] Easton (1965, 273) defined diffuse support as "a reservoir of favorable attitudes or good will that helps members to accept or tolerate outputs to which they are opposed or the effects of which they see as damaging to their wants." Over time, scholars studying the

specific support (rooted in policy disagreement) and, if so, how strongly the two covary (e.g., Bartels and Johnston 2013; Christenson and Glick 2015a; Gibson and Nelson 2014, 2015b; Zilis 2018).[28] This question is sometimes framed in terms of the responsiveness of Supreme Court *legitimacy* to discontent with its policy output. That is, does the Court's legitimacy suffer as a function of disagreeable decisions?

We respect this work – indeed, we have contributed to it – but we argue for a conceptual reorientation. First, concepts such as *institutional legitimacy*, *diffuse support*, and *institutional loyalty* – effectively treated as synonymous in the literature – are difficult to pin down both definitionally and operationally. This has led to inconsistent measurement strategies that confound distinct types of judgment concerning the Court. To wit, the measurement of these concepts has changed quite a bit over the past few decades (e.g., compare Caldeira and Gibson 1992; Gibson, Caldeira, and Spence 2003a; Gibson and Nelson 2015b) and scales measuring them often average over items tapping diverse concepts such as procedural perceptions, trust, and opposition to Court-curbing (see Gibson, Caldeira, and Spence 2003a). Rather than ignore the differences among these concepts, we think it makes sense to keep them distinct, with a primary focus on explaining *support for Court-curbing* – concrete proposals to subvert the Court's power and independence. With this move, our focal dependent variable is both conceptually clean and directly relevant to the questions motivating the literature in the first place: what is the relative power of the Court in American government, and what role does the public play in strengthening or weakening that position? Moreover, by keeping perceptions of the Court's procedural aspects separate, we allow these concepts to move independently of support for Court-curbing rather than impose equivalence by fiat.

Second, while public support for Court-curbing has implications for the Court's institutional legitimacy, it is not a *direct indicator* of legitimacy (or diffuse support or institutional loyalty). We define legitimacy as perceived rightful authority to render rulings for the polity. That means

Supreme Court reconceptualized this concept as related to or synonymous with "legitimacy." More recent work often uses the term "institutional loyalty" synonymously.

[28] Additional work highlights how specific support – approval of or agreement with Supreme Court rulings – influences confidence (Grosskopf and Mondak 1998) and induces changes in Supreme Court support/approval (Hoekstra 2000, 2003). Moreover, Hoekstra (2000, 2003) examines a particular type of Supreme Court awareness or salience by comparing citizens who live in communities in which the Supreme Court case originated with those who live in surrounding communities.

authority is recognized as "rightful" even when those rulings conflict with one's personal preferences. The concept is similar to political tolerance in that it concerns what citizens do when they are placed in the uncomfortable position of disagreeing with the institution and yet being asked to defend its integrity (Sullivan, Piereson, and Marcus 1982). As Gibson and colleagues put it, "legitimacy is for losers" (Gibson 2015; Gibson, Caldeira, and Spence 2002, 2005; Gibson, Lodge, and Woodson 2014; Gibson and Nelson 2016). The same logic can be applied to concepts like diffuse support and loyalty – assessing them requires putting people to a "policy disagreement" test.

In this way, dependent variables that past work has labeled "legitimacy," "diffuse support," or "loyalty" are not clearly or reliably measuring what they intend and may overstate the extent of the public's institutional support for the Court. Indeed, an observational equivalence dilemma plagues attempts at directly measuring these concepts: at any given time, opposition to Court-curbing will include some mix of citizens who genuinely wish to defend the Court for its own sake as well as those who simply agree (or don't disagree) with the current policy direction of the Court. While the former group indicates high levels of perceived legitimacy, the latter indicates low levels of legitimacy because authority is only granted to the Court when it delivers congenial policy outputs – those who grant the Court power today would withhold it next year in the face of uncongenial rulings. This is akin to how early research on tolerance overstated its prevalence by focusing on groups that many citizens supported (Stouffer 1955). Thus, keeping the concepts of legitimacy, diffuse support, and loyalty distinct from support for Court-curbing is crucial for evaluating the policy-based approach, as well as comparing it to the process-based approach. We argue that the Court's legitimacy can only be assessed in light of the *effects* of policy disagreement on support for Court-curbing.

Finally, a shift in focus to Court-curbing allows for an exploration of heterogeneity in how the public responds to different *kinds* of attacks on the Court's power. Prior research on support for the Court's power has largely focused on opposition to long-lasting, fundamental changes to the institution, proposals that we label "broadly targeted Court-curbing." But some of the most important ways in which the Court's authority can be subverted involve less drastic, more circumscribed attacks, such as noncompliance or legislative overrides of individual decisions, which we label "narrowly targeted Court-curbing." We think this distinction is critical for reasons we spell out in detail in Chapter 2. In brief, we argue that broad curbing responds strongly to sustained, long-term policy disagreement with the Court, but responds weakly to policy disagreement with specific Court rulings. The logic is straightforward: narrow curbing can mitigate the consequences of a single bad decision, and if the Court is *generally* producing congenial policy outcomes, then it would be counterproductive to weaken its authority. The solution calls for a scalpel not an axe. If, on the other hand, the Court is deviating from one's policy desires in a more enduring way, then attacking the Court's independence and power more broadly is a reasonable strategy for policy-minded citizens. Thus, we propose that narrow curbing responds strongly to "narrow" disagreement (with specific rulings), while broad curbing responds strongly to "broad" disagreement. We also see a focus on narrow forms of curbing as a return to emphasizing policy acceptance as a key dependent variable in the literature (e.g., Mondak 1990, 1992, 1994; Nicholson and Hansford 2014; Salamone 2014, 2018; see also Zink, Spriggs, and Scott 2009) and as a way to tie the public opinion literature more closely to theories of strategic behavior in the literature on Supreme Court decision-making (e.g., Clark 2011; Epstein and Knight 1998; Nelson and Uribe-McGuire 2017; Rogers 2001; Staton 2010; Vanberg 2005).

Consistent with this discussion, our book focuses on three concepts as dependent variables:

1. Support for lasting and fundamental institutional changes to the Court, or *broadly targeted Court-curbing*
2. Support for proposals to subvert the Court's authority within circumscribed issue areas, or *narrowly targeted Court-curbing*
3. Perceptions of the appropriateness of the Court's decision-making procedures, or *procedural perceptions*

Empirical Foundations

In Chapters 3 through 7, we provide an in-depth empirical examination of the issues raised in previous pages. Our general strategy is to provide multiple, methodologically diverse tests of our policy-based framework. Different research designs – descriptive statistics and temporal patterns, cross-sectional, panel, and experimental designs – have distinct advantages and disadvantages. None of these designs will provide convincing evidence in isolation. Our hope is that our framework shows its worth by surviving many tests with heterogeneous attributes. Our philosophy is that a useful framework makes unique, successful predictions across diverse contexts. We hope to show that ours is useful in this sense.

In Chapter 3, we begin with a descriptive analysis of our three dependent variables. We describe our various datasets and our strategies for operationalizing narrow and broad forms of Court-curbing as well as procedural perceptions. When possible, we also trace these measures through time to provide a picture of the evolution of public opinion of the Court. In Chapter 4, we conduct an in-depth examination of the relationship between sustained policy disagreement and support for broad Court-curbing. These analyses involve cross-sectional datasets and address and expand on conflicting findings in the literature (e.g., Bartels and Johnston 2013; Gibson and Nelson 2015b). The analyses also test the competing effects of process-based factors like democratic values and political engagement. While Chapter 4 focuses on a general form of policy disagreement, Chapter 5 examines the effect of policy disagreement with *specific Supreme Court rulings* on both broad and narrow curbing. In two cases, we report the results of experiments designed to test the impact of specific policy disagreement on both narrow and broad curbing. We also consider three "case studies" using panel data surrounding high-profile Court decisions on health care and same-sex marriage.

In Chapter 6, we turn to the role of partisan polarization in shaping support for Court-curbing. We report the results of two experiments designed to test how intra-party homogeneity and inter-party distance alter the way citizens think about curbing the Court. We also consider the importance of a particularly salient manifestation of mass-level polarization: the degree to which partisans dislike their political opponents. Finally, in Chapter 7, we test our theory of politically motivated reasoning about the appropriateness of how the Court does its business. Specifically, we examine how procedural perceptions – related to the Court's decision-making process – respond to policy-based discontent with the Court's rulings.

WHAT'S AT STAKE?

In Chapter 8, we end with a discussion of the broader implications of our theory and empirical findings. Here, we briefly consider a few reasons why we think this research matters.

First, it matters for our understanding of the balance of power in American government. Theories of strategic interaction among the branches posit the public as guardians of judicial independence, shielding the Court from attacks by elected officials. That is, by making Court-curbing costly, citizens provide incentives for elite actors to respect the Court's authority. If these models are right, then the Court's power relative to the legislature and the executive rests on citizens' willingness to maintain support for judicial power even when it is not in their narrow political interests to do so. In practice, this often entails sanctioning in-partisans and favored political elites for subverting the Court's authority – a largely thankless task. Yet if the process-based approach has the right of it, most citizens rise to the occasion in the name of rule-of-law maintenance, democratic norms and values, and procedural justice. This means that the Court has substantial discretion to generate policy it sincerely prefers. If the policy-based approach is closer to the truth, however, institutional loyalty is fickle, and the Court's discretion is sharply reduced. Citizens support the Court only to the extent it produces desirable outcomes, thus leaving the Court with a reduced menu of viable policy options. Readers may vary with respect to their preferences regarding the relative power of the Court in American politics. But whatever one's preference, the debate matters.

Second, this work has implications for long-standing debates about the sources of institutional stability in democracies. In the literature on democratic values, classic work has raised alarms about the (un)willingness of the public to protect democratic norms, such as respect for freedom of speech and assembly. Some interpret these results to mean that it is elite actors, not the masses, who "carry the creed" forward and protect democratic institutions (McClosky 1964). Yet the Supreme Court literature suggests a quite different conclusion. The received wisdom assumes that elites are happy to subvert the Court's authority when it suits them, and they are held in check only by average citizens and the legitimacy they afford the Court. If the policy-based approach is right, however, an adjustment may be in order. Specifically, we may need to reassess the relative importance of elites in maintaining the Court's integrity and power. If citizen support is fickle, then elite-level support may be more critical to the Court than the received wisdom suggests.

Finally, if our approach is on target, then the Court is not immune from the negative effects of partisan polarization, as others have argued (Gibson 2007). Indeed, our framework suggests that the Court's independence is directly threatened by polarization as left–right conflict comes to dominate other considerations. In a polarized world, citizens may be willing to sacrifice core values and long-standing norms to prevent the opposing side from taking power. Our work thus adds to a burgeoning literature on the degeneration of democratic norms and values in the face of polarization (Hetherington and Rudolph 2015; Iyengar and Westwood

2015; Svolik 2018), though we are, to our knowledge, the first to empirically examine how partisan polarization shapes support for Court-curbing.

CONCLUSION

We write these words following one of the most contentious Supreme Court nominations in living memory. Speculation about the future of the Court and its legitimacy is widespread, and influential commentators are leveling attacks on its institutional integrity. Whatever one's opinion about specific proposals or critiques, there is reason to think these debates will have a lasting impact on the Court and how it is perceived. It is interesting, and a bit tricky, to write a book on a topic that seems to be in flux. On the one hand, we hope our book helps readers to make sense of these events. Indeed, we think our theoretical framework anticipates these developments in a way that the received wisdom does not. Ultimately, though, this is not a book *about* current events (as tempting as it is to try to write that book). Rather, it should be read as a general framework for thinking about the sources and extent of the Court's power relative to other institutions and the implications of this for public policy. Our concerns are bigger than one presidency or even one era of American politics. We wish to make more general claims about the degree to which the Court is bound to public opinion and majoritarian institutions in American politics. Visible confrontations between the Court and other political actors are of obvious importance and make for compelling political theatre. Often, however, what we do *not* see is equally important – that is, the strategic sacrifices to the public will that are taken to avoid such confrontations altogether.

2

Theories of Public Support for Court-Curbing

In this chapter we develop a policy-based theory of public support for Court-curbing. We wish to understand when and why citizens lend their support to actions that reduce the independence and power of the Supreme Court in its interactions with the other branches and institutions of American government. In brief, our argument is that Court-curbing is driven by discontent with the policy implications of the Court's decisions. Citizens support attacks on the Court when doing so will further goals associated with policy preferences, ideology, and political identity. This claim stands in sharp contrast with *process*-based theories which explain Court-curbing as an outgrowth of discontent with the way the Court functions and makes its decisions. To develop a foundation for our alternative perspective, we draw on three general lessons from political psychology.

The first lesson is that there is a substantial gap between the core values citizens endorse in principle and those they reveal in practice – citizens are only "weakly principled." Endorsed values exert *some* constraint on attitudes and behavior, but political expediency typically wins the day. For example, in the abstract, most people endorse values associated with political tolerance – a willingness to allow equal participation rights to political groups that one opposes. When asked about specific groups in specific instances, however, many of these same citizens support restrictions on the rights of disliked groups (Prothro and Grigg 1960; Sullivan, Piereson, and Marcus 1982). For the Court, this lesson suggests that values are unlikely to provide a reliable bulwark against Court-curbing.

The second lesson is that political reasoning is motivated, and citizens seek to balance competing goals when thinking through their options

(Groenendyk 2013; Lavine, Johnston, and Steenbergen 2012). On the one hand, they wish to hold beliefs and attitudes that reflect well on themselves and their political in-group. On the other hand, they wish to hold justifiable opinions that reflect objective reality. These two conditions can often be jointly satisfied through the construction of arguments that rationalize preferences (Haidt 2001; Lodge and Taber 2013). That is, politics has sufficient complexity that a reasonable-sounding argument can be found for many positions in a debate. In the context of the Supreme Court, we argue, citizens will use perceptions of procedural appropriateness in a strategic manner to attack disagreeable decisions and build support for curbing attempts. Conversely, citizens bolster the procedural appropriateness of agreeable decisions to protect the Court from curbing attacks by others. This lesson suggests that procedural perceptions are not exogenous determinants of Court-curbing activity but endogenous rationalizations of the desire to curb or protect the Court and its decisions.

The third lesson is that partisan polarization shapes political cognition. Elite partisans have polarized sharply in the last few decades, and while debate continues over the extremity of public attitudes, most scholars agree that mass partisans dislike their political opponents much more than they used to (e.g., Iyengar, Sood, and Lelkes 2012; Webster and Abramowitz 2017; Mason 2015). Research suggests that both elite and mass polarization increase the power of partisanship in judgment and decision-making and reduce the impact of other considerations (Druckman, Peterson, and Slothuus 2013; Lavine, Johnston, and Steenbergen 2012). The implication for the Supreme Court is that citizens will be less willing to show forbearance in highly polarized contexts because of the high stakes of partisan conflict. In turn, they will follow their favored partisan elites, even when doing so requires a sacrifice of nonpartisan goods, such as democratic values and the institutional integrity of the Court (e.g., Svolik 2018).

We will develop these arguments more fully in the pages to come. Before we get there, however, we must place our theory in the context of existing research on the Court and public opinion. In the first section of this chapter, we review arguments that the Court possesses substantial institutional legitimacy derived from the process by which it reaches its decisions and its special "minoritarian role" as a check on democratic majorities to ensure they are following the rules of the game. This legitimacy fosters a sense of loyalty to the Court and a willingness to forego narrow political benefits to protect its independence and efficacy.

PROCESS-BASED THEORIES OF COURT-CURBING

Conventional wisdom suggests that citizens afford the Supreme Court a high degree of legitimacy – or rightful authority – because of its special role in American government and because of the way it makes its decisions. In this view, citizens are socialized early in life to see the Court as an apolitical branch of government that provides a check on the elected branches. Many citizens subscribe to a "myth of legality": the idea that justices make decisions based on dispassionate legal reasoning in the context of precedent and the Constitution (see Baird and Gangl 2006; Casey 1974; Gibson and Caldeira 2011; Scheb and Lyons 2000; Solberg and Waltenburg 2014).[1] These beliefs and perceptions are reinforced during adulthood as citizens are exposed to the unique and legitimizing symbols of the Court (Gibson, Lodge, and Woodson 2014) and are shielded from the more political aspects of Court decision-making (e.g., no cameras in the Court, legalistic styles of reporting on case outcomes, justices always deliberate and conduct most other business in private). Indeed, in one of the strongest statements of this position, Gibson, Caldeira, and Spence (2003b) argue that even highly contentious decisions – such as *Bush* v. *Gore*[2] – necessarily involve exposure to potent legitimizing symbols and thus reinforce the legitimacy of the Court. Exposure to potentially delegitimizing features of Court decision-making is offset by these powerful positive symbols – a "positivity bias" that serves as a shield from political attacks. In this view, citizens support the Court because it is different from the elected branches, it serves an important and unique role in American government, and it stays above the ideological and political fray.

Conventional wisdom thus suggests that citizens strongly resist Court-curbing attempts from elected representatives or their appointees, ranging from noncompliance with specific decisions to more fundamental changes to the institution, such as Court-packing or jurisdiction stripping (Caldeira and Gibson 1992; Gibson 2007; Gibson, Caldeira, and Spence 2003b; Gibson and Nelson 2014, 2015b; Nicholson and Howard 2003). Such institutional loyalty helps to solve the fundamental "implementation problem": that the Court relies on other institutions of government and the American people to implement and enforce decisions even when those

[1] We use "myth" in its non-pejorative sense to indicate a widely shared belief or narrative within a culture that may or may not be true.

[2] 531 U.S. 98 (2000).

actors may disagree with those decisions. For example, the Court ruled in *Brown* v. *Board of Education of Topeka*[3] that public school segregation is unconstitutional, but the actual process of integration was in the hands of public officials at the state level, many of whom supported segregationist policies. Similarly, in *Obergefell* v. *Hodges*[4] the Court ruled that same-sex couples have a constitutional right to marry, but the process of issuing marriage licenses falls to local government officials, some of whom may oppose same-sex marriage or represent constituencies relatively united in opposition to the ruling.[5] The Court also relies on the forbearance of other actors and institutions with the power to enact punitive alterations to the Court in response to decisions. For example, Congress has the power to alter the Court's jurisdiction in most issue areas.

Formal theorists studying strategic interaction among the branches of government argue that the Court is protected from curbing, in part, by the electoral connection: citizens will punish elected officials at the ballot box if they attack the integrity of the Court or work to undermine its decisions (Carrubba and Zorn 2010; Carrubba 2009; Vanberg 2001, 2005; Staton 2010; Stephenson 2004; see also Friedman 2009). Political elites, in this view, are as virtuous as the people who send them to office in the first place – no more and no less. If citizens care a great deal about preserving the Court's power and independence, political elites who threaten the Court will be an endangered species.

Overall, this body of work suggests a form of "Supreme Court exceptionalism" – the Court has been able to escape the politicized and polarized nature of contemporary American government and politics that has infected so many other facets of American political life because citizens are principled defenders of the judiciary's independence. How did we get to this conventional wisdom? We briefly present this body of work and discuss its three broad "process-based" foundations to legitimacy: (1) procedural perceptions, (2) democratic values, and (3) awareness, knowledge, and positivity bias. We reserve challenges to these claims for subsequent sections.

[3] 347 U.S. 483 (1954). [4] 192 L. Ed. 2d 609 (2015).

[5] The most famous example involved Kentucky clerk Kim Davis, who refused to issue marriage licenses to same-sex couples and went to jail as a result. Flavell, John (November 7, 2018). "Kentucky clerk jailed over gay marriage licenses loses re-election bid." *NBC News*. www.nbcnews.com/feature/nbc-out/kentucky-clerk-jailed-over-gay-marriage-licenses-loses-re-election-n933451.

PROCEDURAL PERCEPTIONS

Rooted in theories of procedural justice and fairness (Tyler 1994, 2006a, 2006b; Tyler and Rasinski 1991), prior work suggests that support for the Court derives from the process by which the Court decides cases. In general, people's willingness to accept decisions that harm their narrow political or policy interests depends on their perceptions that the relevant authorities made the decisions using a fair or just procedure. For example, people obey the law and cooperate with legal authorities more often when they feel that they are treated fairly (Sunshine and Tyler 2003; Tyler 1994, 2006b). Procedural perceptions pertaining to the Supreme Court can range from viewing the Court as ideological and politicized to fair, legalistic, and impartial. Those who view the Court as fair and impartial should ascribe more legitimacy to the Court than those who view the Court in ideological and political terms. In other words, institutional legitimacy is rooted in the perception that the Court is indeed different from the other branches of government and is fulfilling its constitutional role as a neutral arbiter of the law (Gibson and Caldeira 2009b, 141–44). An important implication of this perspective is that perceptions of procedural propriety provide an offset to policy and ideological disagreement: individuals will support the Court, even when they disagree with its rulings, "if they respect the court as an institution that is generally impartial, just, and competent" (Murphy and Tanenhaus 1968, 359; see also Tyler and Rasinski 1991).

While procedural considerations provide an upside for Supreme Court evaluation, they are also the foundation for why people are so *negative* about Congress and government in general (Hibbing and Theiss-Morse 1995, 2001, 2002). Americans are disaffected by a Congress they see as ponderous, byzantine, prone to excessive bargaining and compromise, overly professionalized, and too removed from the people it is supposed to represent. Citizens are turned off by the "sausage-making process." In fact, Hibbing and Theiss-Morse (2002) contend that Americans *prefer* a policymaking process where deliberations are done behind closed doors and out of the public view – many prefer a form of "stealth democracy." Ultimately, the Court receives high levels of support because it is, in many respects, the very opposite of Congress in terms of procedure. Any bargaining and compromise that occurs is known only to the justices and their clerks, decisions are made efficiently, litigants and groups must argue their cases before the bench just like everyone else, and rulings are handed down cloaked in the language of the Constitution. Consistent with these claims, Scheb and Lyons (2000) and Tyler and Rasinski (1991) have shown that positive procedural perceptions, such as subscription to the "myth of legality," are associated with higher levels of support for the Court. Other experimental work suggests that factors such as how a Court ruling is framed, ranging from legal to political (Farganis 2012; Nicholson and Howard 2003; Ramirez 2008), and the closeness or unanimity of a ruling (Salamone 2014, 2018; Zink, Spriggs, and Scott 2009) can influence support for the Court and/or its rulings.[6] While aspects of this view have not gone unchallenged (e.g., Gibson 1989, 1991), a broad conventional wisdom of the importance of procedural propriety to Court support looms large in the literature.

CORE DEMOCRATIC VALUES

A related perspective argues that widespread endorsement of core democratic values rests at the foundation of Supreme Court legitimacy, creating a "reservoir of goodwill" that protects the Court from curbing attacks (Caldeira and Gibson 1992; Gibson 2007; Gibson and Caldeira 2009a, 2009b, 2011; Gibson and Nelson 2015b). Commonly highlighted values concern individual and minority political rights and the nature of constraints on the behavior of elected officials. These typically include some mixture of support for the rule of law, support for a multiparty system of government, tolerance of political minority groups, and support for political and civil liberty over social order (Caldeira and Gibson 1992; Gibson 2007; Gibson and Caldeira 2009a, 56; Gibson and Nelson 2015b). Institutional loyalty to the Court is high, in this view, because most people believe that there are, and should be, constraints on what elected officials can do in the name of the "greater good." There exist basic civil and political rights that are not to be infringed, and it is the Court's role to protect these rights from government overreach. As Gibson and Caldeira (Gibson and Caldeira 2009a, 57) argue, "The Supreme Court is the quintessential minoritarian institution in the American system of government – it is the primary institution empowered to protect minorities against abuse by the majority. Thus, it is not surprising the Court is so firmly embedded within the democratic values belief system."[7] Values function

[6] Benesh (2006) shows how perceptions of procedural fairness influence confidence in state courts.

[7] Once again, our reference to the Court's "minoritarian role" alludes to its function in our political system as a check on democratic majorities. The meaning of "minority" depends

as self-imposed constraints on citizens' behavior in the sense that people pursue these ends even at the expense of their narrow self-interest. Thus, even when it would be politically expedient to attack the Court, citizens will show forbearance and punish their favored elected officials for curbing attempts.

We consider this theory to fall within the broader "process-based" framework because the expectation of a positive relationship between values and legitimacy requires that citizens who endorse these values see the Court as procedurally proper. That is, they afford the Court loyalty to the extent that it executes its role in a fair and just manner. We can thus think of democratic values as a necessary but insufficient condition for loyalty to the Court. Loyalty may require endorsement of these values, but absent procedural approbation, they will not translate into support for the Court. Indeed, we would expect a corrupt version of the Court to receive low ratings from citizens who are most committed to democratic values because such a Court would be violating these basic principles (e.g., the rule of law) by favoring some political groups over others and making decisions based on partisan concerns rather than precedent and the Constitution. Our assessment is not that procedural justice theory and democratic values theory are one and the same but rather that they are complementary. Perceptions of procedural fairness are a factor limiting the translation of values into support for the Court.

Empirically, there is strong evidence for the claim that endorsement of democratic values is associated with institutional loyalty to the Court (e.g., Caldeira and Gibson 1992; Gibson 2007; Gibson and Caldeira 2009a; Gibson and Nelson 2015b). For example, citizens who affirm these principles are more likely to resist fundamental changes to the Court (e.g., jurisdiction stripping), with support for the rule of law and minority political rights being most influential (Gibson and Caldeira 2009a, 57). We will have more to say about values later in the chapter, but we believe the evidence suggests a meaningful role for these in protecting the Court from curbing attacks.

on the context. It can refer to the party out of power, political groups that are underrepresented or unrepresented in government, or racial, ethnic, and religious minorities in the case of civil rights and equal protection issues. The general notion is that the Court has the capacity to invalidate laws and actions enacted by majorities in the elected branches if it deems those laws or actions fall outside of constitutional and statutory boundaries. Some work argues that the Court is frequently in sync with public opinion and majority will more generally (e.g., Friedman 2009; Marshall 1989). That finding does not change the fact that the Court invalidates majority rule with nontrivial frequency.

POLITICAL ENGAGEMENT AND POSITIVITY THEORY

Another related perspective argues that exposure to the Court reinforces procedural approbation. As a result, political engagement – knowledge, interest, attention – is associated with higher levels of institutional loyalty. According to Gibson and colleagues' positivity theory (Gibson and Caldeira 2009a; Gibson, Lodge, and Woodson 2014), the Court is associated with powerful, legitimizing symbols – such as the justices' robes, the building itself, and the legalese used to discuss Court decisions – which reinforce early socialization to the "myth of legality" and the notion that the Court is different from the other, more politicized branches of American government. Citizens who pay more attention to politics and the Court are more likely to be exposed to these symbols and to see the institution as procedurally just. In turn, they are more likely than the politically unengaged to defend the Court from curbing attacks. Importantly, positivity theory argues that even exposure to disliked decisions leads to reinforced perceptions of procedural fairness and institutional loyalty because positive procedural symbols provide a sufficient offset to any negative information (e.g., Gibson, Lodge, and Woodson 2014).

Positivity theory receives empirical support from the long-standing observation that "to know the Court is to love it" – that is, politically knowledgeable citizens show higher levels of institutional loyalty to the Court than less knowledgeable citizens (e.g., Casey 1974; Gibson and Caldeira 2009a; but see Johnston and Bartels 2010 for caveats). Indeed, indicators of political engagement are among the strongest predictors of Court support. Other work also supports the basic claims of positivity theory. Gibson, Caldeira, and Spence (2003b) find that even the contentious decision in *Bush* v. *Gore* had little impact on Supreme Court legitimacy. In a direct test, Gibson, Lodge, and Woodson (2014) find that randomly assigned exposure to legitimizing symbols (e.g., judicial robes) reduces the link between disagreement with a Court decision and citizens' willingness to challenge the ruling. In another experimental study, Baird and Gangl (2006) find that randomly assigned exposure to news articles emphasizing legalistic justifications for Court decisions increases positive procedural perceptions. Taken together, this evidence suggests that exposure to the Court generates perceptions of procedural propriety, which helps to protect the Court from curbing attacks.

SUMMARY OF THE PROCESS-BASED PERSPECTIVE

At the core of this perspective is the notion that citizens can stomach disliked decisions so long as the process by which they are reached is fair and just. Most citizens endorse a set of core democratic values that affirm the rule of law and protect the political rights of individuals and minorities against the intrusion of democratically elected majorities. For most people, what matters is that the Court treats citizens equally and that decisions are made based on legal reasoning in the context of precedent and the Constitution, not political calculation, bargaining and compromise, partisanship, or ideology. Citizens may not agree with the reasoning behind any given decision, they may detest the outcome, and they may even fight hard to elect representatives who will nominate better justices to the Court. But they will accept the decision as legitimate and worthy of deference, and they will protect the Court from curbing attacks.

This perspective suggests that the Court is exceptional in the sense that it floats above the breakdown of democratic norms witnessed in other arenas driven by partisan and ideological polarization and the lack of trust in one's political opponents it entails (Hetherington and Rudolph 2015). In the remainder of this chapter we offer a critique and alternative to the process-based framework. There is much that is important and true in the work described in the previous pages. Still, it is not the whole picture, and the gaps are critical to understanding American political behavior as it relates to the Supreme Court.

A POLICY-BASED THEORY OF COURT-CURBING

A policy-based perspective has emerged to challenge the process-based conventional wisdom. This work argues that left–right orientations – policy preferences, ideology, and partisanship – in interaction with the Court's decision-making, strongly influence how individuals perceive and assess the Court, both in a general sense and in relation to specific Court rulings (e.g., Bartels and Johnston 2013; Christenson and Glick 2015a; Clark and Kastellec 2015; Johnston, Hillygus, and Bartels 2014; Hoekstra 2000, 2003; Nelson and Smith 2015; Nicholson and Hansford 2014; Simon and Scurich 2011; Zilis 2018). In short, citizens care more about policy outcomes than protecting the Court's long-term integrity. In turn, disagreement with the Court's policy output drives support for Court-curbing because there is no "reservoir of goodwill" promoting forbearance. When people dislike the policy implications of a specific ruling, they support measures to mitigate its effects. When people dislike the policy direction of the Court in a more enduring sense, they support broader measures to reduce its power and independence. Institutional support, in this view, is fickle: citizens are only "loyal" to the Court so long as they are getting the policies they want, and they expect this to continue well into the future. This is, of course, a loyalty unworthy of the name.

This perspective provides a portrait of the Court as a fully political institution in the public mind, complementing additional work showing that many Americans tend to perceive the Court in quite political terms (e.g., Bartels and Johnston 2012; Scheb and Lyons 2000, 2001), which is partly rooted in changing media coverage (see Baird and Gangl 2006; Hitt and Searles 2018; Johnston and Bartels 2010; Slotnick and Segal 1998; Solberg and Waltenburg 2014; Spill and Oxley 2003; Strother 2017). The Supreme Court is not exceptional and has not been able to escape the consequences of politicization and polarization that we see in American politics more generally. Instead, support for the Court is more similar in its etiology to that of other institutions and actors than previous scholarship has acknowledged.

To date, however, this alternative is theoretically underdeveloped. Most work in the emerging literature simply seeks to demonstrate a substantively meaningful relationship between political orientations and measures of Supreme Court support or legitimacy (e.g., Bartels and Johnston 2013; Christenson and Glick 2015a) – it is decidedly empirical in flavor. There has been no comprehensive attempt to develop the conceptual and theoretical underpinnings of the policy-based framework such that it can stand as a real alternative to the process-based perspective (but see Nicholson and Hansford 2014).[8] In the remainder of this chapter, we seek to push the literature forward by grounding the policy-based perspective in first principles. We develop in greater depth our three lessons from political psychology and their implications for understanding Court-curbing. On this basis, we generate a series of hypotheses that are tested in the remainder of the book.

Lesson 1: Citizens Are Weakly Principled

We argue that citizens are weakly principled. We agree that the average person endorses a set of core democratic values – rule of law, political

[8] Also, Choper (1980) and Mondak (1992) develop a perspective based on the notion of "exhaustible institutional capital," which argues that the Supreme Court expends its capital (akin to institutional loyalty) to legitimize unpopular policies (see also Zilis 2015). This framework is similar to the process-based perspective in that the Court can generate acceptance of even disagreeable policies based on a reservoir of goodwill (see also Salamone 2014, 2018). It is similar to our perspective in that loyalty is limited and is reduced through exposure to disliked decisions. We will discuss this perspective further, as it relates to our own, in the concluding chapter.

liberty, tolerance – and will tell you so on surveys in a reliable manner (e.g., Gibson and Caldeira 2009a; Gibson and Nelson 2015b; Prothro and Grigg 1960). Consider, for example, data from a 2011 survey that we will use in subsequent chapters (Gibson and Nelson 2015b). Nearly 80 percent of respondents reject the notion that "it is not necessary to obey a law you consider unjust," and nearly 90 percent reject the statement "it is not necessary to obey the laws of a government I did not vote for." The overall scale constructed from five similar items is highly skewed: only about 10 percent of respondents have an average score indicating general agreement with attacks on the rule of law. Similarly, less than 20 percent of respondents agree that "society should not have to put up with those who have political ideas that are extremely different from the majority." In the abstract, then, we see widespread support for the rule of law and civil liberty. We also agree that endorsement of these values is meaningfully associated with opposition to Court-curbing – we will confirm this claim empirically in subsequent chapters. Nonetheless, democratic values are weak, rather than strong (or binding), constraints. They provide some resistance against Court-curbing attacks, but they give way to political expediency under pressure.

In a classic study, Prothro and Grigg (1960) examined support for democratic principles in the abstract, as well as the application of those principles to specific groups. In other words, they first looked at the extent to which citizens endorsed key democratic values and then the extent to which they were willing to follow through on those values when faced with concrete situations. As in our data, they found widespread agreement (over 90 percent) on the value of "minority rights" in the abstract: most people agree that "the minority should be free to criticize majority decisions" and "people in the minority should be free to try to win majority support for their opinions." When asked for their opinions about the rights of *specific* minority groups in specific situations, however, this consensus collapsed. For example, they found that only 44 percent of their sample would allow a communist to give a political speech or run for political office and only 63 percent of their respondents would allow anti-religious speech. The large gap between the percentage of citizens endorsing a value and the percentage applying it to a specific context is a robust finding in the tolerance literature (e.g., McClosky 1964; Stouffer 1955). This is what we mean by weakly principled: there is a high degree of slippage between principle and practice.

One reason for this slippage may be that democratic values are less central and accessible in citizens' belief systems than other objects of concern, such as group identities (Achen and Bartels 2016; Converse 1964; Kinder and Kalmoe 2017; but see Goren 2013 for a conflicting perspective). That is, even if citizens honestly endorse these principles, they may not come to mind in typical situations requiring judgments about relevant topics. On the other hand, strongly held opinions on important issues, and especially group and partisan identities, are very likely to be activated in contexts in which they are relevant (Huckfeldt et al. 1999; Lavine, Johnston, and Steenbergen 2012). This suggests a structural disadvantage for tolerance. As Gibson (1998, 824) argues, "After all, the respondents are often answering difficult and complex questions, and are doing so quickly, perhaps with relatively superficial processing of the stimuli. It would not be surprising, for instance, if respondents were more heavily influenced by the group mentioned in a tolerance question than by the political rights to which the questions refer." Nicholson and Hansford (2014) provide direct evidence for this claim in the context of the Supreme Court. They randomly assigned citizens to read about a recent decision attributed to either the government or the Supreme Court and either with or without party labels attached to supporters and opponents. Despite the long-standing notion that the Court can generate acceptance of its decisions via its legitimizing capacity (Mondak 1994), the authors find that partisanship and partisan cues dominate citizens' responses. In other words, attributing the decision to the Court did not mitigate partisan reasoning about the decision.

Distinct from issues of accessibility, citizens may simply fail to see the relevance of values to a given judgment – a failure of what Higgins (1996) calls "applicability." As Converse (1964, 33) argues:

> while there is widespread support for statements of culturally familiar principles of freedom, democracy, and tolerance in a cross-section sample, this support becomes rapidly obscured when questions turn to specific cases that elites would see as the most direct applications of these principles. In our estimation, such findings are less a demonstration of cynical lip service than of the fact that, while both of two inconsistent opinions are honestly held, the individual lacks the contextual grasp to understand that the specific case and the general principle belong in the same belief system: In the absence of such understanding, he maintains psychologically independent beliefs about both.

This may be particularly true for the application of democratic values to the Supreme Court. For example, it may not be obvious to many citizens that a primary function of the Court is the protection of individual and minority political rights or that a specific case should be interpreted in these terms.

Even when democratic values are activated from long-term memory, and even when citizens recognize their applicability to the judgment at hand, they may still be overwhelmed by other salient concerns. Indeed, research suggests that intolerance rises under pressure, when values strongly conflict with self-interest, political preferences, or important social and political identities (but see Gibson 2006). The classic study is Sullivan, Piereson, and Marcus (1982). They first asked respondents to name their "least liked" political group (e.g., communists, fascists, Ku Klux Klan (KKK)). Follow-up questions then probed respondents' willingness to allow this group to engage in peaceful political activities and participate fully in the democratic process (e.g., run for president, hold public rallies). The idea is that true tolerance requires extending political rights even to those groups we disagree with and dislike the most, but Sullivan et al. find striking levels of support for restricting such rights. For example, only 28 percent of respondents were willing to allow members of their least-liked group to be president, and only 57 percent would allow this group to hold public rallies. In a more recent example, Singer (2018) finds that Latin American citizens who endorse democracy and oppose coups are nonetheless willing to countenance significant attacks on democratic norms and institutions when they identify with the ruling party or are satisfied with the way the country is going economically. Similarly, Svolik (2018) and Graham and Svolik (2018) examine the willingness of voters to punish elected officials and candidates for undemocratic actions and policy proposals; for example, they asked survey respondents to make choices between hypothetical candidates for office in the United States. They found that taking a strongly anti-democratic position on an issue (e.g., prosecuting journalists, ignoring Court orders) cost candidates only 11 percentage points in the final vote tallies. Moreover, strong partisanship and partisan polarization made citizens even less likely to punish anti-democratic candidates. Again, this suggests that democratic values are only a weak constraint on citizens' attitudes and political behavior.

Research also suggests that commitment to democratic values is reduced in conditions of perceived personal or societal threat. When holding firm to democratic principles requires accepting downside risks, citizens tend to abandon their values rather than their (feelings of) security. Indeed, one of the most powerful predictors of intolerance of disliked groups is perceived threat from those groups (Feldman and Stenner 1997; Marcus et al. 1995; Sullivan, Piereson, and Marcus 1982). Citizens are also more willing to accept violations of civil rights when they feel threatened and are more attracted to authoritarianism in such situations (e.g.,

Doty, Peterson, and Winter 1991; Jost et al. 2017; Landau et al. 2004; Merolla and Zechmeister 2009; Vasilopoulos, Marcus, and Foucault 2018). For example, Hetherington and Suhay (2011) find that over 70 percent of citizens who feel "very worried" about terrorism support restricting the media's ability to report on government behavior, and over 60 percent of such people support the government's use of warrantless wiretapping of communications within the United States. Similarly, Peffley, Hutchison, and Shamir (2015) find that persistent terrorist attacks substantially erode *general* political tolerance in Israel. Overall, people seem willing to put aside their commitment to core democratic values in situations where they feel threatened and anxious.

A more general finding is that citizens' political forbearance is "pliable": people can readily be talked out of initially tolerant opinions (Gibson 1998; Peffley, Knigge, and Hurwitz 2001). Citizens often hold competing considerations in long-term memory relevant to tolerance judgments (Zaller and Feldman 1992), such as concerns with the breakdown of social order. Arguments that bring these to the fore or make them seem more important will thus reduce overall levels of tolerance by shifting some initially tolerant people to intolerance (e.g., Nelson, Clawson, and Oxley 1997). Research also suggests that it is easier to convince initially tolerant people to be intolerant than it is to convince initially intolerant people to be tolerant (but see Petersen et al. 2011 for an alternative perspective). This may reflect a more general "negativity bias" in human cognition (e.g., Baumeister et al. 2001). For example, Gibson (1998) asked a set of respondents about their support for preventing a disliked group from full democratic participation. He then provided respondents expressing intolerant judgments with three pro-tolerance arguments and presented those expressing tolerant judgments with three arguments for intolerance. Among the initially intolerant, the counterarguments had little effect – over three-quarters persisted in their opinion. Among the initially *tolerant*, however, positions were more pliable: about 50 percent switched to intolerant opinions. Consistent with our weakly principled claim, endorsement of core democratic values mitigated this effect somewhat but was not a reliable source of forbearance. Indeed, among those endorsing democratic values, over 40 percent of initially tolerant respondents "flipped" to intolerance following exposure to counterarguments. Peffley et al. (2001) find similar results. They examined the persistence of initial tolerance judgments (allowing the KKK to hold a rally in their city) in the face of additional considerations (it will cost the city $100,000). They find that the initially tolerant are about twice as likely to shift their opinions (relative to the initially intolerant) and concluded that "many tolerant citizens find the 'costs' of forbearance borne by the city ... too high."[9]

Importantly, research finds that this gap between principle and practice is prevalent across the political spectrum – intolerance is not solely a conservative or right-wing phenomenon. Indeed, early research on tolerance provided a misleading impression, as it relied primarily on responses to left-wing groups, such as communists, atheists, and socialists (Stouffer 1955). It is not surprising, then, that conservatives seemed less tolerant than liberals. When using more appropriate "content-controlled" designs, however, substantial levels of intolerance are found for left-wing citizens as well (Sullivan, Piereson, and Marcus 1982, 183). Indeed, in recent research, Crawford and Pilanski (2014) show that intolerance of right-wing groups among liberal identifiers is just as prevalent as intolerance of left-wing groups among conservative identifiers (see also Brandt et al. 2014). Similarly, Hetherington and Suhay (2011) find that ideological gaps in opposition to government restrictions on civil liberties disappear when the left and right feel equally threatened by terrorism (see also Vasilopoulos, Marcus, and Foucault 2018).

In sum, the literature on democratic values and tolerance suggests that citizens are weakly principled in the sense that there is a substantial gap between the values they endorse in principle and those they exhibit in their specific attitudes and behavior. This likely has something to do with the lower centrality and accessibility of values relative to other political attitudes and identities and the difficulty some citizens have in connecting values to specific disputes. Moreover, when values conflict with strongly held attitudes against out-groups, and when security and order are threatened, democratic rights and civil liberties give way to political expediency. Finally, citizens can often be talked out of initially tolerant attitudes even when they strongly endorse democratic values.[10]

[9] In an interesting recent study, Petersen et al. (2011) examine the asymmetry hypothesis in Denmark and find that it holds only for certain groups perceived to be particularly prone to violence or hostile to democratic norms.

[10] The long-standing literature on the nature of mass belief systems also provides support for our claim that citizens are weakly principled. As Converse (1964) forcefully argued, citizens' policy attitudes are only weakly constrained by higher-order principles (as indicated by weak intra- and inter-domain correlations). Instead, the average citizen thinks about politics in a more compartmentalized fashion, focusing attention on a small number of personally important issues or on whatever topics happen to be salient in political discourse at the time (Iyengar and Simon 1993). While the degree of Converse's pessimism has been tempered over the years (e.g., Achen 1975;

It is very important to emphasize that our contention is not that citizens' endorsement of core democratic values is empty – citizens seem to feel constrained, to some extent, by their endorsement of such values (e.g., Gibson 1998; Marcus et al. 1995; Peffley, Knigge, and Hurwitz 2001), there are limits to what they are willing to do in the name of partisanship (Lelkes and Westwood 2017), and even apparent violations of political tolerance may sometimes be rooted in what are arguably democratic principles, such as enforcing the social contract and norms of reciprocity (Gibson 1998; Petersen et al. 2011). Nonetheless, values are not strongly binding and are not a reliable source of political forbearance. When push comes to shove – when values conflict with salient concerns related to self-interest, policy preferences, or group identities – they give way to expedient attitudes and policies. The implications for Court-curbing are clear. Disagreement with specific Court decisions is likely to drive support for measures aimed at limiting the impact of those decisions, and longer-term disagreement with the Court will drive support for broader measures aimed at limiting the Court's power and independence. And as we discuss in subsequent sections, both effects should be larger when there is more at stake in terms of partisan and ideological conflict. Indeed, the lessons of the tolerance literature are broad and suggest substantial limits on the willingness of citizens to defend norms and

Ansolabehere, Rodden, and Snyder 2008; Feldman 1988; Goren 2013), the primary conclusion that citizens fall far short of elite levels of constraint persists (e.g., Feldman and Johnston 2014; Kinder and Kalmoe 2017).

The broader literature in mass politics also suggests that values are a weak rather than binding constraint and that they tend to give way when they conflict with strong existing policy preferences or pressure from fellow partisans. Indeed, a robust literature documents citizens' tendency to ignore or abandon core values and ideology when it suits their partisan interests. In a seminal study, Cohen (2003) finds that citizens largely follow party cues on complex policy issues rather than broader ideological principles. For example, conservative identifiers can be induced to prefer a "generous" to a "stringent" welfare policy when Republican elites support the former and Democratic elites support the latter. Other work finds that values and ideology are at least partly endogenous to partisanship and political attitudes. Levendusky (2009), for example, shows that the increasing correlation of partisanship and ideology in American politics is due primarily to citizens shifting their ideological commitments to conform to their partisan identities. Goren and colleagues (Goren 2005; Goren, Federico, and Kittilson 2009) find that core political values (e.g., equal opportunity) are endogenous to partisanship and party cues. And Uhlmann et al. (2009) find that citizens use moral principles in a motivated fashion. That is, they pick and choose from the set of available principles (e.g., utilitarianism versus deontology) with the goal of justifying the action they prefer for other reasons (e.g., group identity).

institutions. The implication is that the Court is less protected by values than previous research suggests.

This does, however, create a problem for citizens who recognize the applicability of values to Court-curbing: their attitudes toward the Court will often conflict with the democratic values they freely endorse, creating a state of cognitive dissonance (Festinger 1957) and leaving those attitudes open to criticism by others who have an interest in protecting the Court's integrity. How do these citizens navigate the tension between their values and partisan interests? How do they justify attacks on the Court without abandoning these principles? Our second lesson from political psychology helps to resolve this puzzle.

Lesson 2: Political Reasoning Is Motivated

Political reasoning is motivated (Flynn, Nyhan, and Reifler 2017; Jost et al. 2003; Leeper and Slothuus 2014; Lodge and Taber 2013; Taber and Lodge 2006). We cannot model citizens as "cold" information-processing machines; rather, we must inquire about their desires. Psychologists distinguish broadly between nondirectional and directional goals (Kruglanski 1989; Kunda 1990, 1999). The former ignores the content of the conclusion that is ultimately reached. For example, people are often motivated to find the most accurate answer to a question, say, the true unemployment rate under an incumbent administration. In this case, the goal is the truth of the matter, whatever it may be.[11] Directional goals, by contrast, create preferences over content. For example, people may wish to maintain their opinions on an issue because they would feel ashamed to learn they made a mistake. Alternatively, they may wish to conclude their own party's position is the best one because they want to be on the winning political team (Kahan 2015). In both cases, the individual prefers a particular conclusion independent of what the available evidence implies.

These goals influence judgment and decision-making via their effect on information gathering and processing. Information search may be open and exploratory when motivated by accuracy, or narrow and biased toward congenial sources in the case of a directional goal (e.g., Iyengar and Hahn 2009; Taber and Lodge 2006); information evaluation may use

[11] Another example of a nondirectional goal is the need for nonspecific closure, which may arise from situational (e.g., time pressure) or dispositional sources (Kruglanski 1989; Webster, Richter, and Kruglanski 1996).

principles of assessment and inference in an even-handed way or may apply these selectively to bolster congenial information and denigrate uncongenial information (Ditto and Lopez 1992; Johnston and Ballard 2016; Kahan, Jenkins-Smith, and Braman 2011); and citizens may integrate new information with prior beliefs in an unbiased manner or by selectively up- and down-weighting information that fits or conflicts (respectively) with what they would like to believe (Hill 2017).

Importantly, research suggests that neither directional nor nondirectional motives always dominate. Rather, political reasoning is driven by attempts at balancing these competing goals (Lavine, Johnston, and Steenbergen 2012; Leeper and Slothuus 2014). As Leeper and Slothuus (2014, 137) note, this stands in contrast to some of the gloomier interpretations of motivated reasoning in political science, in which it "is often treated as a juggernaut – an unstoppable partisan force that blinds everyone to everything, ruining the hopes for an idealized deliberative politics." Citizens will try to generate desirable conclusions even at the expense of accuracy, but they do so within the bounds of what is justifiable. That is, there are constraints on what conclusions can be reasonably attained given the evidence available, and people will not endorse a position that is entirely unacceptable to a reasonable observer. As Kunda (1990, 482–83) explains:

> People do not seem at liberty to conclude whatever they want to conclude merely because they want to. Rather, I propose that people motivated to arrive at a particular conclusion attempt to be rational and to construct a justification of their desired conclusion that would persuade a dispassionate observer. They draw the desired conclusion only if they can muster up the evidence necessary to support it. In other words, they maintain an "illusion of objectivity."

Citizens seek justifiability to maintain a positive view of the self – for example, that one is meeting one's own internalized standards of good citizenship (Groenendyk 2013; Kam 2007) – and to maintain positive standing in one's relationships with people who enforce norms of what constitutes an appropriate conclusion given the evidence (Klar 2014; Lerner and Tetlock 1999). There is thus push and pull between the demands of desired conclusions and those of internally or externally enforced standards of reasonable judgment and decision-making.

The upshot is that directionally motivated reasoning is not unbounded. Citizens tend to seek and process information in a way that confirms their priors and reflects well on their social identities and political in-groups. At the same time, the extent of such bias is limited by the individual's ability to rationalize their desired conclusion. When evidence is clear, or directional reasoning requires violation of important social norms, citizens will not adopt a favored position simply because it is favored. When evidence is mixed, and justifications are easily constructed, however, they will often reach the gratifying position through one route or another, leading to substantial gaps in opinion across partisan and ideological groups.

This brief discussion of the motivated reasoning literature suggests that many citizens will feel the need to justify Court-curbing attacks because most people endorse democratic values related to the Court's role (Gibson and Caldeira 2009a). Adapting Kunda (1990, 482) to the present context, so long as these values are accessible and they recognize the applicability of the values to the Court, people will not feel at liberty to attack the Court merely because that is what would best fulfill their narrow political ends. Rather, they will need to construct an argument that reconciles the action with these values.

In our discussion of the process-based perspective, we argued that, in principle, democratic values work in conjunction with procedural perceptions to constrain Court-curbing. Citizens who endorse the special role of the Supreme Court and see the Court as faithfully executing that role should resist attempts to undermine the Court's decisions and attack its institutional integrity. Put another way, one cannot simultaneously affirm these values, see the Court as procedurally appropriate, *and* support attacks on the Court – something must give. Absent perceptions of fair and just decision-making, however, democratic values should not necessarily translate into institutional loyalty. Thus, among citizens who endorse these values, and recognize their applicability, the procedural propriety of the Court is the factor limiting the justifiability of Court-curbing actions.

To maintain a coherent and defensible set of beliefs and attitudes in the face of disagreement with the Court, citizens can give up (a) their core democratic values, (b) the policy goals and political identity concerns motivating Court-curbing, or (c) their perceptions of the Court's procedural propriety. In general, research suggests that peripheral beliefs and attitudes give way to more central ones (Tesler 2015). This suggests that citizens will attempt to preserve their core democratic values and pursuit of policy and partisanship by altering their procedural perceptions of the Court. It is more gratifying to believe that *the Court* has been corrupted – if only in this one instance – than to accept partisan defeat on an important issue or to acknowledge that one has abandoned critical democratic norms. Moreover, there is enough ambiguity inherent to Court decision-making that such rationalizations should be possible to construct in most cases. Indeed, recent research has successfully applied the motivated reasoning framework to the courts (e.g., Badas 2016; Braman 2006, 2009; Braman and Nelson 2007; Gibson, Lodge, and Woodson 2014; Simon and Scurich 2011). Badas (2016), for example, theorizes and demonstrates that people are more likely to see the justices' decision process as legalistic when they agree with the ruling than when they disagree (see also Strother and Gadarian 2019; see Cann and Yates 2016 for a state-level application).

In sum, the process-based approach argues that procedural perceptions are an *exogenously determined limiting factor* which protects the Court from curbing attacks, even when it is in citizens' narrow interest to support them. The policy-based perspective, by contrast, argues that citizens' policy attitudes and political identities are central in political belief systems. In turn, citizens will seek justifications for attacking the Court when politically expedient, and this is most readily accomplished by delegitimizing the procedures by which the Court reached the offending decision(s). In this view, procedural perceptions are an *endogenous rationalization* of support and opposition to Court-curbing, one that allows citizens to maintain the illusion of support for democratic values and norms. Rather than accept that they are willing to attack legitimate institutions for narrow partisan gain, citizens will rationalize their attitudes and behavior by passing blame to the institutions themselves. Again, of course, this all assumes that citizens endorse these values, have them readily accessible in memory, and recognize their applicability to the issue of Court-curbing. For those who do not make this connection, there should be little motivation to rationalize one's attacks. We return to this issue later in the chapter when we discuss the moderating role of political engagement.

Lesson 3: Polarization Shapes Political Cognition

Our final lesson from political psychology concerns the impact of partisan polarization on political cognition. There is widespread agreement that American political elites have polarized since the 1970s (McCarty, Poole, and Rosenthal 2006). In terms of roll call voting, Democrats and Republicans are more internally homogenous within the parties and more divided between the parties than in the past. At the mass level, things are more complicated. A major point of conflict concerns the extent to which citizens have more extreme policy preferences than in the past. While some scholars argue that citizens remain moderate on most issues (e.g., Fiorina, Abrams, and Pope 2006; Hill and Tausanovitch 2015; Mason 2015, 2018), others see substantial movement to the extremes, especially among politically engaged citizens (Abramowitz 2010; Abramowitz and Saunders 2008). However, there are other ways to think about polarization, and these generate greater agreement.

First, partisans are now better "sorted" than in the past. There is a stronger relationship between partisan identities and issues and ideological identification (Lelkes 2016; Levendusky 2009; Mason 2018). For example, Republicans are much more likely to identify as conservative and hold conservative positions on specific issues than Democrats. Sorting does not imply anything about the *range* of views held within the public (and thus implies nothing about relative extremity). It simply means that Democrats and Republicans are more internally homogenous. People can be more consistent in their views without becoming more radical in the positions they take. Partisans are also better sorted in terms of cultural identities, personality, and lifestyle preferences than in the past, and this creates a sense that Democrats and Republicans are fundamentally different kinds of people (Cizmar et al. 2004, 2004; Hetherington and Weiler 2009; Lakoff 2016; Layman 2001). As Hetherington and Weiler (2009) argue, the rise of several emotionally evocative issues related to race, ethnicity, religion, and law and order has fueled the sorting of citizens into political parties based on competing cultural worldviews. More so than in the past, contemporary partisanship is well predicted by how one prioritizes the values of social order and cohesion relative to individual self-direction, novelty, and diversity, with Republicans placing greater emphasis on the former and Democrats placing more emphasis on the latter. Since these value trade-offs are closely related to basic personality traits (e.g., Jost et al. 2003; Roccas et al. 2002), and because they structure life choices in a variety of areas beyond politics (e.g., residential sorting, consumption, travel), Republicans and Democrats now find it difficult to understand and relate to one another on a social level.

Because of the decline in shared values, preferences, and identities between the parties, mass Republicans and Democrats are more *affectively* polarized than in the past (Iyengar, Sood, and Lelkes 2012; Iyengar and Westwood 2015; Mason 2018; Webster and Abramowitz 2017) – dislike and distrust of the out-party have increased substantially over time. Indeed, Iyengar and Westwood (2015) find that automatic affective biases against the out-party are larger than those observed for racial out-groups, and partisans readily engage in behavioral discrimination against out-party members (but see also Lelkes and Westwood 2017). Thus, regardless of how one resolves the debate over ideological extremity, most scholars agree that mass Democrats and Republicans are more internally homogenous than in the past – both ideologically and culturally – and this has created an affectively charged environment characterized by an intense dislike of one's political opponents.

Critically, research suggests that both elite and mass partisan polarization have important implications for the way citizens reason about politics. Put simply, partisanship and related orientations become more central to political cognition, and other considerations become less important. There are three primary ways in which polarization generates this effect.

First, even if citizens remain moderate in their preferences, polarization suggests larger differences in policy outcomes comparing Democrats to Republicans at the elite level (e.g., Achen and Bartels 2016, 47). This means that there is more at stake in any given partisan battle, and cross-cutting considerations, such as democratic values and institutional loyalty, may seem less important by way of comparison or may simply be insufficient to override these partisan goals (Hetherington and Rudolph 2015; Singer 2018; Svolik 2018; Graham and Svolik 2018). In weighing costs and benefits, the difference in utility comparing a liberal to a conservative outcome may seem so large that it outweighs factors that would otherwise be considered important. For example, as discussed in Chapter 1, prominent left-wing commentators have recently toyed with the idea of "packing" the Supreme Court. The argument seems to be that the expected policy outcomes under the Roberts Court (with Trump's two recent appointments) would be so devastating to liberal interests that the harm to the Court's institutional integrity accompanying a packing scheme is a price worth paying.

Second, partisan polarization increases the informational value of elite partisan cues (Druckman, Peterson, and Slothuus 2013; Hetherington and Rudolph 2015). Polarization is defined by intra-party homogeneity and inter-party distance – the intra-class correlation. This is a measure of the strength of the categorical distinction "Republican versus Democrat" and thus how useful party labels are for making judgments about politics. All else equal, citizens would prefer to make political judgments using less as opposed to more effort, but they nonetheless wish to meet some minimal threshold of confidence. If polarized party cues allow citizens to reach this threshold without further thought or information search, then they will be unlikely to seek out and utilize other considerations (Lavine, Johnston, and Steenbergen 2012). For example, Druckman et al. (2013) find that citizens rely on the quality of arguments when deciding issues in unpolarized contexts, but in polarized environments they prefer the in-party's position, no matter how weak the argument in its favor. A similar point applies to mass-level affective polarization. Research suggests that when citizens feel unambivalent about their partisanship they bring fewer considerations to bear on judgment and decision-making than when they have both positive and negative feelings toward each party (Lavine, Johnston, and Steenbergen 2012). In affectively polarized environments, citizens feel quite confident in judgments based on partisanship alone.

In the context of the Court, citizens learn at least two things from party cues. First, many people possess weakly structured belief systems and fail to recognize the partisan and ideological implications of issues (Converse 1964; Kinder and Kalmoe 2017). This means there is a large gap between the attitudes of elites, which largely fall along a single dimension, and citizens, whose attitudes take on a multidimensional structure (e.g., Feldman and Johnston 2014; Treier and Hillygus 2009). When issues become salient, however, elite partisans teach the public "what goes with what" (Converse 1964), which increases the association between left–right political identities and specific issue attitudes (e.g., Lenz 2012; Levendusky 2009; Zaller 1992). This is especially true for complex issues over which citizens have weak prior opinions (Carmines and Stimson 1980; Johnston and Wronski 2015). While some cases before the Court are affect-laden (e.g., gay marriage), others are less likely to elicit strong attitudes independent of elite cues (e.g., campaign finance). Thus, elite partisans play an important role in teaching their co-partisans in the mass public which side of a case they *should* be on (Nicholson and Hansford 2014). Second, elites play an important role in defining norms for appropriate behavior in a democracy. Is it OK to call the justices "activist"? Is it OK to support noncompliance, Court-packing, or stripping the Court's jurisdiction? These are complex issues, and citizens will look to knowledgeable elites for cues to what is acceptable behavior. If elite partisans support Court-curbing actions, this makes it much more likely that their attentive co-partisans will as well.

Finally, polarization increases the costs to partisan defection. Taking a position that deviates from those of one's fellow partisans is always difficult, but it is especially tough when the two sides are sharply divided. Psychologically, defection causes substantial cognitive dissonance, which people generally seek to avoid (Festinger 1957; Heider 1958). There are also social costs to deviating from the partisan in-group. When positions on salient issues become associated with partisan labels, position-taking becomes a badge of membership – a signal that one is a group member in good standing (Johnston, Lavine, and Federico 2017; Kahan 2015). Taking a position contrary to the in-group may result in loss of reputation or standing within the group (Sinclair 2012), or it may simply cause tension with others whose companionship is valued for reasons that have little to do with politics (Mutz 2006). As Baddeley (2018, 64) explains, "Failing to conform generates awkwardness and can lead to confrontation and confusion. Conformity is much easier: it provides psychological reassurance, and is psychologically satisfying, especially if it means we can minimize interpersonal conflicts." Citizens will thus be motivated to develop "habits of mind" that credibly signal conformity to current partisan norms (Kahan 2015). This research suggests that polarization activates the pursuit of partisanship for its own sake – positive political identities become ends in themselves (e.g., Mason 2018). This implies that citizens may support Court-curbing actions in response to decisions they do not even disagree with, because agreement and disagreement with the decision are tightly linked to identity, and party members work to signal their status within the group through increasingly extreme attitudes and actions.

In sum, polarization increases the importance of partisanship – and left-right orientations tied to partisanship – in political cognition and reduces the relative importance of other considerations, such as core democratic values. Empirical support for this idea comes from a survey experiment conducted in Venezuela. Svolik (2018) finds, first, that all voters care to some degree about democratic principles in the sense that candidates are penalized for proposals that subvert democratic institutions. Importantly, however, this commitment to democratic values is too weak to constrain strong partisans from pursuing their narrow political interests. They may like their own candidate a bit less for proposing anti-democratic reforms, but they still prefer that candidate – even when the opposing party vows to protect these institutions (see also Graham and Svolik 2018; Singer 2018). This work illustrates two of our lessons from political psychology: citizens are only weakly principled, and partisan polarization exacerbates this problem. As Svolik (2018, 1) concludes, "voters in polarized societies are indeed willing to trade off democratic principles for partisan interests and their willingness to do so increases in the intensity of their partisanship."

Conceptualizing (and Distinguishing) Support for Court-Curbing

Our book focuses on *support for Court-curbing*, or citizens' willingness to undermine and diminish the Court's independence and power in the

American political system. This is a departure from much recent research. Contemporary work often begins with the Eastonian (1965) distinction between "specific" and "diffuse" support. Specific support is approval or performance satisfaction and is thought to move considerably over time in response to Court decision-making. Like presidential approval, specific support taps whether citizens think the current justices are doing a good job. It is thus natural and expected for specific support to respond to policy disagreement with the Court. Diffuse support, by contrast, is an enduring institutional loyalty – an unwillingness to make fundamental changes to the Court, even when one disagrees with its rulings. Diffuse support is primarily rooted in perceived legitimacy: when citizens see the Court as possessing rightful authority, they defend the institution, even if they dislike its rulings for policy-related reasons. These conceptual definitions seem uncontroversial, but problems arise in their operationalization and use in practice.

First, legitimacy and diffuse support are notoriously amorphous concepts and thus difficult to operationalize. The most popular solution is to average many diverse items, all of which are thought to be related to these terms in one way or another. This measurement strategy seeks to cover the breadth of the conceptual space and has the added advantage of producing reliable measures.[12] In practice, researchers have combined items tapping support for Court-curbing (e.g., doing away with the Court), perceptions of procedural propriety (e.g., the Court is "too mixed up in politics"), and general trust in the Supreme Court (e.g., Bartels and Johnston 2013; Christenson and Glick 2015a; Gibson and Caldeira 2009a, 2009b; Gibson, Caldeira, and Spence 2003a; Gibson and Nelson 2015b; Zilis 2018).

The problem, we think, is that Court-curbing, procedural perceptions, and trust are meaningfully distinct, and it is not clear what we are measuring when we average across them. The gain in breadth and reliability comes at a steep price: a loss of conceptual clarity. Further, both process-based and policy-based theories highlight a unique and important role for procedural perceptions in understanding Court-curbing. For process-based theories, these perceptions are an important predictor of willingness to curb the

[12] From a measurement perspective, breadth is related to content validity, while reliability in multi-item scales is associated with internal consistency (or inter-item correlations) among items. A related example involves how scholars work with "ideology," another notoriously difficult concept to operationalize. For example, by averaging many diverse policy items, one can generate reliable measures that cover the broad conceptual space of "liberalism" or "conservatism" (e.g., Ansolabehere, Rodden, and Snyder 2008).

Court, while in our policy-based approach, perceptions are used to rationalize attacks on the Court. Averaging support for curbing with procedural perceptions makes it impossible to test these theories. We think the right approach is to keep them separate. If multi-item scales are used to increase reliability, the items should respect these conceptual boundaries.

Second, scholars and commentators often consider opposition to Court-curbing to be a *direct* measure of legitimacy and diffuse support. The logic is that these concepts imply an unwillingness to make fundamental changes to the Court, so if most citizens oppose Court-curbing, most citizens must be loyal to the institution. The problem with this reasoning is that citizens may oppose Court-curbing for two very different reasons: (a) they believe the Court has rightful authority and thus strongly value its institutional integrity as an end in itself or (b) they agree with the policies generated by the Court's rulings and thus have a partisan interest in protecting the Court's power. The former is the essence of perceived legitimacy and (its consequence) institutional loyalty. The latter, by contrast, implies a fickle and merely instrumental support for the Court; that is, opposition to curbing is conditional on the delivery of congenial outcomes. This observational equivalence problem means that opposition to Court-curbing, on its own, is not a valid indicator of legitimacy or diffuse support because those who oppose curbing today may support it as soon as the ideological winds change.

The upshot is that legitimacy and diffuse support must be inferred by comparing citizens' opposition to Court-curbing when they agree with the Court's decisions to their opposition when they disagree. Like tolerance, we need to place citizens in situations where support for the Court is costly to their policy, partisan, or ideological interests. This is not a new claim. Gibson and colleagues, for example, have argued for the importance of an "objection precondition" in studies of legitimacy and make a similar point with their quip "legitimacy is for losers" (Gibson 2015; Gibson, Caldeira, and Spence 2002, 2005; Gibson, Lodge, and Woodson 2014). Nonetheless, the literature often falls into the trap of equating levels of opposition to Court-curbing with institutional legitimacy, loyalty, or diffuse support.[13] In sum, while we cannot measure these latter concepts directly, the *effects* of policy disagreement on support for Court-curbing tell us something important about citizens' perceptions of legitimacy and diffuse support for the Court. If citizens believe the Court has rightful

[13] We have been guilty of this as well (Bartels and Johnston 2013).

authority, support for Court-curbing should be both low *and* resistant to change in the face of uncongenial rulings.

Broadly Targeted and Narrowly Targeted Court-Curbing

We argue that there are at least two distinct types of Court-curbing actions that differ in how they respond to disagreement with Court decision-making. Specifically, we distinguish between *narrowly targeted* (or *narrow*) and *broadly targeted* (or *broad*) forms of Court-curbing. Narrowly targeted Court-curbing involves actions designed to minimize the consequences of a small number of decisions – perhaps only one. In such cases, the goal is not to alter the Court in a fundamental way but to mitigate the negative implications of the Court's jurisprudence within an issue area. The most commonly observed forms of narrow Court-curbing are legislative overrides, overt or subtle noncompliance with decisions, the removal or sanctioning of judges based on specific cases or issues, and the stripping of the Court's jurisdiction to hear cases within a narrowly circumscribed issue area (e.g., marriage cases). The defining aspect of these actions is that the Court's efficacy is threatened within a small area and is left untouched in other areas. Broadly targeted curbing, by contrast, is defined by actions that reduce the Court's power and independence in a more general and enduring way, across many or all issue areas. Common examples of broad curbing include a mandatory retirement age, retention elections for justices, Congressional vetoes or public referenda on Court decisions, greater executive control over appointment and retention of justices, and doing away with the Court altogether.

We believe this distinction between narrow and broad curbing has real consequences for understanding how citizens respond to the Court. To understand why, consider what we should expect if the policy-based perspective is entirely correct – that is, if citizens care *only* about getting desirable outcomes and not at all about the institutional integrity of the Court. Under what conditions will they support narrow and broad forms of Court-curbing? The answer, we think, depends a great deal on whether citizens dislike the Court's general ideological trajectory or only a subset of decisions. If the Court is expected to deviate from the individual's preferences on a wide array of issues over the long run, then broadly targeted measures make a lot of sense. In this case, the Court is a fundamentally hostile political institution and policy-concerned citizens can only benefit by constraining the Court's independence from the majoritarian institutions of government. The worst-case scenario is that the majority also agrees with the Court, in which case they are no worse off than with a completely independent Court. But the upside is that the elected branches will be able to rein in the Court to some degree and the Court may even feel pressure to moderate its decision-making to avoid these attacks altogether.

What about a case where citizens strongly dislike a single decision but believe the Court is furthering their policy goals as a general matter? Here it would not make sense to support broadly targeted Court-curbing measures – one would be constraining the power of an institution that is generally producing favorable policy outcomes. Rather than reduce the Court's independence, the goal should be to mitigate the negative consequences of the decision, for example, by pushing strongly for legislative override of one sort or another, supporting noncompliance, or perhaps even seeking a removal of the Court's jurisdiction in the relevant issue area. Indeed, we saw several examples of such proposals in Chapter 1.

Should there be any relationship at all between single disliked decisions and support for broad curbing? We think so, but it should be weaker than for narrow curbing. Broad curbing responds to perceptions of disagreement with the Court's general ideological tendencies. A single decision provides some information about this – after all, liberal decisions are typically made by a liberal Court. If citizens update their perceptions of the Court's ideology based on individual decisions, then support for broadly targeted Court-curbing may also respond to single decisions. However, the movement should be small because the information is noisy – liberal decisions are sometimes made by a conservative Court. To the extent citizens do update their perceptions, we should see small changes in support for broad curbing measures in response to even one decision. But again, it is narrow curbing measures that should respond most strongly.

The literature to date has largely ignored this distinction and its implications. By focusing on the highly abstract concepts of legitimacy and diffuse support, scholarship has not considered the possibility that different forms of disagreement have different consequences for the Court's power and independence. For example, recent work (including our own) makes the same prediction for how support for the Court changes in the face of both general ideological disagreement as well as disagreement with single decisions (Bartels and Johnston 2013; Christenson and Glick 2015a). By focusing on the more concrete concept of Court-curbing, and by breaking this concept down into multiple facets, we offer a more nuanced perspective on how citizens respond to Court decision-making.

One could also view the distinction between narrow and broad Court-curbing as an attempt to revitalize *decision acceptance* as a focal dependent variable in this literature. Recent work is largely concerned with whether citizens support fundamental changes to the Court – broad curbing in our terminology (e.g., Bartels and Johnston 2013; Christenson and Glick 2015a; Gibson, Caldeira, and Spence 2003b; Gibson and Nelson 2015b; Zilis 2018). However, an important line of work is concerned with the *legitimizing capacity* of the Supreme Court – with its ability to generate acceptance of its decisions, even when people initially disagree with the policy implications (e.g., Choper 1980; Bartels and Mutz 2009; Christenson and Glick 2015b; Clawson and Waltenburg 2009; Clawson, Kegler, and Waltenburg 2001, 2003; Franklin and Kosaki 1989; Fontana and Braman 2012; Gibson, Caldeira, and Spence 2005; Hoekstra and Segal 1996; Mondak 1990, 1994; Nicholson and Hansford 2014; Salamone 2014, 2018; Stoutenborough, Haider-Markel, and Allen 2006; Woodson 2015; Zilis 2015). Decision acceptance – and the "implementation problem" more generally – is also focal in the formal literature on the Court's interaction with other branches (e.g., Carrubba 2009; Carrubba and Zorn 2010; Staton 2010; Stephenson 2004; Vanberg 2001, 2005). As discussed in Chapter 1, these models show that public resistance to narrow curbing constrains the ability of elected officials to confront the Court and thus expands the set of viable policies that the Court can consider on any given issue.

The focus of recent work on fundamental changes to the Court is understandable given the profound implications such changes would have for the institution. But this emphasis obscures other ways in which the Court's power and independence are constrained by a fickle public. Citizens need not threaten to destroy the institution; the Court's efficacy can be substantially reduced if citizens fail to punish their elected officials for intransigence or hostility on specific decisions or issues (Carrubba and Zorn 2010; Rosenberg 1992; Vanberg 2001). We argue for a return to focus on these narrower forms of Court-curbing in the public opinion literature, but not at the expense of a consideration of broad forms. Rather, a full understanding of the public's response to Court decision-making requires giving each dimension its due and recognizing the differences between the two.

The Role of Political Engagement

To this point we have treated citizens as largely homogenous, but there is reason to think that our expectations should be conditional on citizens' knowledge of, and attention to, American politics – that is, on their level of *political engagement*. There is perhaps no more important moderator of political attitudes and behavior (Abramowitz 2010; Carpini and Keeter 1996; Zaller 1992). However, the way in which engagement alters citizens' support for Court-curbing is unclear, because process-based and policy-based theories generate conflicting expectations.

First, political engagement is associated with belief systems that more closely approximate the left–right divide at the elite level (Abramowitz 2010; Converse 1964; Zaller 1992) and with stronger political identities and greater investment in one's political opinions and beliefs (Huddy, Mason, and Aarøe 2015; Johnston, Lavine, and Federico 2017). For example, engaged citizens are more likely to say that they use "we" instead of "they" when discussing their favored party. They are also more likely to agree that their political attitudes and beliefs are an important reflection of who they are as people. Overall, engaged citizens care more about political conflicts and seek out the information necessary to learn where the parties, and other important political groups, stand on the issues. We thus expect that engaged citizens will also care more about what goes on at the Supreme Court and will see larger stakes for any given Court decision. They will be more attentive to news and commentary about big decisions and are more likely to understand the implications of decisions for their favored groups and issues and for competition between the two major parties. Moreover, their stronger partisan identities imply greater responsiveness to partisan polarization (e.g., Slothuus and de Vreese 2010). These considerations suggest that political engagement should increase the effect of policy disagreement with the Court on support for Court-curbing.

Process-based theories of Court-curbing view the role and implications of political engagement much differently. A long line of research suggests that "to know the Court is to love it" – that is, political sophistication and exposure to the Supreme Court increase perceptions of the Court's legitimacy and thus heighten institutional loyalty (Caldeira and Gibson 1992; Casey 1974; Gibson and Caldeira 2009a). In this view, citizens who know more about politics in general also have a better understanding of the Court's unique minoritarian role in American politics and are more likely to be exposed to the legitimizing symbols of the institution. Process-based theories thus make a conflicting prediction: political engagement should *decrease* the effect of policy disagreement on support for Court-curbing. From this perspective, the engaged are one of the most important bulwarks against attacks on the Court.

We think both perspectives make important points. Engaged citizens have stronger political identities and are more invested in Court outcomes, but they are also more knowledgeable about the Court, its unique role in American politics, and how it is different from the overtly political branches. They are more motivated to attack the Court in response to disliked decisions but are also more likely to recognize the constraints implied by their endorsement of core democratic values. This conflict could lead to less support for Court-curbing in the face of disliked decisions, as process-based theories expect. Our first two lessons, however, suggest that this conflict could also generate more directionally motivated reasoning aimed at justifying support for Court-curbing. That is, engaged citizens may be no less likely to support Court-curbing compared to the unengaged but may feel a greater need to rationalize these attacks. Indeed, there is substantial evidence that politically attentive and knowledgeable citizens are both more motivated and more skilled at generating arguments that justify their prior opinions and partisan proclivities (Kahan et al. 2017; Lavine, Johnston, and Steenbergen 2012; Slothuus and de Vreese 2010; Taber and Lodge 2006; Zaller 1992). It is often our most politically attentive citizens who are the most biased by their political predispositions.

This leaves us with a bit of a puzzle. There are reasons to believe that engagement will both increase and decrease the impact of policy disagreement with the Court on support for Court-curbing. We therefore examine the moderating role of engagement on curbing in an exploratory fashion. We do, however, have stronger expectations regarding the relationship between engagement and directionally motivated reasoning. Here we agree with the process-based perspective that engaged citizens will experience greater conflict when considering Court-curbing. First, they are more likely to understand and endorse the Court's unique role in American government and to recognize the applicability of widely shared democratic values to judgments about the acceptability of Court-curbing. In turn, they are more likely to recognize that their support for Court-curbing conflicts with important norms and are thus more likely to feel the need to rationalize their support. The unengaged, by contrast, should experience less dissonance when considering Court-curbing measures. It is also clear from the political science literature that politically attentive and knowledgeable citizens are better able to rationalize their political attitudes and beliefs. For both reasons, we expect procedural perceptions to respond more strongly to decision disagreement among the engaged than among the unengaged. *When* engaged citizens support Court-curbing, they will be more motivated and more competent at rationalizing this support through attacking the Court's procedural legitimacy.

HYPOTHESES

It is useful to end this chapter by outlining a set of hypotheses to be tested in subsequent chapters. Our first set of hypotheses concerns the relationship between policy disagreement with the Court and support for Court-curbing:

1. Disagreement with specific Supreme Court decisions ("specific policy disagreement") will be strongly associated with support for narrowly targeted Court-curbing measures, such as issue-specific jurisdiction stripping, noncompliance, and legislative override.
2. Specific policy disagreement will be weakly, but positively, associated with support for broadly targeted Court-curbing measures, such as doing away with the Court altogether, reducing its independence, or instituting mandatory retirement ages or retention elections for justices.
3. Disagreement with the general ideological trajectory of the Supreme Court ("general policy disagreement") will be strongly associated with support for broadly targeted Court-curbing measures.[14]
4. Partisan polarization will strengthen the relationship between policy disagreement with the Court and support for narrow and broad forms of Court-curbing.

Our final two hypotheses concern how procedural perceptions respond to disagreement with the Court via directionally motivated reasoning:

5. Specific and general policy disagreement will be strongly associated with negative procedural perceptions of the Court ("perceptions of politicization").
6. The relationship between policy disagreement and perceptions of politicization will be larger for politically engaged citizens relative to unengaged citizens.

CONCLUSION

In this chapter we reviewed the process-based perspective on Court-curbing and offered an alternative, policy-based framework. We argue that citizens care more about furthering their narrow political interests

[14] Note that we do not test for the impact of general policy disagreement on narrowly targeted curbing. By definition, we use policy disagreement with a specific decision any time we analyze narrow curbing.

than protecting the Court's institutional role in American government and thus seek to curb the Court in response to disliked decisions. The nature of this Court-curbing, however, varies with the nature of citizens' disagreement with the Court. When disagreement is limited to a small number of decisions or issues, citizens seek narrow forms of curbing that mitigate their impact but preserve the Court's institutional integrity. It is only when citizens disagree with the longer-term ideological trajectory of the Court that they support measures aimed at reducing the Court's countermajoritarian capacity. As argued by process-based theorists, both forms of Court-curbing conflict with citizens' endorsement of core democratic values. We argue that politically engaged citizens resolve this discord through the construction of arguments that attack the procedural propriety of the Court. If the justices are failing in their role as fair and objective interpreters of the Constitution, then curbing attacks may be justifiable. Finally, we have argued that elite and mass partisan polarization exacerbate these dynamics. In contexts where the parties are sharply divided, in terms of both policy and feelings toward one's opponents, citizens find it much more difficult to exhibit forbearance by sacrificing narrow political victories for the longer-term goal of protecting the Court's integrity.

3

A Deep Dive into Supreme Court Evaluation and Support

Many scholars and commentators argue that the US Supreme Court enjoys a robust "reservoir of goodwill" within the public. In this chapter we take a deep dive into measures of support for the Supreme Court to assess the validity of this received wisdom. While our book's core objective is to examine theories of Court-curbing, this chapter provides a descriptive account of the level of support – across multiple facets of evaluation – that the Court has secured in the last few decades. An important contribution of our book is an emphasis on conceptually clean outcomes of interest when it comes to public assessments of the Supreme Court. We thus present descriptive evidence for several distinct concepts, including (1) job approval and confidence, (2) procedural perceptions, (3) trust, and (4) both narrow and broad forms of Court-curbing. Subsequent chapters will focus on Court-curbing and procedural perceptions as the key dependent variables in our story. This chapter also gives us the opportunity to introduce the data and measures we will use in subsequent chapters.

Court-curbing contains "broadly targeted" and "narrowly targeted" components. The former relates to enduring attacks on the Court's independence and power in American government, for example, by restricting tenure or imposing additional veto points on Court decisions. Broad curbing items are often included as indicators of legitimacy and diffuse support, as in Caldeira and Gibson's (1992) seminal work. By contrast, narrow curbing refers to subverting the Court's authority on specific issues, for example, through noncompliance, jurisdiction stripping, or legislative override. It has also been referred to as policy legitimacy or decision acceptance (e.g., Mondak 1990, 1994).

Procedural perceptions entail beliefs about the Court's decision-making process. They range from politicized, partisan, and ideological to legalistic, fair, and impartial. Recent work has tended to combine procedural perceptions and Court-curbing into a single measure of diffuse support, legitimacy, or institutional loyalty (Bartels and Johnston 2013; Christenson and Glick 2015a; Gibson 2007; Gibson and Caldeira 2009a; Gibson, Caldeira, and Spence 2003a, 2003b; Gibson and Nelson 2015b; Nelson and Smith 2015; Zilis 2018). This muddying of concepts is less than ideal from a theoretical perspective. In process-based theories, procedural perceptions are a primary foundation of institutional support or legitimacy (Tyler and Rasinski 1991), while in our policy-based approach such perceptions serve as an important mechanism of rationalization for Court-curbing. In either case, procedural perceptions must be treated as an independent facet of Court evaluation. They are an important part of the bigger story, but they are conceptually distinct from citizens' preferences over curbing the Court.

Consistent with past work, we also distinguish curbing from *job approval* – a facet of Court assessment often referred to as "specific support" (a la Easton 1965) or "performance satisfaction" (Gibson and Nelson 2014, 2015b). In this chapter, we also examine "confidence" and "trust" in the Court, which Gibson et al. (2003a) have conceptualized as falling into the realm of specific support.

DATA DESCRIPTION

In the following we describe aggregate levels and trends for various facets of Supreme Court opinion. For job approval and confidence, we rely on several commercial polls described later. For concepts that are central to our book – and which play an important role in subsequent chapters – we rely on academic surveys. Some of these were designed by others, and some were designed by us. To ease discussion in this and subsequent chapters, we summarize all the datasets that will be analyzed in the book in Table 3.1. We will subsequently refer to these datasets by their designated nicknames, which are listed in the table. More detailed information regarding each survey can be found in the appendix to this chapter. Harvard Dataverse houses the book's reproduction archive.

We emphasize both the quantity of data sources (seven) and the range of research designs: three experimental studies (using national samples) and four observational studies, one of which contains a long-term panel component (i.e., surveying the same respondents multiple times). By

TABLE 3.1 *Characteristics of surveys analyzed in this book*

Year	Title	Nickname	Type of study	Study characteristics	Chapters
2005	Annenberg Supreme Court Survey	2005 ASCS	Observational, cross-sectional	National sample of 1,504 US adults. Conducted by Annenberg Public Policy Center. Interviews 3/17/2005-4/18/2005.	3, 4, 7
2006	Alito Confirmation Survey (merged with 2005 Citizenship, Involvement, and Democracy)	2006 Alito	Observational, cross-sectional	National sample (PIs: James Gibson and Gregory Caldeira), wave 2 reinterview of 335 US adults from the 2005 CID, 1/19-2/13/2006.	3, 7
2009	Time-sharing Experiments in Social Sciences Survey	2009 TESS	Experimental	National sample of 1,061 US adults conducted by Knowledge Networks. Contains survey experiment designed by authors. 2/7-2/17/2009.	3, 5, 7
2011	Freedom and Tolerance Survey	2011 FTS	Observational, Cross-sectional	National sample of 750 US adults fielded for Washington University (PI: James Gibson) by Abt-SRBI. 4/26-7/7/2011.	3, 4, 7
2012–2016	The American Panel Survey	TAPS	Observational, cross-sectional and panel	National panel survey (sample sizes vary by months and types of analyses) conducted for Weidenbaum Center at Washington University (PI: Steven Smith) by	3, 4, 5, 7

				Knowledge Networks/Gfk. Monthly panel survey from 2012–2016.	
2016	YouGov Study	2016 YGS	Experimental	National sample of 2,500 US adults. Contains survey experiment designed by authors. 5/17-5/24/2016.	3, 5, 6, 7
2017	Qualtrics Study	2017 QS	Experimental	National sample of 1,597 US adults. Contains survey experiment designed by authors. 6/15-6/23/2017.	3, 6

Note: The book's data and reproduction archive is housed at the Harvard Dataverse.

examining cross-sectional, panel, and experimental data across diverse sampling strategies and multiple distinct measures of key constructs, we offer an especially comprehensive test of our core hypotheses. While each study has its own set of strengths and drawbacks, the combination of multiple studies with heterogeneous attributes allows for stronger inferences. The conclusions do not rest on any particular study or dataset. In addition to the datasets listed in Table 3.1, we rely (in this chapter only) on descriptive reports from Gibson (2007), who uses the following data sources:

1. 1987 Freedom and Tolerance Survey (in conjunction with the General Social Survey) (Gibson 1987) (1987 FTS)
2. 1995 Gibson and Caldeira survey (1995 GC)
3. 2001 Gibson, Caldeira, and Spence survey (conducted after the *Bush* v. *Gore* ruling) (2001 GCS)
4. 2005 Citizenship, Involvement, Democracy Study (2005 CID)[1]

JOB APPROVAL AND CONFIDENCE OVER TIME

Figure 3.1 reports data on approval, confidence, and satisfaction with Supreme Court policymaking. The job approval numbers are constructed primarily from Gallup – which covers 2000 to present – and supplemented with several other commercial polls to extend the series back to the 1980s. These supplemental data were retrieved from the Roper Center's iPOLL archive.[2] While the data bounce around somewhat from survey to survey, the smoothed series suggests a secular decline in the percent of citizens who approve of the way the Supreme Court is handling its job, from its peak in the mid-1980s (at about 60 percent) to its nadir in the 2010s (45–50 percent). This decline in approval appears to accelerate beginning in the late 1990s or early 2000s with less than half of the public approving of the Court in recent years. Thus, the decline in approval over the last three decades is meaningful, if modest. There was, however, a slight uptick in 2017 and 2018, and we await additional data to see if this constitutes the beginning of a new trend.

[1] As Table 3.1 indicates, the 2006 Alito study that we analyze in this chapter and Chapter 7 is a reinterview (panel) study of a subset of survey respondents from the 2005 CID study.

[2] Gallup data for all three series are available at the Gallup website via their "Supreme Court" site: https://news.gallup.com/poll/4732/supreme-court.aspx. Data for all three series, including the supplemental data we collected via the Roper Center's iPOLL database, are available in our book's data archive.

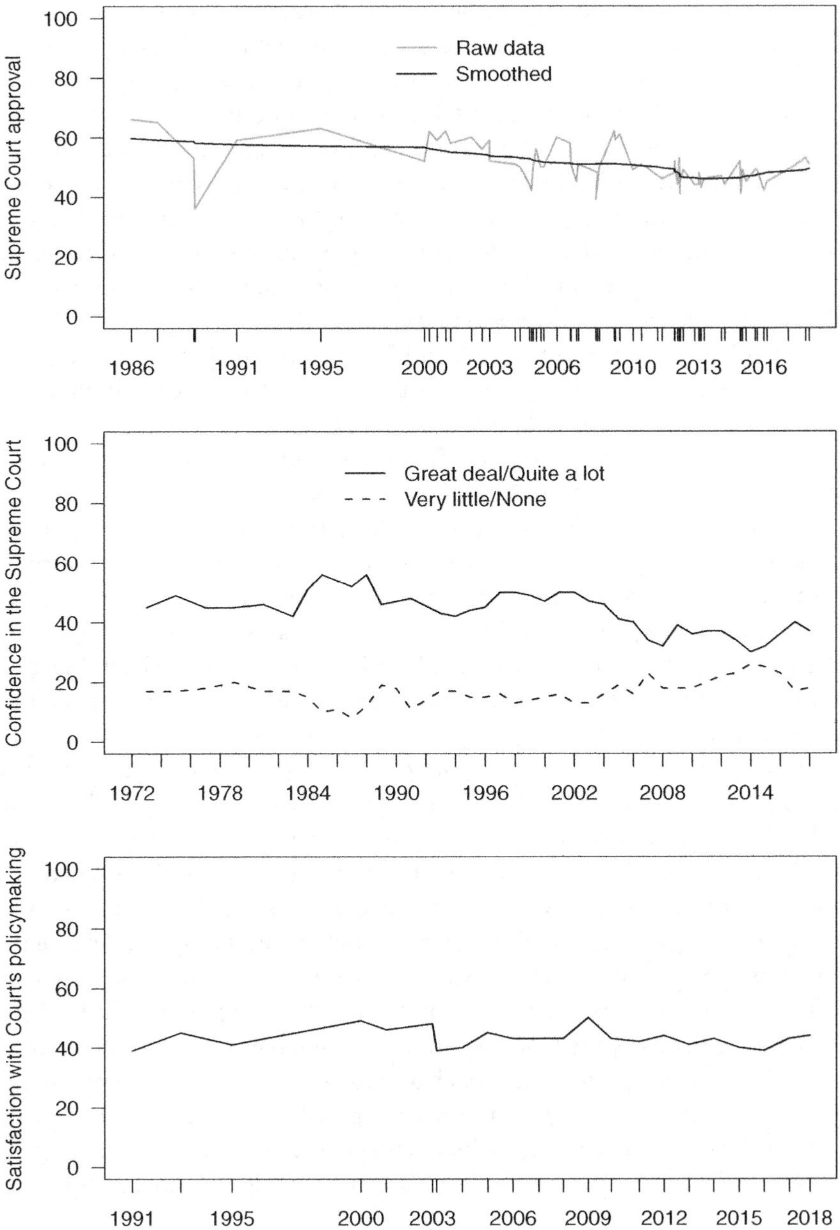

FIGURE 3.1 Aggregate approval, confidence, and policy satisfaction for the Supreme Court over time

Moving to "confidence" in the Court, we rely on data gathered from Gallup. The middle panel of Figure 3.1 reports trends from 1973 to 2018. We add together the percent of respondents indicating "a great deal" and "quite a lot" of confidence, and we do the same for "very little" and "none."[3] The percent of the public expressing high confidence hovers between the low 40s and the mid-50s from the beginning of the series through the 1990s, with a peak in the mid-1980s. Like the approval series, however, confidence declines meaningfully beginning in the early 2000s. By 2014, only 30 percent of the public express high levels of confidence in the institution and 26 percent express very little or no confidence. There has also been a slight uptick in confidence in recent years – peaking in 2017 – and the series ends in 2018 with 37 percent expressing high levels and 18 percent expressing low levels of confidence.

The bottom panel of Figure 3.1 reports Americans' assessment of whether the Court is "too liberal," "too conservative," or "about right" (via Gallup). We refer to this facet as satisfaction with the Court's policy-making. In Chapter 4 we return to this variable as one of multiple measures of policy disagreement. The last option ("about right") is an expression of "approval" in the sense that the respondent is satisfied with the Court's policy direction. Overall, satisfaction is relatively stable and shows no obvious trend, ranging between 40 and 50 percent over the entire period.

Taken together, these results show that on approval or "performance satisfaction" grounds, the Court does not enjoy an unusually large or robust "reservoir of goodwill." For example, rarely does a majority of the public express high levels of confidence in the institution. Further, there has been a meaningful decline in approval and confidence in the last two decades (though perhaps with a small uptick in recent years). Aggregate levels of approval do not shift drastically from one year to the next, which is to be expected. Approval is theoretically closely related to individual preferences vis-à-vis the Court's outputs. While partisans and ideologues at the *individual level* may shift back and forth over time in response to the Court's decisions, average changes among different partisan groups can offset each other to an extent, which tempers the variance of the aggregate series. Still, it will be interesting to see if what appear to be slow but

[3] The responses do not sum to 100 percent because respondents could also choose "Some" confidence or state that they "Don't know." Those latter responses are not directly included in the graph, but they are included in the denominator for purposes of estimating the percentages for high and low confidence.

secular declines in approval beginning in the early 2000s continue forward into the future or whether the recent uptick is the start of a new trend.

PROCEDURAL PERCEPTIONS OVER TIME

We next review aggregate data on how Americans perceive the process by which the Supreme Court and its justices make decisions and go about their business.[4] One measure that has been used across several surveys is whether the Supreme Court "gets too mixed up in politics." The top panel of Figure 3.2 reports the percentage of respondents who agree and disagree with this item in the 2001 GCS, 2005 CID, 2005 ASCS, 2011 FTS, and five years of TAPS. For the TAPS surveys, this item is measured two or three times per year. We use data that precede the Court's typical spree of significant rulings that are announced in June. In 2012, 2015, and 2016, we use the May wave, and in 2013, we use the January wave; 2014 contains the July wave, since the variable was not measured before then in 2014. For all surveys, the response scale is a five-category agree–disagree scale. We combine the "strongly" and "somewhat" categories for both agree and disagree responses. Those who are neutral (neither agree nor disagree) are not included in the graph, but they are included in the denominator for purposes of generating agree versus disagree percentages. In all cases, "agree" indicates that the respondent sees the Court as too mixed up in politics.

In 2001, roughly equal shares agreed and disagreed that the Court gets too mixed up in politics. The percent agreeing shoots up to 65 (CID) and 72 (ASCS) in the two 2005 surveys – clearly, many Americans saw the Court in political terms during the period surrounding the Roberts and Alito nominations. While the percent agreeing that the Court is too mixed up in politics declines in subsequent years, the percent *disagreeing* never recovers to its pre-2005 levels. Indeed, from 2013 onward, less than 20 percent of the public disagrees with this statement and more than 40 percent agrees with it. Overall, and in line with past work, a significant share of the public sees the Court as politicized and, perhaps just as important, less than 30 percent disagree that the Court is too mixed up in politics.

We also have descriptive data on perceptions of how the Court makes decisions. Are cases decided based on politics, partisanship, and ideology,

[4] All descriptive statistics reported in this chapter use post-stratification survey weights provided with the survey. The one exception is our 2017 QS.

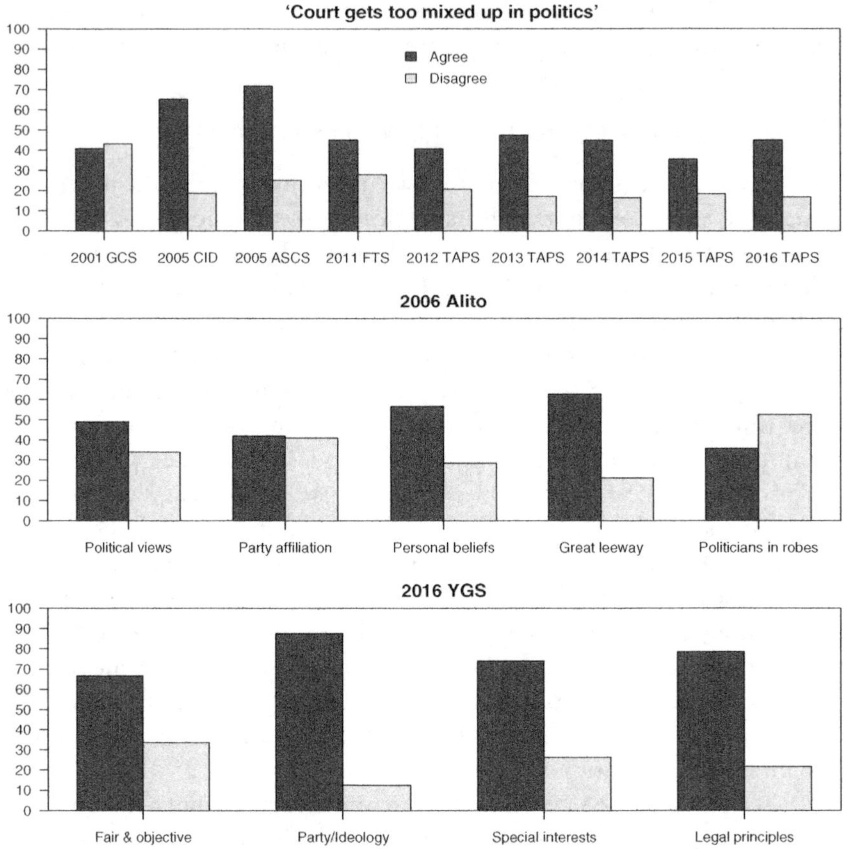

FIGURE 3.2 Procedural perceptions of the Supreme Court. The top panel shows percentage agreement and disagreement that the Supreme Court "gets too mixed up in politics" across several datasets (see Table 3.1 for information about each dataset); the middle panel shows agreement and disagreement with several statements in the 2006 Alito survey concerning the degree of politicization of judicial decision-making; the bottom panel shows agreement and disagreement that several factors influence judicial decision-making in the 2016 YGS (note that agreement with "Fair & objective" and "Legal principles" indicates low levels of perceived politicization); the denominator for each bar includes any neutral responses, "don't knows," and refusals.

or the Constitution, the law, and dispassionate legal principles? Are justices fair in their decision-making or are they politically motivated? Does the Court favor some groups over others or cater to partisan or ideological interest groups?

We take a deeper dive into these dynamics by looking at multiple questions from two surveys – the 2006 Alito study and the 2016 YGS. The first survey, conducted by Gibson and Caldeira as a part of their Alito confirmation study (Gibson and Caldeira 2009a, 2009b), asked respondents about whether the following factors had an influence on justices' decision-making: (1) values and political views, (2) party affiliations, and (3) personal beliefs versus the law and the Constitution. The survey also asked (4) whether justices have a great deal of leeway in constitutional interpretation and (5) whether justices are merely "politicians in robes." Each item uses a five-point agree–disagree scale. The middle panel of Figure 3.2 reports the percent of respondents who agree with the "political" response versus the percent who agree with the "nonpolitical" response.[5] Across the first four items, the percent of political responses is greater than the percent of nonpolitical responses. Nearly 50 percent believe that justices base their decisions on their values and political views, and 57 percent agree that justices base their decisions on their personal beliefs even when they say their decisions are based on the law and Constitution. A little over 40 percent disagree that justices' party affiliations had "little to do with how they decide cases," while greater than 60 percent agree that the Constitution gives the justices "a great deal of leeway" in making decisions. While just under 40 percent perceive that justices are merely "politicians in robes," only about 50 percent explicitly reject the idea (with the remainder being uncertain).

These descriptive statistics reveal that many in the public see the justices as political and ideological decision-makers, at least to an extent. These findings serve as the basis for Gibson and Caldeira's (2011) work on whether Americans have increasingly embraced "legal realism," the opposite of a subscription to the "myth of legality." The findings also support related work by Scheb and Lyons (2000) on decreasing subscription to the myth of legality (see also Bartels and Johnston 2012). Moreover, it is again worth emphasizing the low levels of explicit rejection of these politicized perceptions. Except for the "politicians in robes" item, less than 50 percent of the public – and in some cases, less than 30 percent – see the Court in highly legalistic terms.

In our 2016 YGS, reported in the bottom panel of Figure 3.2, we asked respondents similar questions, including (1) whether the Court makes

[5] Once again, "neutral" (neither agree nor disagree) responses are not included in the graphs but are included in the denominator for purposes of estimating agree and disagree percentages.

decisions fairly and objectively and whether the Court's decisions are influenced by (2) partisanship and ideology, (3) special interests, and (4) legal and constitutional principles. These descriptive statistics average over all the experimental treatments (we discuss these in greater depth in subsequent chapters). We use six-point agree–disagree response scales, where the middle options are "agree a little" and "disagree a little." Figure 3.2 combines all three agree responses and all three disagree responses. The descriptive statistics show not only that many Americans do perceive the Court in political terms but also that many perceive a "hybrid" model of Supreme Court decision-making. In other words, when given the opportunity, many believe the Court tries to be fair and objective and is influenced by legal and constitutional principles, but they also believe that the Court's decisions are shaped by partisanship, ideology, and special interests. In sum, many Americans believe that the Court is influenced by both political *and* legal considerations (see Bybee 2010; Gibson and Caldeira 2011).

TRUST

We now move to trust in the Supreme Court. While trust has been considered a core component of legitimacy or diffuse support in past research (Gibson, Caldeira, and Spence 2003a; see also Tyler and Rasinski 1991), recent work has argued that it is a distinct dimension of evaluation (Gibson 2011). We think trust likely falls somewhere between approval and support for Court-curbing. It is distinct from curbing because it does not involve supporting or opposing an action taken against the Court's power. At the same time, it is not quite the same thing as approval as it suggests more general beliefs about the extent to which the Court is properly executing its role. For these reasons we will largely ignore the concept of trust in the remainder of the book. Given its use in past work, however, we consider here its distribution over time.

Figure 3.3 reports data over seven years for the question of whether the Court can "usually be trusted to make decisions that are right for the country as a whole." We report percentages for those who register at least some agreement or some disagreement with that statement (respondents could also indicate uncertainty). Explicit distrust is low across the entire period, peaking at a bit above 25 percent in 1995 and again in 2011. Perhaps surprisingly, trust peaks (at nearly 80 percent) in 2001 in the aftermath of the *Bush* v. *Gore* ruling but hovers between 50 and 60 percent in recent years, which is a substantial decline from its highest values.

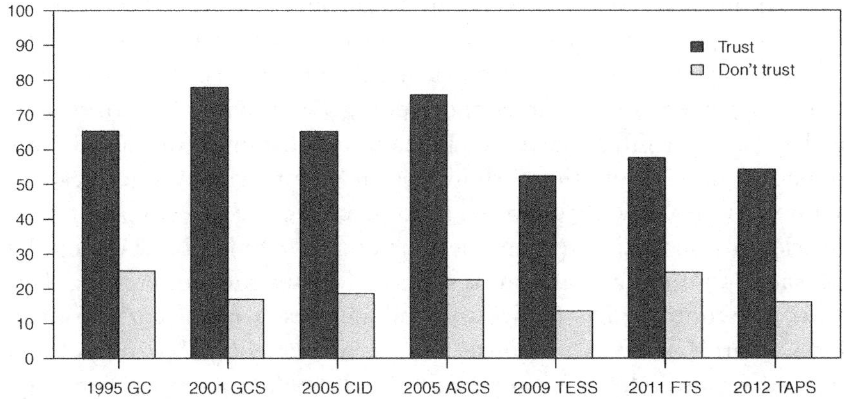

FIGURE 3.3 Trust in the Supreme Court. The figure shows the percentage of respondents who agree and disagree that the Supreme Court can "usually be trusted to make decisions that are right for the country as a whole" across several surveys (see Table 3.1 for information about each dataset); the denominator for each bar includes any neutral responses, "don't knows," and refusals.

COURT-CURBING

Now we turn to our primary outcome of interest: support for curbing the Supreme Court. Recall that we distinguish between two variants of Court-curbing. The first is broadly targeted Court-curbing, which centers on reducing the Court's power and independence in the political system. We refer to the second variety as narrowly targeted Court-curbing, which is aimed at reducing the Court's authority on a specific policy issue.

As we have discussed, Court-curbing has a strong connection to past conceptualizations and operationalizations of legitimacy, which is defined generally as rightful authority to render rulings for a polity. However, as we made clear in Chapters 1 and 2, legitimacy is not indicated directly by levels of opposition to Court-curbing at a given point in time. Instead, citizens' loyalty must be put to the test in the face of policy disagreement (see also Gibson 2015; Gibson, Caldeira, and Spence 2002, 2005). In subsequent chapters, we examine how both those in disagreement and those in agreement with Supreme Court policy render judgments on Court-curbing. We use evidence from these analyses to discuss implications for the Court's legitimacy.

It is nonetheless interesting to examine baseline levels of support for Court-curbing across both narrow and broad types and across time.

Even if high levels of opposition to curbing do not guarantee the Court's legitimacy, levels do tell us something about the Court's relative vulnerability to different types of curbing actions. If, for example, only 10 percent of people support doing away with the Court altogether, we can infer that it would take a substantial deviation from public opinion before this curbing option became viable, since baseline support is very low. By contrast, if 40 percent of people support tenure restrictions on justices at baseline, it may only require a few unpopular decisions to build a coalition of support for this form of curbing. Past work, by contrast, has tended to combine these various curbing items into additive indexes to bolster the measurement properties of key dependent variables – an approach we also take in subsequent chapters. Advantages notwithstanding, something is lost in the process of averaging many unique items. We lose both a sense of the concrete content of what we are discussing – that is, the specific policies, such as removing the Court's jurisdiction – and a sense of scale, since individual scores have primarily *relative* meaning in the context of an index. It is worthwhile to take a step back and see what is going on under the hood. What types of curbing actions find meaningful levels of support within the citizenry at baseline? Where are the Court's primary weak points?

Broadly Targeted Court-Curbing

We examine support for broad curbing in two ways. First, we examine items for which we have several years of data over time. Second, we examine specific data sources that include additional measures beyond the standard variables used in the literature. Table 3.2 summarizes the broadly targeted Court-curbing measures we use across our primary surveys. Note that the table refers to nicknames for each item. For some items (e.g., "do away with" and "issues reduced"), the question wording changed slightly from survey to survey, but the items are comparable. Once question wording stabilizes, we simply include the nickname in column two instead of the full question wording.

Figure 3.4 reports descriptive statistics for five broad curbing items for which we have data spanning at least five years: (1) do away with, (2) issues reduced, (3) less independent, (4) remove justices, and (5) stronger control. Nearly all items are based on five-category agree–disagree formats. We combine the two "agree" (strongly and somewhat) and "disagree" options into two categories: support for or opposition to curbing.

TABLE 3.2 *Broadly targeted Court-curbing survey items*

Survey	Items
1987 FTS*	1. If the Supreme Court continually makes decisions that the people disagree with, it might be better to do away with the Court altogether. (*Do away with*)
	2. The right of the Supreme Court to decide certain types of controversial issues should be limited by the Congress. (*Issues reduced*)
1995 GC*	1. If the US Supreme Court started making a lot of decisions that most people disagree with, it might be better to do away with the Supreme Court altogether. (*Do away with*)
	2. The right of the Supreme Court to decide certain types of controversial issues should be reduced. (*Issues reduced*)
2001 GC*	1. If the US Supreme Court started making a lot of decisions that most people disagree with, it might be better to do away with the Supreme Court altogether. (*Do away with*)
	2. The right of the Supreme Court to decide certain types of controversial issues should be reduced. (*Issues reduced*)
2005 CID*	1. *Do away with*
	2. *Issues reduced*
2005 ASCS	1. If the Supreme Court started making a lot of rulings that most Americans disagreed with, it might be better to do away with the Court altogether. (*Do away with*)
	2. Do you think there should be a mandatory retirement age for Supreme Court Justices, or not? (*Retirement age*)
	3. Do you think the Court should allow television cameras in the courtroom so that others can see and hear the arguments? (*Cameras*)
	4. Do you feel that the US Supreme Court has too much power, too little power or about the right amount of power? (*Too much power*)
	5. Do you think Supreme Court nominees should be required to state their personal views on controversial issues or do you think that they should be allowed to refuse to state their views? (*Nominees' views*)
	6. When the president chooses a Supreme Court nominee, should he only consider that person's legal qualifications and background or should he also consider how that nominee might vote on controversial issues? (*President views*)

TABLE 3.2 *(continued)*

Survey	Items
	7. When the Senate is reviewing the president's nominee for the Supreme Court, should the Senate only consider that person's legal qualifications and background or should the Senate also consider how that nominee might vote on controversial issues? (*Senate views*)
2009 TESS	1. *Do away with*
	2. *Issues reduced*
	3. The US Supreme Court should have the right to say what the Constitution means, even when the majority of the people disagree with the Court's decision. (*Constitution means*)
2011 FTS	1. *Do away with*
	2. *Issues reduced*
	3. The US Supreme Court ought to be made less independent so that it listens a lot more to what the people want. (*Less independent*)
	4. Judges on the US Supreme Court who consistently make decisions at odds with what a majority of the people want should be removed from their position as judge. (*Remove justices*)
	5. It is inevitable that the US Supreme Court gets mixed up in politics; therefore, we ought to have stronger means of controlling the actions of the US Supreme Court. (*Stronger control*)
TAPS	1. *Do away with*
	2. *Issues reduced*
	3. *Less independent*
	4. *Remove justices*
	5. *Stronger control*
	From June 2012 wave only: How strongly would you support or oppose:
	6. Making it easier to remove judges from the Supreme Court if their decisions go against what the majority of the people want. (*Easier to remove*)
	7. Making it easier to change the constitution when the Supreme Court interprets the constitution wrongly. (*Easier to change Constitution*)
2016 YGS	1. *Do away with*
	2. *Issues reduced*
	3. *Less independent*
	4. *Remove justices*
	5. *Constitution means*

TABLE 3.2 *(continued)*

Survey	Items
2017 QS	1. Some people have proposed a Constitutional amendment that would allow the public to vote to overturn Supreme Court decisions on controversial issues. Do you support or oppose this amendment? (Branching used to get four-point response scale) (*Referenda*) 2. Which of the following comes closest to your view? Supreme Court appointees should be vetted to ensure they will vote the right way on important issues, or Supreme Court appointees should be selected based on legal qualifications alone. (Branching used to get four-point response scale) (*Nominees vetted*) 3. Some people have proposed a Constitutional amendment that would put in place retention elections for Supreme Court justices. This means that, every few years, citizens would vote on whether a justice gets to stay on the Supreme Court, or whether the President should nominate a new justice. Do you support or oppose this amendment? (Branching used to get four-point response scale) (*Retention*)

* *Note:* Items in the first four datasets are included in Chapter 3 only, not the subsequent chapters. Unless otherwise noted, all items use agree–disagree response scales.

Nearly all surveys include a neutral option (e.g., "neither agree nor disagree"), and some include "don't know." For all descriptive statistics reported here, these latter options are included in the denominator. In other words, the percentages reported in Figure 3.4 are the percent supporting or opposing curbing among all respondents in the survey. We interpret the percent *opposing* Court-curbing proposals as a reasonable measure of the Court's "reservoir of goodwill" or baseline institutional support. Again, it is important not to conflate this with "legitimacy" – these individuals may simply agree with the Court's current policymaking – but it does give an idea of how hard it would be to build a coalition of support for each type of curbing.

Figure 3.4 reports trends for the "do away with" item, which represents the most extreme form of broad curbing. It taps whether respondents want to take a giant axe, as opposed to a scalpel, to the Court. In comparative context, especially in democratizing countries in which

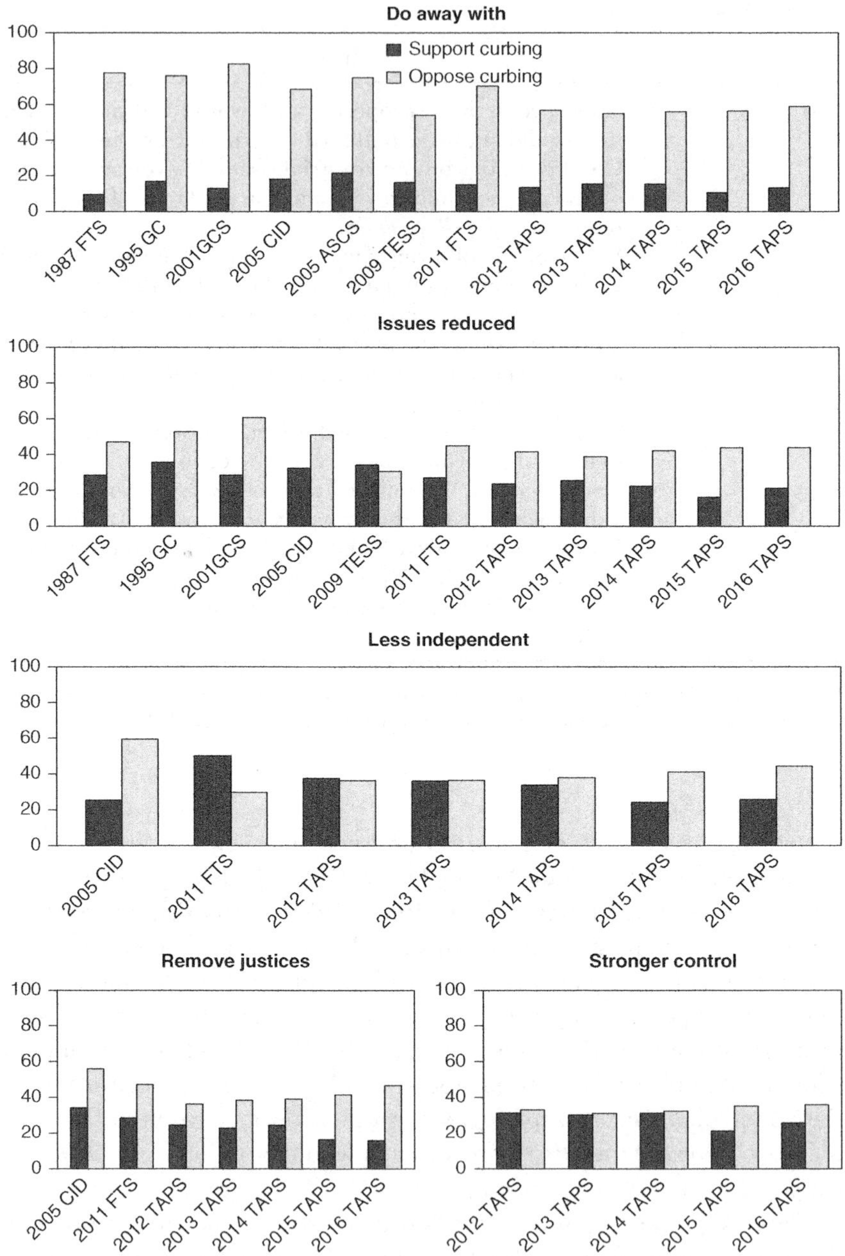

FIGURE 3.4 Support for broadly targeted Court-curbing across time. See Table 3.1 for information about each dataset and Table 3.2 for question wording of each curbing item; the denominator for each bar includes any neutral responses, "don't knows," and refusals.

courts have short histories of genuine authority, this question is not at all far-fetched. Indeed, one sign of "democratic backsliding" is the derogation of the rule of law and an accompanying diminution of judicial authority (e.g., Gibler and Randazzo 2011).

Support for this extreme form of curbing is quite low across surveys, ranging from 10 to 20 percent. But these numbers alone do not show the decrease over time in *opposition* to doing away with the Court – recall that some respondents give a neutral option or don't know. Opposition was between 70 percent and just north of 80 percent in the first five surveys (1987 through 2005). Except for the 2011 FTS, however, opposition rates are meaningfully lower in later surveys than earlier ones, dropping to only 55 to 60 percent from 2009 onward. This is important because it is more difficult to convince opponents than undecideds to support Court-curbing. Thus, despite a lack of increase in support for doing away with the Court over time, the decline in opposition is perhaps troubling for the justices, because it indicates that even this most extreme curbing option may be "on the table" for upwards of 40 percent of the public.

The second panel of Figure 3.4 reports trends for the "issues reduced" item. This item taps support for taking away the Court's power to hear controversial issues. It is "broad" curbing in our sense because the item does not refer to specific issues and thus involves reducing the Court's independence in a more general sense. In other datasets, we consider narrowly targeted jurisdiction stripping as well. Opposition to this type of Court-curbing ebbs and flows throughout this period, ranging from under 50 percent in 1987 up to 60 percent in 2001. It then plummets down to just 30 percent in the 2009 TESS survey and rebounds to around 40 percent for 2011 onward. Explicit support for reducing the Court's jurisdiction to hear controversial issues averages about 30 percent from 1987 to the 2008 TESS data, then decreases to an average of about 20 percent from 2011 onward. These patterns imply that those in the neutral category increase during the latter period. Thus, the Court's baseline institutional support on this dimension is low, many citizens are unsure about this form of curbing, and the Court never enjoys a sustained period of majority opposition to substantially reducing the Court's jurisdiction.

The "less independent" measure is a direct indicator of support for attacks on judicial independence. While only about one-fourth of the public preferred a less independent Court in 2005, half thought the Supreme Court should be made less independent in 2011. That number drops to, and stays, between 30 and 40 percent over the next four surveys and drops again to about 25 percent in the final two years of our series. As with the prior two items, however, opposition to this form of curbing never reaches majority levels after 2005. Many citizens are simply unsure about the importance of judicial independence.

A similar pattern emerges for the "remove justices" item. Like the previous items, baseline opposition to this form of curbing is weak, and only in the 2005 CID survey is there majority opposition. On the other hand, support for removal has decreased over time – from a high of over 30 percent in 2005 down to an average of about 25 percent from 2012 to 2014 to about 15 percent in 2015 and 2016.

Finally, we report five years of data for the "stronger control" measure. Support for more control of the Court is about 30 percent for the first three years and drops to between 20 and about 25 percent in the final two years. Meanwhile, opposition to this type of curbing levels out at about 30 percent across the five years, which again suggests a large portion of the public who do not have an opinion, one way or the other, on the matter.

On the whole, this descriptive evidence is certainly at odds with received wisdom about the Court possessing a substantial "reservoir of goodwill." One could argue the Court comes close to achieving such a threshold for the "do away with" measure, though opposition to this extreme form of curbing just clears 50 percent in several more recent surveys. While explicit support for broad curbing in many of these classic measures is not high, opposition is also weak. There are many in the public who simply do not register an opinion when it comes to these proposals, leaving the remainder of the public divided. This is not a boon to the Court. While we argue that even opponents of curbing can be moved to support based on contemporary events or elite cues, those who respond "don't know" or "neutral" are easier to shift. Thus, the decline in firm opponents of broad curbing in recent decades is an important signal of the Court's vulnerabilities in the current polarized era. The Court's baseline institutional support is far weaker than suggested in previous research.

2005 Annenberg Supreme Court Study

In addition to the "do away with" item already discussed, the 2005 ASCS contains additional questions that have not traditionally been used in diffuse support or legitimacy-oriented support scales. We nonetheless consider these items to fall within the broadly targeted Court-curbing category in that they reflect meaningful changes to the institutional status quo aimed at reducing the independence of the Court. They include measures concerning (1) retirement age, (2) cameras in the courtroom, and (3) the Court having too much power as a general matter. The survey also asked about changes to practices in the Supreme Court appointment process. One item asks about support for changing the process so that justices are considered based on personal views rather than simply legal qualifications (see Bartels and Johnston 2012). Of course, the status quo permits justices to refuse to state their views on legal issues so that they do not prejudge cases that may come before them in the future. The other appointment-related items, all listed in Table 3.2, pertain to whether the president and the Senate should consider how nominees may vote on controversial issues.

We report descriptive statistics for these six items in the top panel of Figure 3.5. The figure shows that curb rates range from just under 40 percent to nearly 60 percent, which again suggests that the Court does not necessarily enjoy a deep reservoir of goodwill. Indeed, about 60 percent prefer a mandatory retirement age, suggesting majority opposition to the notion of life tenure on the Court, and almost 40 percent say that the Court has too much power. About 40 percent prefer televised oral arguments, which can be viewed as an indicator of support for greater transparency. Finally, many respondents prefer a process where nominees state their views explicitly. Just over 50 percent think that nominees should be required to state their views, and nearly 50 percent agree that the president and Senate should consider nominees' views on controversial issues. This represents a distinct break from the norms that representatives at least profess to follow in the appointment process.

June 2012 TAPS

In addition to the five broad curbing items discussed in Figure 3.4, the June 2012 wave from TAPS has two additional items. The items are reported in Table 3.2. Respondents were asked if they supported or opposed: (1) "Making it easier to remove judges from the Supreme Court if their decisions go against what the majority of the people want," and (2) "Making it easier to change the constitution when the Supreme Court interprets the constitution wrongly." Both items use a four-point support-oppose scale, with no middle/neutral option, and we combine the two categories for oppose and the two for support. Just over 40 percent support the proposal to make it easier to remove justices whose decisions go against the public will, while over 50 percent oppose it. Around 30 percent would support a proposal to make it easier to

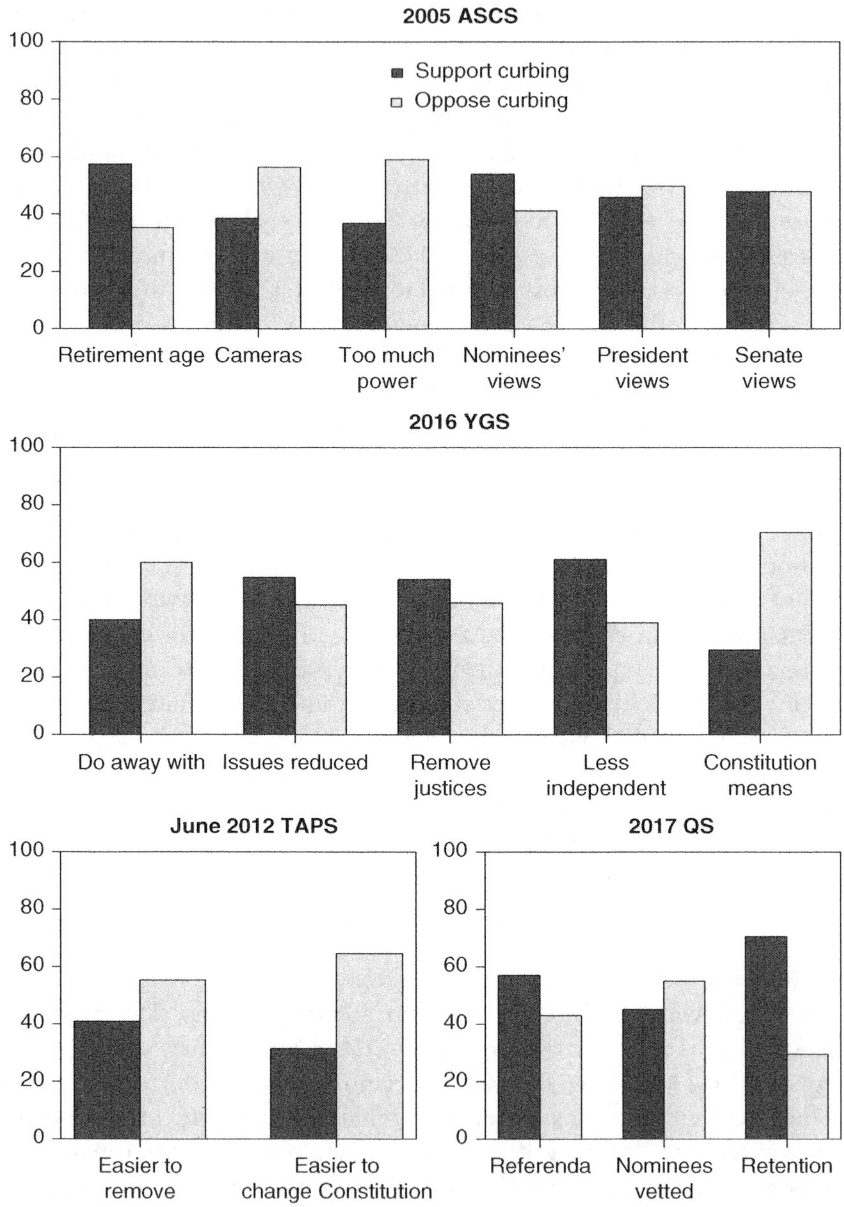

FIGURE 3.5 Support for broadly targeted Court-curbing in four surveys. See Table 3.1 for information about each dataset and Table 3.2 for question wording of each curbing item; the denominator for each bar includes any neutral responses, "don't knows," and refusals.

change the Constitution for wrongly decided rulings, which represents a challenge to judicial supremacy. On the other hand, over 60 percent oppose such a proposition. On the whole, the results resemble what we see in Figure 3.4.

2016 YGS

Our 2016 YGS also includes broadly targeted Court-curbing items commonly used in the literature. We discuss this survey's Court-curbing items separately from the others since they are quite recent and also because we employ slightly different response options relative to past studies. Like past items, we employ agree–disagree formats, but to discern whether those who may be inclined to respond "neutral" or "neither agree nor disagree" may lean one way or the other, we provided six response options: agree strongly, agree somewhat, agree a little, disagree a little, disagree somewhat, and disagree strongly. Our descriptive statistics combine the three agree responses and the three disagree responses. We note that when combining just the top two responses – both curb and no curb, respectively – the general patterns are similar. The inclusion of the "leaners" changes the levels but not the overall patterns. This study also includes two survey experiments with multiple experimental conditions pertaining to procedural and polarization considerations and liberal-conservative policy treatments. Those experimental aspects will be analyzed in depth in Chapters 5, 6, and 7. Figure 3.5 presents descriptive statistics for the entire sample, while averaging over the experimental treatments. Wordings for the five items are listed in Table 3.2.

Consistent with the other surveys, descriptive statistics from this survey show that the Court does not enjoy a deep and wide reservoir of goodwill among the American public. First, almost 40 percent of respondents show some level of agreement with getting rid of the Court altogether if it starts making decisions most Americans disagree with. This level of agreement is quite staggering and a marked departure from the descriptive statistics reported in Figure 3.3. While it is impossible to draw firm conclusions (given differences in sampling), these results suggest that many respondents who state "don't know" or "unsure" on the "do away with" item may lean toward doing away with the Court if it drifts too far from the median voter.

For the next two items – reducing the power of the Court to hear controversial issues and removing justices who are out of line with the public – support for curbing surpasses opposition (around a 55 to 45 split). For both items, "leaners" break more in the direction of support for curbing than opposition.

The last two items present opposing patterns. On independence, over 60 percent support curbing the Court's independence, while about 40 percent oppose such a measure. Leaners break toward the curbing option in this instance. The opposite pattern holds for the last item regarding the Court's right to say what the Constitution means. For this item, the Court does seem to enjoy a higher baseline level of support. Roughly 70 percent oppose curbing this power (about 20 percent of whom are leaners), while about 30 percent support curbing on this measure. Thus, on the matter of giving the Court robust authority to say what the Constitution means, aggregate opinion opposes curbing. This is an intriguing result because it seems to conflict with the implications of the other items, such as removing justices or reducing the Court's jurisdiction. Indeed, support for the Court is higher on this item than the "do away with" question. One possibility is that the wording of "Constitution means" leaves ambiguity in intent. Specifically, the item could be interpreted as stating that the Court should have the right to pass judgment, but this does not necessarily imply that its decisions should be treated as the final say or even followed.

2017 QS

We designed the 2017 QS survey experiment with the intention of expanding the range of Court-curbing measures. While the Qualtrics sample is nationally drawn, the sample providers use a variety of methods to obtain respondents (e.g., pop-up ads on social media) that make it difficult to infer representativeness. We thus stress caution in drawing firm inferences from the descriptive statistics here. Moreover, the ultimate value of this study is its experimental component, which will be analyzed in Chapter 6. Nonetheless, the survey is useful in that it asks about curbing actions that have rarely – if ever – been considered in the literature to date. For the three items listed in Table 3.2, we report statistics that average over the study's experimental conditions.

Figure 3.5 represents the percent of survey respondents who support or oppose each measure. Looking to the first item, a clear majority of the sample (58 percent) supports a constitutional amendment giving the people the ability to overturn Supreme Court rulings. Support for this item is a significant blow to notions of judicial supremacy – that the Court has the final word on constitutional meaning for everyone. These data suggest that many citizens want more control over constitutional meaning (as well as a say on other legal questions of national importance) or at least the ability to provide a direct check on the Supreme Court.

Similar to what we found regarding some of the 2005 ASCS items, about 44 percent of respondents support more "policy vetting" to make sure appointees "will vote the right way on important issues." A majority of the sample rejects that proposition and prefers nominees be evaluated based on legal qualifications alone. Yet many want judges who would vote like they would vote. It suggests substantial support for a confirmation process based on politics and prospective voting as opposed to qualifications and credentials alone. Many in the public crave more "policy accountability" mechanisms for justices.

Finally, over two-thirds of the Qualtrics sample supports the idea of holding retention elections for justices. Along with the first item, this suggests robust support for greater accountability of justices to public opinion. Many in the public prefer greater majoritarian control over the Court – that justices be subject to electoral mechanisms, an idea which has gained popularity in state court systems.

Overall, the Qualtrics sample provides converging evidence that the Court's reservoir of goodwill is weaker than suggested by previous research. Many citizens support measures that would significantly curb the Court's extant authority in the political system. While support for curbing varies across different types of items, there seems to be a general pattern of enthusiasm for stronger majoritarian constraints on the Court. Moreover, rarely do we find supermajority *opposition* to fundamental changes to the Court in American politics.

Narrowly Targeted Court-Curbing

Three of our original studies – 2009 TESS, 2016 YGS, and 2017 QS – contain measures of narrowly targeted Court-curbing which involve attacks on the Court's authority on specific policies as opposed to the institution itself. We list all narrow curbing items in Table 3.3. For each of these studies, narrow curbing is asked in the context of an experimental treatment about a liberal or conservative Court ruling. Importantly, this means that the results here are limited in what they can tell us. They average over agreement and disagreement with the manipulated decision, variation we explore in Chapters 5 and 6. Like the broad curbing items, the marginals reported here provide an indication of the public's baseline

TABLE 3.3 *Narrowly targeted Court-curbing survey items*

Survey	Items
2009 TESS	1. How much authority do you think the Court's decision should have over the other branches of government and the American people? (complete authority, some authority, not that much authority, no authority at all) (*Authority*) 2. To what extent should Congress and the President comply with the Court's ruling? (Should fully comply, should comply with most aspects, should comply with only some aspects, should not have to comply with the ruling) (*Compliance*) 3. Do you feel as if the Supreme Court's ruling should be accepted as the final word on this issue? (yes, no) (*Final word*)
2016 YGS	(All respondents who received these questions received information on Supreme Court rulings. See Chapter 5 for more details.) 1. The Supreme Court's ruling should not be the final word on the matter and there ought to be an effort to overturn the ruling. (Agree–disagree scale) (*Final word*) 2. All Americans (including elected officials nationwide) should comply with the Supreme Court's ruling. (Agree–disagree scale) (*Compliance*)
2017 QS	(Respondents who received information on campaign finance and same-sex marriage rulings received this language. Respondents in control group (no information about a ruling) received these questions with generic reference. 1. Some people argue that it is extremely important for citizens and politicians to obey the Supreme Court's order [re: campaign finance or same-sex marriage], even if they disagree with the decision. Others argue that it is not at all important for citizens and politicians to obey the Court's order. And others have opinions somewhere in-between. How important do you think it is for citizens and politicians to obey the Supreme Court's order? (Extremely important, Very important, Somewhat important, Not too important, Not at all important) (*Compliance*) 2. The Constitution gives Congress the power to determine the Supreme Court's jurisdiction, that is, the types of issues the Court may and may not decide. Some people argue that Congress should take away the Court's power to decide [campaign spending or same-sex marriage] issues. Others

TABLE 3.3 *(continued)*

Survey	Items
	argue that Congress should not limit the Supreme Court's jurisdiction. Which of the following comes closest to your view? (Branching used to create six-category response scale) (*Strip issue*)
	3. Some people argue that the Supreme Court should have the final say on the issue of (corporate campaign spending or same-sex marriage). Others argue that Congress should have the final say on this issue. Which of the following comes closest to your view? (Branching used to create six-category response scale) (*Court v. Congress*)

level of support for the Court across different types of curbing policies. Weaker enthusiasm for a given curbing proposal suggests greater difficulty in convincing citizens to attack the Court in that fashion. This variation in baseline opposition to curbing is itself of interest.

2009 TESS

In our 2009 TESS study, respondents were randomly assigned to a liberal or conservative Court ruling on the issue of governmental surveillance of emails and phone conversations to combat terrorism. As we discuss in Chapter 5, there are also "procedural" treatments in this study. For the descriptive statistics we present here, we simply average over all experimental conditions. Figure 3.6 presents results on the narrow curbing items from Table 3.3. Across the three items, the Court finds only moderate levels of baseline loyalty and support. Only 15 percent of respondents believe that the Court's ruling should have "complete authority over the other branches of government and the American people," only one-third of respondents believe that Congress and the president should "fully comply" with the ruling, and a minority of respondents affirm judicial supremacy and the idea that the "Court's ruling should be accepted as the final word on this issue."

Instead, we see a willingness to attack the Court's authority at the margin. While few citizens reject the Court's authority altogether, large proportions question that authority and suggest that only partial compliance by the other branches of government is acceptable. A majority believe that the Court's ruling should *not* be the final word on the matter. And remember that we are

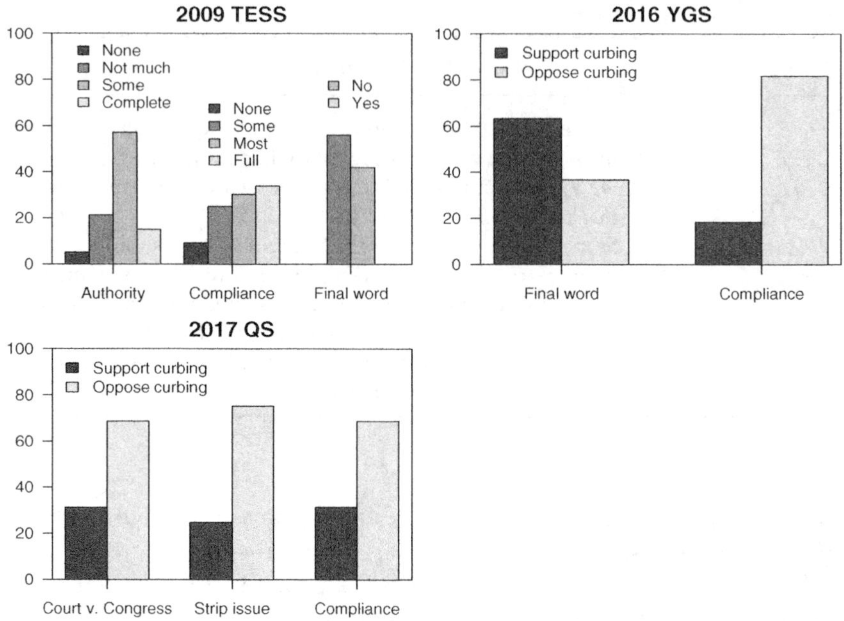

FIGURE 3.6 Support for narrowly targeted Court-curbing. See Table 3.1 for information about each dataset and Table 3.3 for question wording of each curbing item. Denominators for each bar include refusals.

averaging over agreement and disagreement with the ruling itself – many citizens will oppose narrow curbing simply because they like the decision outcome. Like the results for the broad curbing items discussed previously, various forms of narrow curbing are "on the table" for many (if not most) citizens. In Chapters 5 and 6 we will directly examine how support for these policies moves in response to decision dissatisfaction.

2016 YouGov Study

As discussed, this study contains two survey experiments (respondents were first randomly assigned to one module or the other). In both studies, respondents are randomly assigned to receive a liberal or conservative Court ruling. After this, subjects are randomly assigned to receive one of four rulings from the areas of race, search and seizure, free expression, and the death penalty. An advantage of this study (discussed in greater depth in Chapters 5, 6, and 7) is that any inferences we make are generalizable across these four issue areas. The other experimental factors in each experiment are elite polarization and procedural fairness, and we report descriptive statistics in this chapter that average across all experimental conditions. We analyze the two narrow curbing items from Table 3.3. We used six-category agree–disagree formats (like for the broad curbing items from the same survey), and we combined the three "agree" responses and the three "disagree" responses to generate support and opposition to curbing for each item.

These results are reported in the middle panel of Figure 3.6. Averaging over the various decisions and treatment conditions in this experiment, close to two-thirds of respondents agree that the Court should *not* have "the final word on the matter and there ought to be an effort to overturn the ruling." As with the 2009 TESS, baseline support for judicial supremacy is rather weak. On the other hand, people overwhelmingly agree that others, including elected officials, should comply with the Court's ruling. The binarized version of this item does hide variation in the strength of this commitment, however. Only 37 percent of respondents strongly agree that others should comply, while 27 percent agree somewhat, and 18 percent agree only a little. Nonetheless, in these data at least, baseline support for compliance is fairly high.

2017 Qualtrics Study

Our Qualtrics study also asks about narrowly targeted curbing items, but in a different way than the previous two studies. As discussed, the study involves an experimental component which varies the ideological direction of the ruling (on campaign finance and same-sex marriage) and partisan intensity. There is a control group that does not receive any Court ruling/policy direction (we discuss this further in Chapter 6). For comparability to the other two experimental studies, we report results only for respondents who received a Court ruling ($n = 1{,}266$). We average across liberal (same-sex marriage) and conservative (campaign finance) rulings, as well as the partisan cues treatments.

As seen in Table 3.3, the first item concerns whether the Court or Congress should have the final say on the issue,[6] the second concerns stripping the Court's jurisdiction on the issue, and the third asks about compliance. The third panel of Figure 3.6 presents the descriptive statistics for these three items. For the compliance item, about two-thirds of

[6] The reference to Congress in this and the "take away the Court's power to decide" items is important for the polarization aspect of that experiment (see Chapter 5). Again, our goal with the additional studies is to expand the range of Court-curbing items in the literature.

respondents believe that it is either “extremely” or “very important” for citizens and politicians to obey the ruling, while about one-third express significant skepticism about the importance of compliance. When respondents are given a choice of whether to give Congress or the Court the final say, about 70 percent choose the Court while just over 30 percent choose Congress. It is a bit hard to interpret this baseline support for the Court. These results conflict with those of the 2009 TESS and 2016 YGS, where a majority opposed giving the Court the final say. The difference is likely due to the explicit reference to Congress in the 2017 item. Congressional approval is quite low as a general matter, and many citizens may be skeptical that the current partisan configuration of Congress will work in their interests. This again suggests the importance of examining how support for narrow curbing *changes* as a function of disagreement with specific decisions – a task we undertake with these data in Chapter 6. We see similar results when asked if Congress should remove the Court’s authority to hear the policy issue: about 75 percent reject such a removal while about 25 percent are in favor.

Summary

In sum, when examining aggregate support for narrowly targeted Court-curbing across three surveys, we see significant variation across policies. Few citizens reject the Court’s policy authority entirely, but many appear willing to consider significant forms of Court-curbing. Similarly, when posed in a binary manner, less than one-third of citizens countenance noncompliance with the Court’s rulings, but a substantial portion indicates support for partial noncompliance when that option is available, and few are strongly committed to compliance. Further, citizens are far less supportive of giving the Court the “final say” on policy matters (though support increases if the alternative explicitly mentions “Congress”). This is interesting because noncompliance is not necessarily a stronger attack on the Court’s independence than legislative overrides. Indeed, much of the literature on public opinion of the Court is motivated by the importance of the Court’s legitimizing capacity to its efficacy.

Finally, we emphasize again that aggregate patterns of support for narrow Court-curbing can be deceiving, because they average over agreement and disagreement with the ruling. Citizens who agree with a ruling would not be expected to support narrow curbing measures, *even if* they afford the Court low levels of legitimacy. Still, this initial glimpse at narrow curbing does suggest variation in how citizens think about their options for getting around disagreeable decisions: noncompliance and jurisdiction stripping, for many citizens at least, are more drastic steps than passing legislation to mitigate the consequences of the decision. Further, it seems that the way in which these narrow curbing questions are posed may matter quite a bit. For example, respondents are wary of noncompliance when posed as a stark, binary choice, but they seem to be more comfortable when noncompliance is framed as *partial* compliance. This, of course, is still a substantial attack on judicial supremacy. Deeper examination of the importance of question wording for narrow Court-curbing support must await future research.

CONCLUSION

This chapter accomplished two goals. First, we introduced our datasets and key measures. We will refer to these throughout the remainder of the book. Second, we took a deep dive into baseline public support for the Court. While our primary research questions revolve around *variation* in support for Court-curbing, an examination of aggregate opinion can answer interesting questions. For example, we find that support for the Court appears to have declined meaningfully over the last two decades. This is true of approval, confidence, and several measures of broad curbing. We also find substantial variation in levels of support for different Court-curbing options. Within broad forms of Court-curbing, there is a surprising degree of support for direct, majoritarian control over the Court, such as public referenda on Court decisions or retention elections for justices. Within narrow forms of curbing, we find high levels of opposition to giving the Court the last word on constitutional issues, but more modest support for noncompliance and jurisdiction stripping. Although even here, there is variation in support as a function of framing: noncompliance may be more acceptable if it is framed as partial compliance.

But the most important conclusion to emerge in this chapter is that, contrary to received wisdom, the Court does not enjoy an exceptionally high level of support. For most broad curbing policies, only a minority of citizens show unambiguous support for the institution. That is, a majority either support broad curbing measures or are uncommitted one way or the other. This is evidence against a wide and deep reservoir of goodwill because aggregated opposition to curbing is effectively an upper bound on the public's institutional loyalty: many people who oppose Court-curbing at a given point in time may simply agree with the Court's policymaking. It is thus critical to examine how support for Court-curbing changes as a function of policy disagreement. How many citizens remain loyal to the Court when policy, partisan, and ideological interests are at stake? We begin this investigation in the next chapter.

APPENDIX: METHODOLOGY FOR NATIONAL SURVEYS

While Table 3.1 in the main text briefly describes each survey we analyze in this book, this appendix provides more details on sampling and methodology used by the survey firms to gather those samples. We draw on (and sometimes paraphrase) the descriptions provided by the sponsors and the firms themselves.

Annenberg Supreme Court Survey (2005 ASCS): The survey, directed by the Annenberg Public Policy Center, obtained telephone interviews with a sample of 1,504 US adults. The interviews were conducted in English by Princeton Data Source, LLC, from March 17 to April 18, 2005. The sample was designed to represent all continental US telephone households. The telephone sample was provided by Survey Sampling International, LLC (SSI), according to PSRAI specifications. The sample was drawn using standard list-assisted random digit dialing (RDD) methodology. As many as ten attempts were made to contact every sampled telephone number. The response rate was estimated at 41 percent.

Alito Confirmation Survey, merged with 2005 Citizenship, Involvement, and Democracy (CID) Study (2006 Alito): The 2005 CID is a door-to-door survey that was fielded from May 16 to July 19, 2005, resulting in 1,001 completed interviews. Interviews were conducted by International Communications Research (ICR) of Pennsylvania. The study used a cluster design (stratifying by census regions and metropolitan status) with the intent to retrieve a representative sample of the US adult population. Response rate was estimated at 40.03 percent. Directed by PIs Gibson and Caldeira, reinterviews were conducted via telephone for 335 of these 1,001 respondents between January 9, 2006, and February 13, 2006 (surrounding the Judge Alito confirmation process). For more details, see Gibson and Caldeira's ICPSR archive (#31841, "Assessing the Consequences of Politicized Confirmation Processes, 2005–2006").

2009 TESS Study: The study was conducted by Knowledge Networks (now GfK/Knowledge Networks). For our study, Knowledge Networks used its KnowledgePanel. Panel members are randomly recruited via random digit dialing (RDD) and are provided with access to the Internet and hardware if needed. Knowledge Networks surveys are based on a sampling frame which includes both listed and unlisted numbers; it is not limited to current Web users or computer owners. Once people are recruited to the panel, they can be contacted by e-mail (instead of by phone or mail). Knowledge Networks used this methodology to conduct 1,061 interviews from February 7 through February 17, 2009. For more details on methodology, see: www.tessexperiments.org/data/zip/Simas675/Knowledge%20Networks%20Methodology.pdf.

2011 Freedom and Tolerance Study (2011 FTS): The survey was fielded for Washington University by Abt SRBI, which used RDD for both land-line and cell phone frames. The telephone sample was provided by Survey Sampling International, LLC (SSI). A total of 750 interviews were conducted. The Supporting Information file for Gibson and Nelson's (2015) article (see *American Journal of Political Science* website) is not clear on the interview dates, though we attempt to estimate it using variables in the dataset; our best guess is April 26 through July 7, 2011. The response rate was estimated at 27 percent.

The American Panel Survey (2012–2016 TAPS): TAPS is a monthly panel study that began surveying respondents in fall 2011. The sample is intended to be representative of US adults. The sample was attained via random selection of residential addresses (stratified by age and ethnic group). A panel of more than 2,000 adults was initially recruited. TAPS surveys were administered online by GfK/Knowledge Networks. Panelists who did not have a computer or online service were provided computer and internet access by TAPS. We rely on select monthly surveys conducted between 2012 and 2016. For more details on TAPS methodology, see https://taps.wustl.edu/technical.

2016 YouGov Study (2016 YGS): The YouGov panel is a proprietary opt-in survey panel and comprised of 1.6 million US residents who have agreed to participate in YouGov's Web surveys. Panel members are recruited by a number of methods to help ensure diversity in the panel population. Recruiting methods include Web advertising campaigns (public surveys), permission-based email campaigns, partner-sponsored solicitations, telephone-to-Web recruitment (RDD based sampling), and mail-to-Web recruitment (voter registration–based sampling). The primary method of recruitment for the YouGov panel is Web advertising campaigns that target respondents based on their keyword searches. After a double opt-in procedure, where respondents must confirm their consent again by responding to an email, the database checks to ensure the newly recruited panelist is in fact new and that the address information provided is valid. Between May 17 and May 24, 2016, YouGov interviewed 2,619 respondents who were then matched down to a sample of 2,500 to produce the final dataset. The respondents were matched to a sampling frame on gender, age, race, education, ideology, and political interest. The frame was constructed by stratified sampling from the full 2010 American Community Survey (ACS) sample with selection within strata by weighted sampling with replacement (using the person weights on the public use file). Data on voter registration status and turnout were matched to this frame using the November 2010 Current Population Survey. Data on interest in politics and party identification were then matched to this frame from the 2007 Pew Religious Life Survey. The matched cases were weighted to the sampling frame using propensity scores. The matched cases and the frame were combined and a logistic regression was estimated for inclusion in the frame. The propensity score function included age, gender, race/ethnicity, years of education, voter registration, ideology, and non-identification with a major party. The propensity scores were grouped into deciles of the estimated propensity score in the frame and post-stratified according to these deciles.

2017 Qualtrics Study (2017 QS): We and two other researchers collected a non-probability sample of 1,597 US adults using Qualtrics Panels. The survey was fielded between June 15 and June 23, 2017. Quotas for age, education, gender, and race were used to obtain a sample similar to that of the general population on these characteristics. Specifically, we requested that no more than 40 percent of the sample hold a bachelor's degree, no more than 73 percent of the sample identify as white, and additionally requested between 51 percent and 53 percent female identifiers, 24 percent between the ages of 18 and 29, 45 percent between 30 and 54, and 31 percent over 55. The final percentage of females is 54 percent because we include in our final sample 85 respondents who finished the survey after quotas were filled. Respondents obtained through Qualtrics Panels typically receive points for their participation. The survey includes additional questions for an unrelated study on respondents' beliefs about conspiracy theories (see Lopez and Hillygus 2018), but all such questions were asked after our treatment and dependent variables.

4

General Policy Disagreement and Broadly Targeted Court-Curbing

This chapter tests the impact of general policy disagreement on citizens' support for broadly targeted Court-curbing. By "general policy disagreement," we mean an enduring form of policy divergence, not simply discontent with one or a small number of decisions. We are interested in what happens when citizens see the Court drifting away from their broader political orientations and identities for an extended period. For instance, an individual describing herself as liberal but who sees the Court as generally conservative is in strong general disagreement with the Court. Our focus is thus on *subjective perceptions* of divergence.[1] The value of this conceptualization and measurement strategy is that it taps how people *actually* perceive the Court in policy terms. Perceptions may be grounded in incomplete information – in some cases they might even be wildly off-base – but it is ultimately citizens' subjective impressions of the Court's decision-making that matter for behavior.

Indeed, our prior work demonstrates that citizens may have rational bases for perceiving the contemporary Supreme Court as conservative, moderate, or even liberal depending on the types of rulings to which they are paying most attention (Bartels and Johnston 2013). While the Court's output has been center-right in recent decades, a majority of the Court's most salient rulings have actually been decided in the liberal direction (Bartels and Johnston 2013; see also Bartels 2015). Consistent with these points, we find substantial variation in perceptions of the Court's ideological tenor. Taking perceptions into account is crucial for our purposes

[1] In prior work, we referred to this concept as "subjective ideological disagreement" (Bartels and Johnston 2013; see also Bartels, Johnston, and Mark 2015).

because they moderate the direction of the relationship between political preferences and support for Court-curbing. For example, Republicans will only support curbing at higher rates than Democrats if they see the Court as producing liberal policy outcomes. If, instead, they see the Court as conservative, it will be *Democrats* who support curbing at higher rates. The upshot is that ignoring variation in perceptions leads to the erroneous conclusion that left–right orientations are unrelated to support for Court-curbing, because these two effects have opposite signs and thus cancel out in the aggregate (see Bartels and Johnston 2013; Christenson and Glick 2015a).[2] Previous work has often erroneously rejected the importance of partisanship and ideology to Supreme Court legitimacy for just this reason (e.g., Gibson 2007).

There are different ways to operationalize the concept of general policy disagreement. For example, a measure we used in prior work (from the 2005 ASCS) first asks whether individuals think that the Court is liberal, conservative, or "making decisions more on a case-by-case basis." We interpret that latter option to mean that citizens perceived the Court to be charting a moderate policy course, while Gibson and Nelson (2015b) argue it is picking up nonideological factors, such as perceptions of impartiality or legalism (see also Christenson and Glick 2015a). Gibson and Nelson thus use a different measure, which calculates the proximity of the respondent to the Court based on the respondent's placement of the self and the Court in ideological space. Another strategy is to simply ask citizens directly whether they see the Court as generally "too liberal," "too conservative," or "about right" in its decision-making. We think there are advantages and disadvantages to each of these strategies – there is no perfect measure of general policy disagreement. The best approach is thus to consider a range of operationalizations across multiple datasets. If the results are consistent, we will have more confidence that we are onto something important.

Our operationalizations of support for broad Court-curbing are described in detail in Chapter 3, Table 3.2. We will briefly reiterate how we measure this construct in each study, but the reader should use Chapter 3 as a reference when needed. We include a common set of control variables, when possible, for regression models: age in years, sex (female = 1), black or African-American self-identification, Hispanic or Latino self-identification, five dummy variables for educational attainment ("less than high school

[2] Mondak and Smithey's (1997) dynamic model of Supreme Court support also emphasizes a similar aspect.

degree" is the excluded category), household income,[3] religiosity,[4] and political engagement.[5] When available, we also include measures of various democratic values, such as liberty over order, commitment to the rule of law, and tolerance. We will describe these measures in greater detail when they appear. In the 2005 ASCS (described in the next section), we also include a measure of trust in government as an additional control to be consistent with our previous analysis of these data (Bartels and Johnston 2013). This choice makes no difference to our results.

Our primary hypothesis is straightforward – we expect that general policy disagreement will substantially increase support for broad forms of Court-curbing. Recall from Chapter 2 that we are also interested in the interaction of disagreement with political engagement. In all datasets to follow we have examined the relevant interactions. Simply put, we find no support for an interaction of these two variables in *either* direction. That is, engagement does not consistently enhance or reduce the impact of policy disagreement on support for Court-curbing. As we noted in Chapter 2, there are competing predictions regarding the conditioning role of engagement. The process-based approach seems to imply that engagement will mitigate the negative consequences of disagreement for institutional support, while the policy-based approach suggests the opposite. It is possible that these competing effects wash out in the aggregate. It is also possible that neither theory has the right of it. In any case, given the inconclusive results, we do not consider these results further in this chapter. Future research is needed to delve more deeply into this issue.

2005 ANNENBERG SUPREME COURT STUDY

As discussed in Chapter 3, there are seven measures of Court-curbing from the 2005 ASCS. In addition to the standard "do away with" item, there are additional items not commonly used in the literature but which we believe capture interesting and heretofore underappreciated elements of broadly

[3] Household income often displays high nonresponse rates. In such cases, we impute missing values based on a regression model which predicts income from age, sex, educational attainment, race and ethnicity, and the interaction of education and sex and education and race and ethnicity.

[4] Indicators of religiosity vary across datasets. When available, we average items for the importance of religion to the respondent, church attendance, frequency of prayer, and biblical literalism.

[5] Indicators of political engagement vary across datasets. When available, we average objective political knowledge and indicators of subjective political interest and attention.

targeted curbing. To review, these include (1) mandatory retirement age, (2) cameras in courtroom, and (3) whether the Court has too much power. They also include measures of how justices are selected and appointed that tap general policy accountability: (4) nominees should be required to state their views on controversial issues, and both the (5) president and (6) senate should consider how a nominee will vote on controversial issues. These latter six items are binary, while the "do away with" item is a four-point agree–disagree response scale. We first build a scale that simply counts the number of "curb" responses for each respondent ("do away with" is recoded to be binary). We recoded the scale to range from 0 to 1 and estimate linear regression models which adjust for post-stratification weights.[6]

Before we describe independent variables, we address a difference between this analysis and our past work (Bartels and Johnston 2013) on the effect of policy/ideological disagreement. In this prior work, we created a "legitimacy scale" (our dependent variable) that reflected recommendations from Gibson et al. (2003a). That scale included the "do away with" item, two "trust" items, and two items which we refer to in this book as "procedural perceptions" (i.e., "mixed up" and "favors some groups more than others"). Our goal in this book is to create conceptually clean distinctions between Court-curbing, procedural perceptions, and trust, and to clearly distinguish between support for Court-curbing and legitimacy.[7] Thus, we do not use this scale and focus instead on support for and opposition to Court-curbing. To this end, we have expanded substantially (beyond "do away with") the number of curbing items included in our dependent variable.

We use two operationalizations of general policy disagreement in the 2005 ASCS. First, in order to make connections to prior work, we use the same four-point nominal measure we used in Bartels and Johnston (2013). That measure crossed an individual's ideology (using a three-category measure: liberal, moderate, conservative) with the individual's perception of the Supreme Court's ideology (liberal, conservative, or "case-by-case"). To review, the measure's four categories are:

[6] Since all items are binary and the scale is essentially a count, Cronbach's alpha is not an ideal measure of the internal consistency in the traditional sense. For this scale, however, alpha = 0.56, which is on the low side. We subsequently estimate separate models for each variable and the effect of policy disagreement is fairly stable (in sign and statistical significance) across the items. Estimating count models which account for over-dispersion gives substantively similar results.

[7] The "trust" concept strays from our conceptualization of Court-curbing. Recent work also argues that it likely reflects performance satisfaction rather than core diffuse support (Gibson 2011).

1. *Strong Agreement*: Individual ideology matches up with the perception of Court ideology (including moderates who say the Court decides on "case-by-case" basis).
2. *Tacit Agreement*: Liberals and conservatives who say the Court decides on "case-by-case" basis.
3. *Moderate Disagreement*: Moderates who perceive the Court as liberal or conservative.
4. *Strong Disagreement*: Liberals who perceive the Court as conservative and conservatives who perceive the Court as liberal.

We operationalize the measure as a nominal variable and include dummy variables (present or not) for categories two through four such that the effects of these dummies are relative to strong agreement.

Given concerns about validity which center on the "case-by-case" option, we use a second, interval-level measure that focuses only on respondents who perceive the Court as either liberal or conservative. Our measure takes respondent ideology (measured on a five-point scale) and recodes it so that higher values always indicate greater ideological disagreement with the Court.[8] For those who perceive the Court as liberal, "very conservative" respondents are high on the scale and "very liberal" respondents low. For those who perceive the Court as conservative, liberals are high on the scale and conservatives low. We thus expect this variable to be positively associated with support for curbing. An alternative approach (one which we consider in later chapters) is to always code respondent ideology in the same direction but estimate separate models for those who see the Court as liberal and those who see it as conservative. The latter strategy allows the effect of ideology to vary as a function of perceptions, while the approach we adopt averages over any such heterogeneity. The advantage of the latter is efficiency, and given that we have relatively little data in the ASCS, we opt for this approach.

While the 2005 ASCS does not measure democratic values, which is an important concept in the process-based approach, it does include general political trust.[9] We also create a political engagement scale combining

[8] Throughout the book, to reduce missing data, we recode "don't knows" to the ideology question to the middle of the scale, i.e., at "moderate." This choice is not consequential for our results or conclusions.

[9] The measure is based on this survey question: "Generally speaking, how much do you trust the federal government as a whole to operate in the best interests of the American people – a great deal, a fair amount, not too much or not at all?" The variable is a four-category ordinal variable, where higher values represent higher trust.

political knowledge items, subjective awareness of the Court, and how closely one follows the Supreme Court.[10] Finally, we control for basic demographic variables: sex, race, education, income, age, and religiosity.[11]

Full model results are included in the Appendix (Table A4.1). Figure 4.1 reports the effect of general policy disagreement on support for broad Court-curbing. Points are estimated effects and extended lines are 95 percent confidence intervals. The latter can be used to conduct significance tests: confidence intervals that do not cross the vertical dotted line at 0 are statistically significant with a two-tailed test and $\alpha = 0.05$.

The results provide strong support for the hypothesis that general policy disagreement exhibits substantively important effects on citizen support for Court-curbing. Looking first at the nominal measure of disagreement, citizens in strong and moderate disagreement with the Court are significantly more supportive of broad Court-curbing measures than those in strong agreement (the baseline category) by a bit over 10 percentage points. The results also indicate that those in tacit agreement are slightly more supportive of Court-curbing than those in strong agreement. When using our alternative, interval-level measure of disagreement, the results again suggest that greater policy disagreement leads to significantly more support for Court-curbing. In this case, a change from low to high disagreement entails an increase in support for broad curbing of about 15 percentage points.

Table A4.1 lists the marginal effects of other model variables. Some of the effects differ when comparing these two models, and we refer to the results from the model with the four-point policy disagreement measure,

[10] Knowledge items include whether the respondent knows (1) who the chief justice is, (2) who the women justices are, (3) whether the Court can invalidate an act of Congress, (4) whether the founders intended to divide up power between branches, and (5) whether a 5–4 ruling is declarative. We created a summative knowledge scale (alpha = 0.62). Subjective knowledge was measured by asking respondents how well they understand the Court's ruling (based on a four-point scale). Attention to the Court is based on how closely one follows the Court's decisions (four-point scale). All three variables were recoded to range from 0 to 1 and then averaged together to create a political engagement scale (alpha = 0.64).

[11] Education is operationalized as a four-category nominal variable: high school or less, some college, college graduate, and graduate degree. We include dummies for the last three categories; high school or less is the baseline category. Income is based on categories of family income; missing data are imputed. Age is measured in years. Religiosity is measured as frequency of church attendance based on a five-point scale (ranging from "never" to "more than once a week"). All independent variables are recoded to range from 0 to 1.

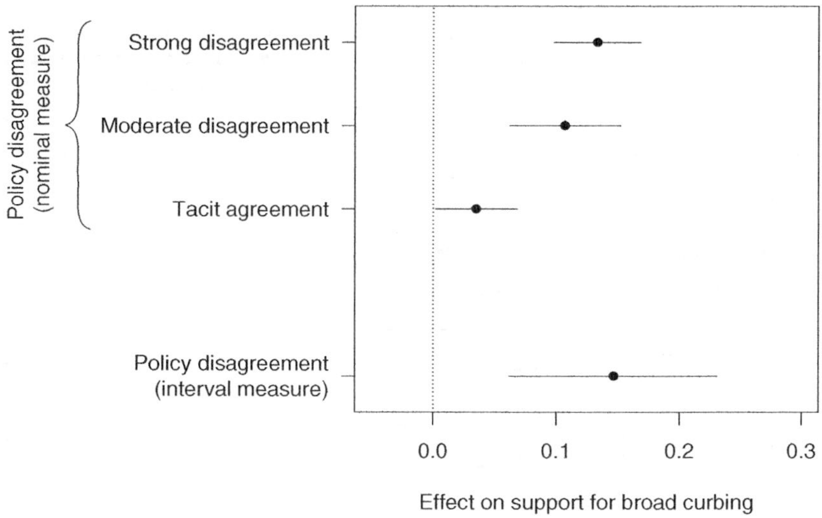

FIGURE 4.1 The effect of general policy disagreement on support for broad curbing, 2005 ASCS. The estimate for the interval measure is the percentage point change in support for broad curbing for a change in general policy disagreement from minimum to maximum; the estimates for the nominal measure represent differences in support for curbing comparing each category to "strong agreement"; extended lines are 95 percent confidence bounds; see Table 3.2 for the items that make up the broad curbing scale; this figure is based on model estimates in Table A4.1; the effects of the two policy disagreement variables come from two separate models.

since those are based on the full sample. In line with past work, those with greater political engagement, political trust, and more than a high school degree are significantly less supportive of Court-curbing than their counterparts. Religious individuals and black identifiers are significantly more supportive of Court-curbing, while higher family income is associated with less support. These additional model variables also allow us to place the effect of ideological disagreement in comparative context. Specifically, disagreement is the strongest predictor of support for Court-curbing in the model and even exceeds the process-related variables of political engagement, education, and general political trust in impact. These variables matter, which is consistent with the process-based approach, but general policy disagreement is at least as important in understanding support for broad forms of Court-curbing.

We also report how general policy disagreement influences each Court-curbing item individually. It is useful to consider (1) what types of curbing

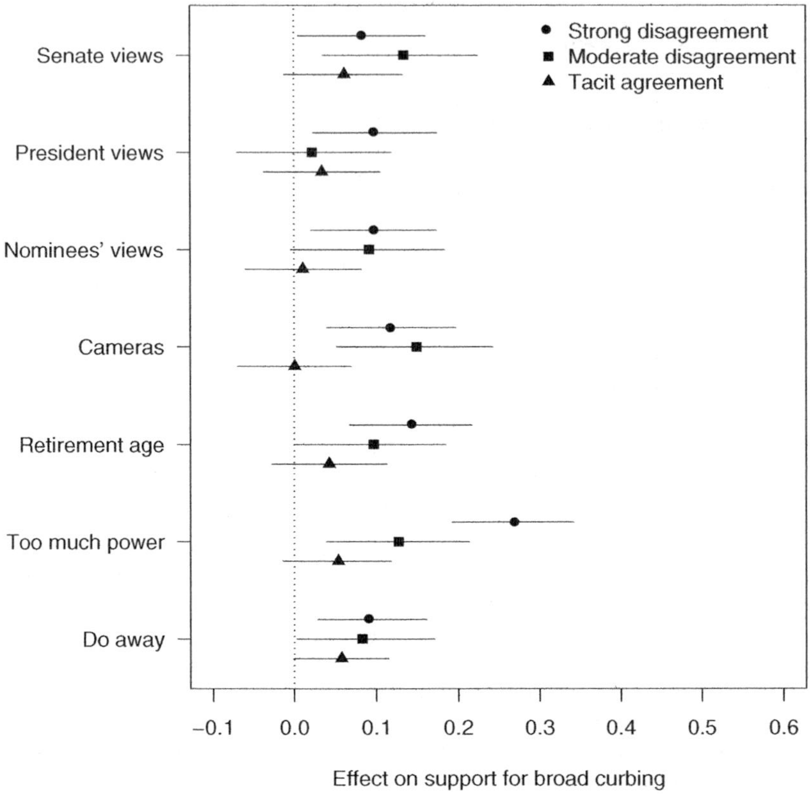

FIGURE 4.2 The effect of general policy disagreement on the probability of support for several broad curbing proposals, 2005 ASCS. Points represent first differences in the probability of supporting a given proposal comparing each disagreement category to "strong agreement"; extended lines are 95 percent confidence bounds; see Table 3.2 for the wording of each curbing item; this figure is based on model estimates in Table A4.2.

items elicit stronger or weaker effects of policy disagreement and (2) the *levels* of support for curbing across the range of disagreement. Figure 4.2 reports the effects of the four-category general policy disagreement measure across the seven Court-curbing dependent variables. Recall that each dependent variable is binary, so the results are from logit models.[12] More specifically, this figure reports the average change in the probability that

[12] We treat the "do away with the Court" item as binary in this analysis, even though it is originally measured on a four-point agree–disagree scale. We collapse the two agree options as well as the two disagree options in this analysis.

a respondent supports a given curbing policy as a function of moving from "strong agreement" to each of the other categories of our key independent variable.[13] Full results are presented in the appendix (Table A4.2).

The effect of strong disagreement (relative to strong agreement) is statistically significant in all seven models. Strong policy disagreement with the Court significantly increases the probability of supporting each Court-curbing measure. The effects are quite large for some models and range from a low of 8 percentage points to a substantial 28 points. Strong disagreement has the smallest effect on the "do away with" item, which might be expected given that this is the most extreme form of Court-curbing. Importantly, however, policy disagreement has the largest effect on citizens' beliefs about how much power the Court should have in the United States. Compared to strong agreement, respondents in strong disagreement with the Court are nearly 30 percentage points more likely to agree that the Court has "too much power" in American government. This is striking and provides strong support for our theory – there are few items that capture in so straightforward a manner the concept of broad curbing as we have defined it. Those in moderate disagreement are significantly more likely than their strong agreement counterparts to support five of the seven Court-curbing items. Interestingly, in many cases, strong and moderate disagreers are indistinguishable in their support for Court-curbing. This could suggest that the "action" for many of these items involves strong agreers increasing their institutional support for the Court, but we cannot draw firm conclusions on this point with these data. Finally, there are no significant differences across the individual items between tacit and strong agreement.

Figure 4.3 looks at these results in a slightly different manner. We plot, for each model, the predicted probability of Court-curbing support as a function of policy disagreement. The results build on Figure 4.2 by showing differences in the strength of the effect across items and also differences in average *levels* of support for various curbing actions. Once again, the effect is strongest for the "too much power" item. The probability of a "too much power" response ranges from less than 0.3 for those in strong agreement to nearly 0.6 for those in strong disagreement. Thus, general policy disagreement shifts the public from majority disagreement

[13] In all cases, throughout the book, we use the "observed value" approach to generating post-estimation quantities of interest, as opposed to the "average case" approach (see Hanmer and Kalkan 2013). The observed value approach calculates the quantity for each unit in the data and then calculates the average over all observations. This provides an estimate of the average value of the quantity in the population.

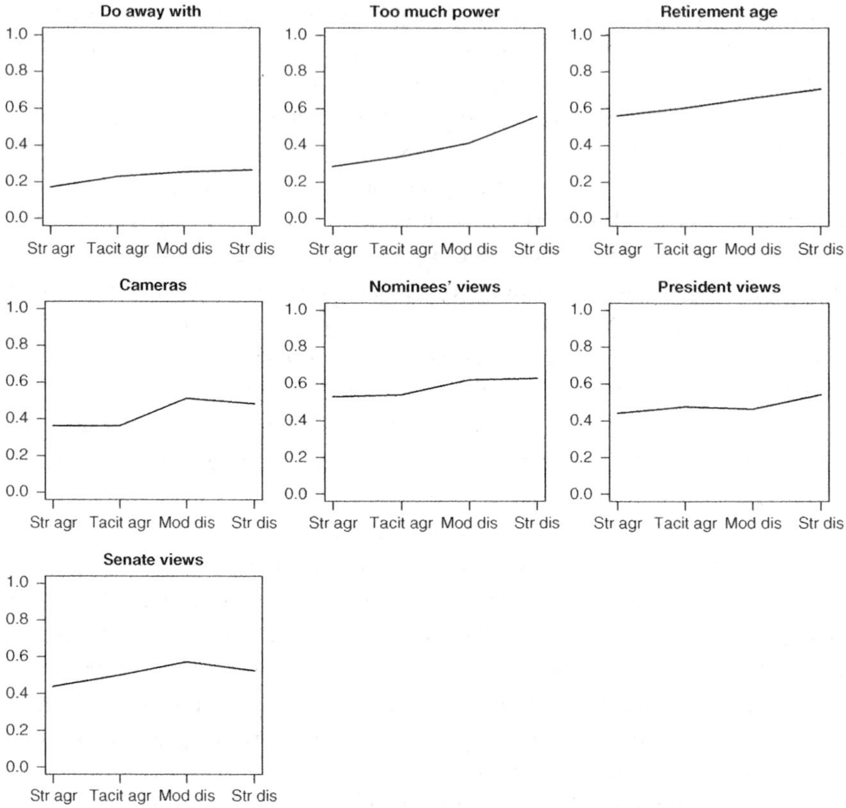

FIGURE 4.3 The predicted probability of support for several broad curbing proposals across general policy disagreement, 2005 ASCS. The y-axis is the probability of supporting each proposal; on the x-axis: "Str agr" = strong agreement, "Tacit agr" = tacit agreement, "Mod dis" = moderate disagreement, and "Str dis" = strong disagreement; see Table 3.2 for the wording of each curbing item; this figure is based on model estimates in Table A4.2.

to majority agreement with the claim that the Court is too powerful. The effect of general policy disagreement on the "do away with" item, though statistically significant, is not substantial, and the overall baseline for this extreme form of Court-curbing is also quite low. For those in strong disagreement, the probability of wanting to do away with the Court is just shy of 0.3, up from just south of 0.2 for those in strong agreement.[14]

[14] Of course, the Court may not find it comforting to learn that over one-fifth of the public supports doing away with the Court altogether.

On the other hand, the baseline of support for mandatory retirement age is quite high – greater than 0.5 for those in strong agreement – and general policy disagreement increases support for this action all the way up to 0.7. The results for "too much power" and "retirement age" make clear that significant attacks on the Court may be "on the table" for many citizens. The most popular broad curbing item in the literature has been "do away with," and this may have led to the mistaken impression that few citizens are willing to make lasting changes to the institution. We hope to dispel this myth in both this and subsequent chapters. There is often substantial support for major changes to the Court and policy disagreement pushes this support to levels that constitute a real threat to the institution. Turning to other items, policy disagreement enhances support for cameras in the courtroom quite substantially, moving from a low propensity of support (just above 0.3) for those in strong agreement to a probability of about 0.5 among those in moderate and strong disagreement. For the appointment items, the effects of policy disagreement are of similar magnitude. For each, greater policy disagreement enhances support for more policy accountability in the appointment process. In other words, the more one disagrees with the policy direction of the Court, the more one wants individuals to be chosen for the bench on the basis of their views on legal policy issues. Note also the quite high baseline of support for requiring nominees to state their views on controversial issues.

In sum, the results support our contention that general policy disagreement significantly and meaningfully increases citizen support for broadly targeted Court-curbing measures. The more people disagree with the policy and ideological direction of the Court's policymaking, the more they want to check the Court's power and independence by making it accountable to majoritarian institutions. We also find that political engagement reduces support for Court-curbing, which is in line with the "to know the Court is to love it" effect. General political trust also reduces support for Court-curbing, which resembles findings in the literature (which we test more directly in the following sections) about the positive effects of democratic values on Court support. In these data, however, it is policy disagreement that exhibits the strongest effects on support for curbing.

2011 Freedom and Tolerance Study

The 2011 Freedom and Tolerance Study (FTS), as analyzed in Gibson and Nelson (2015b), contains multiple measures of general policy disagreement and five broadly targeted Court-curbing items. They include (1) do away with, (2) issues reduced, (3) justices removed, (4) less independent, and (5) stronger control. All items are five-category agree-disagree response scales. We first build a Court-curbing scale averaging the five items.[15] The survey also contains process-related variables – democratic values and political engagement.

We use two different measures of general policy disagreement. First, Gibson and Nelson created a policy disagreement measure similar to our four-point scale (from the 2005 ASCS) in that it combines perceptions of the Court's ideology with the respondent's self-placed ideology. Whereas our 2005 ASCS measure of perceived Court ideology contained a middle option ("case-by-case" basis), Gibson and Nelson employed a four-category measure of perceived Supreme Court ideology: very conservative, somewhat conservative, somewhat liberal, and very liberal. In addition, some respondents (about 3 percent) volunteered a middle, moderate option. They combine this measure with a nine-point citizen ideology scale to generate a policy disagreement measure (see Gibson and Nelson 2015b). We use this measure in the interest of continuity with past literature. The primary drawback to this measure is that Court ideology and individual ideology are not measured on the same scale. Gibson and Nelson attempt to align citizens' assessments of the Court's ideology and their own ideology to create a measure of perceived ideological distance from the Court. The final measure ranges from 0 to 1 but is very positively skewed: the 95th percentile has a value of 0.64. Higher values indicate greater perceived distance.

Second, given the drawbacks of both distance-based measures, we take advantage of the opportunity to use an alternative: self-reported judgments regarding whether people think the Court is too liberal, too conservative, or about right. This measure taps subjective policy disagreement directly. A downside to this measure is that it has restricted range and cannot distinguish between people who see the Court as *much* too ideological in one direction or the other. But overall, the measure provides a clean assessment and viable alternative to the proximity approach. We operationalize the variable as a three-category nominal variable, including

[15] For this scale, Cronbach's alpha = 0.81. We note that Gibson and Nelson build a "legitimacy" scale with these five items plus two others that we do not consider "Court-curbing" items: (1) "Supreme Court justices are just like any other politicians; we cannot trust them to decide court cases in a way that is in the best interests of our country" and (2) the "too mixed up in politics" item. We categorize both as procedural perceptions and examine them in Chapter 7.

the "too liberal" and "too conservative" options and specifying "about right" as the baseline category.

Like Gibson and Nelson, we include values measures as independent variables, including support for (1) the rule of law,[16] (2) political tolerance,[17] and (3) liberty over order.[18] We also include a political engagement scale based on knowledge items and self-reported awareness of the Court.[19] Each variable is recoded to range from 0 to 1. Both the values and engagement measures are negatively skewed; many respondents in this sample are very high on these scales. This skewness can make the effects of these variables look bigger than they actually are.[20]

16 A summative rule of law scale was generated based on the following five items (alpha = 0.64), answered via a five-category agree–disagree format: (1) it is not necessary to obey a law you consider unjust; (2) sometimes it might be better to ignore the law and solve problems immediately rather than wait for a legal solution; (3) the government should have some ability to bend the law in order to solve pressing social and political problems; (4) it is not necessary to obey the laws of a government I did not vote for; and (5) when it comes right down to it, law is not all that important; what's important is that our government solve society's problems and make us all better off.

17 The survey asked whether respondents thought four groups should be able to hold a public demonstration: radical Muslims, a group of people who are against all churches and religion, US communists, and religious fundamentalists. The question is: "Next, let's suppose that [GROUP] wanted to hold public rallies and demonstrations in your community to advance their cause, but that the authorities decided to prohibit it. How would you react to such a ban by the authorities of a public demonstration by [GROUP]? Would you strongly support the ban, support the ban, oppose the ban, or strongly oppose the ban?" We create a summative scale based on these four items (alpha = 0.79).

18 A summative scale was generated based on three items (alpha = 0.66): (1) society should not have to put up with those who have political ideas that are extremely different from the majority; (2) it is better to live in an orderly society than to allow people so much freedom that they can become disruptive; and (3) free speech is just not worth it if it means that we have to put up with the danger to society of extremist political views.

19 Knowledge items include (1) whether justices are appointed or elected, (2) whether justices serve life or limited terms, (3) who has the final say over conflicts on constitutional meaning, (4) how many decisions the Court rules on each year, and (5) whether the Court's rulings are final or whether they can be appealed. We created a summative knowledge scale recoded to range from 0 to 1 (alpha = 0.69). Subjective awareness is based on a four-point scale (recoded to range from 0 to 1) measuring how aware of the Court's rulings the respondent is. Our political engagement scale is an average of knowledge and subjective awareness (ranging from 0 to 1; $r = 0.32$). Gibson and Nelson (2015b) include "performance satisfaction," or job approval, as an independent variable in their model. Inclusion of this variable induces post-treatment bias (performance satisfaction is an outcome that is subsequent to general policy disagreement), which poses a threat to valid inferences about the effect of general policy disagreement. Therefore, we do not include performance satisfaction as an independent variable in any of our analyses.

20 When we perform log transformations on these somewhat skewed variables, the results are substantively similar. Once again, the key issue is attaining effects for realistic ranges of these variables.

The regression coefficients represent predicted changes in the dependent variable for changes in independent variables from minimum to maximum (0 to 1), when in reality most of the variation is restricted to a narrower space – the fifth percentiles for rule of law, tolerance, liberty, and political engagement are 0.40, 0.25, 0.19, and 0.33, respectively. To show effects for more realistic ranges, we report predicted changes in the dependent variable when varying these variables from their 5th to 95th percentiles.

Finally, we include similar controls as our last analysis: sex, race, education, age, and religiosity.[21] While income is not measured in the survey, we include a home ownership variable. All models use post-stratification weights provided in the survey. All variables are recoded to range from 0 to 1. Full model results are in the appendix (Table A4.3).

We note that these data have some additional limitations relative to other datasets we analyze in the book. First, the sample size ($n = 750$) is relatively small. Second, the sampling frame for the survey is quite long in temporal terms. Using the "cdate" variable in the original data, the sampling frame runs from April 26, 2011, through July 7, 2011 – almost two and a half months. As seen in Table 3.1, most sampling frames are between two weeks and one month. Moreover, this sampling frame for the 2011 FTS covers the period in June when many Supreme Court rulings are announced. That poses potential problems in terms of respondents experiencing different information flows at different time points. However, we did not find any obvious time-specific effects.

Results

Figure 4.4 presents results from a linear regression model displaying the effects of the two policy disagreement variables (from separate models) as well as democratic values and political engagement (for comparison). For the distance-based disagreement measure (used by Gibson and Nelson 2015b), we report the first difference when moving that variable from its 5th to 95th percentile. We do the same when reporting the effects of democratic values and political engagement, which are from the model

[21] Education is a five-category nominal variable: less than high school (baseline), high school degree, some college, college degree, and postgraduate degree. Religiosity is measured as an average of church attendance and whether respondent is a born-again Christian (r = 0.36).

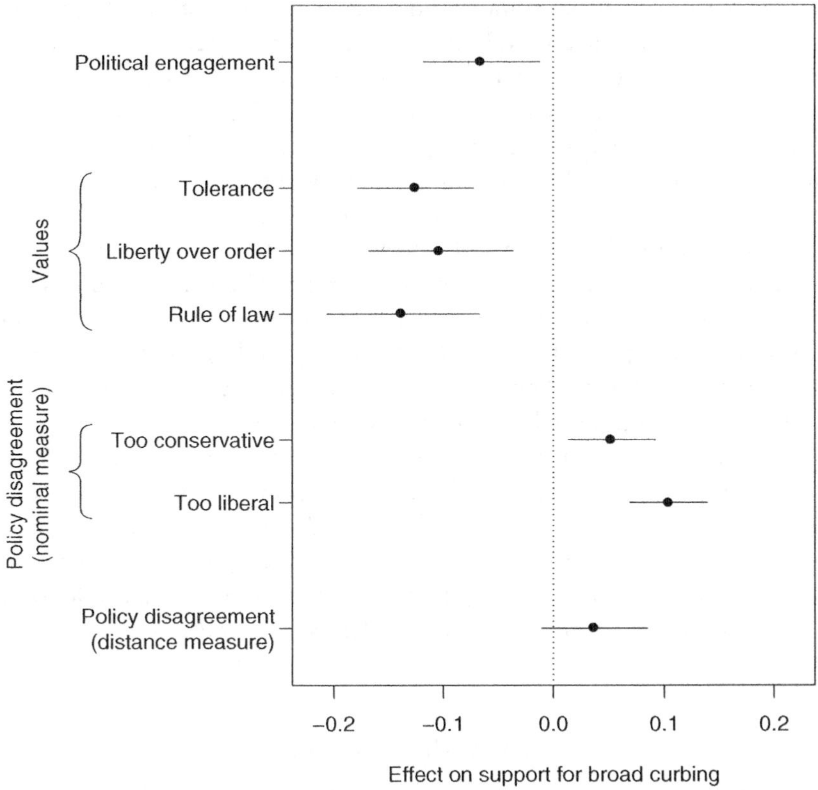

FIGURE 4.4 The effects of political engagement, democratic values, and general policy disagreement on support for broad curbing, 2011 FTS. Points for political engagement, the distance measure of general policy disagreement, and all three values measures represent estimated effects of moving each variable from its 5th to its 95th percentile; for the nominal measure of disagreement, points represent differences in support for curbing comparing each category to "about right"; extended lines are 95 percent confidence bounds; see Table 3.2 for the items that make up the curbing scale; this figure is based on model estimates in Table A4.3; the effects of the two policy disagreement variables come from two separate models; the effects of political engagement and values are from the model using the distance measure of policy disagreement.

with the distance-based policy disagreement measure (though results are quite similar across models).

First, we find that the distance-based measure of policy disagreement is positively associated with support for broadly targeted Court-curbing, but the effect is not statistically significant. The results for the nominal, direct measure of disagreement, however, show statistically significant and substantively meaningful effects. Those who perceive the Court as "too liberal" are about 10 percentage points more likely to support Court-curbing measures relative to those who think the Court is "about right" in its policymaking. The effect for "too conservative" is also significant but smaller than the "too liberal" effect (about five points). Looking now at the process-related variables, support for the rule of law, liberty over order, and political tolerance each decrease support for broadly targeted Court-curbing, as expected by past research. These effects are all of a similar magnitude to one another and to the effect of seeing the Court as too liberal. Support for the rule of law has the largest effect at about fourteen points. Political engagement also significantly decreases support for Court-curbing, though the effect is a bit smaller.

Together, these data provide mixed support for our expectations. On the one hand, the distance-based measure of policy disagreement is only weakly (and insignificantly) related to broad curbing. Our second measure, however – which asks directly about ideological disagreement – promotes support for Court-curbing at levels that are comparable to the "usual suspects" from prior work: democratic values and political engagement.

Item-by-Item Analyses

As we did for the 2005 ASCS, we a take a deeper dive into the individual Court-curbing items and examine whether any of these curbing measures elicit stronger policy responses from the public. Given that the distance-based measure was only weakly tied to curbing, we use the too liberal, too conservative, or about right measure for these analyses.

We estimated the same model from the previous section, but separately for each of the five individual Court-curbing measures. The results are quite similar to the analysis using the Court-curbing scale.[22] The effect of too liberal (relative to "about right") is positive and statistically significant across all five items. Perceptions that the Court is too conservative significantly increase support for Court-curbing in all models but "remove justices." The effect of policy disagreement seems to have its strongest impact on making the Court less independent. The process-

[22] We do not report these particular results in figures or tables. These results can be reproduced from the materials provided at the book's reproduction archive and are also available from the authors by request.

based variables exhibit fairly stable effects across models, with some exceptions.[23]

Five-category agree–disagree items are typically treated as ordinal or continuous measures, and the "neutral/uncertain" or "neither agree nor disagree" item is forced to be the midpoint of the scale. Another way to model these items is to operationalize Court-curbing as a nominal (unordered) dependent variable: support curbing, oppose curbing, and uncertain or neither support nor oppose. This specification is more flexible because it does not force the middle option to fall between curbing and no curbing responses. For example, ideological disagreement may have different effects on moving from uncertain to support for curbing relative to opposition. The continuous and ordinal approaches restrict these changes to be identical. The linear models reported in previous pages are also difficult to interpret substantively: what does a 10-percentage-point change in support for broad curbing mean really? Interpretation inevitably becomes comparative, looking for relative importance compared to other variables in the model. Treating the dependent variable as nominal (curb, don't curb, or uncertain) makes it easier to interpret the substantive impact of policy disagreement. By how much does policy disagreement increase the probability of generating a "curb" relative to a "don't curb" response? Does policy disagreement influence the probability of revealing "uncertain/neutral" responses? To find out, we estimated multinomial logit models for each of the five Court-curbing measures using the same independent variables as in previous pages. The results generate important new insights about the effects of policy disagreement on institutional support for the Court.[24]

[23] Support for the rule of law potently reduces support for the first four Court-curbing measures, particularly the "do away with" item. It does not significantly reduce support for exerting stronger control over the Court. Support for liberty over order significantly reduces support for curbing in all models except for the "issues reduced" model. Support for political tolerance consistently reduces support for Court-curbing across all five models, though its potency is reduced in the "do away with" and "remove justices" models. Political engagement exhibits more inconsistent effects than expected. Engagement significantly reduces support for Court-curbing in three of the five models. Engagement does not significantly reduce support for the most extreme form of curbing, doing away with the Court. Nor does it reduce support for reducing the Court's ability to decide certain controversial issues. However, engagement does significantly reduce support for making the Court less independent, removing justices, and exerting more control over the Court.

[24] In this book, we do not report tables of regression coefficients for multinomial logit models. These tables can be reproduced from the materials provided at the book's reproduction archive and are also available from the authors by request.

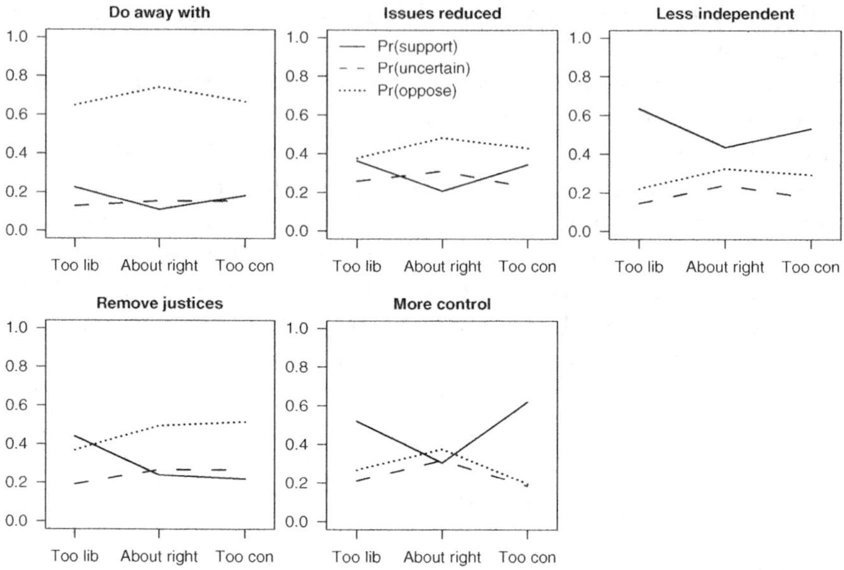

FIGURE 4.5 The predicted probability of support for several broad curbing proposals across perceptions of the Court's policymaking, 2011 FTS. The lines in each panel represent the probability that the respondent supports, opposes, or is uncertain about each curbing proposal; multinomial logit model estimates used to produce this figure can be obtained from the reproduction materials for this book; see Table 3.2 for the wording of each curbing item.

Figure 4.5 reports, for each model, the average probability of each discrete response as a function of general policy disagreement (using the "too liberal/too conservative/about right" measure). For the "do away with" item, the most extreme form of curbing, Figure 4.5 reports a low baseline probability of supporting this form of curbing, but the probability does increase significantly and meaningfully as respondents move from about right to either too liberal or too conservative.[25] Nonetheless, most people are averse to this rather extreme form of Court-curbing, even those who express general policy disagreement.

The remaining items reveal the power of general policy disagreement in shaping judgments about Court-curbing. First, the results for "issues

[25] Each of those changes is statistically significant, though not especially large. Conclusions about whether policy disagreement exhibits a statistically significant impact on the probability of supporting versus opposing curbing are made based on calculations not reported in Figure 4.5. We test whether the first differences in the probabilities (between different values of policy disagreement) are statistically significant.

reduced" again show the "v-shaped" effect of policy disagreement on support for curbing. Citizens who view the Court's policymaking as too liberal or too conservative are significantly more likely to support reducing the Court's ability to decide controversial issues compared to those in the about right category. General policy disagreement also reduces the probability of opposing this type of curbing (and significantly so for the too liberal response). Among those who view the Court as about right in its policymaking, support for curbing is the lowest-likelihood response, opposition is the highest, and uncertain/neutral is in the middle. Those relative orderings change, however, in the face of policy disagreement. Among those in the too liberal category, curbing support and opposition are equal in response propensity, while the uncertain/neutral response falls to third place. A similar dynamic occurs among those in the too conservative category, though the probability of opposition is slightly higher than the probability of support. In sum, policy disagreement elevates support for curbing at the expense of the other response options. Policy disagreement makes support for curbing nearly equal to opposition and it reduces the extent of uncertainty over curbing within the population.

This pattern is even more stark for the less independent and more control items. Indeed, the effect size for policy disagreement for both items is very large. For example, a change from "about right" to "too liberal" is associated with an increase in support for restricting the Court's independence of over 20 percentage points and a similar change to "too conservative" is associated with an increase in support for exerting more control over the Court of over 30 points. Interestingly, support for reducing the Court's independence has the highest baseline response propensity. Even among those who are generally satisfied with the direction of the Court's policymaking, support for less independence is the most popular response category, followed by opposition and then uncertainty. Yet policy disagreement exacerbates this pattern, driving up support for reducing the Court's independence to over 60 percent of the public in the too liberal category and over 50 percent of the public in the too conservative category. A similar pattern is seen for the "more control" item. In this case, the stronger response is from those who see the Court as too conservative, though both directions of disagreement have potent effects on support for curbing at the expense of the other response options. In short, policy disagreement makes support for exerting political control over the justices (by far) the most likely response. Thus, in both cases, policy disagreement leads to majority support for fundamental changes aimed at reducing the political independence of the Supreme Court.

There is greater asymmetry in the remove justices item. Policy disagreement in the direction of "too liberal" has a quite large and significant effect on support for curbing, while disagreement in the "too conservative" direction has a null effect (relative to "about right"). It also has a null effect on opposition to curbing. The relative orderings are distinct, too. While those in the about right category are highly likely to oppose removal of justices, those who believe the Court is too liberal are more likely to support this measure than oppose it. However, disagreement in the conservative direction does not alter the relative ordering of response options in terms of aggregate popularity.

For comparison, we show the effects of values and engagement on the "less independent" item (treated as nominal). The results are presented in Figure 4.6. Because of the distributions of these variables (discussed earlier), the x-axes on the figures range from the 5th to 95th percentile. The first three graphs show that support for democratic values decreases support for Court-curbing; those effects are statistically significant. Political engagement also decreases curbing support, but the change is not statistically significant. Each of these variables also significantly increases opposition to this form of curbing. Thus, when using this operationalization for the curbing dependent variables, the effects of policy disagreement are roughly on par with those of classic process-related measures.

In sum, our results from the 2011 FTS show that general policy disagreement increases support for broadly targeted Court-curbing, while the process-based variables decrease that support. We noted some drawbacks to this dataset: a fairly small sample size, a wide survey sampling time frame, and a less-than-ideal distance-based measure. That latter measure did not exhibit a statistically significant effect on support for broadly targeted Court-curbing; however, our alternative measure showed statistically significant and sizable effects of general policy disagreement that often rival the effects of process-based factors. Further, when treated as nominal, our item-by-item analysis of the Court-curbing items reveals new insights into both the public's baseline support for different methods of curbing the Court and the potent effects of general policy disagreement. In some instances, policy disagreement makes support for Court-curbing the most likely response category. And in two cases, policy disagreement generates majority support for restricting the Court's independence. It is also worth noting that our direct measure of policy disagreement does not distinguish strong from weak divergence. We would expect these effects to be even larger among citizens who *strongly* disagree with the direction of the Court's policymaking.

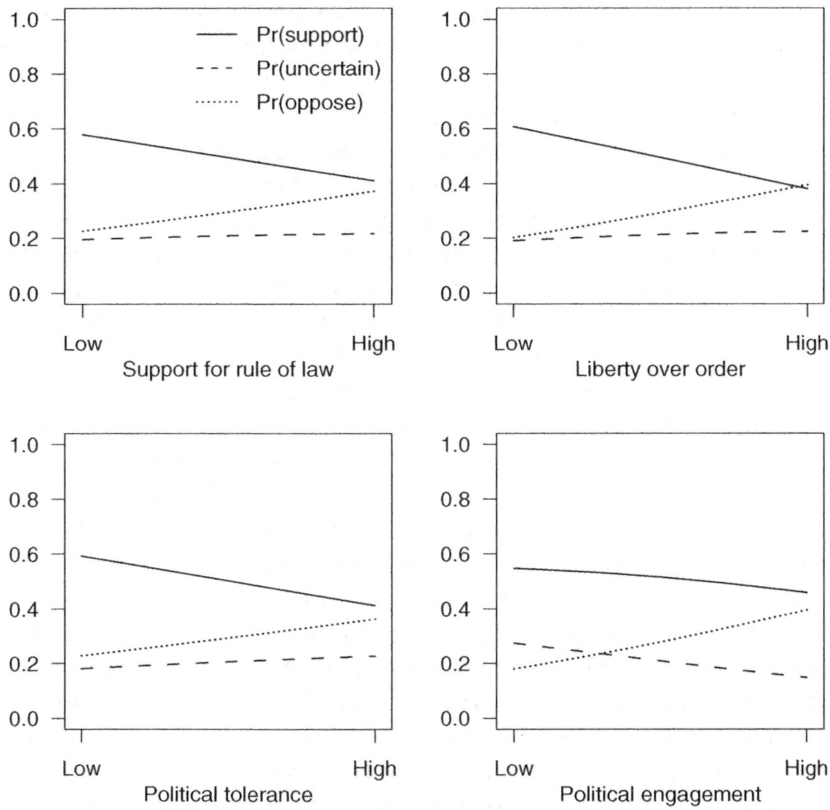

FIGURE 4.6 The predicted probability of support for making the Supreme Court less independent across democratic values and political engagement, 2011 FTS. The lines in each panel represent the probability that the respondent supports, opposes, or is uncertain about each curbing proposal; the x-axes range from the 5th to the 95th percentile of each variable; multinomial logit model estimates used to produce this figure can be obtained from the reproduction materials for this book.

JUNE 2012 TAPS

The 2012 TAPS contains perhaps the best distance-based measure of general policy disagreement available and also the best test of policy versus process-based factors when it comes to broadly targeted Court-curbing. As discussed in Chapter 3, TAPS is a monthly panel study that began in late 2011 and continued into 2012 and beyond. The study is sponsored by the Weidenbaum Center at Washington University in

St. Louis and administered by Knowledge Networks (now GfK). The data we analyze in this chapter come from the June 2012 wave, which was conducted on the eve of the Court's landmark healthcare ruling (*National Federation of Independent Business* v. *Sebelius*). We analyze that issue (and others) in more detail in Chapter 5. In the June 2012 wave, 1,475 panelists answered numerous questions about the Supreme Court. These include seven Court-curbing items (summarized in Table 3.2): (1) do away with, (2) issues reduced, (3) remove justices, (4) less independent, (5) stronger control, (6) easier to remove, and (7) change Constitution. Note that the first five items are the same as those in the 2011 FTS.

We note that 73 of the 1,475 respondents in the June 2012 wave completed the interview after the Affordable Care Act (ACA) ruling was announced on the morning of June 28, 2012. We have excluded these 73 individuals from all analyses so as not to confound the effects of our variables of interest in this study (we examine the effect of the decision itself in the next chapter). Finally, all analyses employ post-stratification weights (with internet adjustment) for all respondents.

Like in each of the prior two studies, we use two measurement strategies for tapping general policy disagreement. The first is a distance-based measure. The survey contains a measurement experiment tapping the ideological tenor of the Supreme Court, which partly resolves the controversy between Bartels and Johnston (2013) and Gibson and Nelson (2015b) over the treatment of the middle response category. Respondents were randomly assigned to receive one of two survey items tapping the Court's ideological tenor. The difference between the two items is in the number of response options. The first question asks about the ideological tenor of the Court using a seven-point scale. Importantly, it uses the same verbal labels as those used in the individual ideology measure (e.g., very liberal, liberal, slightly liberal, moderate). The second question asks the exact same question but uses a four-point scale instead (i.e., very liberal/conservative and somewhat liberal/conservative with no "moderate" option).

To measure general policy disagreement using the seven-point measure, we simply recode both the Court measure and individual ideology (also on seven-point scale) to range from 0 to 1 (higher values conservative) and then we take the absolute value of the difference between these two measures. To measure ideological disagreement using the four-point scale, we first recode the Court measure to range from 0 to 1 (higher values conservative). In comparison to individual ideology, 0 and 1 represent "very liberal" and "very conservative," respectively, for both measures. "Somewhat liberal/conservative" for the Court question takes on the same value as "slightly liberal/conservative" for individual ideology (i.e., 0.333 for liberal and 0.667 for conservative). Again, we take the absolute value of the difference between the two measures. Since respondents were randomly assigned to receive one of the Court ideology measures, we can test whether the difference in response scales for the Court measure has any impact on the effect of policy disagreement on support for Court-curbing. Our second measure of general policy disagreement is the same nominal operationalization we use for the 2011 FTS: whether the respondent thinks the Court is "too liberal," "too conservative," or "about right." We dummy out the three categories and the effects are again relative to the "about right" baseline category.

Our models use similar independent variables to those in the 2011 FTS. We include the same values measures – rule of law, political tolerance, and liberty over order. These are measured using the same items as the 2011 FTS (and we refer the reader to the prior measurement discussion for details). We measure political engagement using (1) political knowledge items, (2) self-reported Court awareness, (3) general political interest, and (4) how frequently the respondent discusses politics.[26] Finally, we include standard controls used in prior models: age, sex, race, education, religiosity, and income.[27]

We first tested whether the two different response scales for the Court's ideological tenor make a difference in predicting Court-curbing from policy disagreement. We "stacked" these two measures into one policy disagreement variable and created a dummy variable indicator for whether individuals received the seven-point or four-point response scale for perceptions of the Court's ideological tenor. An interaction between general policy disagreement and the dummy thus provides an empirical test of whether there is a practical difference between the two response scales. That interaction term is not statistically significant ($p = 0.49$). The impact of policy

[26] The knowledge items included 7 questions from the January 2012 wave and 9 from the June 2012 wave, including 4 that are Supreme Court specific. Core results do not change substantially when using different subsets of these knowledge items. We created a summative scale based on the number of correct answers (alpha = 0.81). Awareness of the Court is a four-category measure (ranging from haven't heard of to very aware). Political interest is based on a four-point scale reflecting general interest in politics and public affairs (ranging from not at all interested to very interested). Frequency discussing politics is based on self-reported frequency (seven-point scale ranging from never to every day). All four measures were recoded to range from 0 to 1 and then averaged together to create a political engagement scale (alpha = 0.78).

[27] Religiosity is a scale combining four items: church attendance, belief in a god, frequency of prayer, and frequency of saying grace before meals (alpha = 0.86). Education is a five-category nominal variable: less than high school (baseline), high school degree, some college, college degree, and post-graduate degree. Income is based on self-reported categories of family income. We imputed missing values based on demographic characteristics.

disagreement is the same whether one uses the seven-point or four-point Court ideology scale. Thus, we use the stacked measure for our primary analysis. Full model results are included in the appendix (Table A4.4).

Figure 4.7 presents the effects of our variables of interest: general policy disagreement (both the stacked distance-based and nominal operationalizations) and process-related variables. Once again, since values and political engagement are sparsely populated at their low ranges, we report first differences for these variables as they range from their 5th to 95th percentiles.[28] We do the same for the continuous policy disagreement variable.[29] While we report the effects of both policy disagreement variables in Figure 4.7, they are derived from two separate models (as seen in Table A4.4). The effects of the process-based variables are very similar across models, and we report the effects from the model using the distance-based measure of policy disagreement.

The results show that distance-based policy disagreement exhibits a robust and statistically significant effect on support for Court-curbing. Those with greater degrees of policy disagreement are significantly more supportive of Court-curbing than those with lower degrees of disagreement by about 10 percentage points. Like in the 2011 FTS, the effects of the democratic values variables are potent as well and, on average, slightly more impactful than policy disagreement. Political engagement exhibits a potent effect and is on par with the values measures. Thus, as expected by past work, process-related variables significantly and meaningfully reduce support for Court-curbing. General policy disagreement – using this distance-based measure – exhibits an effect somewhat smaller than the process-based variables but overall on par with those effects.

Figure 4.7 also reports results using our second, nominal measure of general policy disagreement – the "too liberal/conservative" versus "about right" measure. The general nature of the effect of this second measure replicates what we reported from the 2011 FTS. First, those who perceive the Court as either too liberal or too conservative are significantly more likely to support broad curbing than those who perceive the Court as "about right" in its policymaking. Second, support for Court-curbing is more strongly connected to those in the "too liberal" relative to "too conservative" camp.

[28] Like in the 2011 FTS, reporting raw effects varying from 0 to 1 reveals an exaggerated effect since there are few respondents at the very low ends of the distributions of these variables. The 5th percentiles for rule of law, liberty, tolerance, and engagement are 0.4, 0.25, 0.17, and 0.30, respectively.

[29] Recall that the variable ranges from 0 to 1. The 5th percentile is 0 and the 95th percentile is 0.83.

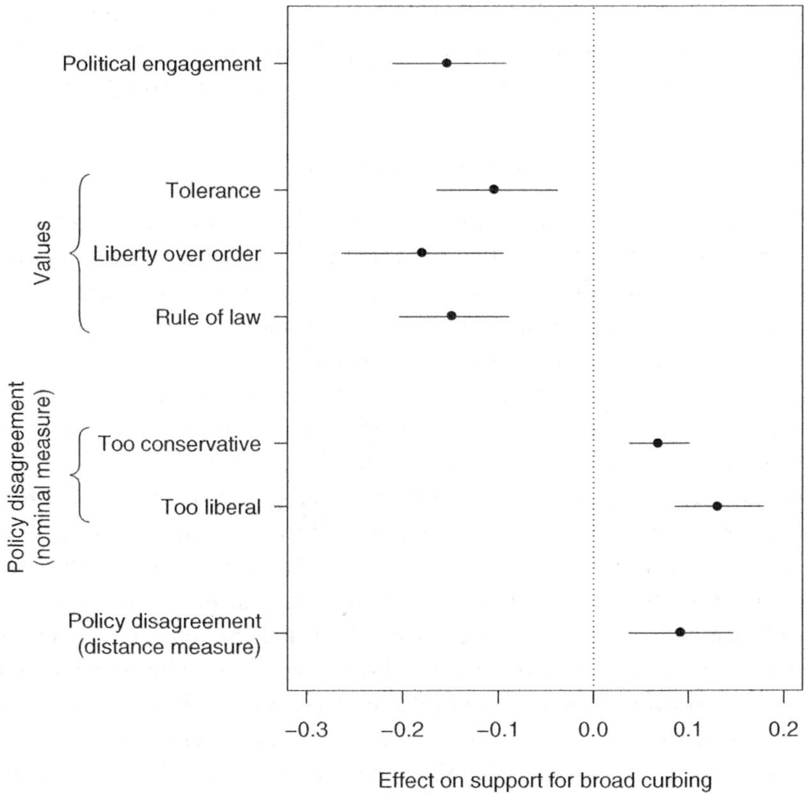

FIGURE 4.7 The effects of political engagement, democratic values, and general policy disagreement on support for broad Court-curbing, 2012 TAPS. Points for political engagement, the distance measure of general policy disagreement, and all three values measures represent estimated effects of moving each variable from its 5th to its 95th percentile; for the nominal measure of disagreement, points represent differences in support for curbing comparing each category to "about right"; extended lines are 95 percent confidence bounds; see Table 3.2 for the items that make up the curbing scale; this figure is based on model estimates in Table A4.4; the effects of the two policy disagreement variables come from two separate models; the effects of political engagement and values are from the model using the distance measure of policy disagreement.

A change from "about right" to "too liberal" entails a change in support for curbing of about thirteen points, while the same change to "too conservative" is associated with an increase of about seven points. Once again, there is greater movement in support for curbing among conservatives who believe the Court is too liberal than among liberals who believe the Court is too conservative. The effects of the process-based variables are similar to the previous model. Importantly, the effect of policy disagreement – particularly in the too liberal direction – rivals the effects of values and engagement.

Item-by-Item Analyses

As we did for the 2011 FTS, we delve more deeply into the magnitude of policy disagreement's impact by treating the first five Court-curbing items as a three-category discrete and nominal choice: support curbing, oppose curbing, or uncertain/neither support nor oppose.[30] This allows us to estimate (1) the extent to which the predicted probability of each response changes as a function of general policy disagreement (while averaging over other variables) and (2) the relative orderings of each response type (curb, no curb, uncertain) given low and high levels of disagreement. For the last two curbing items (easier to remove and change Constitution), we create binary measures since these were originally measured with four-point response scales (with no "neutral" option). We discuss the results using the distance-based policy disagreement measure, displayed in Figure 4.8. While we do not report analogous results using the nominal policy disagreement measure, we note that (1) those results generally converge with what we reported from the 2011 FTS analysis and (2) the conclusions are generally similar to those using the interval measure reported below.[31]

We present the results from all models in Figure 4.8. Throughout this analysis, we stress caution about inferences at the highest end of policy disagreement, at which there are not many respondents.[32] For the "do away with" item, Figure 4.8 shows high baselines of opposition to curbing and low baselines of support. Policy disagreement significantly increases the probability of supporting this extreme form of curbing, but even among those in disagreement, the probability of support is quite low.[33] Disagreement also

[30] As we did for the 2011 FTS, we first estimated separate linear regression models for each item, with the same specification as the models using the Court-curbing scale. Those analyses generate patterns that do not deviate from our scale-based analysis, so we jump right to the analysis using the alternative discrete-choice coding of the Court-curbing items.

[31] An equivalent figure for the nominal measure of policy disagreement can be generated using the reproduction materials for Chapter 4.

[32] As discussed, the 95th percentile of the proximity-based policy disagreement variable in the 2012 TAPS data is 0.83. The value "1" is at the 99th percentile, so at the upper reaches of the sample distribution.

[33] Our conclusions about statistical significance in this analysis are based on additional calculations for the average effects of policy disagreement on both the probabilities of supporting and opposing curbing.

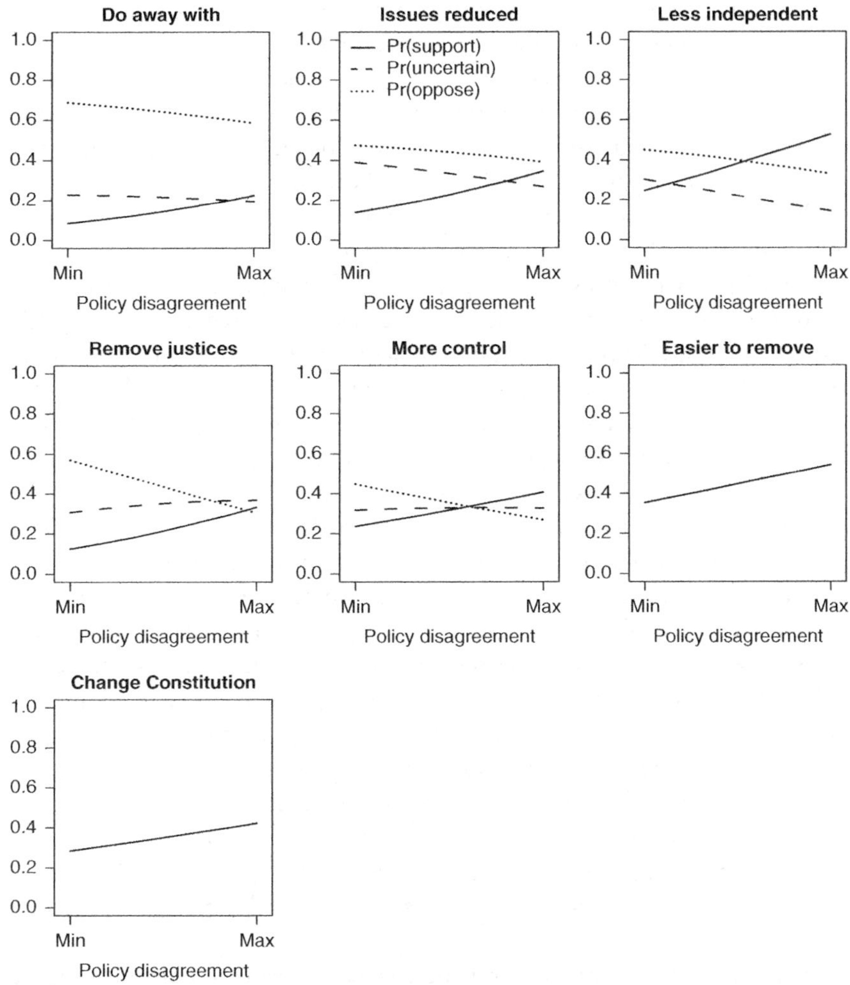

FIGURE 4.8 The predicted probability of support for several broad curbing proposals across general policy disagreement, 2012 TAPS. The lines represent the probability that the respondent supports, opposes, or is uncertain about each curbing proposal; the x-axis represents degrees of policy disagreement with the Court based on the distance measure; multinomial logit (first five figures) and logit (last two models) estimates used to produce this figure can be obtained from the reproduction materials for this book; see Table 3.2 for the wording of each curbing item.

significantly decreases opposition to curbing, but that magnitude is not particularly large. While policy disagreement does reduce the response propensities between relative orderings, the highest probability response across the board is opposition to doing away with the Court. On the other hand, at the highest levels of disagreement, the probability of opposition is about 0.6.

For the "issues reduced" item, general disagreement significantly enhances the probability of supporting a reduction of the Court's ability to hear controversial issues and decreases (though not at a statistically significant level) opposition to this form of broad curbing. The potent role of disagreement is also demonstrated by how it elevates support for this measure to just shy of the most likely response.

Figure 4.8 again shows the quite potent effect of policy disagreement on support for making the Court less independent. Disagreement significantly and substantially increases support for reducing the Court's independence and significantly decreases opposition to this form of curbing. Like in the 2011 FTS, disagreement makes the curbing response the most likely by far. Policy disagreement has the most potent effect, then, on this form of curbing.

For the "remove justices" measure, we see an effect similar to that for the "issues reduced" item. Disagreement generates a significant and potent increase in the probability of supporting removal and an equally potent decrease in opposition. Increasing policy disagreement closes the gulf between response likelihoods and makes support for curbing just as likely a response as opposition. The results reveal the substantial influence of policy disagreement in both altering response propensities and closing the gap in relative likelihoods of supporting versus opposing Court-curbing.

For the "stronger control" model, Figure 4.8 again shows how policy disagreement significantly increases support for Court-curbing and decreases opposition. Like with the less independent item, as policy disagreement increases (particularly toward higher ends of that spectrum), support for curbing becomes the most likely response over both opposition and uncertainty.

Finally, for the last two items, general policy disagreement enhances the probability of supporting making it easier to remove justices and changing the Constitution in light of disagreeable rulings.[34] That effect is more potent in the first model, with policy disagreement driving support for this measure to 0.5 at higher levels of disagreement. The effect is not as strong for the "easier to change Constitution" item.

In sum, the results from the July 2012 TAPS study support prior analyses in this chapter: general policy disagreement exhibits robust effects on support for broadly targeted Court-curbing, often rivaling the effects of process-based

[34] The effect of disagreement on "making it easier to remove justices" is statistically significant ($p < 0.05$). For "easier to change Constitution," the effect is marginally significant ($p = 0.087$).

variables like support for democratic values and political engagement. Our item-by-item analyses reveal new insights as well. In some cases, policy disagreement elevates support for curbing to the most likely, or close to the most likely, response in comparison to no curbing and uncertainty. And with only two exceptions, we observe less than 50 percent opposition to these fundamental changes among those in strong policy disagreement with the Court.

CONCLUSION

Using multiple measures of general policy disagreement across a variety of Court-curbing items and several distinct datasets, we find that general policy disagreement exhibits a consistently significant and substantively meaningful effect on support for broadly targeted Court-curbing. Indeed, the effects of disagreement rival – and in some cases exceed – those of process-related variables (democratic values and political engagement). In line with past work, support for democratic values and political engagement increase institutional support for the Court. Importantly, however, these factors do not dominate citizens' thought about Court-curbing. Consistent with our claim that citizens are weakly principled, general policy disagreement matters despite widespread endorsement of core democratic values.

These results have implications for our understanding of the Supreme Court's legitimacy. If we think of legitimacy as rightful authority, then such authority should be granted to the Court regardless of whether one agrees or disagrees with its rulings on policy grounds. Yet our results present a very clear pattern that support for Court-curbing is a function of general policy disagreement. The more citizens disagree with the policy direction of the Court, the more likely they are to support Court-curbing measures. Moreover, the effect of disagreement is not moderated by political engagement. Thus, even the most politically engaged citizens are willing to attack the Court in the face of policy drift. This is critical because engaged citizens are most likely to hold their representatives accountable at the voting booth. The Court relies on this group for protection of its independence, yet policy disagreement has the same effect on curbing support as for the unengaged. Overall, the importance of policy disagreement to curbing undermines the idea that the Court has legitimacy in the sense of perceived rightful authority because citizens only conditionally accept the independence of the institution. The Court is strongly protected from political attacks only by those who agree with its current ideological direction.

Particularly concerning for the Court is the fact that many broad curbing policies appear to be "on the table" for a substantial proportion of citizens. The prevailing narrative in the public opinion literature is that the Court enjoys substantial baseline support – a deep reservoir of goodwill. Thus, even moderate shifts in favor of Court-curbing would not be a threat (Gibson and Nelson 2015b). As we have shown, however, many curbing items generate non-negligible baseline levels of support, and for some items, policy disagreement generates majority support for restricting the Court's power and independence. This is quite striking and reinforces the importance of the policy-based model in future assessments of the Court's status in the public mind and among the other institutions of American government.

APPENDIX

TABLE A4.1 *Models of broadly targeted Court-curbing, 2005 ASCS*

	(1)	(2)
Intercept	0.43 (0.05)	0.49 (0.03)
Age	0.04 (0.05)	0.06 (0.03)
Female	0.01 (0.02)	0.02 (0.01)
Black	0.07 (0.04)	0.08 (0.02)
Hispanic	0.00 (0.05)	0.01 (0.03)
Some college	−0.03 (0.03)	−0.05 (0.02)
BA degree	−0.04 (0.03)	−0.07 (0.02)
Post-grad	−0.00 (0.04)	−0.05 (0.02)
Income	−0.09 (0.05)	−0.08 (0.03)
Engagement	−0.10 (0.06)	−0.11 (0.04)
Political trust	−0.05 (0.04)	−0.10 (0.02)
Religiosity	0.13 (0.03)	0.05 (0.02)
Policy disagreement (interval)	0.15 (0.04)	
Policy disagreement (nominal)		
Tacit agreement		0.04 (0.02)
Moderate disagreement		0.11 (0.02)
Strong disagreement		0.13 (0.02)
R^2	0.10	0.13
N	605	1435

Notes: Data are from the 2005 ASCS (see Chapter 3 for descriptions of all datasets). Entries are ordinary least squares estimates and standard errors (in parentheses). The dependent variable is the Court-curbing scale; higher values indicate greater support for Court-curbing. Post-stratification weights are used in both analyses.

TABLE A4.2 *Models of broadly targeted Court-curbing, item-by-item, 2005 ASCS*

	Do away	Power	Retire	Cameras	Nom. views	Pres. views	Sen. views
Intercept	−0.31 (0.33)	0.17 (0.29)	0.90 (0.32)	0.19 (0.28)	0.27 (0.28)	−0.29 (0.28)	−0.08 (0.28)
Age	−0.19 (0.34)	0.27 (0.30)	1.67 (0.32)	0.37 (0.30)	0.74 (0.30)	0.27 (0.29)	0.11 (0.29)
Female	0.22 (0.16)	−0.00 (0.14)	0.08 (0.13)	−0.24 (0.13)	0.12 (0.13)	0.34 (0.13)	0.26 (0.13)
Black	0.36 (0.25)	0.45 (0.23)	0.44 (0.24)	0.43 (0.21)	0.21 (0.23)	0.34 (0.22)	0.19 (0.22)
Hispanic	−0.01 (0.31)	0.45 (0.27)	0.29 (0.27)	0.17 (0.26)	−0.24 (0.26)	−0.42 (0.26)	−0.13 (0.25)
Some college	−0.31 (0.19)	−0.35 (0.17)	−0.19 (0.17)	−0.52 (0.17)	−0.08 (0.16)	−0.03 (0.16)	−0.20 (0.16)
BA degree	−0.49 (0.21)	−0.44 (0.18)	−0.33 (0.17)	−0.36 (0.17)	0.10 (0.17)	−0.30 (0.17)	−0.39 (0.17)
Post-grad	−0.41 (0.28)	−0.76 (0.27)	−0.18 (0.23)	−0.52 (0.24)	−0.07 (0.23)	0.04 (0.22)	0.03 (0.22)
Income	−0.66 (0.32)	−0.55 (0.29)	−0.59 (0.29)	−0.30 (0.28)	−0.28 (0.28)	−0.57 (0.27)	−0.45 (0.27)
Engagement	−1.79 (0.42)	−0.60 (0.36)	−1.16 (0.37)	−0.48 (0.34)	−0.41 (0.34)	−0.56 (0.34)	−0.53 (0.34)
Political trust	−0.23 (0.29)	−1.59 (0.25)	−0.76 (0.25)	−0.29 (0.23)	−0.59 (0.23)	0.25 (0.23)	0.09 (0.23)
Religiosity	−0.02 (0.23)	0.55 (0.21)	−0.02 (0.20)	−0.22 (0.19)	0.34 (0.19)	0.47 (0.19)	0.36 (0.19)
Policy disagreement (nominal)							
Tacit agreement	0.38 (0.20)	0.28 (0.17)	0.19 (0.16)	0.00 (0.16)	0.04 (0.15)	0.15 (0.16)	0.26 (0.16)
Moderate disagreement	0.53 (0.26)	0.62 (0.22)	0.44 (0.22)	0.63 (0.21)	0.39 (0.21)	0.09 (0.21)	0.55 (0.21)
Strong disagreement	0.59 (0.21)	1.26 (0.19)	0.68 (0.18)	0.51 (0.17)	0.42 (0.17)	0.42 (0.17)	0.35 (0.17)
Pseudo-R^2	0.05	0.10	0.07	0.04	0.03	0.03	0.02
N	1397	1383	1347	1364	1370	1383	1381

Notes: Data are from the 2005 ASCS. Entries are logit estimates and standard errors (in parentheses). For each dependent variable, 1 = curb and 0=do not curb. Post-stratification weights are used in each analysis.

TABLE A4.3 *Models of broadly targeted Court-curbing, 2011 FTS*

	(1)	(2)
Intercept	0.83 (0.05)	0.81 (0.05)
Age	−0.03 (0.04)	−0.03 (0.03)
Female	0.03 (0.02)	0.03 (0.02)
Black	−0.03 (0.02)	−0.01 (0.02)
Hispanic	0.04 (0.03)	0.02 (0.03)
HS degree	0.06 (0.03)	0.04 (0.03)
Some college	−0.01 (0.03)	−0.02 (0.03)
BA degree	−0.05 (0.03)	−0.07 (0.03)
Post-grad	−0.10 (0.04)	−0.11 (0.03)
Homeowner	0.00 (0.02)	−0.00 (0.02)
Engagement	−0.10 (0.04)	−0.10 (0.04)
Rule of law	−0.23 (0.06)	−0.22 (0.05)
Liberty over order	−0.14 (0.04)	−0.13 (0.04)
Tolerance	−0.17 (0.04)	−0.16 (0.03)
Religiosity	0.02 (0.03)	0.00 (0.02)
Policy disagreement (distance-based)	0.06 (0.04)	
Policy disagreement (nominal)		
SC too liberal		0.10 (0.02)
SC too conservative		0.05 (0.02)
R^2	0.35	0.37
N	697	730

Notes: Data are from the 2011 FTS. Entries are ordinary least squares estimates and standard errors (in parentheses). The dependent variable is the Court-curbing scale; higher values indicate greater support for Court-curbing. Post-stratification weights are used in both analyses.

TABLE A4.4 *Models of broadly targeted Court-curbing, June 2012 TAPS*

	(1)	(2)
Intercept	0.96 (0.05)	0.95 (0.05)
Age	0.08 (0.05)	0.10 (0.05)
Female	0.03 (0.02)	0.03 (0.02)
Black	0.03 (0.03)	0.05 (0.03)
Hispanic	−0.02 (0.02)	−0.00 (0.02)
HS degree	−0.01 (0.03)	0.00 (0.03)
Some college	0.01 (0.03)	0.02 (0.03)
BA degree	−0.03 (0.03)	−0.03 (0.03)
Post-grad	−0.05 (0.03)	−0.05 (0.03)
Income	−0.04 (0.04)	−0.04 (0.04)
Engagement	−0.25 (0.05)	−0.27 (0.05)
Rule of law	−0.27 (0.05)	−0.25 (0.05)
Liberty over order	−0.24 (0.06)	−0.23 (0.05)
Tolerance	−0.12 (0.04)	−0.13 (0.04)
Religiosity	−0.02 (0.03)	−0.04 (0.03)
Policy disagreement (distance-based)	0.11 (0.03)	
Policy disagreement (nominal)		
SC too liberal		0.13 (0.02)
SC too conservative		0.07 (0.02)
R^2	0.40	0.44
N	1211	1216

Notes: Data are from the June 2012 wave of TAPS. Entries are ordinary least squares estimates and standard errors (in parentheses). The dependent variable is the Court-curbing scale; higher values indicate greater support for Court-curbing. Post-stratification weights are used in both analyses.

5

Specific Policy Disagreement and Support for Court-Curbing

The last chapter presented multiple empirical tests of the effect of general policy disagreement on support for broadly targeted Court-curbing. In this chapter, we examine the effect of disagreement with *specific rulings* on support for both broad and narrow Court-curbing. We present several tests of our hypotheses using multiple research designs, including a panel study and two survey experiments. These two designs – and the experimental studies in particular – also address important limitations of the previous chapter's reliance on cross-sectional data, namely concerns about the possible endogeneity of policy disagreement (and its reliance on subjective perceptions of the Court's ideological tenor) to support for Court-curbing. Like the last chapter, each study examines the effects of rival factors. Importantly, this chapter also presents two experimental tests of the effects of procedural characteristics pertaining to the Court's rulings – an important aspect of process-based approaches. We begin with our panel data analysis using TAPS, which examines public opinion surrounding several salient Supreme Court rulings.

CHANGE IN SUPPORT FOR COURT-CURBING AFTER BLOCKBUSTER RULINGS

Can single Supreme Court rulings, especially highly salient ones, alter support for broadly targeted Court-curbing? Our primary goal in this section is to examine how individual-level support for Court-curbing changes after a salient ruling and how policy disagreement with that ruling shapes the direction of those changes. We also examine the duration of changes: whether individuals revert in the long run to pre-decision levels of support for the Court. We focus on two highly salient rulings: (1) the 2012 decision in *National Federation of Independent Business* v. *Sebelius* (hereinafter *NFIB*), in which the Supreme Court upheld the core of the Affordable Care Act (ACA, or "Obamacare")[1] and (2) the 2015 same-sex marriage ruling in *Obergefell* v. *Hodges* (hereinafter *Obergefell*) in which the Court struck down several state bans on same-sex marriage and declared that the Constitution's 14th Amendment compels all states to recognize the legality of same-sex marriages. Both cases were blockbuster rulings that captured the attention of many Americans.

We also analyze the effects of what we call "off-setting" rulings, i.e., salient rulings decided in close temporal proximity but that cut in different policy directions (one liberal, one conservative). June 2013 provides such an opportunity to examine two blockbuster cases that generate countervailing policy signals.[2] First, on June 25, 2013, the Court in *Shelby County* v. *Holder* (2013) (hereinafter *Shelby*) struck down a key provision of the 1965 Voting Rights Act (VRA) regulating which Southern states with a history of racial discrimination must undergo federal oversight of any changes to their voting laws. The Court ruled that conditions of racial discrimination that existed back in the 1960s and 1970s rendered the formula for determining federal oversight inapplicable today.[3] Second, the following day (June 26, 2013), the Court issued its first major same-

[1] The case (567 U.S. 519) was announced on June 28, 2012. It upheld the insurance mandate portion of the ACA, President Obama's signature domestic achievement. In a bitter 5–4 ruling, conservative Chief Justice Roberts (appointed by President George W. Bush) wrote the majority opinion and argued that the penalty for not obtaining health insurance amounted to a tax that Congress has the constitutional power to impose. The dissenters in the case, led by Justice Kennedy, wanted to strike down the entire ACA law as unconstitutional. The Court did strike down the Medicaid expansion requirement, which means that the ruling did deliver a conservative policy output as well. However, for the most part, the media and political elites portrayed the ruling as a significant political victory for President Obama and Democrats.

[2] Obviously, other rulings were issued in 2012 and 2015 as well, but *NFIB* and *Obergefell* were far more salient. They were also decided on the last two days of the term. The other high-profile decision was *Fisher* v. *University of Texas* (decided June 24, 2013), which was an affirmative action case involving a challenge to the use of race in university admissions. However, the Court did not rule on the underlying constitutionality of the affirmative action program. Instead, it vacated the lower court ruling because it did not apply the appropriate legal standard (strict scrutiny). In 2016 (in *Fisher* II), the Supreme Court would uphold the university's use of race in admissions.

[3] More specifically, the Court struck down Section 4b of the VRA, which contains the formula for ascertaining whether changes to voting procedures need to be federally reviewed. The Court did not strike down the "preclearance standard" in Section 5, though without a formula that standard is not enforceable.

sex marriage ruling. In *Windsor* v. *U.S.* (hereinafter *Windsor*), the Court struck down the Defense of Marriage Act (DOMA), thus declaring a fundamental constitutional right for same-sex marriage at the *federal* level.[4] That same year, the Court declined to rule on the substantive merits of California's Proposition 8 regarding whether the Constitution prohibits states from banning same-sex marriages.[5] The Court ruled that the defenders of Proposition 8 did not have standing, which meant that a federal district court ruling declaring same-sex marriage legal was the policy for California. Of course, the question of whether same-sex marriage was a constitutionally protected right was settled for all states two years later in *Obergefell*.

This combination of a conservative ruling in *Shelby* and a liberal ruling in *Windsor* – decided just one day apart – allows us to test whether the effects of these two rulings cancel each other out.[6] Liberals may disagree with a conservative ruling today and become more supportive of Court-curbing, but then they may agree with a liberal ruling tomorrow and become less supportive. And vice versa for conservatives. In this story, Court-curbing judgments are in flux with the receipt of new policy pronouncements, but an even balance of liberal and conservative rulings can create the appearance of stability in Court-curbing support for individuals over time. But as the dynamics surrounding *Obergefell* and *NFIB* will show, if the Court were to generate an onslaught of rulings in one direction or another, we may witness a more sustained backlash among the losing side.

This section also provides a glimpse into the Court's support across the political spectrum in an era where the justices have produced a great deal of liberal policy on salient issues. As we have previously noted, the contemporary Supreme Court, which is typically dubbed "conservative," has generated a plethora of significant liberal rulings over the past several years (Bartels 2015; Bartels and Johnston 2013). Though it has generated its fair share of significant conservative policy as well, the most salient

[4] DOMA was signed into law in 1996 by President Clinton after it passed both Republican-controlled chambers of Congress. It said that the federal government would not legally recognize same-sex marriages from states.

[5] That case was *Hollingsworth* v. *Perry* (2013).

[6] Christenson and Glick's (2019) innovative panel design was in the field immediately following *Shelby* and before *Windsor*. They find evidence of a "negativity bias," where those opposed to a ruling punish the Court more than supporters reward it. Unlike their study, our analysis is not capable of assessing the fine-grained changes following each ruling. But we can make comparisons and conclusions about the total and "canceling out" effect of both rulings.

cases since the Obama era are surely the upholding of the ACA and the legalization of same-sex marriage at both the federal and state levels. We show how the cumulative effect of this liberal shift – peppered with "conservative interruptions" – alters left–right divisions in support for Court-curbing across time.

Our findings are capable of addressing differences in substantive conclusions across extant studies of how citizens update their views of the Court in light of significant rulings (e.g., Christenson and Glick 2015a, 2019; Clawson and Waltenburg 2009; Gibson 2015; Gibson, Caldeira, and Spence 2003b; Gibson, Pereira, and Ziegler 2017; Woodson 2018; Zilis 2018). While past work, like Gibson et al.'s (2003b) prominent study of the *Bush* v. *Gore* (2000) ruling,[7] essentially focused on aggregate change in the Court's legitimacy, more recent studies have examined how individuals change their Court support in light of policy disagreement. For instance, Christenson and Glick's (2015a) analysis of the impact of the Court's *NFIB* ruling concludes that changes (within subject) in ideological proximity generate changes in Supreme Court legitimacy. This finding has received general validation from Nelson and Smith (2015). Moreover, while we examine whether the conflicting signals of *Shelby* and *Windsor* essentially cancel each other out among liberals and conservatives, we draw comparisons to Christenson and Glick's (2019) innovative panel study that assesses change after *Shelby* and *before Windsor*. They report expected decision disagreement effects after each ruling, but they find evidence of a negativity bias: Those who disagree with a ruling punish the Court more than those who agree.

Woodson (2018) argues that a "multiple modes theory" accounts for change in light of *NFIB*: policy agreement and disagreement influences Court support among those who perceive that the Court makes decisions on ideological bases, but it does not matter among those who perceive the Court as principled or tied to public opinion.[8] Gibson et al. (2017) challenge the underpinnings of these general results by concluding that many citizens do not have the capacity or knowledge to engage in this systematic "rule, learn, update" model of reasoning (see also Gibson 2015). In addition to testing core theoretical propositions in our book,

7 Kritzer (2001) reports evidence that Supreme Court approval – distinct from diffuse support, of course – significantly diminished among Democrats and increased among Republicans after *Bush* v. *Gore*. This suggests that partisans moved in accord with the pattern of policy (or partisan) disagreement.

8 Questions exist, especially in the TAPS observational data, about how truly independent the decision-making modes are from both policy disagreement and support for the Court.

our analysis revisits some of these related issues concerning individual-level change in response to rulings.

Research Design, Data, and Measures

The TAPS data allow us to examine *changes* in support for Court-curbing from just before to just after a major ruling. This design sidesteps the risk of reverse causality present in cross-sectional data in which it is possible that support for Court-curbing shapes perceived policy disagreement. Specifically, we measure policy preferences and political identity *prior* to the ruling and examine their relationship with *changes* in Court-curbing support. With this approach, reverse causality is not possible. Yet panel data do not provide the same degree of causal leverage as our experiments, where we randomly assign the ideological direction of a ruling to respondents. We cannot infer that all changes in Court-curbing judgments before and after a ruling are due to that specific ruling itself. The Court tends to issue several rulings each June (and sometimes earlier in Spring), and many of these receive substantial discussion, so other rulings and events may factor into any changes we observe. This limitation notwithstanding, the *NFIB* and *Obergefell* rulings were blockbuster events and one would be hard pressed to conclude that other decisions issued around the same time exerted a larger pull on people's discussion regarding the Court. To further assuage such concerns, however, we examine changes in support for Court-curbing as a function of decision-specific policy preferences (in addition to broader measures of political orientation).

For each of the three case studies, we examine pre-to-post ruling changes using panel waves as close to the decisions as possible given data availability. When possible, we then examine the longer-term stability of changes in attitudes. For the *NFIB* analysis, we use TAPS data from May 2012 (pre-ruling), July 2012 (post-ruling), and January 2013 (longer-term). For the *Obergefell* ruling, we use data from the May 2015 wave (pre-ruling), July 2015 (post-ruling), and March 2016 (longer-term). For the *Shelby* and *Windsor* rulings, the closest wave before the ruling containing Court-curbing questions is January 2013. The post-ruling wave is July 2013. Unfortunately, we are unable to examine durability and reversion for *Shelby*/*Windsor* because the next wave containing Court-curbing questions at least a few months after the rulings was not until July 2014, which is after another "cycle" of Supreme Court rulings that are released in June. For all analyses, we use post-stratification weights. Since these are change analyses, we use the weights from the second wave forming the change measure for the dependent variable. For instance, in examining change from the May to July wave, we use weights from the July wave.

For all analyses, our dependent variable is *change in support for broadly targeted Court-curbing* from one wave to the next. We use the five broad curbing items discussed in Table 3.2 (do away with, issues reduced, less independent, remove justices, and stronger control). We create Court-curbing scales for each wave, where higher values represent greater support for Court-curbing (recoded to range from 0 to 1).[9] For the immediate effects of the ruling, we subtract the pre-decision Court-curbing measure from the post-decision measure. Positive values represent increases in support for Court-curbing, and negative values represent decreases in support for Court-curbing. To assess whether immediate changes are durable or subject to reversion, we subtract post-decision support for Court-curbing from the same variables measured in a wave several months later (for *NFIB* and *Obergefell* only). This second analysis tests whether any changes that occurred in July because of the ruling stick or revert to pre-ruling levels. Values near 0 suggest persistence of post-ruling changes, while values opposite in sign to the original change suggest reversion.

We use two strategies for operationalizing policy disagreement. First, for all three case studies, we average the seven-point partisanship and ideological identification scales to create a measure of *left–right identity* ($rs \approx 0.70$). We recode these to range from 0 to 1, with higher values representing more conservative/Republican leanings.[10]

For the *Shelby* and *Windsor* rulings, we use the left–right identity measure only.[11] For the other two decisions, we also rely on ruling-specific policy items. For *NFIB*, TAPS asked two relevant questions in the May 2012 wave: (1) "Do you approve or disapprove of the requirement that every American must buy health insurance or pay a fine?" A five-point response scale was used,[12] and we coded the variable so

[9] For all scales, Cronbach's alpha exceeds 0.88.

[10] For the *NFIB* ruling, left–right identity relies on party identification measured in April 2012 and ideology measured in May 2012. For *Shelby/Windsor*, both party identification and ideology come from November 2012. For Obergefell, party identification comes from January 2015 and ideology comes from May 2015.

[11] For the *Shelby/Windsor* analysis, we measured policy preferences on same-sex marriage using the first item used for *Obergefell*. Results using that measure are almost identical to what we see when using the broader left–right orientations measure. To our knowledge, TAPS has no analogous measure for the *Shelby* ruling.

[12] Strongly approve: 8.5%; approve: 14.1%; neither: 11.4%; disapprove: 27.6%; strongly disapprove: 35%. Don't know or refused: 3.4%.

that it ranges from 0 (strongly approve) to 1 (strongly disapprove). (2) "Concerning the requirement that every American must buy health insurance or pay a fine, do you think that this is (un)constitutional?" Three options were given: constitutional, unconstitutional, or "don't know."[13] We coded this as a three-point scale with "constitutional" equal to 0, "don't know" in the middle (0.50), and "unconstitutional" equal to 1. We combined the two policy preference items into a single "health insurance preferences" scale ($r = 0.70$), with higher values representing more disagreement with the mandate aspect of the ACA.

For the *Obergefell* ruling, the September 2014 wave of TAPS included the item "The federal government should recognize the validity of a same-sex marriage where state law does." A five-point agree–disagree response scale was used, which was recoded to range from 0 to 1 such that higher values represent greater opposition to same-sex marriage. Note how this item is more closely tailored to the *Windsor* (DOMA) case,[14] which involved whether the federal government should recognize same-sex marriages. Though *Obergefell* was related to marriage at the state level, we think this measure still captures the overarching dimension of support for or opposition to same-sex marriage. In addition, the March 2014 wave included the item "Regardless of whether or not you think it should be legal, please indicate whether you personally believe gay or lesbian relations is morally acceptable or morally wrong." A three-point scale was used (morally acceptable, depends on the situation, or morally wrong; "not sure" was combined with the middle category). We recoded this item to range from 0 to 1 and then created a "same-sex marriage preferences" scale that is the average of the two items ($r = 0.73$) such that higher values are more conservative on this issue and therefore in greater policy disagreement with the Court's *Obergefell* ruling.

For controls, we include the same variables we have used in prior analyses, including our prior analysis of TAPS data in Chapter 4: democratic values (rule of law, liberty over order, tolerance), political engagement, age, sex, race, education, religiosity, and income.[15] We measure

[13] Constitutional: 19.4%; unconstitutional: 67.7%; don't know or refused: 12.9%.

[14] That item was also asked in 2013 before the DOMA ruling.

[15] Our measures of these variables rely on the same survey questions we employed in the 2012 July TAPS wave from Chapter 4. Since these items are measured periodically throughout the panel waves, we measure them as close to, but not after, the three cases. For question wordings, we refer the reader to Chapter 4. For the specific waves in which questions were asked, we refer the reader to our reproduction materials. Cronbach's alphas for rule of law scales are 0.76 (for *NFIB* and *Shelby/Windsor* analyses) and 0.75

values and engagement from the TAPS wave closest to the pre-decision wave (that also precedes or coincides with that wave), where we first measure support for Court-curbing.

For political engagement, we create three separate scales (one for each ruling). Each scale uses some combination of political knowledge, political interest, how often one discusses politics, and Supreme Court awareness (self-reported). For *NFIB* and *Obergefell*, we average political knowledge, frequency of discussing politics, and political interest.[16] For *Shelby/Windsor*, we use a knowledge scale, Supreme Court awareness (self-reported), political interest, and frequency of discussing politics.[17] Note that as new items arise (in subsequent waves), we use the most recent items that precede or coincide with the initial pre-decision wave for which we measure Court-curbing.

Results

We first estimate models for each ruling using both decision-specific policy preferences and broader left–right identity, which include all individuals in the survey. The appendix (Tables A5.1 and A5.2) reports the full results for the models. Figure 5.1 presents the key estimates. In each panel, the y-axis represents the predicted change in support for broad Court-curbing from before to after each ruling. Each graph includes a horizontal zero line, which represents no change in support for curbing from pre- to post-decision. Points above this line indicate increases in support for curbing, while points below the line indicate decreases in support. The x-axis represents either policy preferences or left–right identity, with higher values indicating more conservative/Republican preferences. We also include the 95 percent confidence interval around each line which, in

(for the *Obergefell* analysis). Alphas for liberty scales are 0.70 for all analyses. Alphas for tolerance scales are 0.86 (*NFIB* and *Shelby/Windsor*) and 0.85 (*Obergefell*). Alphas for religiosity scales are 0.86 (*NFIB*), 0.87 (*Shelby/Windsor*), and 0.86 (*Obergefell*).

16 *NFIB*: For knowledge, we create a scale based on ten knowledge items from January 2012 (alpha = 0.76). Interest and discuss politics also come from January 2012. For the full engagement scale, alpha=0.78. *Obergefell*: For knowledge, we create a scale based on sixteen knowledge items from May 2014 (alpha=0.83). Interest comes from January 2015, and discuss politics also come from May 2015. For the full engagement scale, alpha=0.70.

17 For *Shelby/Windsor*, we create a knowledge scale based on thirteen knowledge items from January 2012 and June 2012 (alpha=0.81). Subjective awareness of the Court and political interest are from June 2012, while discuss politics is from January 2012. For the full engagement scale, alpha=0.78. Once again, we refer readers to our reproduction file for precise items used and in what waves.

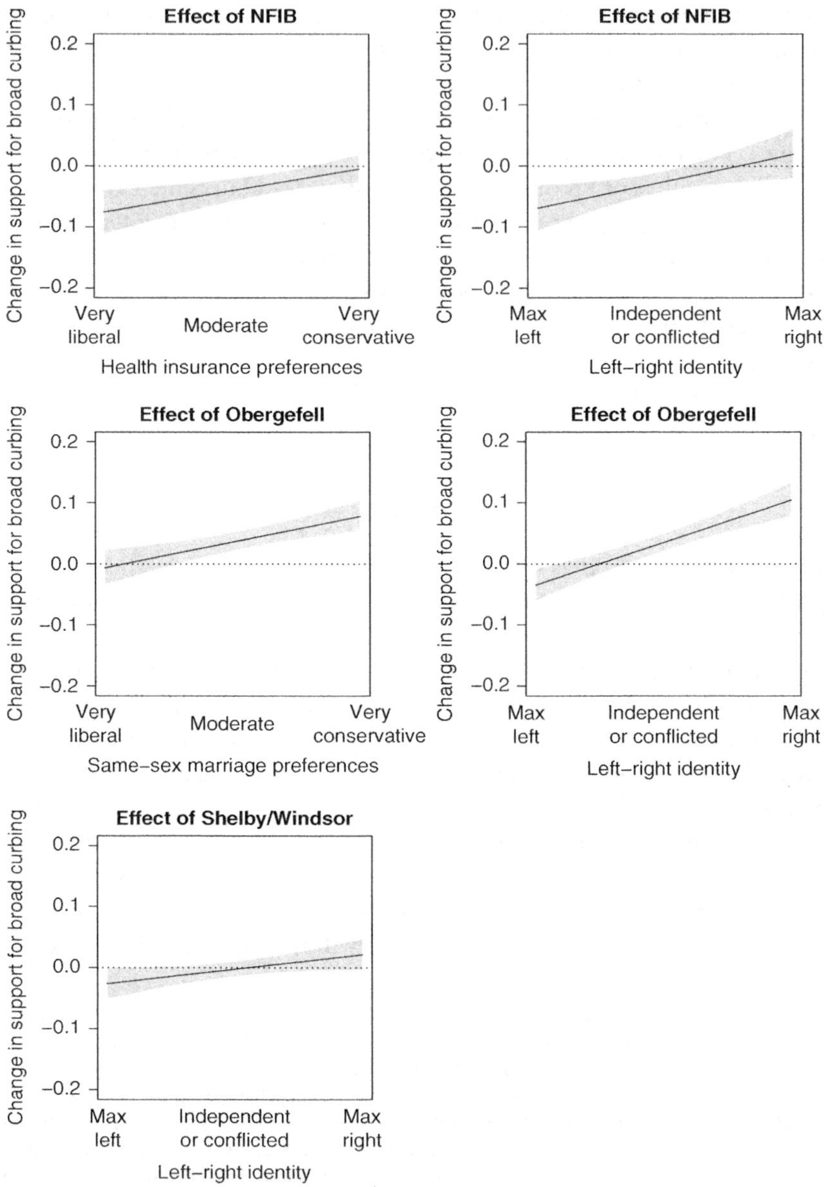

FIGURE 5.1 The effects of Supreme Court decisions on support for broad curbing across policy preferences and left–right identity, TAPS. The solid lines represent the predicted change in support for broad curbing from pre- to post-decision at each level of policy preferences or left–right identity; the grey bands are 95 percent confidence bounds; see Table 3.2 for the items that make up the curbing scale; the theoretical range of the dependent variable is −1.0 to 1.0; this figure is based on model estimates in Tables A5.1 and A5.2.

conjunction with the horizontal line at zero, tests whether the change in support for broad curbing at a particular point on the left–right spectrum is statistically significant. The slope of each line represents the effect of policy preferences and left–right identity on updating. The larger the slope, the larger the difference in updating across these variables.[18]

Starting with the *NFIB* analysis (the first two panels in the top row), the results reveal that changes in support for Court-curbing from pre- to post-ruling are conditional on health insurance preferences and left–right identity. Citizens who were generally supportive of the mandate provisions in the ACA, along with liberal and Democratic identifiers, became significantly less supportive of broad Court-curbing measures following the *NFIB* ruling. By contrast, citizens who opposed the mandate, along with conservative and Republican identifiers, show little to no change in support for curbing over this period.[19] The effect size for citizens on the left is modest though meaningful at about 8 percentage points, which is consistent with our theoretical and conceptual framework. A salient ruling allows citizens to update their perceptions of the Court's ideological tenor, but it is just one ruling and must be integrated with other information citizens possess about the Court. Our general expectation is that policy agreement and disagreement with a single ruling has a small, but reliable, effect on support for broad curbing. This is exactly what we observe. Thus, while any one decision may not lead to large changes in the Court's standing among different subsets of the public, these results suggest that the *accumulation* of salient rulings can drive substantial changes in support for curbing. The effects we report generally coincide with Woodson's (2018) "aggregate" effects (averaging over decision-making modes) and are distinguished

18 All slopes in Figure 5.1 are statistically significant.

19 Past work examining the effects of decisions has confined analysis to those who have heard about the ruling and/or who know the direction in which the Court ruled (Franklin and Kosaki 1989; Gibson 2015; Nelson and Smith 2015). We were able to measure "awareness of the Court's ruling" for *NFIB* only. Subsequent panel waves (for *Shelby/Windsor* and *Obergefell* or other rulings) do not contain comparable measures. In the July 2012 wave, TAPS asked two questions to validate whether respondents knew: (1) if "the Supreme Court ruled on whether it is constitutional to require Americans to have health insurance" (yes, no, not sure) and (2) if yes, "is the requirement that American have health insurance or pay a penalty constitutional or unconstitutional?" From these questions, 62.4 percent of the sample correctly knew the ruling. When we include only the respondents who heard about the *NFIB* ruling (and knew the correct direction of the ruling), the results, using both measures, are nearly identical to what we have reported above.

from Christenson and Glick's (2015a) more nuanced finding about change resulting from the *NFIB*.[20] Moreover, for *NFIB*, we do not find evidence of a negativity bias – losers punish the Court more so than winners reward it – suggested by Christenson and Glick (2019).

The results for *Obergefell* provide additional support for our hypotheses. Both measures of policy disagreement exhibit statistically significant effects on changes in support for broad curbing, which again suggest that liberals and conservatives update in different ways. Those opposed to same-sex marriage, along with conservatives and Republicans, became significantly more supportive of Court-curbing in light of the Court's landmark ruling in *Obergefell*. These effect sizes are similar in magnitude to those for *NFIB*, but in the opposite direction. Thus, while conservatives did not punish the Court for the ruling on the ACA, they did punish for the legalization of same-sex marriage. Interestingly, while liberals and Democrats were more prone to update in the negative direction after the ACA ruling, they essentially refrain from updating in light of the congenial *Obergefell* ruling. Only at the most liberal point on the general left–right identity measure is there significant updating in the "oppose" direction, and that change is not especially large. Thus, after *Obergefell*, we do find evidence suggesting a negativity bias (Christenson and Glick 2019). This asymmetry across the two rulings is striking and we have no good explanation for the differences observed. As discussed previously, there are limitations to panel data that make firm causal inferences difficult to draw. Thus, further research is needed to understand why the effects of single decisions may vary from one context or issue to the next. Nonetheless, the results for both *NFIB* and *Obergefell* provide support for our framework. In both cases, we observe changes in support for broad Court-curbing that are consistent with citizens punishing and rewarding the Court for uncongenial and congenial policy outcomes.

Moving to the offsetting *Shelby* and *Windsor* rulings from 2013, the results show minimal degrees of updating. While the coefficient for left–right identity is statistically significant – indicating differential updating across political orientation – the magnitudes of the effects are quite small, as shown in Figure 5.1. Citizens on the left are significantly less supportive of curbing after the decisions, while those on the right are slightly (though insignificantly) more supportive. This accords with our expectations

[20] Recall that Christenson and Glick (2015a) find that the ruling led people to update their general ideological disagreement with the Court, which in turn led to changes in legitimacy.

regarding the countervailing nature of temporally proximate policy signals sent by *Shelby* on one day and *Windsor* on the next. If anything, the results suggest that *Windsor* may have been slightly more impactful than *Shelby*, which is generally consistent with Christenson and Glick (2019).[21] That could also be due to the fact that *Windsor* was announced the day after *Shelby*. Given the small effect sizes, we do not want to overstate the case.[22]

Reversion

We next examine the longer-term impacts of any changes in Court-curbing from before to after a major decision. Do attitudes toward Court-curbing revert to pre-decision levels soon after the ruling, or do changes stick for longer periods of time? Recall that we are limited to analyzing reversion for *NFIB* and *Obergefell*. We report full model results in the appendix (Tables A5.1 and A5.2). Figure 5.2 reports analogous graphs as Figure 5.1.

Looking first at the *NFIB* ruling, changes are minimal across the board. The top panels of Figure 5.2 show that over the year following *NFIB*, liberals move in the direction of pre-decision levels of support for Court-curbing. However, these changes are small and statistically insignificant, and the 95 percent confidence bounds do not contain coefficients large enough to fully offset the effects of *NFIB* and return liberal citizens fully to pre-decision levels of support for Court-curbing. Thus at least a portion of

[21] Christenson and Glick (2019), who gathered more fine-grained data before and after both *Shelby* and *Windsor*, show that liberals and Democrats punished the Court more for *Shelby* than they rewarded it for *Windsor* (i.e., negativity bias). Analogously, conservatives and Republicans punished the Court more for *Windsor* than they rewarded it for *Shelby*. We are essentially measuring the net change after both rulings.

[22] The panel analyses are one of the few places where we find evidence of interactions between policy disagreement and political engagement. However, we also found that the results were conditional on the use of post-stratification weights. In the unweighted analysis, the interactions are intuitive: engaged citizens are generally more likely to respond to decisions than the unengaged. In the weighted analysis, however, the unengaged show updating in the opposite direction to the engaged, which is difficult to understand, theoretically. Importantly, engagement in TAPS is skewed toward the high end of the scale, leaving relatively few unengaged citizens to estimate these conditional effects. The use of weights can exacerbate this problem as a small number of observations can carry a large amount of influence shaping the conditional effect estimates. For these reasons, we are hesitant to draw firm conclusions regarding differences across engagement, though there is some suggestive evidence that engaged citizens update more strongly in the expected direction than unengaged citizens. The interactive models can be estimated using our reproduction materials for Chapter 5.

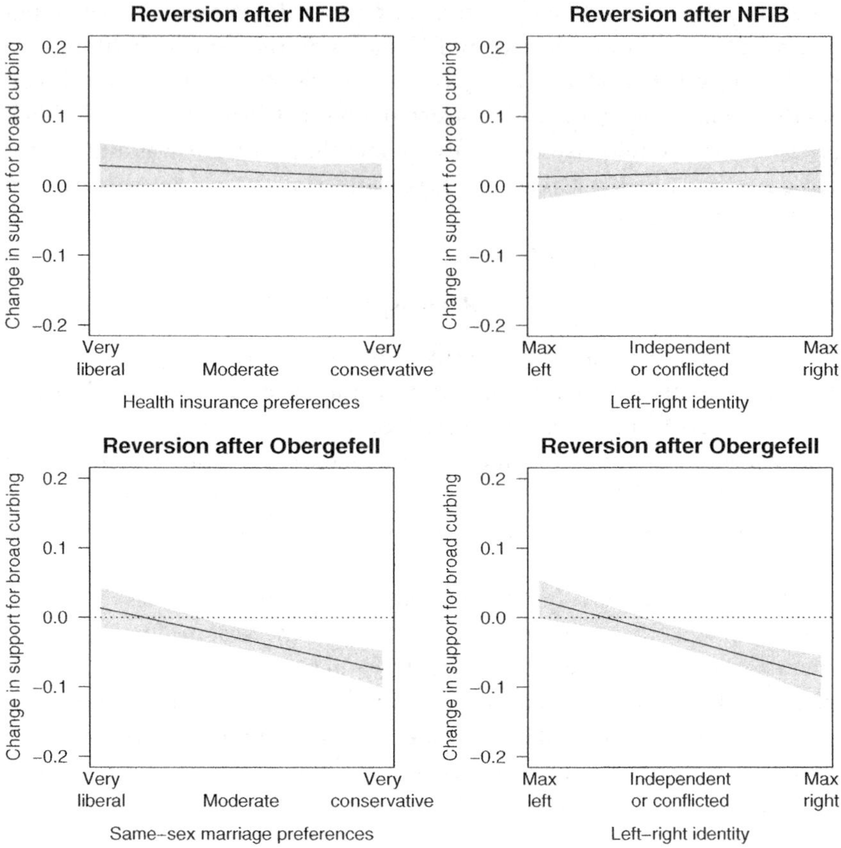

FIGURE 5.2 Reversion of support for broad curbing following two Supreme Court decisions, TAPS. The solid lines represent the predicted change in support for broad curbing from just after each decision to several months later at each level of policy preferences or left–right identity; the grey bands are 95 percent confidence bounds; see Table 3.2 for the items that make up the curbing scale; this figure is based on model estimates in Tables A5.1 and A5.2.

the negative effect of *NFIB* among citizens on the left persists many months later.[23] Conservative/Republican citizens also exhibit small positive changes over this period, but recall they did not update much in response to the *NFIB* and are thus relatively stable across the entire time period.

[23] Woodson (2018) reports evidence of considerable persistence of the effects of *NFIB*.

The results from *Obergefell* indicate substantially more reversion over a similar length of time. The bottom two panels of Figure 5.2 show that the effect of *Obergefell* among citizens on the right is almost entirely eliminated over the next year. This same effect occurs using both same-sex marriage policy preferences and broader left–right orientations, and both effects are statistically significant. Little to no reversion occurs among liberals and Democrats, though recall they did not update significantly in light of *Obergefell* and are thus stable across this period.

One complicating and potentially confounding factor for these reversion effects involves the politics surrounding the Supreme Court vacancy left by the death of Justice Scalia in February 2016. Immediately after Scalia's death, Senate Republicans, led by Majority Leader Mitch McConnell, pledged to block any nomination to the Supreme Court made by President Obama. Senate Republicans argued that because the presidential election campaign had started, the winner of the next election – not President Obama – should fill that seat. Given that an Obama nominee could have given liberals a solid five-justice majority on the Court, the Senate pledge to block any Obama nomination surely pleased Republicans. On March 16, 2016, President Obama nominated Judge Merrick Garland to fill the vacancy, but the Senate never considered the nomination. Thus, changes in support for Court-curbing from the *Obergefell* decision to the March 2016 TAPS could be confounded with these events, which we would expect to please conservatives and Republicans.

Overall, our conclusions regarding the persistence of the effects of single decisions on support and opposition to broad Court-curbing are tentative and mixed. For both *NFIB* and *Obergefell*, we found significant and substantively meaningful changes in support for Court-curbing from before to after the decisions. In the case of *NFIB*, citizens on the left became less supportive of Court-curbing in response to the decision preserving the ACA. In the case of *Obergefell*, citizens on the right became more supportive of Court-curbing after the ideologically uncongenial ruling on same-sex marriage. In the former case, we find that the effect of the decision persisted many months later, suggesting that even single decisions can have a lasting impact on citizens' attitudes toward fundamental changes to the Court. In the latter case, however, we find just the opposite: the effect of *Obergefell* on conservatives was almost entirely erased by Spring of the following year. Moreover, our analysis of reversion is possibly confounded by other important events concerning the Supreme Court over this period. While we believe these results are useful, more research on the effects of single decisions on broad curbing is clearly needed. We will add several more findings relevant to this issue when we consider our experimental studies below and in the next chapter, but it would also be useful to have further research "in the field" to increase external validity and examine persistence across time.

Exploring Left–Right Divides in Support for Court-Curbing over Time

In this section, we investigate the cumulative effect of the Court's decision-making over the period from 2012 to 2016. Drawing on ten of the TAPS panel waves between 2012 and 2016, we examine how the relationship between left–right identity and support for Court-curbing has changed over time. These are *cross-sectional* results – they estimate the relationship between left–right identity and Court-curbing *within* each TAPS wave. Some respondents are included in multiple waves, but we treat these as separate observations.[24]

Between 2012 and 2015, the Supreme Court produced three blockbuster rulings in the liberal direction: *NFIB* in 2012, *Windsor* in 2013, and *Obergefell* in 2015. These decisions are likely quite disappointing to an American right expecting a generally conservative Court in the contemporary era. Conversely, the rulings give liberals hope that a center-right Court can generate liberal legal change, especially with a swing justice like Anthony Kennedy. But the Court also generated important conservative policy outcomes during this period, including *Shelby County* in 2013, which we discussed as a "policy offset" to *Windsor*. In 2014, the Court handed down multiple rulings that were congenial to conservative and Republican interests, including (1) striking down aggregate limits on campaign contributions to political candidates and parties,[25] (2) upholding prayer to open a town board meeting,[26] (3) ruling that religious objections can exempt corporations from the ACA's requirement to pay contraceptive coverage for employees,[27] and (4) giving abortion protesters more latitude to protest outside abortion clinics.[28] The Court also

[24] We use the same independent variables for this analysis: democratic values (rule of law, liberty, tolerance), political engagement, age, sex, race, education, religiosity, and income. As discussed previously, we measure left–right identity, values, engagement, and religiosity from the TAPS wave most closely preceding or coinciding with the wave measuring Court-curbing. Post-stratification weights are used for each wave.

[25] *McCutcheon* v. *FEC*. [26] *Town of Greece* v. *Galloway*.

[27] *Burwell* v. *Hobby Lobby*. [28] *McCullen* v. *Coakley*.

issued liberal rulings that same year, including restrictions on the use of the death penalty[29] and requiring warrants to search cell phones after an arrest.[30] We suspect that *Obergefell* dominated people's Court-related mindset in 2015 to the extent they were following any rulings. The balance of the remaining significant rulings in 2015 also appears to lean in the liberal/Democratic direction.[31] And 2016 followed suit, with rulings that upheld the use of affirmative action in college admissions[32] and struck down state abortion regulations that burden a woman's right to an abortion.[33] On the whole, over the period from 2012 to 2016, 62 percent of the Court's most salient rulings – those that appeared on the front page of *New York Times* the day after the ruling (Epstein and Segal 2000) – were decided in the *liberal* direction.[34] That figure accords with our prior work as well (Bartels 2015; Bartels and Johnston 2013).

Our core results are presented in Figure 5.3, which, for each wave, presents the relationship between left–right identity (on the x-axis) and support for broad curbing (on the y-axis).[35] The results are striking. First, in May 2012, on the eve of the Court's historic ACA ruling, there is no left–right divide in support for Court-curbing. Recall that in the June 2012 wave we analyzed in Chapter 4, there was a significant impact of general policy disagreement (one's own ideology relative to perceptions of the Court's ideology). But in May 2012, liberals and conservatives in general do not evince significantly different levels of support for broad curbing. As expected from the change results, the effect of left–right identity on broad curbing is statistically significant in July 2012 *after* the ruling in *NFIB* such that conservatives and Republicans are significantly more supportive of Court-curbing than liberals and Democrats. This left–right division persists into 2013 (and is even a bit larger at that time), suggesting a longer-term effect of the *NFIB* ruling. Recall that the degree of reversion in January 2013 (relative to July 2012) was quite small, with only a small amount of reversion among those on the left. As the *Shelby* and *Windsor* rulings can be viewed as "policy offsets," they do not change this left–right

[29] *Hall* v. *Florida*. [30] *Riley* v. *California*.

[31] See, e.g., https://www.nytimes.com/interactive/2015/us/major-supreme-court-cases-in-2015.html (accessed October 8, 2018).

[32] *Fisher* v. *University of Texas*. [33] *Whole Women's Health* v. *Hellerstedt*.

[34] Liberal and conservative directions were coded in accord with the Supreme Court Database (http://scdb.wustl.edu/). Salience was coded by the authors.

[35] The regression tables used to construct these figures can be generated using the reproduction materials for Chapter 5.

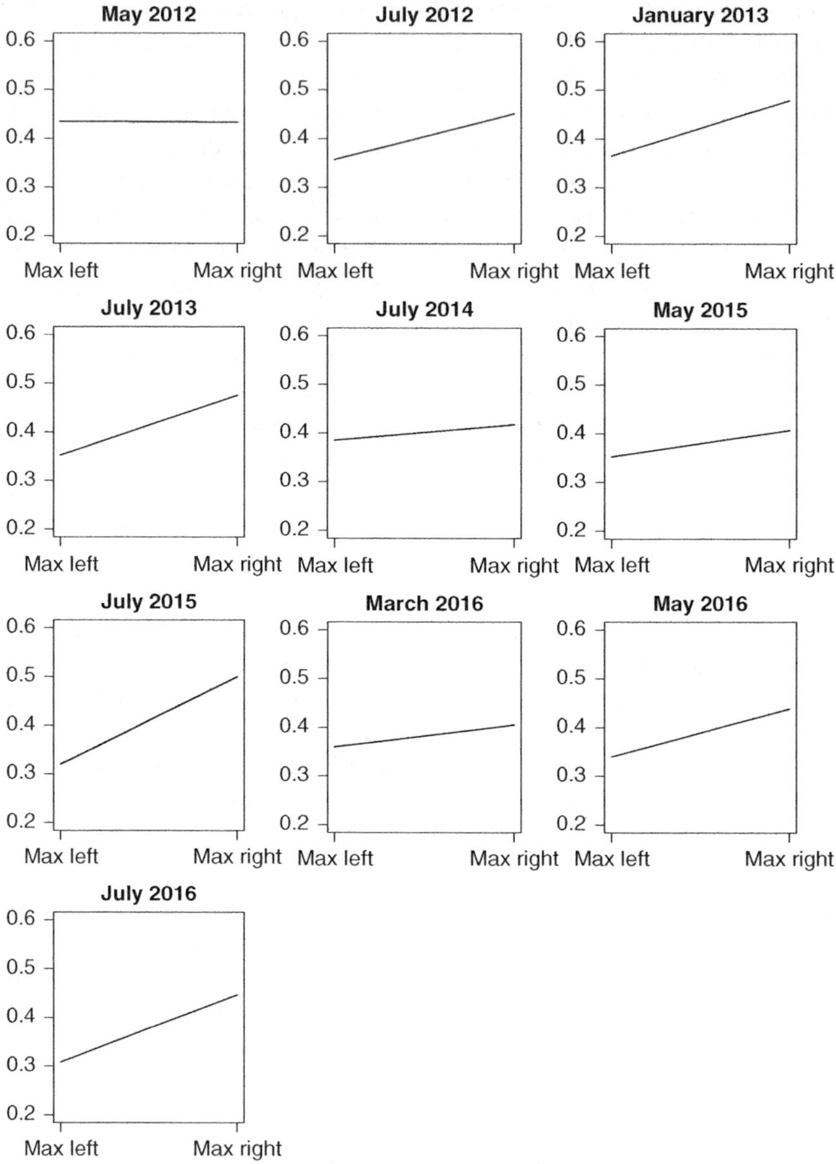

FIGURE 5.3 Support for broad curbing across left–right identity from 2012 to 2016, TAPS. See Table 3.2 for the items that make up the curbing scale, which ranges from 0 to 1; model estimates used to produce this figure can be obtained from the reproduction materials for this book.

division, and the effect size of left–right identity remains similar into July of 2013.

The first panel wave measuring Court-curbing in 2014 is July 2014. Recall that this wave comes after a mix of rulings which favor conservative and Republican interests on balance. As expected, then, the left–right divide in support for broad curbing is attenuated and is statistically insignificant in July 2014. In May 2015, on the eve of the blockbuster *Obergefell* ruling, that left–right divide remains statistically insignificant, suggesting that the Court redeemed itself among conservatives and Republicans after the 2014 season. However, immediately following the *Obergefell* ruling, the left–right divide opens to its largest extent in the series. As we also show in the change results, conservatives significantly increase their support for Court-curbing in light of this landmark liberal ruling, though these results suggest the possibility that citizens on the left may have moved in the direction of greater opposition to curbing as well. The sum of these changes is a strikingly large relationship between left–right identity and support for Court-curbing: those on the far right are about 20 percentage points more supportive of broad curbing than those on the far left.

By March 2016 there is reversion to the left–right divide we saw pre-*Obergefell*, which is consistent with our previous panel analysis, and the effect of left–right orientations in March 2016 is statistically insignificant. As we discussed, this wave coincided with Senate Republicans' refusal to consider any Supreme Court nomination made by President Obama after Justice Scalia's death. We suspect that conservatives viewed this as (at least) a short-term victory for Republican and conservative interests. On the other hand, by May 2016, the left–right divide once again becomes statistically significant, with conservatives significantly more supportive of broad curbing than liberals. One possibility is that voters assume at that point that Hillary Clinton will win the presidential election and be able to appoint the next justice, which is thus viewed as a victory for liberals, though this is obviously speculative. After more liberal rulings, like *Fisher* and *Hellerstedt*, the left–right divide remains robust and statistically significant in July 2016, the last panel wave for which we have measures of Court-curbing support.

Thus, by this last panel wave, there is a clear left–right divide in support for broad curbing that seems to reflect cumulative effects of policymaking by a Court that leaned liberal in terms of both its blockbuster rulings and the ideological balance of its other salient rulings. The theoretical implications are important. At any given time, we may not observe a large effect of left–right identity on support for attacks on the Court's institutional integrity. But a given null result may obscure an important role for policy disagreement. When we look *across* time, we find that the relationship between political orientation and support for Court-curbing varies substantially in ways consistent with the Court's policymaking. Moreover, in some periods, the relationship between left–right identity and Court-curbing is very strong indeed.

EXPERIMENTAL STUDIES OF SPECIFIC POLICY DISAGREEMENT

In this section, we examine two national survey experiments to test for the effects of policy disagreement with specific Supreme Court decisions on both broadly and narrowly targeted Court-curbing. This is our first examination of narrow curbing, and the next chapter also analyzes this variable. Our experiments resolve some of the causal issues endemic to general policy disagreement measures from Chapter 4 and the panel analysis in the prior section of this chapter. General policy disagreement relies on self-reported perceptions of the Court's ideological tenor, thus posing questions about causal direction – are people's perceptions endogenous to their support for Court-curbing? – and there are other measurement issues associated with distance-based measures (see Nelson and Gibson 2017). One of the strengths of our book is our reliance on multiple research designs with heterogeneous attributes. Our observational studies have high external validity but raise questions of causal identification. Our experimental studies, by contrast, *randomly assign* individuals to a liberal or conservative ruling and thus have high internal validity, though this causal leverage may come at the expense of realism. Our hope is that the cumulative evidence is stronger than any of the studies taken individually.

In the experimental studies reported in the remainder of the chapter, we test whether the effect of left–right identity and policy preferences on support for narrow and broad Court-curbing judgments reverses direction for liberal versus conservative rulings. If specific policy disagreement matters, then liberals should support Court-curbing measures more than conservatives in the face of a conservative ruling, and conservatives should support Court-curbing more than liberals in the face of a liberal ruling. Since we randomly assign respondents to decision direction, we can be confident that any changes in the relationship of political orientation to curbing are due to the decision itself.

This section also tests an important aspect of the process-based approach: whether procedural characteristics of the Court's ruling influence citizens' Court-curbing judgments. Our experimental design is similarly advantageous in this context in that we do not have to rely on self-reports of procedural perceptions (e.g., Gibson and Nelson 2017; Tyler and Rasinski 1991; see also Mondak 1993). In observational studies, if policy disagreement simultaneously influences both procedural perceptions (see Chapter 7) and Court-curbing judgments, then we may erroneously conclude that perceptions are driving Court-curbing. In contrast, we randomly assign respondents to read about process-related facets of the Court's rulings, thus ensuring exogeneity of procedural variables. Our work builds on past experiments, some of which have found evidence that process-related aspects of decisions influence support for the Court (e.g., Baird and Gangl 2006; Farganis 2012; Salamone 2014, 2018; Zink, Spriggs, and Scott 2009) and others which have found null effects (e.g., Mondak 1991, 1993). Our data come from two survey experiments discussed in Chapter 3 (see Tables 3.1, 3.2, and 3.3): the 2009 TESS and 2016 YGS.

2009 TESS

The 2009 TESS contains 1,061 respondents and was fielded in 2009 by Knowledge Networks via a grant from the Time-sharing Experiments in Social Sciences (TESS) program. The experiment is a 2 [direction of ruling] × 5 [procedural factors] full-factorial design. Thus, subjects are randomly assigned to one of ten experimental conditions. For the first experimental factor, individuals were randomly assigned to receive either a liberal or conservative ruling on the issue of government monitoring of citizens' email and phone messages in the context of terrorism investigations. The second experimental factor manipulated information about the decision process driving the outcome. In the control condition, no additional information (aside from the ruling itself) was provided; in the counter-majoritarian condition, the ruling overturned a popular federal law; in the ideological condition, the justices split along ideological lines and decided based on policy preferences; in the politicized condition, members of the two major political parties in Congress successfully influenced the decision-making of their respective justices; and in the legalistic condition, the justices adhered to precedent and were guided primarily by the law. All conditions describe fictional rulings, and respondents were debriefed to this fact following the study. We list the text for all conditions in Table 5.1.

TABLE 5.1 *Treatments in the 2009 TESS study*

Ideological direction conditions

Conservative: "The Supreme Court ruled today that federal law enforcement agents have the authority to monitor citizens' communications, including e-mail messages and phone conversations, in investigations of terrorism and related crimes."

Liberal: "The Supreme Court ruled today that federal law enforcement agents do not have the authority to monitor citizens' communications, including e-mail messages and phone conversations, in investigations of terrorism and related crimes."

Process-related conditions

Control: No process information provided.

Counter-majoritarian: "The decision strikes down a federal law passed by Congress last year that greatly [restricted (conservative ruling) or expanded (liberal ruling)] the FBI's ability to monitor an individual's communications. Many experts agree that the Court exercised a significant amount of power in overturning a law that received widespread public support and was passed by large majorities in the House and Senate."

Ideological: "The justices split strongly along ideological lines, with conservatives supporting vigorous monitoring measures and liberals opposing them. Many experts agree that instead of following long-standing legal precedents that oppose such strong measures, the justices based their decisions on their personal policy preferences." (*Note: We included "conservatives supporting" first for the conservative ruling and "liberals opposing" first for the liberal ruling.*)

Politicized: "The Court's decision had the appearance of being politicized, given the insertion of partisan politics into the decision. Members of Congress from both parties attempted to influence the justices through written arguments. Many experts agree that these arguments contributed to the stark differences in voting between Republican-appointed justices and Democrat-appointed justices." (*Note: We included "Republican-appointed" first for the conservative ruling and "Democrat-appointed" first for the liberal ruling.*)

Legalistic: "The Court adhered to long-standing legal precedents that prohibit strong investigation measures even when national security concerns arise. Many experts agree that the justices were strongly guided by prior law, evidenced by the fact that several justices who typically disagree with each other joined together to produce the Court's decision."

Our dependent variables are support for broadly targeted and narrowly targeted Court-curbing. From Table 3.2, recall that we use three broad curbing items: do away with, issues reduced, and Constitution means. From Table 3.3, we use three narrow curbing items: ruling's authority, compliance, and final word. For each, we build summative scales; they range from 0 to 1, where higher values reflect greater support for Court-curbing.[36] In our statistical models, we include the four procedural treatments as dummies and exclude the control group. To measure policy disagreement, we rely on two measures of individuals' left–right orientations: (1) policy-specific preferences on the government monitoring issue and (2) general left–right identity. For policy preferences, we asked, "When it comes to investigations of terrorism, do you favor or oppose the ability of the federal government to monitor citizens' e-mail messages and phone conversations?" A four-category response scale was used: strongly favor, somewhat favor, somewhat oppose, strongly oppose. The variable was recoded to range from 0 to 1, where higher values are more favorable toward monitoring (i.e., conservative). The identity measure combines a seven-point ideology measure with a seven-point party identification measure. We averaged the two ($r = 0.57$) and recoded the resulting scale to range from 0 to 1 such that higher values indicate conservative Republicans.

We use two strategies for operationalizing policy disagreement with the decision based on these measures.[37] First, we report average policy disagreement by averaging across liberal and conservative decision conditions. For this measure, we code both policy preferences and general left–right identity so that higher values represent greater policy disagreement. In other words, for those in the liberal ruling treatment, policy preferences and left–right identity are coded so that higher values are more conservative/Republican. For those in the conservative ruling treatment, we do the reverse – policy preferences and left–right identity are coded so that higher values are more liberal/Democratic. Second, we show how the effects of policy preferences and left–right identity *change direction* based on the direction of the Court's ruling. Among those receiving a liberal court ruling, conservatives and Republicans should demonstrate more support for Court-curbing than liberals and Democrats. Among those receiving a conservative ruling, this relationship should flip. All

[36] For narrow curbing, Cronbach's alpha=0.76. For broad curbing, alpha=0.59, which is lower than usual for such scales used in the literature.

[37] A separate analysis shows that the direction of ruling treatment was understood by the subjects in the way we intended, which suggests that our policy disagreement measures (based on this treatment) are valid. This is supported by very strong effects of both policy disagreement operationalizations on specific approval of the ruling, which is another variable we measured after the treatments. Citizens on the right (using both policy preferences and left–right identity) were substantially more approving of the conservative ruling than those on the left and vice versa for the liberal ruling.

models include the procedural condition dummies along with controls for age, gender, race, education, and income.[38]

We note that for this second strategy, we estimate separate regression models for each direction of ruling treatment condition (liberal versus conservative).[39] By estimating separate models, we implicitly interact the treatment factor with our key independent variable (policy preferences or left–right orientation) as well as all other controls in the models. The alternative – estimating a single model without the additional treatment by control variable interactions – could lead to excluded variable bias in estimates of our focal interaction. We employ this method for analogous models of experimental data throughout the book.

Full regression results are in Appendix Tables A5.3 and A5.4. Figure 5.4 reports the key results for both narrow and broad curbing using the first policy disagreement measurement strategy (average effect of policy disagreement). We estimated separate models for disagreement measures using policy preferences and left–right identity. Across both narrow and broad curbing, the effect of policy disagreement is statistically significant and in the predicted direction – the more one disagrees with the specific ruling, the more supportive one is of both narrow and broad Court-curbing measures. Interesting differences emerge, however, in line with expectations from Chapter 2. For both political identity and policy preferences, the effect of policy disagreement is much stronger for narrow than broad curbing. For narrow curbing, the effect of policy disagreement is about 30 percentage points or close to one-third of the scale of the dependent variable. This is a very large treatment effect. For broad curbing, by contrast, the effect of disagreement is 5 to 10 percentage points, which is consistent with what we found using the TAPS panel data. In the face of disagreement with a specific ruling, citizens are more willing to attack the authority of the ruling than the institutional integrity of the Court itself. As discussed in Chapter 2, this makes good sense even if citizens care *only* about policy outcomes and not at all about the Court's integrity for its own sake. Since single decisions provide some, but not a lot of information about the Court's ideological direction, they have more modest effects on support for broad curbing.

[38] Age is measured in years and recoded to range from 0 to 1. Education is a five-category nominal variable with the following categories: no high school diploma (excluded category), high school graduate, some college but no four-year college degree, college degree, and post-graduate degree. Income is measured based on nineteen categories reporting family income and recoded to range from 0 to 1.

[39] Post-estimation quantities and statistical tests are generated using simulation from the respective sampling distributions for each model.

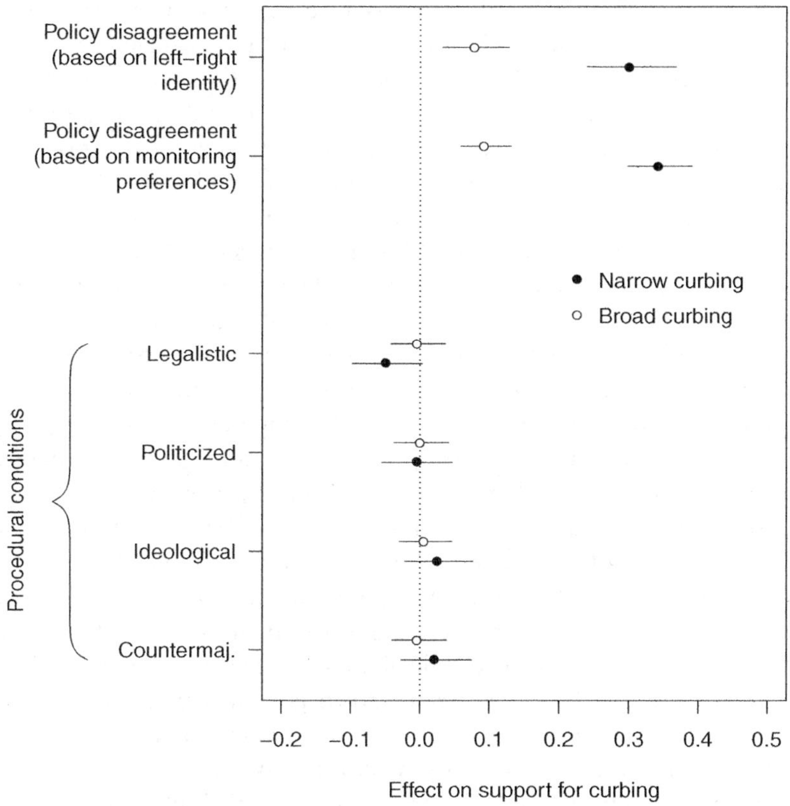

FIGURE 5.4 The effects of specific policy disagreement and procedural information on support for narrow and broad curbing, 2009 TESS experiment. The dependent variables are scales of support for narrow (solid circles) and broad (open circles) Court-curbing, recoded from 0 to 1; points for both measures of specific policy disagreement show the effect of moving each variable from its minimum to its maximum; points for the procedural conditions show the difference in support for each type of curbing relative to the control condition; extended lines are 95 percent confidence bounds; see Tables 3.2 and 3.3 for the items that make up the curbing scales; this figure is based on model estimates in Tables A5.3 and A5.4; for each dependent variable, the effects of the two disagreement variables come from two separate models; the effects of procedural conditions are from the model using the monitoring preferences measure of disagreement.

There is also a slightly larger effect of policy disagreement based on specific policy preferences compared to left–right identity, but this difference is not large or statistically significant.

The other important result from our survey experiment is that the process factors, in general, do not matter, which is evidence against the process-based approach. We plot these results for the models using monitoring preferences to operationalize policy disagreement in Figure 5.4.[40] For narrow curbing, the effects of "negative" process information – the counter-majoritarian, politicized, and ideological conditions – have statistically insignificant and minimal effects on support for both broad and narrow curbing. For broad curbing, the effect of positive (legalistic) process information is also small and insignificant. However, we do see that legalistic information reduces support for narrow curbing though the effect size is much smaller than that of policy disagreement (about 5 to 7 percentage points; see Table A5.3). Thus, the Court's policy authority is enhanced somewhat when its ruling is framed as following long-standing legal precedents. While the three negative procedural factors have no impact on narrow curbing, we find that at least one *positive* process element reduces support for narrow curbing. These results are consistent with experimental work by Baird and Gangl (2006), who find a similar asymmetry.

In our second set of models, we regress support for broad and narrow curbing directly on policy preferences and left–right identity. These results are shown in Figure 5.5. The solid lines show the results for the liberal decision condition (the Court strikes down government monitoring) and the dotted lines show the results for the conservative condition (the Court upholds monitoring). Among those who received the liberal ruling, policy preferences and left–right identity have positive, statistically significant, and large effects on support for narrow curbing such that conservatives are much more supportive of curbing than liberals. For those who received the conservative ruling, we observe the exact opposite pattern: a negative, statistically significant, and large effect of policy preferences and left–right identity on support for narrow curbing such that liberals are much more supportive than conservatives.

It is worth emphasizing the magnitude of these effect sizes. For example, in the liberal decision condition, a change from strongly oppose to strongly support government monitoring is associated with an increase in support for narrow curbing of over thirty-five points. In the conservative ruling condition, the same change in policy preferences is associated with a *decline* in

[40] The two sets of models lead to the same conclusions. The one difference of note is that the effect of the legalistic condition is statistically significant using left–right identity to operationalize policy disagreement but is only marginally significant when using policy preferences.

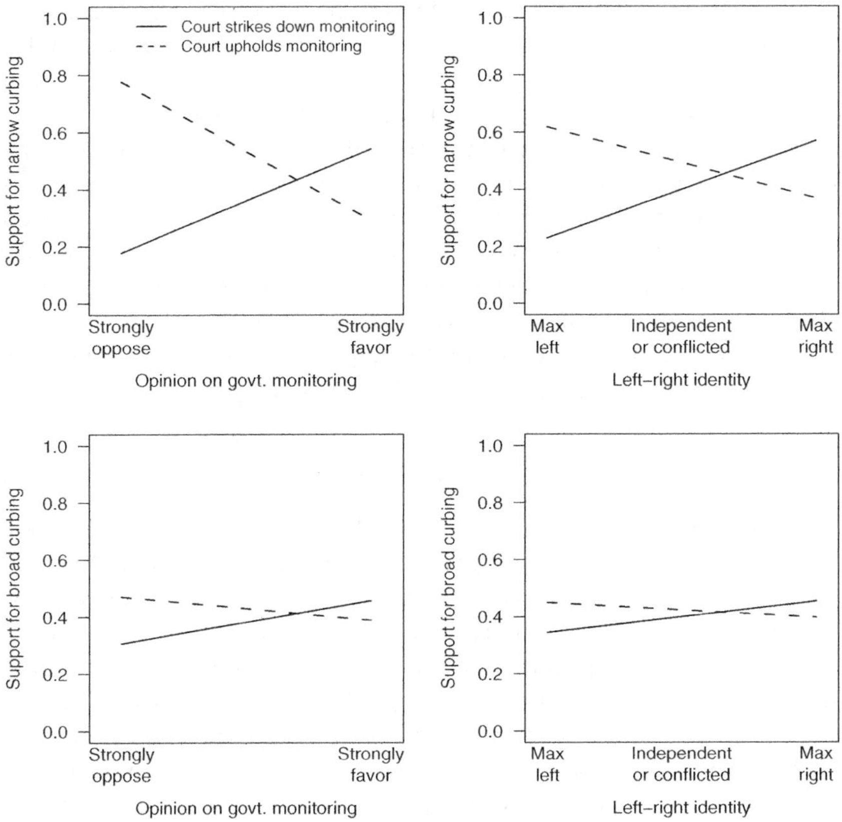

FIGURE 5.5 Predicted support for narrow and broad curbing across policy preferences, left–right identity, and decision treatment conditions, 2009 TESS experiment. See Tables 3.2 and 3.3 for the items that make up the curbing scales; this figure is based on model estimates in Tables A5.3 and A5.4.

support for narrow curbing of about fifty points. No other model predictors come close to these effect sizes. When it comes to attacking the Court's policy authority on a specific issue, citizens on the left and right turn on a dime as a function of the policy direction of the Court's ruling. Those who strongly opposed curbing the Court in ideologically congenial conditions are strongly supportive of curbing after uncongenial rulings. Simply put, this is strong evidence against the claim that the public sees the Court as highly legitimate and worthy of deference.[41]

[41] Specific policy disagreement based on policy preferences has a greater effect on narrow curbing for the conservative ruling, while disagreement based on left–right identity has

For broadly targeted curbing, the results converge with the general story from Figure 5.4. Like narrow curbing, the effect of policy preferences flips across decision conditions and is statistically significant in both. Yet these results again suggest that specific policy disagreement is much more consequential for narrow than broad Court-curbing. The size of the effect of policy preferences on broad curbing is 10 to 15 percentage points, which is comparable to what we observe in Figure 5.3 in several of the TAPS waves. Turning to left–right identity, the effect is positive and statistically significant for the liberal ruling condition, but it is negative and not statistically significant ($p = 0.14$) among those receiving the conservative ruling condition. However, the effect sizes comparing policy preferences to left–right identity are also statistically indistinguishable.[42]

Item-by-Item Analysis

As we have done in prior analyses, we analyze the curbing items separately to explore possible heterogeneity based on the specific content of curbing proposals. We estimated models with each curbing item as a dependent variable using the policy disagreement measure based on policy preferences as our key independent variable (i.e., always coded so higher values indicate disagreement with the ruling). For the three narrow curbing items, which were on four-point scales (no "uncertain/neutral" option), we recode these as binary variables, where 1 = curb and 0 = no curb.[43] For these, we estimated logit models using the same independent variables as above, and the estimates are shown in Appendix Table A5.5. For the broad curbing items, which contain middle options ("neither agree nor

a greater effect for a liberal ruling. We have no explanation for this asymmetry and we think it should be treated carefully without replication in other settings.

[42] When estimating the treatment effect of decision direction on support for broad curbing, it is positive (0.10) and statistically significant among liberal/Democratic citizens: a conservative ruling elicits significantly greater support for curbing than a liberal ruling. For conservative/Republican citizens, the treatment effect is negative (−0.02) but not statistically significant. That is, a conservative ruling does not elicit significantly lower curbing than a liberal ruling. This asymmetry in effect size across political orientation is consistent with some additional evidence we present in Chapter 6.

[43] We also examined these dependent variables using their full extent. Due to space considerations, we do not display these specific results, but note that the impact of disagreement is especially strong on the "final word" item. Converging with prior analyses, disagreement's effects on the broad curbing items are lower than the effects on narrow curbing. However, the effect of policy disagreement is positive and statistically significant across all models.

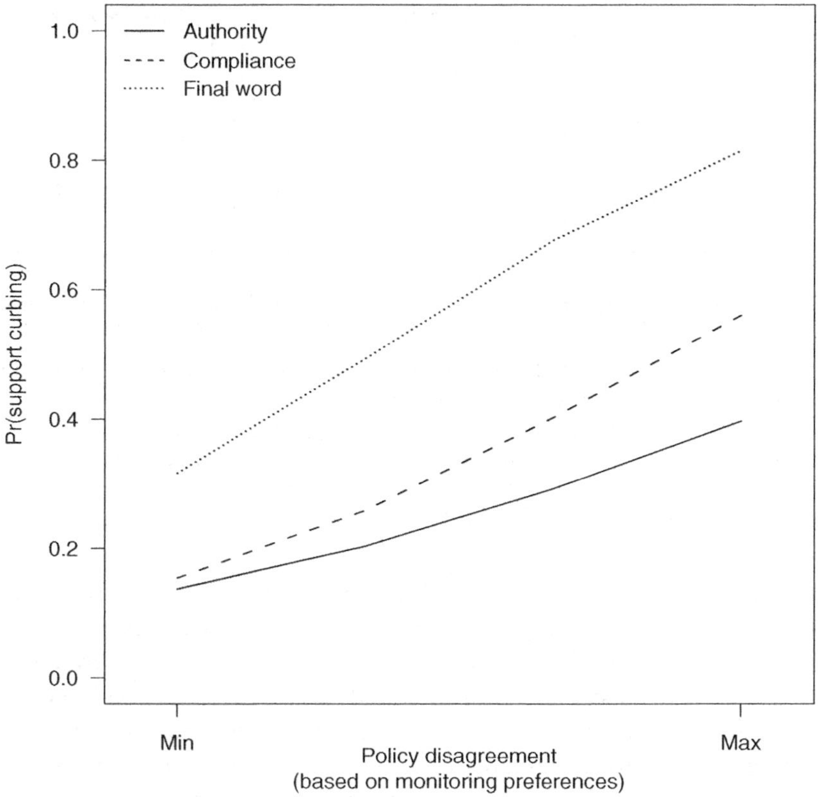

FIGURE 5.6 The predicted probability of support for three forms of narrow curbing across specific policy disagreement, 2009 TESS experiment. See Table 3.3 for the wording of each curbing item; this figure is based on model estimates in Table A5.5.

disagree"), we code them as three-category nominal variables and estimate multinomial logits.[44]

Figure 5.6 plots the average probability of support for narrow curbing proposals as a function of specific policy disagreement. First, we see that specific policy disagreement strongly increases the likelihood of subverting the Court's policy authority. Among those who strongly agree with the Court's decision (the minimum of the scale), the probability of subversion is quite low at about 0.15, but the probability rises to over 0.35 among those who strongly disagree (the maximum). The results are even larger

[44] These estimates can be obtained from the reproduction materials for Chapter 5.

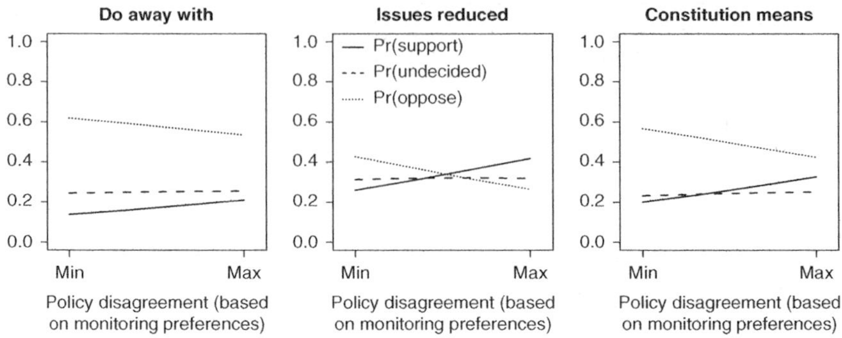

FIGURE 5.7 The predicted probability of support for several broad curbing proposals across specific policy disagreement, 2009 TESS experiment. The lines represent the probability that the respondent supports, opposes, or is undecided about each curbing proposal; see Table 3.2 for the wording of each item; multinomial logit model estimates used to produce this figure can be obtained from the reproduction materials for this book.

for support for noncompliance and whether the Court's ruling represents the final word on the matter. Support for noncompliance rises from about 0.15 among those who strongly agree with the decision to over 0.50 among those who strongly disagree. And opposition to giving the Court the final word on the matter increases from about 0.30 to about 0.80, moving from strongly disagree to strongly agree. In stark contrast to a deferential public, these results reveal that specific policy disagreement strongly influences support for undermining the Court's policy authority. Indeed, on two of the three items we see majority support for narrow curbing among those who strongly disagree with the ruling.

Figure 5.7 considers support for broad curbing. The lines represent the average predicted probability of each available response (curb, no curb, uncertain/neutral) as a function of specific policy disagreement. First, note how results from the "do away with" model resemble results from Chapter 4. For this extreme form of broad curbing, opposition is the most likely response across the board, though policy disagreement both significantly increases support for and significantly decreases opposition to this form of curbing. But specific policy disagreement has a potent impact on support for reducing the Court's power to hear controversial issues. Support for this form of curbing is less than 0.30 among those in strong agreement with the ruling but rises to over 0.40 among those in strong disagreement. Policy disagreement also significantly decreases *opposition* to this form of curbing such that, among those who strongly disagree with the ruling, support for reducing the Court's jurisdiction is the most likely response of the three. Specific policy disagreement also significantly increases support for and decreases opposition to curbing the Court's right to say what the Constitution means. Among those in strong agreement with the Court's ruling, "oppose curbing" is the most likely response, but policy disagreement substantially closes this gap. In sum, single rulings matter for broad curbing – for some types of curbing proposals quite a bit – but to a smaller extent compared to narrow curbing.

The item-by-item results also confirm the null effects of process variables for the most part. All "negative" political process variables are statistically insignificant across both narrow and broad items. A ruling framed as legalistic and following prior precedents decreases narrow curbing for the authority item but is insignificant in the "comply" and "final word" models. Across all three broad curbing models, the process variables fail to exhibit any statistically significant effects. Overall, the results reveal the primacy of policy disagreement over procedural characteristics tied to a ruling.

Summary

In sum, these results show that policy disagreement with a specific Supreme Court decision has significant and substantively important consequences for both broadly and narrowly targeted Court-curbing. Our experimental design, which randomly assigns the policy direction of the ruling, generates strong causal evidence of the effect of policy disagreement. In addition, our analysis highlights the importance of studying narrowly tailored Court-curbing, which we show is moved to a much greater extent than broad curbing. While broad curbing is obviously an important construct that has been studied extensively, narrow curbing captures an element of judicial evaluation – policy authority and judicial supremacy – that is crucially important for understanding the Court's power and efficacy in the political system. Finally, our experimental results cast doubt on the importance of procedural aspects of single rulings, though they suggest the possibility that positive procedural aspects may have small negative effects on support for some forms of narrow Court-curbing.

2016 YGS

We conducted another experiment capable of testing the effects of policy disagreement and procedural characteristics of Supreme Court rulings. Our 2016 YGS actually contains two experimental "modules." One is a polarization experiment, which is analyzed in depth in Chapter 6, and the other is a procedural experiment, analyzed here and again in Chapter 7. In total, 2,500 subjects were randomly assigned to only one of the two experiments. There are thus 1,250 respondents in the procedural experiment discussed here.

The original goal of the YGS procedural experiment was to examine motivated reasoning in the formation of procedural perceptions about the Court (see Chapter 7). This includes testing the role of policy disagreement and procedural information (experimentally manipulated, like in the 2009 TESS study) on subsequent perceptions of the Court as political and ideological versus legalistic and fair. Our initial dependent variables immediately following the delivery of treatment information are the procedural perception variables. After those variables, we measured both narrowly and broadly targeted Court-curbing. In this chapter, we examine the Court-curbing dependent variables only. We emphasize the nature of this study because examining the Court-curbing-dependent variables was a secondary goal of this particular experiment.

The general nature of the experiment is similar to the 2009 TESS. It has two experimental factors: (1) direction of a court ruling (liberal or conservative) and (2) variation in procedural characteristics of the ruling (no procedural information, positive procedural information, or negative procedural information). It also has a "global" control group that gets no information at all on either factor. For both the polarization and procedural experiments, we introduce an innovation in the "direction of ruling" treatment. We first randomly assigned individuals to receive either a liberal or conservative ruling. Within each of these conditions, we then randomly assigned individuals to receive one of four rulings related to issues of free speech, race, the death penalty, or search and seizure. The treatments described real Court decisions, but we did not refer to the case names. On each issue, we attempted to find rulings in different policy directions (liberal versus conservative) that were roughly comparable. In the analyses, we then distinguish between liberal and conservative rulings while averaging over the issues. The advantage of this approach is an increase in generalizability compared to a design that examines only a single issue.

When the direction of ruling and process conditions are crossed, we have a 2 × 3 design with six total experimental conditions. As discussed, we also included a seventh condition that is a true control group, which receives neither information about a ruling nor procedural information. We list the exact text for the four liberal and four conservative ruling conditions in Table 5.2 and the exact text for the two procedural

TABLE 5.2 *Ideological direction treatments for the 2016 YGS experiment*

"There has been a lot of discussion over the years about how the Supreme Court goes about making decisions on such important issues as . . . ."

Liberal conditions

"… the ability of anti-abortion protesters to express their views outside of abortion clinics and engage in discussions with patients of those clinics. The Supreme Court has ruled that anti-abortion protesters do **not** have the right to engage in counseling or literature distribution with patients entering or leaving an abortion clinic."

"… whether giving the death penalty to minors (under the age of 18) is "cruel and unusual punishment" in violation of the Constitution. The Supreme Court has ruled that the death penalty **cannot** be given to offenders who were under the age of 18 when their crimes were committed."

" . . . using affirmative action in college admissions to increase racial diversity. The Supreme Court has ruled that college and university administrators **can** use an individual's race as one of several factors in admissions decisions if it advances an institution's goal of generating a racially diverse student body."

"… appropriate types of action police officers may take when investigating an individual suspected of breaking the law. The Supreme Court has ruled that the police may **not** draw blood from drunk driving suspects to test their blood alcohol level without a search warrant, even if there is probable cause."

Conservative conditions

"… whether corporations should be limited in their ability to spend money in elections. The Supreme Court has ruled that corporations **can** spend as much money as they want to help political candidates win elections."

"… whether lethal injection as a means of carrying out a death sentence is "cruel and unusual punishment" in violation of the Constitution. The Supreme Court has ruled that lethal injection is **not** "cruel and unusual punishment" and has rejected death row inmates' challenges that certain lethal injection drugs cause severe pain and suffering."

"… whether U.S. states with a history of racial discrimination should still be monitored by the federal government to ensure that changes to their electoral laws are free from racial bias. The Supreme Court has ruled that the federal government **cannot** require states with a history of racial discrimination to secure federal government approval of changes to their election laws."

"… whether incriminating evidence against a criminal suspect can be admitted in court if the police search that uncovered the evidence was illegal and a violation of a suspect's constitutional rights. The Supreme Court has ruled that evidence gathered from an illegal police search **can** be used in court as long as the search violation was not intentional."

treatment conditions in Table 5.3. The text of the procedural conditions always followed the text describing the ruling (the process control group receives no additional text other than the ruling).

TABLE 5.3 *Procedural treatments for the 2016 YGS experiment*

Procedurally positive condition
"On this and other decisions, legal experts who watch the Court up close argue that its decisions are made fairly and objectively, are not influenced by partisanship, ideology, or special interests, and are based on legal and constitutional principles – even when there's disagreement among the justices."

Procedurally negative condition
"On this and other decisions, legal experts who watch the Court up close argue that its decisions are not made fairly and objectively, are heavily influenced by partisanship, ideology, and special interests, and are not based on legal and constitutional principles."

As discussed in Chapter 3 (in relation to Tables 3.2 and 3.3), the 2016 YGS contains two narrow Court-curbing items (final word and compliance) and five broad curbing items (do away with, issues reduced, remove justices, less independent, and Constitution means). Recall from Chapter 3 that all curbing items are measured on 6-point agree–disagree scales. For each dependent variable, we create summative scales, where higher values represent greater support for curbing.[45] Note that the survey questions for narrow curbing are tied to the policy depicted in the ruling, so the "true control" group does not receive these survey questions.

To measure policy disagreement, we again use our "left–right identity" measure, which combines ideological identification and partisanship (r = 0.60). Our measure of left–right identity averages the two together, such that the measure ranges from very liberal, strong Democrats on one end to very conservative, strong Republicans on the other. In this study, we did not measure policy-specific preferences, so this is our only measure of disagreement. We note, however, that we are still tapping a form of "specific policy disagreement" since respondents are confronted with only one ruling.

Note that the true control group allows us to capture a baseline relationship between left–right identity and support for broad curbing. Recall from our TAPS analysis in this chapter that the baseline effect was positive and statistically significant by May 2016 – conservatives and Republicans are more supportive of broad curbing than liberals and Democrats – which is also when this survey is conducted.

[45] For narrow curbing, the correlation between the two items is 0.38. For the broad curbing scale, Cronbach's alpha=0.80.

As with the 2009 TESS, our models use two strategies for operationalizing policy disagreement. First, we code our left–right identity variable so that higher values represent greater policy disagreement. For those in the liberal ruling treatment, left–right identity is coded so that higher values are more conservative/Republican. For those in the conservative ruling treatment, we do the reverse – higher values are more liberal/ Democratic. When using this measure, we use the 2 × 3 full-factorial design without the true control group since that group does not receive a treatment for direction of ruling.

Second, we test whether the direction of ruling treatment switches the direction of the left–right identity effect. If policy disagreement matters, among those receiving a liberal court ruling, conservative Republicans will support Court-curbing more than liberal Democrats. Among those receiving a conservative ruling, liberal Democrats will support Court-curbing more than conservative Republicans. For narrow Court-curbing, when using this measure, we use the 2 × 3 full-factorial design without the true control group because narrow curbing is not measured for that condition. However, when using this measure in the broad curbing model, we are able to use all seven experimental conditions. The relationship between left–right identity and support for broad curbing for the true control group serves as a baseline of comparison.[46] All models include one of the two measurement strategies for policy disagreement, the process condition variables (with the process control group as the baseline), and controls for political engagement, age, gender, race, education, religiosity, and family income.[47] Respondents are

[46] Evidence suggests that our liberal and conservative rulings were, on average, received by subjects as we intended. Since we strove for generalizability via multiple issues, there is always the risk that some citizens do not perceive a particular ruling the way we intended (i.e., as liberal or conservative). After the treatment information, we asked, "Do you agree or disagree with the Supreme Court's ruling that you read about?" A six-category agree–disagree format was used. The direction of ruling treatment flips the sign of the left–right identity effect as predicted. For those in the liberal ruling treatment, conservative Republicans have significantly lower levels of decision agreement with the ruling than liberal Democrats. For those in the conservative ruling treatment, conservative Republicans have significantly higher levels of agreement with the ruling than liberal Democrats. The former effect is stronger, suggesting a degree of asymmetry. For the most part, the direction of ruling treatment was received as intended.

[47] For engagement, we generated a scale (alpha=0.75) based on five multiple choice knowledge questions, including whether people knew (1) length of US Senate terms, (2) on which issue the federal government spends the least, (3) who the current Chief Justice is, (4) who the current Prime Minister of the United Kingdom is, and (5) who is the current Speaker of the House. Religiosity was measured using both frequency of church

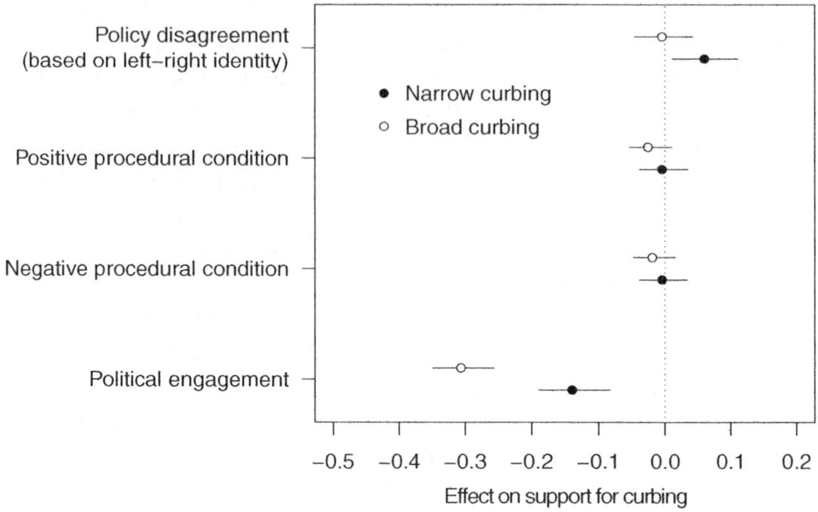

FIGURE 5.8 The effects of specific policy disagreement and procedural information on support for narrow and broad curbing, 2016 YGS experiment. The dependent variables are scales of support for narrow (solid circles) and broad (open circles) Court-curbing, recoded from 0 to 1; points for specific policy disagreement and political knowledge represent the effect of moving each variable from its minimum to maximum; points for the procedural conditions show the difference in support for each type of curbing relative to the control condition; extended lines are 95 percent confidence bounds; see Tables 3.2 and 3.3 for the items that make up the curbing scales; this figure is based on model estimates in Table A5.6.

nested within issues (eight of them), so we include dummies for seven of these issues to eliminate clustering of errors. Estimates were obtained via ordinary least squares.

All regression estimates for the 2016 YGS are in Table A5.6. We focus here on our hypotheses and again present results graphically. Our first analysis uses the first measurement strategy for policy disagreement. The results are reported in Figure 5.8. Policy disagreement via left–right identity significantly increases support for narrow Court-curbing, but

attendance (six options ranging from never to more than once a week) and whether one was a "born again" Christian (yes or no). Education is five categories: no high school diploma, high school diploma, some college but no college degree, college degree, and post-graduate degree. Income was measured based on seventeen categories; missing values were imputed based on demographics.

unlike the results from prior analyses, it does not have an impact on support for broad curbing. The effect is essentially zero for broad curbing and not especially large for narrow curbing, though it is statistically significant.

The procedural manipulations have null effects on support for curbing – results that generally converge with our 2009 TESS results. Receipt of positive or negative information about how the Court made its decision neither decreases nor increases (respectively) support for either form of Court-curbing. What appears to matter is political engagement, which significantly reduces support for both narrow and broad curbing. Thus, while procedural information about the Court's ruling fails to influence Court-curbing judgments, the broader process-based factor, political engagement, plays a potent role in diminishing support for curbing. Those who are more knowledgeable and engaged are more protective of the Court's authority, which is consistent with positivity theory. In line with our prior analyses, we tested for the interaction between engagement and policy disagreement and that interaction was not statistically significant in our models. Another finding of interest includes religiosity's positive and significant effects; religious individuals are more likely to support both narrow and broad curbing measures. No other variables exhibit much of an effect, though income significantly reduces support for broad curbing.

Results using our second measurement strategy – where we examine how the effect of left–right identity changes as a function of the direction of ruling treatment – shed light on the effects of policy disagreement just reported. Figure 5.9 reports predicted values of support for narrow and broad curbing as a function of left–right identity conditional on the direction of the Court's ruling. Recall that the control group does not receive the narrow curbing questions while they do receive broad curbing items. If policy disagreement matters like we expect (and like we found in the 2009 TESS study), we should observe a positive effect of left–right orientations for the liberal treatment (meaning conservative Republicans are more supportive of curbing) and a negative effect for the conservative treatment (conservative Republicans less supportive of curbing). Were it not for our dynamic TAPS analysis reported earlier in this chapter, we would expect a null effect of left–right identity for the control group since it is not relative to any policy signal from the Court. However, as mentioned, the cumulative effect of Supreme Court rulings tilting in the

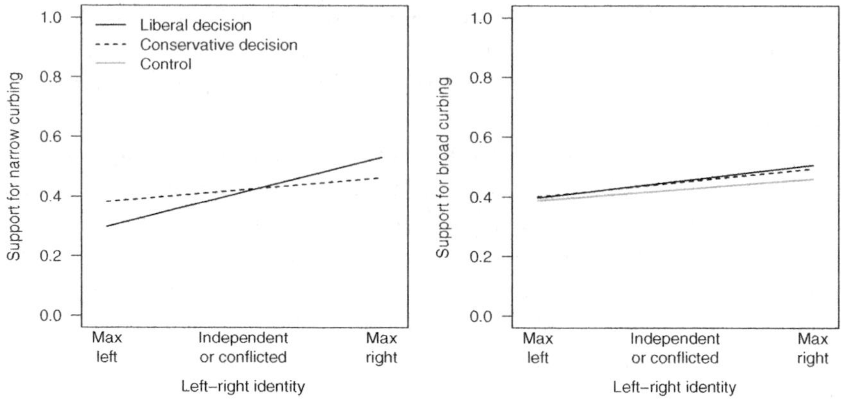

FIGURE 5.9 Predicted support for narrow and broad curbing across left–right identity and decision treatment conditions, 2016 YGS experiment. See Tables 3.2 and 3.3 for the items that make up the curbing scales; this figure is based on model estimates in Table A5.6.

liberal direction appears to have elicited more support for broad curbing from conservatives and Republicans compared to liberals and Democrats during this period. Thus, subjects arguably bring priors to the experiment based on significant Court rulings on salient topics such as same-sex marriage and health care.

For narrow curbing, the results for the liberal treatment are in line with expectations: In the face of a liberal Court ruling, conservatives and Republicans are more supportive of subverting the Court's policy authority than liberals and Democrats. That effect is statistically significant and quite large at about 20 percentage points. However, in the face of a conservative ruling, though we would expect liberal Democrats to be more supportive of Court-curbing than conservative Republicans, we see the opposite. Conservative Republicans are significantly more supportive of narrow curbing than liberal Democrats even in the face of a conservative Court ruling. Nonetheless, there are significant changes among liberal Democrats and conservative Republicans comparing the two treatment conditions. Moving from the liberal decision to the conservative decision condition, we see a significant increase in support for narrow curbing among citizens on the left, while we see the opposite pattern among those on the right. While our policy disagreement expectations receive a semblance of support, the results for conservative rulings defy expectations to an extent. One possibility is that conservatives and Republicans do not fully recognize the conservative nature of the conservative rulings and require elite cues to map the decisions to their own political beliefs and attitudes.[48] As we will see in Chapter 6, this hypothesis finds strong support in our 2016 YGS polarization study.

Turning to broad curbing, Figure 5.9 shows that in the face of a liberal ruling, conservative Republicans are significantly more supportive of broad curbing than liberal Democrats – a result we again expect from a policy disagreement perspective. However, as with narrow curbing, in the face of a conservative ruling, conservative Republicans continue to be more supportive of broad curbing than liberal Democrats, and the two effects of identity are indistinguishable statistically. Moreover, neither slope is distinguishable from the control condition. Thus, for broad curbing, the treatments had no effect on the relationship between left–right identity and curbing.

Item-by-Item Analysis

Like we did for the prior analyses, we conducted item-by-item analyses, using linear regression and multinomial logit for three-category (curb, no curb, middle) dependent variables. Unlike past analyses in which interesting comparisons and new findings emerged, we do not find any patterns or effects that differ substantially from the linear regressions using the narrow curbing and broad curbing scales and employing both measurement strategies for policy disagreement. Given this relative uniformity across items, we refrain from reporting item-by-item results.

CONCLUSION

While Chapter 4 revealed a robust effect of general policy disagreement on broadly targeted Court-curbing, this chapter analyzed the effect of policy disagreement with a specific ruling on support for both broad and narrow curbing. Our analyses – using both panel data and experimental designs – generate evidence in support of our theoretical contentions. Specific policy disagreement leads citizens to support Court-curbing, but the effect is stronger for narrow curbing

[48] This possibility is also consistent with the asymmetry in how the direction of ruling treatment was received, as reported in Footnote 46.

than broad curbing. This occurs because citizens, when in disagreement with a specific ruling, do not necessarily feel the need to take an axe to the Court but are willing to use a scalpel to subvert the Court's policy authority on that issue. This point notwithstanding, we do find evidence – in the TAPS panel and the 2009 TESS – that single rulings can shape support for broad curbing to a meaningful degree and that these effects can accumulate over time.

Our experiments also gave us the chance to test an important part of the process-based approach: whether negative and positive procedural information boosts and deflates support for broad and narrow curbing. In contrast to prior work relying on procedural perceptions in cross-sectional analyses (Gibson and Nelson 2017; Ramirez 2008; Tyler and Rasinski 1991; but see Baird and Gangl 2006), we manipulated procedural characteristics of the ruling. Across the two experiments, we find minimal effects of procedural information (in the 2009 TESS study we find a small, negative effect of legalistic perceptions on support for narrow curbing). In the 2009 TESS study, then, policy disagreement far eclipses the effect of procedural considerations. In the 2016 YGS, policy disagreement significantly increases support for narrow (but not broad) curbing, but procedural considerations exhibit null effects on both narrow and broad curbing. Political engagement (based primarily on knowledge) exhibits the largest effect in this study, which is consistent with positivity theory. The results from both experiments suggest that exposure to positive or negative procedural information related to a Court ruling exhibits no substantial effects on opposition to Court-curbing.

In sum, the results from our Chapter 5 studies generally support our theoretical framework and suggest that the Court's capacity for policy legitimation may be weaker than previously thought. In our 2016 YGS study, however, the effects of policy disagreement were much weaker than in our 2009 TESS study. One possibility is that citizens often require elite guidance to figure out which side of a decision they should be on. In Chapter 6, we seek to both replicate the findings from Chapter 5 in two independent samples and explore the possibility that elite cues and partisan polarization magnify the effect of policy disagreement on support for Court-curbing.

APPENDIX

TABLE A5.1 *Models of change in support for broadly targeted Court-curbing as a result of* NFIB *v.* Sebelius *(2012 ACA Health Care Ruling), 2012–2013 TAPS*

	Change	Reversion	Change	Reversion
Intercept	−0.05 (0.06)	0.07 (0.06)	−0.01 (0.06)	0.05 (0.05)
Age	0.01 (0.05)	0.05 (0.04)	0.01 (0.05)	0.05 (0.04)
Female	−0.01 (0.02)	−0.00 (0.02)	−0.00 (0.02)	−0.00 (0.02)
Black	−0.10 (0.03)	0.06 (0.03)	−0.09 (0.04)	0.07 (0.03)
Hispanic	−0.05 (0.02)	0.03 (0.02)	−0.04 (0.02)	0.03 (0.02)
HS degree	−0.02 (0.04)	0.02 (0.03)	−0.02 (0.04)	0.02 (0.03)
Some college	−0.02 (0.04)	−0.00 (0.03)	−0.03 (0.04)	0.00 (0.03)
BA degree	−0.05 (0.04)	0.02 (0.03)	−0.05 (0.04)	0.02 (0.03)
Post-grad	−0.04 (0.04)	0.01 (0.03)	−0.05 (0.04)	0.02 (0.03)
Income	0.06 (0.04)	−0.03 (0.03)	0.05 (0.03)	−0.03 (0.03)
Engagement	0.03 (0.04)	−0.04 (0.04)	0.00 (0.04)	−0.03 (0.04)
Rule of law	0.05 (0.06)	−0.06 (0.06)	0.04 (0.06)	−0.07 (0.06)
Liberty over order	−0.12 (0.05)	0.05 (0.04)	−0.12 (0.05)	0.05 (0.04)
Tolerance	0.04 (0.04)	−0.03 (0.03)	0.04 (0.04)	−0.02 (0.03)
Religiosity	−0.01 (0.03)	−0.02 (0.02)	−0.02 (0.03)	−0.03 (0.03)
Policy disagreement (health ins. pref.)	0.07 (0.02)	−0.02 (0.02)		
Policy disagreement (left–right identity)			0.09 (0.03)	0.01 (0.03)
R^2	0.08	0.04	0.08	0.04
N	1249	1167	1249	1167

Notes: Data are from the TAPS panel survey. Entries are ordinary least squares estimates and standard errors (in parentheses). For the "Change" models, the dependent variable is change in support for Court-curbing from May 2012 to July 2012 (Court-curbing scale from July 2012 minus the scale from May 2012); higher values indicate greater support for Court-curbing as a result of *NFIB*. For the "Reversion" models, the dependent variable is change in support from July 2012 to January 2013 (Court-curbing scale from January 2013 minus that scale from July 2012); higher values indicate greater support in January compared to July (see text and graphs for more interpretation). Health insurance preferences mean our "policy disagreement" measure is based on specific policy preferences related to the ACA/health insurance mandate (higher values conservative). "Left–right identity" means the policy disagreement measure is based on the average of ideological identification and party identification (higher values more conservative/Republican). Post-stratification weights are used in all analyses.

TABLE A5.2 *Models of change in support for broadly targeted Court-curbing as a result of* Obergefell *v.* Hodges *(2015 ruling making same-sex marriage legal across states) and "Offsetting Rulings" of* Shelby County *v.* Holder *(2013 voting rights act ruling) and* Windsor *v.* U.S. *(2013 same-sex marriage ruling striking down DOMA), TAPS*

	Obergefell				*Shelby/Windsor*
	Change	Reversion	Change	Reversion	Change
Intercept	−0.01 (0.05)	−0.05 (0.04)	−0.04 (0.04)	−0.04 (0.04)	−0.13 (0.05)
Age	0.09 (0.04)	−0.04 (0.05)	0.10 (0.04)	−0.05 (0.05)	0.02 (0.04)
Female	−0.02 (0.02)	0.02 (0.02)	−0.02 (0.02)	0.02 (0.02)	0.02 (0.01)
Black	−0.01 (0.02)	0.03 (0.03)	0.04 (0.03)	−0.01 (0.03)	0.02 (0.02)
Hispanic	0.01 (0.02)	−0.01 (0.03)	0.02 (0.02)	−0.02 (0.02)	−0.02 (0.02)
HS degree	0.02 (0.03)	0.01 (0.03)	0.02 (0.03)	0.01 (0.03)	0.03 (0.03)
Some college	−0.03 (0.03)	0.03 (0.03)	−0.03 (0.03)	0.03 (0.03)	0.07 (0.03)
BA degree	−0.01 (0.03)	0.02 (0.03)	−0.01 (0.03)	0.02 (0.03)	0.07 (0.03)
Post-grad	−0.06 (0.03)	0.03 (0.03)	−0.05 (0.03)	0.03 (0.03)	0.07 (0.03)
Income	0.08 (0.04)	−0.07 (0.04)	0.06 (0.04)	−0.06 (0.04)	0.01 (0.03)
Engagement	−0.09 (0.04)	0.05 (0.04)	−0.11 (0.04)	0.07 (0.04)	−0.02 (0.04)
Rule of law	0.09 (0.06)	−0.02 (0.05)	0.09 (0.06)	−0.03 (0.05)	0.11 (0.04)
Liberty over order	−0.02 (0.05)	0.01 (0.04)	−0.03 (0.05)	0.02 (0.04)	−0.05 (0.03)
Tolerance	−0.04 (0.03)	0.05 (0.03)	−0.04 (0.03)	0.05 (0.03)	0.02 (0.03)
Religiosity	−0.02 (0.03)	0.05 (0.03)	−0.02 (0.03)	0.03 (0.03)	−0.02 (0.02)

Policy disagreement (same-sex mar. pref.)	0.08 (0.02)	−0.09 (0.02)			
Policy disagreement (left–right identity)			0.14 (0.02)	−0.11 (0.03)	0.05 (0.02)
R^2	0.13	0.09	0.14	0.08	0.06
N	1027	956	1050	974	1107

Notes: Data are from the TAPS panel survey. Entries are ordinary least squares estimates and standard errors (in parentheses). For the "Change" models for *Obergefell*, the dependent variable is change in support for Court-curbing from May 2015 to July 2015 (July 2015 scale minus May 2015 scale); higher values indicate greater support for Court-curbing as a result of *Obergefell*. For the "Reversion" models, the dependent variable is change in support from July 2015 to March 2016 (March 2016 scale minus July 2015 scale); higher values indicate greater support in March compared to July (see text and graphs for more interpretation). For *Shelby/Windsor*, the dependent variable is change in support for Court-curbing from January 2013 to July 2013 (July 2013 scale minus January 2013 scale); higher values indicate greater support for Court-curbing as a result of the rulings. "Policy preferences" means our "policy disagreement" measure is based on specific policy preferences related to same-sex marriage (higher values more conservative). "Left–right identity" means the policy disagreement measure is based on the average of ideological identification and party identification (higher values more conservative/Republican). Post-stratification weights are used in all analyses.

TABLE A5.3 *Models of narrowly targeted Court-curbing, 2009 TESS*

	Combined model	Combined model	Strikes monitoring	Strikes monitoring	Upholds monitoring	Upholds monitoring
Intercept	0.28 (0.04)	0.31 (0.05)	0.16 (0.06)	0.19 (0.06)	0.79 (0.06)	0.71 (0.07)
Age	0.03 (0.04)	0.06 (0.04)	0.01 (0.05)	0.11 (0.06)	0.08 (0.05)	0.01 (0.06)
Female	0.02 (0.02)	0.02 (0.02)	0.00 (0.02)	0.01 (0.02)	0.03 (0.02)	0.04 (0.02)
Black	−0.03 (0.03)	−0.01 (0.03)	−0.08 (0.04)	−0.01 (0.05)	0.03 (0.04)	0.00 (0.05)
Hispanic	0.07 (0.03)	0.05 (0.03)	0.06 (0.04)	0.06 (0.05)	0.06 (0.04)	0.04 (0.04)
HS degree	0.02 (0.03)	0.01 (0.03)	0.03 (0.04)	0.04 (0.04)	0.01 (0.04)	−0.02 (0.05)
Some college	0.03 (0.03)	0.02 (0.03)	0.02 (0.04)	0.03 (0.05)	0.02 (0.04)	−0.02 (0.05)
BA degree	−0.02 (0.03)	−0.04 (0.04)	−0.02 (0.05)	−0.04 (0.05)	−0.02 (0.04)	−0.06 (0.05)
Post-grad	−0.07 (0.04)	−0.07 (0.04)	−0.05 (0.05)	−0.05 (0.05)	−0.10 (0.05)	−0.10 (0.06)
Income	−0.07 (0.04)	−0.07 (0.04)	0.00 (0.06)	0.01 (0.06)	−0.11 (0.05)	−0.12 (0.06)
Procedural experimental conditions						
Legalistic	0.02 (0.03)	−0.01 (0.03)	0.01 (0.04)	−0.02 (0.04)	0.02 (0.03)	0.00 (0.04)
Politicized	0.03 (0.02)	0.01 (0.03)	0.02 (0.03)	−0.00 (0.04)	0.04 (0.03)	0.02 (0.04)
Ideological	−0.00 (0.03)	−0.02 (0.03)	0.00 (0.04)	−0.02 (0.04)	−0.01 (0.03)	−0.01 (0.04)
Counter-majoritarian	−0.05 (0.03)	−0.08 (0.03)	−0.02 (0.04)	−0.05 (0.04)	−0.07 (0.03)	−0.11 (0.04)
Policy disagreement (monitoring pref.)	0.34 (0.02)					

Policy disagreement (left–right identity)		0.30 (0.03)				
Monitoring preferences			0.36 (0.04)		−0.48 (0.03)	
Left–right identity				0.34 (0.05)		−0.25 (0.05)
R^2	0.20	0.11	0.21	0.14	0.36	0.12
N	1049	1056	531	534	518	522

Notes: Data are from the 2009 TESS study. Entries are ordinary least squares estimates and standard errors (in parentheses). The dependent variable is the narrowly targeted Court-curbing scale; higher values indicate greater support for Court-curbing. For the combined models, each left–right variable (monitoring preferences and left–right identity) is measured relative to the direction of the ruling treatment (see text for clarification); higher values indicate greater policy disagreement. In the remaining models, separate models are estimated for "strikes" and "upholds" monitoring and the two left-right measures are measured as is (higher values conservative).

TABLE A5.4 *Models of broadly targeted Court-curbing, 2009 TESS*

	Combined model	Combined model	Strikes monitoring	Strikes monitoring	Upholds monitoring	Upholds monitoring
Intercept	0.51 (0.03)	0.52 (0.03)	0.45 (0.05)	0.47 (0.05)	0.64 (0.05)	0.63 (0.05)
Age	−0.08 (0.03)	−0.07 (0.03)	−0.10 (0.04)	−0.06 (0.04)	−0.07 (0.04)	−0.08 (0.04)
Female	0.03 (0.01)	0.03 (0.01)	0.02 (0.02)	0.03 (0.02)	0.04 (0.02)	0.04 (0.02)
Black	−0.01 (0.02)	−0.01 (0.02)	−0.01 (0.03)	0.01 (0.03)	−0.02 (0.04)	−0.02 (0.04)
Hispanic	0.04 (0.02)	0.03 (0.02)	0.05 (0.03)	0.04 (0.03)	0.03 (0.03)	0.02 (0.03)
HS degree	−0.03 (0.02)	−0.03 (0.02)	−0.04 (0.03)	−0.03 (0.03)	−0.04 (0.04)	−0.05 (0.03)
Some college	−0.07 (0.02)	−0.07 (0.02)	−0.06 (0.03)	−0.05 (0.03)	−0.09 (0.04)	−0.10 (0.04)
BA degree	−0.12 (0.03)	−0.12 (0.03)	−0.10 (0.04)	−0.11 (0.04)	−0.14 (0.04)	−0.14 (0.04)
Post-grad	−0.19 (0.03)	−0.18 (0.03)	−0.16 (0.04)	−0.16 (0.04)	−0.22 (0.04)	−0.22 (0.04)
Income	−0.11 (0.03)	−0.11 (0.03)	−0.08 (0.04)	−0.07 (0.04)	−0.14 (0.04)	−0.14 (0.04)
Procedural experimental conditions						
Legalistic	−0.00 (0.02)	−0.01 (0.02)	−0.01 (0.03)	−0.03 (0.03)	0.01 (0.03)	0.00 (0.03)
Politicized	0.01 (0.02)	0.00 (0.02)	0.01 (0.03)	0.00 (0.03)	0.00 (0.03)	−0.00 (0.03)
Ideological	0.00 (0.02)	−0.00 (0.02)	−0.01 (0.03)	−0.02 (0.03)	0.02 (0.03)	0.02 (0.03)
Counter-majoritarian	−0.00 (0.02)	−0.01 (0.02)	−0.00 (0.03)	−0.02 (0.03)	−0.01 (0.03)	−0.01 (0.03)
Policy disagreement (monitoring pref.)	0.10 (0.02)					

Policy disagreement (left–right identity)		0.08 (0.02)				
Monitoring preferences			0.15 (0.03)		−0.08 (0.03)	
Left–right identity				0.11 (0.03)		−0.05 (0.04)
R^2	0.14	0.12	0.15	0.11	0.15	0.14
N	1046	1052	529	532	517	520

Notes: Data are from the 2009 TESS study. Entries are ordinary least squares estimates and standard errors (in parentheses). The dependent variable is the broadly targeted Court-curbing scale; higher values indicate greater support for Court-curbing. For the combined models, each left–right variable (monitoring preferences and left–right identity) is measured relative to the direction of the ruling treatment (see text for clarification); higher values indicate greater policy disagreement. In the remaining models, separate models are estimated for "strikes" and "upholds" monitoring and the two left-right measures are measured as is (higher values conservative).

TABLE A5.5 *Models of narrowly targeted Court-curbing (item by item), 2009 TESS*

	Authority	Compliance	Final word
Intercept	−1.44 (0.38)	−1.68 (0.37)	−1.20 (0.36)
Age	0.47 (0.35)	0.32 (0.33)	0.35 (0.32)
Female	0.09 (0.15)	0.18 (0.14)	−0.06 (0.14)
Black	−0.08 (0.29)	−0.24 (0.28)	−0.26 (0.26)
Hispanic	0.26 (0.27)	0.42 (0.26)	0.64 (0.27)
HS degree	−0.22 (0.25)	−0.06 (0.25)	0.48 (0.25)
Some college	−0.43 (0.27)	−0.02 (0.26)	0.71 (0.27)
BA degree	−0.73 (0.30)	−0.49 (0.29)	0.51 (0.29)
Post-grad	−1.04 (0.36)	−0.82 (0.34)	0.24 (0.32)
Income	−0.48 (0.35)	−0.34 (0.34)	−0.37 (0.33)
Procedural experimental conditions			
Legalistic	0.26 (0.23)	0.41 (0.22)	0.04 (0.22)
Politicized	0.01 (0.23)	0.28 (0.21)	0.18 (0.21)
Ideological	0.08 (0.23)	−0.00 (0.22)	−0.01 (0.22)
Counter-majoritarian	−0.25 (0.24)	−0.23 (0.23)	−0.18 (0.22)
Policy disagreement (monitoring preferences)	1.46 (0.22)	2.02 (0.22)	2.30 (0.21)
Pseudo-R^2	0.07	0.10	0.11
N	1046	1040	1045

Notes: Data are from the 2009 TESS study. Entries are logit estimates and standard errors (in parentheses). The dependent variables are the three narrowly targeted Court-curbing items; 1=support curbing, 0=oppose curbing. "Policy disagreement" is based on monitoring preferences and is measured relative to the direction of the ruling treatment (see text for clarification); higher values indicate greater policy disagreement.

TABLE A5.6 *Models of broadly and narrowly targeted Court-curbing, 2016 YGS*

	Combined model (narrow curbing)	Combined model (broad curbing)	Lib decision (narrow curbing)	Con decision (narrow curbing)	Lib decision (broad curbing)	Con decision (broad curbing)	Control condition
Intercept	0.40 (0.05)	0.59 (0.04)	0.38 (0.06)	0.39 (0.06)	0.54 (0.06)	0.58 (0.05)	0.47 (0.06)
Age	0.05 (0.04)	0.05 (0.03)	−0.02 (0.05)	0.09 (0.05)	−0.04 (0.05)	0.12 (0.04)	−0.08 (0.05)
Female	−0.04 (0.02)	−0.02 (0.01)	−0.01 (0.02)	−0.05 (0.02)	0.01 (0.02)	−0.03 (0.02)	−0.00 (0.02)
Black	−0.01 (0.02)	−0.03 (0.02)	0.08 (0.03)	−0.03 (0.04)	0.02 (0.03)	−0.04 (0.03)	0.02 (0.04)
Hispanic	−0.01 (0.03)	0.01 (0.02)	−0.00 (0.04)	0.02 (0.04)	0.02 (0.03)	0.04 (0.03)	−0.08 (0.04)
HS degree	0.03 (0.04)	0.03 (0.03)	−0.02 (0.05)	0.06 (0.05)	0.06 (0.05)	0.00 (0.04)	0.16 (0.05)
Some college	0.01 (0.04)	−0.02 (0.03)	−0.01 (0.05)	0.01 (0.05)	0.02 (0.05)	−0.05 (0.04)	0.07 (0.05)
BA degree	−0.02 (0.04)	−0.04 (0.03)	−0.07 (0.06)	0.04 (0.05)	−0.02 (0.05)	−0.05 (0.04)	−0.01 (0.06)
Post-grad	−0.01 (0.04)	−0.06 (0.04)	−0.02 (0.06)	0.00 (0.06)	−0.01 (0.06)	−0.11 (0.05)	0.02 (0.06)
Income	−0.12 (0.07)	−0.17 (0.06)	−0.17 (0.09)	−0.01 (0.11)	−0.23 (0.08)	−0.05 (0.09)	0.08 (0.11)
Religiosity	0.10 (0.02)	0.06 (0.02)	0.07 (0.03)	0.06 (0.03)	0.04 (0.03)	0.02 (0.03)	0.03 (0.04)
Engagement	−0.14 (0.03)	−0.30 (0.02)	−0.14 (0.04)	−0.12 (0.04)	−0.31 (0.03)	−0.29 (0.03)	−0.36 (0.04)
Negative procedural	−0.00 (0.02)	−0.02 (0.02)	−0.02 (0.03)	0.01 (0.03)	−0.01 (0.02)	−0.04 (0.02)	
Positive procedural	−0.00 (0.02)	−0.02 (0.02)	−0.01 (0.03)	0.01 (0.03)	−0.04 (0.02)	−0.01 (0.02)	
Policy disagreement	0.06 (0.03)	−0.00 (0.02)					

TABLE A5.6 *(continued)*

	Combined model (narrow curbing)	Combined model (broad curbing)	Lib decision (narrow curbing)	Con decision (narrow curbing)	Lib decision (broad curbing)	Con decision (broad curbing)	Control condition
Left–right identity			0.23 (0.04)	0.08 (0.04)	0.11 (0.03)	0.09 (0.03)	0.07 (0.04)
R^2	0.09	0.26	0.19	0.07	0.33	0.24	0.36
N	1071	1071	542	529	542	529	353

Notes: Data are from the 2016 YGS. Entries are ordinary least squares estimates and standard errors (in parentheses). The dependent variables are narrowly and broadly targeted Court-curbing scales; higher values indicate greater support for Court-curbing. For the combined models, left–right identity is measured relative to the direction of the ruling treatment (see text for clarification); higher values indicate greater policy disagreement. In the remaining models, separate models are estimated for "liberal" and "conservative" rulings and left–right identity is measured as is (higher values conservative/Republican).

6

Partisan Polarization and Support for Court-Curbing

In the previous chapter we provided strong causal evidence for the effect of specific policy disagreement on support for Court-curbing. In two distinct experiments, we showed that citizens respond to an uncongenial decision by supporting actions aimed at minimizing the ruling's impact – what we have termed "narrowly targeted Court-curbing." In some cases, at least, a disliked decision even increases support for broader forms of curbing aimed at limiting the Court's autonomy. These studies are important evidence in support of our theoretical framework and suggest that the Court has less institutional support in the public than previously thought.

Yet our experimental explorations to this point have been rather bloodless, devoid of the intensity and emotion that defines the present moment in the United States. They have missed the hard-charging partisan elements that often accompany discourse about the Supreme Court. For example, nomination battles and salient Court decisions are typically supported and opposed by homogenous blocks of party elites, Democratic and Republican politicians often attack the Court's authority after an unfavorable ruling, and citizens have never seemed more tribal in their partisan and ideological attachments. We have thus side-stepped two of the most important factors shaping mass politics: political identity and partisan polarization (e.g., Druckman, Peterson, and Slothuus 2013; Iyengar, Sood, and Lelkes 2012; Lavine, Johnston, and Steenbergen 2012; Mason 2018). Our strategy to this point is not without intention – we have sought to establish several facts regarding Court-curbing in a relatively "pristine" environment – but it is time to add nuance to the analysis.

We argue that partisan polarization – at both the elite and mass levels – threatens judicial independence and power. This follows from the argument developed in Chapters 1 and 2, which we review briefly here. Standard theories in political science place the foundation of judicial independence in the public's willingness to sanction their elected officials for attacks on the Court, even when doing so requires a sacrifice of narrow political gain. In practice, this means a willingness to sanction one's fellow partisans, and perhaps even to side with the *opposing* party, on important issues. Indeed, this is the very essence of the legitimacy concept: to believe an institution has rightful authority is to put its integrity above narrow partisan concerns and policy benefits – it is only credible if it hurts. Our argument is that polarization reduces the proportion of citizens willing to sanction their co-partisan elected officials in the face of attacks on the judiciary. From the perspective of electorally minded elite actors, a drop in such costs raises the incentive to attack the courts. The electoral connection cuts both ways.

We have argued that there are three ways in which polarization has this effect – extremity of political outcomes at the elite level, the informativeness of party cues, and the psychological and social costs of partisan defection. First, as the parties polarize at the elite level, the cost of opposing the in-party grows, because the distance between the expected policy outcomes under the two parties increases. In a polarized environment there is more at stake, and citizens may be willing to sacrifice democratic norms for political victories (Svolik 2018). Second, polarization increases the informational value of partisan cues and citizens' propensity to rely on political identity alone when reasoning about politics (e.g., Druckman, Peterson, and Slothuus 2013; Lavine, Johnston, and Steenbergen 2012). Party cues teach citizens which side of each decision they should be on and what types of attitudes and behavior toward the Court are acceptable. Polarization increases the influence of such cues and reduces the importance of other considerations, such as democratic values. Finally, polarization increases the costs of partisan defection. Political identity is more than a reflection of one's policy stances; it is a psychological and social investment in a group (Huddy, Mason, and Aarøe 2015). Standing up for the Court, and against one's in-group, requires foregoing the comradery and righteous indignation that are a large part of what makes political participation valuable to citizens (e.g., Haidt 2012; Huddy, Mason, and Aarøe 2015; Johnston, Lavine, and Federico 2017; Kahan 2015; Schuessler 2000). Defection from a valued identity causes substantial dissonance, which citizens generally seek to avoid (Festinger 1957;

Heider 1958), and taking positions against the in-party may cause tension with close others or lead to loss of reputation and status within one's social networks (e.g., Sinclair 2012). As the parties have grown more distinct along several dimensions, politics has become more tribal, and the pressure to conform to the party line has intensified.

In sum, we expect that partisan polarization at both the elite and mass levels will reduce citizens' willingness to stand up for the Court and against their narrow partisan interests. Testing this hypothesis, however, is difficult. In the real world, we observe a single, upward trend in polarization over time and we do not have good measures of Court-curbing across time. As discussed in Chapter 3, confidence and approval in the Supreme Court have declined in recent decades, but this is tenuous evidence for a causal effect of partisan polarization on Court-curbing. Instead, we turn to experimentation, which has two virtues relevant to our goals. First, experiments allow the researcher to create environments that are theoretically relevant – in the sense that one's theory makes strong predictions about what should happen – but which are difficult or impossible to observe in the real world (Morton and Williams 2010). This is valuable if existing observational data are not able to distinguish among competing perspectives. For example, declining confidence in the Court since 2000 could be due to partisan polarization or the decision in *Bush v. Gore*. Second, experiments allow for strong causal inference through random assignment and carefully constructed controls. As we will see, this allows us to make claims regarding the effect of polarization per se, as distinguished from the effect of mere partisan branding and policy disagreement. We have conducted two national survey experiments with the explicit purpose of testing our theory of partisan polarization and Court-curbing. We report these in turn.

THE 2016 YOUGOV EXPERIMENT (2016 YGS)

Our first experiment was designed to disentangle the effects of specific policy disagreement, partisan branding, and partisan polarization on public support for Court-curbing, both narrow and broad. The basic design – discussed in greater detail later – assigned subjects to read about a Supreme Court decision that was either liberal or conservative in direction and contained either (1) no additional party cues, (2) unpolarized party cues, or (3) polarized party cues. Based on the results discussed in Chapter 5, we expect that exposure to Court rulings that conflict with political identity will boost support for narrow Court-curbing measures, with perhaps a smaller effect on support for broad measures. Republicans and conservatives will be more likely to attack the Court after liberal than conservative rulings, while Democrats and liberals will show the opposite pattern. The question for this chapter is whether adding partisan polarization to the mix amplifies this pattern. We consider three possibilities.

First, citizens may not care about partisanship above and beyond policy disagreement. That is, once they know the direction of the decision, information regarding the partisan distribution of support and opposition to the decision may not matter. In this world, political identity (partisanship and ideological identification) is a mere summary of one's positions on the issues (e.g., Fiorina 1981). If this is true, we should observe no differences among the three treatment conditions – disagreement is disagreement. Second, partisanship may add value above and beyond the direction of the decision, but polarization may not matter. In this case, citizens would only use information about the partisan distribution of support and opposition in a coarse way. For example, they might use a "one good reason" heuristic (Gigerenzer and Goldstein 1999): choose the side that contains more members of one's own party. Such a rule could imply effects of partisanship beyond policy disagreement but would not imply any additional role for polarization. In this case, we would observe a difference when comparing each party cue treatment to the decision-only treatment, but no difference when comparing the party cues treatments to each other. Finally, polarization may be what *drives* the effect of party cues through the three mechanisms discussed above (Druckman, Peterson, and Slothuus 2013). If this is the case, we should observe little difference between the decision-only and the unpolarized party cues treatments but a large difference between the polarized cues treatment and the other two conditions. In this way, the design of the study allows us to make strong causal claims regarding the role of elite polarization while controlling for alternative theories. In line with our theory, we expect this final possibility to be realized in the data.

Data and Design

The data for this study were collected by YouGov from May 17 to 24, 2016.[1] Of the 2,500 respondents available in the overall sample, 1,250 participated in this study.[2] The experiment is a 2 (Court decision outcome:

[1] See Chapter 3 for a more detailed discussion of this sample.

[2] The second half of the sample participated in a different study, the "procedural module," which is analyzed in Chapters 5 and 7.

liberal or conservative) × 3 (party cues: no party cues, unpolarized party cues, or polarized party cues) between-subjects design with a dangling control group that received no information related to Court decision-making. Thus, each subject was randomly assigned to one of seven possible conditions; however, we will focus our attention on the six decision treatments and mention the control only when relevant.[3]

We randomly assigned subjects to receive one of eight Court decisions depending on whether they were assigned to read about a liberal or conservative outcome. Subjects assigned to receive a liberal outcome read about one of the following cases: the rights of anti-abortion protestors to distribute literature at abortion clinics, the death penalty for crimes committed as a minor, the use of race as one of several factors in college admissions decisions, and police drawing blood to test for drunk driving without a search warrant. Subjects assigned to receive a conservative outcome read about one of the following cases: corporate campaign spending, lethal injection as cruel and unusual punishment, rollback of the Voting Rights Act, and the use of evidence in cases of unintentional illegal police searches. In all cases, the stimulus materials were descriptions of actual decisions made by the Supreme Court. Our goal in using multiple cases for each of the two outcome treatments is to increase the external validity of our study. That is, our design alleviates concerns that any conclusions reached are due to the choice of specific cases, rather than generalizable conclusions about American public opinion. Importantly, we designed this study with the intention of averaging over any issue-specific variation in results. This means that we do not have the statistical power to examine differences across issues. Accordingly, we will not do so. Our focus is on average patterns. The exact text of all decisions is provided in Chapter 5, Table 5.2.

The party cues factor has three possible conditions and is modeled directly on the experimental design in Druckman, Peterson, and Slothuus' (2013) seminal study of polarization and persuasion. In the no party cues condition, respondents received only the text of one of the decisions listed in Table 5.2, with no other accompanying information. In the unpolarized party cues condition, respondents received not only the same decision text

[3] Since the control group did not receive a decision, we could not ask directly about narrow Court-curbing (though we attempt to solve this problem in the next study). Thus, the control group received only the broadly targeted curbing items. As we will see, the control group results suggest that the decision and polarization treatments had no clear systematic effects on broadly targeted Court-curbing.

but also an accompanying message describing the fact that "Republicans nationwide" tend to favor one side of the issue, while "Democrats nationwide" tend to favor the other side. In all cases, Democrats supported liberal decisions and Republicans supported conservative decisions. However, subjects were also told that the "partisan divide is not stark" and that members of each party can be found on both sides of the issue. This message operationalizes the notion of a small intra-class correlation and weak polarization. Finally, in the polarized party cues condition, subjects received the same basic treatment as in the unpolarized cues condition, but the added text stated that "the partisan divide is stark" and "most members of each party are on the same side as the rest of their party." This operationalizes the notion of a high intra-class correlation and strong polarization. The exact text of these three conditions, provided in the context of the abortion case, is provided in Table 6.1.

The items measuring narrow and broad Court-curbing were described in Chapter 3 and are shown in Tables 3.2 and 3.3. We averaged the two narrow items (final word and compliance) to form a single scale, with higher values indicating greater support for Court-curbing ($r = 0.38$), though we will also examine these separately. For broad Court-curbing, we have five items (do away with, issues reduced, less independent, remove justices, and Constitution means), which were again averaged to form a single scale, with higher values indicating greater support for Court-curbing ($\alpha = 0.82$).

Since our focus in the present chapter is on the effects of political identity and partisan polarization, we use *left–right identity* as our key independent variable, which is the average of the seven-point partisanship and ideological identification measures ($r = 0.63$).[4] The lowest values of this scale correspond with very liberal, strong Democrats, and the highest values correspond with very conservative, strong Republicans. The midpoints of the scale are occupied by moderate independents and those with conflicting political identities. This measure has two virtues for our purposes. First, we argue that the combined scale is a more reliable measure of political identity in contemporary American politics than either component taken in isolation. For example, some people may be loath to identify directly with a party but may nonetheless harbor a latent partisan attachment (Klar and Krupnikov 2016). We expect that liberal independents, for instance, are more likely than conservative independents to take cues from

[4] As discussed in Chapter 5, the 2016 YGS does not contain any questions regarding issue-specific attitudes.

TABLE 6.1 *Example polarization treatments in 2016 YGS experiment*

No party cues (abortion protests)

"There has been a lot of discussion over the years about the ability of anti-abortion protesters to express their views outside of abortion clinics and engage in discussions with patients of those clinics.

The Supreme Court has ruled that anti-abortion protesters do **not** have the right to engage in counseling or literature distribution with patients entering or leaving an abortion clinic."

Unpolarized party cues (abortion protests)

"There has been a lot of discussion over the years about the ability of anti-abortion protesters to express their views outside of abortion clinics and engage in discussions with patients of those clinics. Republicans nationwide tend to favor the ability of anti-abortion protesters to engage in these practices, while Democrats tend to oppose these practices. However, the partisan divide is not stark as the parties are not too far apart. Also, while Republicans tend to be in favor and Democrats opposed, members of each party can be found on both sides of the issue.

The Supreme Court has ruled that anti-abortion protesters do **not** have the right to engage in counseling or literature distribution with patients entering or leaving an abortion clinic."

Polarized party cues (abortion protests)

"There has been a lot of discussion over the years about the ability of anti-abortion protesters to express their views outside of abortion clinics and engage in discussions with patients of those clinics. Republicans nationwide tend to favor the ability of anti-abortion protesters to engage in these practices, while Democrats tend to oppose these practices. Moreover, the partisan divide is stark as the parties are far apart. Also, not only do Republicans tend to be in favor and Democrats opposed, but most members of each party are on the same side as the rest of their party.

The Supreme Court has ruled that anti-abortion protesters do **not** have the right to engage in counseling or literature distribution with patients entering or leaving an abortion clinic."

Democrats. Our measure captures such variation. Second, recent research suggests that converging partisan and ideological identities – so-called partisan-ideological "sorting" – may be a primary force driving political tribalism. Citizens with consistent identities (liberal Democrats and conservative Republicans) are angrier and more biased than their conflicted counterparts, and they respond more strongly to political threats from their opponents (Mason 2015, 2018). It is thus important to distinguish, for example, strong Democrats who identify as liberal from those who identify as moderate or conservative. In our measure, fully sorted partisans occupy the endpoints of the scale. These arguments notwithstanding, we note that the results in this chapter are nearly identical if we use partisanship alone.[5]

In all models, we include controls for age, gender, black/African-American and Hispanic/Latino identification, educational attainment (operationalized as a set of dummy variables), household income, political engagement, and religiosity.[6] All variables were recoded to range from 0 to 1 prior to analysis.

Policy Disagreement, Polarization, and Court-Curbing

Our theory makes several predictions. First, the more strongly one identifies with political groups generally opposed to the policy direction of the Court's decision, the more one will support measures to curb the Court. Moreover, we expect the size of this relationship to be much larger for narrowly targeted curbing than for broadly targeted curbing. This is just a restatement of our specific policy disagreement hypotheses tested in Chapter 5. Importantly, however, we expect the *size* of this relationship to be much larger in the polarized party cues condition than in either of the other two conditions (i.e., unpolarized party cues and no cues). When the parties are sharply divided, citizens will feel a strong pressure to take positions consistent with the in-group's goals.

To test these hypotheses, we first recoded left–right identity in the following way: in treatment conditions where the Court made a liberal decision, the scale ranges from very liberal, strong Democrats to very conservative, strong Republicans; in conservative decision conditions the scale is coded in the reverse direction. Thus, higher values of this measure always correspond to increases in identification with groups expected to *disagree* with the Court's decision. We will refer to this measure as "policy disagreement" to be consistent with previous chapters and to distinguish it from the original left–right identity scale. We then estimated six regression models: one model for each polarization condition (no cues, unpolarized cues, polarized cues), for each dependent

[5] The difference is in effect size. Since partisanship treats strong partisans with consistent ideological identities as equivalent to those with conflicting ones, it restricts the range of possible variation. The effect sizes for partisanship alone are nonetheless substantial and can be generated using our reproduction materials for Chapter 6.

[6] See the last empirical section of Chapter 5 for a discussion of variable operationalizations in the 2016 YGS.

variable (narrow v. broad curbing). Each of the six models regresses support for Court-curbing on policy disagreement along with the set of controls described earlier.[7] Let's consider what this approach accomplishes and what its limitations might be.

Policy disagreement encodes information regarding the ideological direction of the Court's decision and its relationship to left–right identity – higher values always indicate conflict between the respondent's political identity and the policy direction of the decision. Since the dependent variables are coded such that higher values indicate support for Court-curbing, we always expect a positive coefficient for policy disagreement. The advantage of modeling the data this way is an increase in efficiency: if we break the conditions down further by the ideological direction of the Court's decision, we cut our sample in half (twelve regression models rather than six). By averaging over liberal and conservative decision conditions, we get estimates of key parameters that contain less uncertainty. The downside to this approach is that we lose information regarding possible heterogeneity in how political groups respond to disliked decisions and partisan polarization. That is, one group may respond more strongly than the other in terms of changes in support for Court-curbing across treatment conditions. We consider this possibility in a subsequent section. Finally, as we noted in Chapter 5, by estimating separate models for the three polarization conditions, we are implicitly interacting the party cues factor with *all* independent variables, not just policy disagreement. This is important, because we wish to ensure that changes in the effect of disagreement across treatment conditions are not spurious (i.e., due to something correlated with disagreement, such as education or age).

The preliminaries complete, we turn to the results of the experiment. Regression estimates are shown in Table A6.1 and the key quantities of interest are shown in Figure 6.1. Each point in Figure 6.1 represents the effect of policy disagreement on support for either narrowly targeted Court-curbing (the left three points) or broadly targeted Court-curbing (the right three points). Positive values mean that liberal Democrats support curbing more than conservative Republicans in the conservative decision condition, while conservative Republicans support curbing more than liberal Democrats in the liberal decision condition. Circles

[7] Respondents are nested within issues (eight of them), and we include dummies for seven of these issues to eliminate clustering of errors. Estimates were obtained via ordinary least squares.

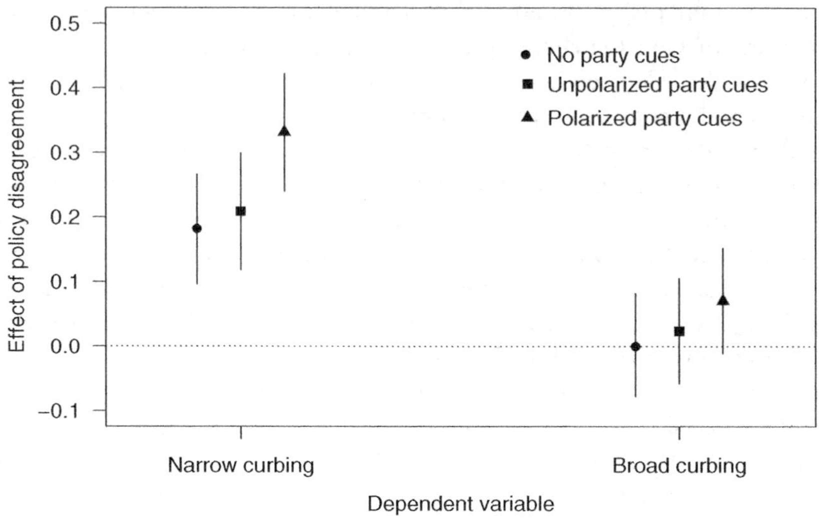

FIGURE 6.1 The effects of specific policy disagreement on support for narrow and broad curbing across treatment conditions, 2016 YGS experiment. The points represent the change in support for narrow or broad curbing for a change in specific policy disagreement from minimum to maximum; extended lines are 95 percent confidence bounds; see Tables 3.2 and 3.3 for the items that make up the curbing scales; this figure is based on model estimates in Table A6.1.

represent the no party cues condition, squares the unpolarized party cues condition, and triangles the polarized party cues condition. The extended vertical lines are 95 percent confidence bounds on these estimates. Since all variables are coded from 0 to 1, the estimates represent percentage point changes in the dependent variable for a change in policy disagreement from minimum to maximum.

First, policy disagreement has a positive, substantively meaningful, and statistically significant effect on support for narrow Court-curbing but has no statistically significant effect on broad curbing. Moreover, the null results for broad curbing are precisely estimated (given the large sample size), and the 95 percent confidence bounds do not include any of the estimates for narrow curbing. Put another way, the largest effect of policy disagreement on broad curbing (in the polarized cues condition) is very likely smaller than the *smallest* effect of disagreement on narrow curbing (in the no cues condition). We again find strong support for the importance of distinguishing narrow from broad Court-curbing, as well as our expectation that single decisions have much smaller effects on the latter.

Second, we find support for the importance of partisan polarization as a moderator of the effect of policy disagreement on support for narrow Court-curbing. The difference in the effect of disagreement, comparing the polarized cues to the no cues condition, is large (15 percentage points) and statistically significant.[8] In the no cues condition, a change in policy disagreement from minimum to maximum is associated with an increase of 18 percentage points in support for narrow Court-curbing. In the polarized cues condition, the effect is 33 percentage points. Importantly, the results also suggest that polarization itself matters, above and beyond simple partisan branding of positions on the case. First, the difference in the effect of disagreement comparing the unpolarized cues condition to the no cues condition is small and statistically indistinguishable from zero. In other words, simple partisan cues do not enhance the effect of policy disagreement above and beyond a context with no parties at all. The effect of disagreement in the polarized cues condition, however, is 12 percentage points larger than in the unpolarized cues condition, and this difference is statistically significant. Thus, partisan polarization strengthens the relationship between disagreement with the Court's ruling and the willingness of citizens to support narrow Court-curbing measures. Mass partisans are much more likely to attack the Court after an uncongenial decision when the parties are sharply divided on the issue.[9]

Overall, this first experiment provides strong support for the importance of partisan polarization in shaping the way citizens respond to Supreme Court decisions. Compared to contexts with no partisan cues (as in Chapter 5), policy disagreement in polarized contexts is a much stronger predictor of support for narrow Court-curbing. Our experiment also suggests that polarization enhances the effect of simple party branding, which is consistent with past work (Druckman, Peterson, and Slothuus 2013).[10] It is

[8] See the reproduction materials for Chapter 6 for these significance tests, which were conducted via simulation from the sampling distributions of the respective models.

[9] We also examined the interaction between policy disagreement and political engagement across conditions for both dependent variables. In contrast to previous chapters, we found a significant interaction in the unpolarized and polarized cues condition (but not in the no cues condition) for narrow Court-curbing. The direction of both interactions is positive, which means that political engagement *increases* the size of the relationship between disagreement and support for narrow curbing in the presence of partisan cues. We do not emphasize this interaction because it is the only time it has emerged, and it does not replicate in the 2017 QS (discussed later in this chapter).

[10] As discussed previously, there are several possible mechanisms that could explain this moderating effect of polarization, but it is beyond the scope of the present study to disentangle these.

important to note, however, that policy disagreement still matters quite a bit for narrow curbing in the other two conditions. Indeed, in the no cues condition, only education and political engagement rival the effect of policy disagreement. Having a post-graduate degree (relative to less than a high school degree) reduces support for curbing by 17 percentage points, and a change from minimum to maximum engagement reduces support by 12 points. In the unpolarized cues condition, only religiosity and political engagement rival policy disagreement. A change from minimum to maximum religiosity is associated with a 14-point increase in support for narrow curbing, while the same change in engagement is associated with 10 point drop in support. Thus, even without elite polarization, policy disagreement has a substantial effect on support for narrow Court-curbing. This study thus provides an independent replication of the experimental findings in Chapter 5. Moreover, the effect size in the control condition for the present study is more than twice as large as the effect size found for the first 2016 YGS experiment reported in Chapter 5, despite having a similar design. The only significant difference between these studies is that the Chapter 5 version asked respondents about their procedural perceptions prior to asking about Court-curbing. It is possible that these items interacted with the treatment in some way, but this is purely speculative.

Finally, we find no significant effects of policy disagreement with the Court's decision on support for broad curbing measures. In the 2009 TESS study, reported in the previous chapter, these effects were smaller for broad than narrow curbing, but were still meaningful for the former. Here, we find no significant relationship at all. There seems to be a slight trend in the positive direction moving from the no cues to the polarized cues condition – and the effect in the latter approaches significance – but in no case are the estimates particularly large, and the differences across conditions are not statistically significant.

Item-by-Item Results

The advantage of combining individual policy items into an overall scale of support for Court-curbing is efficiency: there is less measurement error and we obtain more precise regression estimates. The downside to this practice is interpretability: what does a thirty-point change in support for narrow curbing mean in practice? For this reason, we end this section with a consideration of the two narrow curbing items taken individually.

We estimated three models like those above, but we substituted support for noncompliance and for overturning the decision in place of our narrow curbing scale. Since both items are measured on a six-point scale, we used ordered logistic regression models.[11] We then translated the regression estimates into predicted probabilities of supporting Court-curbing across levels of policy disagreement.[12] The regression estimates are shown in Table A6.2 and the predicted probabilities of supporting narrow curbing are shown in Figure 6.2. The x-axes range from minimum to maximum policy disagreement, and the y-axes represent the predicted probability of supporting curbing for each item. The solid line represents the no party cues condition, the dashed line represents the unpolarized cues condition, and the dotted line represents the polarized cues condition. While the effect of disagreement is statistically significant in all conditions for both items, it increases substantially moving from the no cues to the polarized cues condition.

Looking first at noncompliance, at the low end of disagreement, support for curbing is quite low in all three conditions (0.12). At high levels of disagreement, by contrast, support for noncompliance exceeds 20 percent for all conditions and 30 percent in the polarized party cues condition. In other words, when Republicans and Democrats are sharply divided on

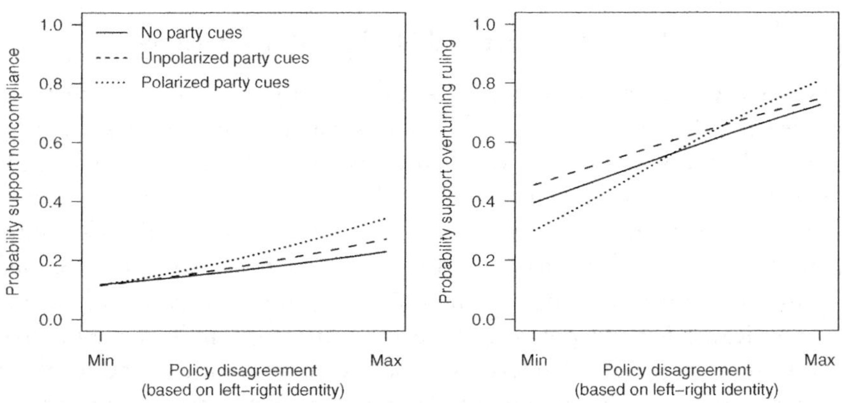

FIGURE 6.2 The predicted probability of support for two forms of narrow curbing across specific policy disagreement and polarization conditions, 2016 YGS experiment. See Table 3.3 for the wording of each item; this figure is based on model estimates in Table A6.2.

[11] To deal with clustering of errors by issue, we again included dummy variables for seven of the eight issue conditions. Estimates were obtained via maximum likelihood.

[12] We defined "support for curbing" as responses indicating agreement with the curbing statements ("agree strongly," "agree moderately," or "agree a little").

a Court decision, nearly one out of every three strongly disagreeing citizens supports noncompliance with the Court's decision. This is striking and suggests that the Court may be less capable of legitimizing decisions in polarized contexts than classic work on public legitimacy suggests (Mondak 1994; Tyler and Rasinski 1991).[13]

Looking now at the second panel, we find even larger effects of policy disagreement and polarization. The effect of disagreement is statistically indistinguishable for the no cues and unpolarized cues conditions, at about 30 percentage points. In these conditions, at low levels of disagreement, citizens are more likely than not to think that the Court's decision should be the final word. By contrast, at high levels of disagreement, nearly 75 percent support efforts to overturn the ruling. The effect size for disagreement increases substantially in the polarized cues condition to 50 percentage points. At low levels of disagreement, only 30 percent of respondents support curbing, while at high levels of disagreement 80 percent are in support. This is a truly massive treatment effect and these results strongly question the prevailing wisdom that the Court is capable of legitimizing policy through its decision-making and that it is immune to the effects of partisan polarization.

A Look at Partisan and Ideological Asymmetries

As noted previously, recoding left–right identity to policy disagreement increases efficiency but potentially hides asymmetries in how different political groups respond to disliked decisions – liberals and Democrats may respond more strongly than Republicans and conservatives, or vice versa. In this final section of the first study, we consider this possibility. Specifically, we substituted the original left–right identity scale (coded from very liberal, strong Democrats to very conservative, strong Republicans) for the policy disagreement measure and then estimated twelve new regression models – six each for narrow and broad forms of Court-curbing.[14] The six models for each dependent variable correspond with the six possible conditions defined by the crossing of decision direction (liberal or conservative) and partisan polarization (no cues, unpolarized cues, polarized cues). Since political identity is coded from left to right, we expect that it will be positively associated with support for

[13] Though these findings are consistent with more recent research (Nicholson and Hansford 2014).

[14] We again included fixed effects for issue assignment to deal with clustering of errors.

Court-curbing in the liberal decision conditions and negatively associated with support for Court-curbing in the conservative decision conditions. Again, however, we expect this dynamic to be much stronger for narrow than broad forms of curbing. Finally, we expect that it will be larger in the polarized party cues condition relative to the two other cues conditions. We have no expectations for partisan asymmetries, and so this aspect of our investigation is entirely exploratory.

Regression estimates are shown in Tables A6.3 (for narrow curbing) and A6.4 (for broad curbing). We plot the key results in Figure 6.3. The top three panels correspond to the no cues, unpolarized cues, and polarized cues conditions for the narrow curbing dependent variable, while the bottom three panels correspond to the same three conditions for the broad curbing variable. Within each panel, the y-axis represents the predicted value of support for Court-curbing, with the solid line representing liberal decision conditions and the dashed line representing conservative decision conditions. The x-axes range from very liberal, strong Democrats ("Max

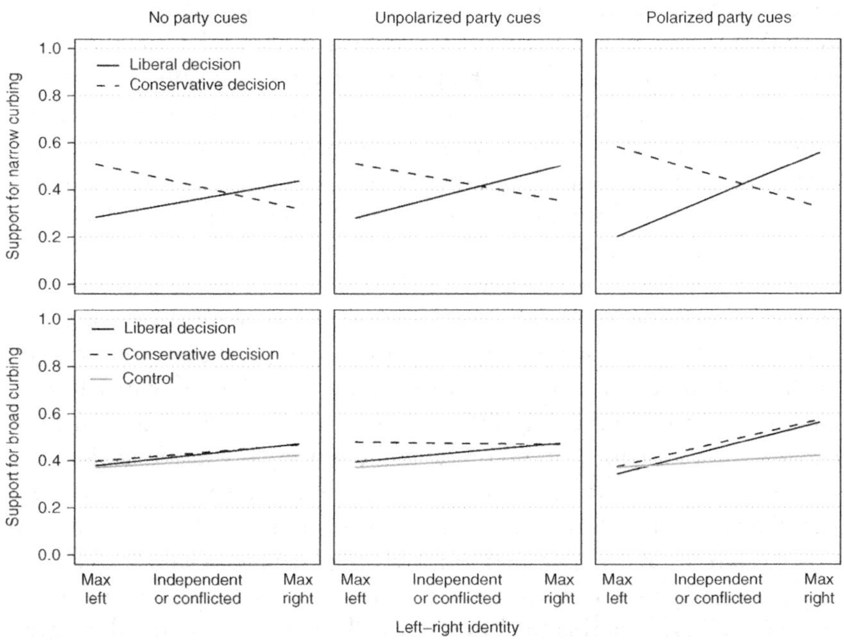

FIGURE 6.3 Predicted support for narrow and broad curbing across left–right identity, decision direction, and polarization conditions, 2016 YGS experiment. See Tables 3.2 and 3.3 for the items that make up the curbing scales; this figure is based on model estimates in Tables A6.3 and A6.4.

left") to very conservative, strong Republicans ("Max right"), with moderate independents and conflicted identities in the middle regions ("Independent/conflicted").

Looking first at the top three panels, we again see strong support for the interactive role of left–right identity and decision outcomes in shaping support for narrow forms of Court-curbing. This should not be surprising: the averages of the absolute values of the slopes of the two lines within each panel are essentially the estimates in Figure 6.1. What is perhaps more interesting is a possible asymmetry in response to liked and disliked decisions comparing left– and right-wing identifiers. Indeed, we see some evidence that liberal Democrats respond more strongly than conservative Republicans. For example, in the polarized party cues condition, for liberal Court decisions, very liberal, strong Democrats have an estimated support for narrow curbing of only 0.20, but that support rises to about 0.60 in the conservative decision condition – a change of nearly 40 percentage points. Right-wing identifiers, by contrast, show a more muted response to ideologically divergent decisions. In the conservative decision condition with polarized cues, very conservative, strong Republicans have an estimated support of 0.32 for narrow curbing, while in the liberal condition support is 0.56 – a change of twenty-four points. Put another way, average levels of support for narrow Court-curbing are about the same for the left and right, but liberal Democrats show greater *responsiveness* to single decisions, and thus greater variance around the average.

Turning now to broadly targeted Court-curbing, we see results consistent with Figure 6.1: single decisions just don't matter much. In each case, there is a tendency for citizens on the right to be more supportive of curbing than those on the left – and this is particularly true in the polarized condition – but there is no pattern of differential partisan response to the ideological direction of the decisions. Moreover, the effect of left–right identity is only significantly different from the control condition (indicated in grey) for liberal outcomes in the polarized cues condition. The difference in the effect of identity appears driven by conservative Republicans, who show higher levels of support for broad curbing in this condition. We would caution against placing too much weight on this one significant effect without replication. Given the number of models estimated, it is inevitable that an effect will emerge by chance alone every so often, and there is no difference in support for Court-curbing among conservative Republicans comparing liberal and conservative decisions in the polarized condition. For now, we think the most justified conclusion from these data is that the decision treatments had little effect on support for broad curbing, but that conservatives in 2016 were more supportive of broad curbing measures than liberals.[15] We note also that this general finding accords with what we found in Chapter 5 from the TAPS panel analysis – the accumulation of significant liberal rulings by 2016 left conservatives more supportive of broad curbing than liberals.

Summary of the 2016 YGS

In this first study we find strong support for the role of partisan polarization in shaping citizens' support and opposition to narrowly targeted Court-curbing measures. When the parties are internally homogenous and far apart on the issues, the effect of political identity on support for Court-curbing is much stronger than when party cues are absent altogether or when partisans are not sharply divided. This implies that polarization matters above and beyond mere partisan branding and is thus a threat to the Court's independence.

THE 2017 QUALTRICS STUDY (2017 QS)

The 2016 YGS established the importance of partisan polarization for Court-curbing, above and beyond the role of partisan branding and simple policy disagreement. Our second experiment, contained in the 2017 Qualtrics study (2017 QS), was designed to increase realism at the expense of control over the role of polarization relative to party cues. Our goal in this second study was to put citizens to the test by placing them in a context approximating a highly publicized Supreme Court decision on a controversial issue, a situation in which tempers flare, elites attack the Court with harsh rhetoric, and members of the "losing" party call for Court-curbing measures. In the previous experiment, citizens read about the distribution of partisan support for the decision and considered curbing measures proposed as hypotheticals. In this experiment, they see and feel what it means for the parties to be sharply divided, and curbing measures are attributed directly to partisan elites. We view this experiment as a tough test of institutional loyalty, and, as discussed in the introduction to this chapter, one that is increasingly relevant to the

[15] This latter conclusion is supported by averaging over all conditions, including the control. With this modeling approach, very conservative, strong Republicans are 11 percentage points more supportive of broad curbing measures than very liberal, strong Democrats, and this effect is statistically significant and precisely estimated.

American judiciary: how do citizens respond when protecting the Court requires opposing the partisan in-group – and perhaps supporting the out-group – in the context of a heated battle over an important issue?

Data and Design

The data for this study were collected between June 16 and 23, 2017, by Qualtrics Panels.[16] The design of this study is 2 (decision outcome condition; liberal or conservative) × 2 (polarization condition; no party cues or polarized party cues) with a dangling control group that received no information at all. Noncontrol respondents were randomly assigned to one of two decision conditions in which they read about either a conservative Supreme Court ruling (*Citizens United* v. *FEC*) or a liberal ruling (*Obergefell* v. *Hodges*). They were also assigned to one of two polarization conditions. In the first, no party cues or additional information (beyond the decision itself) were provided. In the second, we provided additional language related to partisan polarization, as in the 2016 YGS study. In this case, "Republicans and conservatives" and "Democrat and progressives" were said to be sharply divided and internally homogenous on the issue. We display all four conditions in Table 6.2. Control respondents received no decision or partisan information at all.

There are two other important differences between the no party cues and polarized party cues treatments. In the latter, following the decision description, respondents read four quotes from partisan legislators who supported the decision, and then four quotes from partisan legislators who opposed the decision. In the *Citizens United* condition, supporting legislators were Republicans and opposing legislators were Democrats. In the *Obergefell* condition, these were reversed. All sixteen quotes are actual statements made by prominent Democrats and Republicans following the actual decisions. Supporters are all laudatory and speak of the Court in legitimizing terms. Opponents, by contrast, are vitriolic and aggressive and use strongly delegitimizing language. Again, it is important to emphasize that these quotes are actual statements made by prominent public officials. We list all sixteen in Table 6.3.

Finally, as in the control and no party cues conditions, respondents in the polarized cues conditions received several narrow curbing items and then several broad curbing items (see Chapter 3, Tables 3.2 and 3.3).

[16] Further details for this sample are provided in Chapter 3, including the survey methodology appendix at the end of Chapter 3.

TABLE 6.2 *Decision treatments for 2017 QS experiment*

Citizens United* v. *FEC
In *Citizens United* v. *Federal Election Commission*, the Supreme Court ruled that corporate political spending is Constitutionally protected speech, and that federal and state governments cannot restrict independent political spending by corporations.

Obergefell* v. *Hodges
In *Obergefell* v. *Hodges*, the Supreme Court ruled that the right to marry someone of the same sex is Constitutionally protected, and that all states must allow and recognize same-sex marriages.

No party cues condition
Many people believe it was the right decision, while many others believe it was the wrong decision. Politicians have stated their opinions about the decision publicly, and those who believe it was the wrong decision sometimes make harshly critical statements about the Supreme Court and its decision.

Polarized party cues condition:
The two parties are sharply divided on this issue. Most [Republicans and conservatives/Democrats and progressives] believe it was the right decision, but most [Democrats and progressives/Republicans and conservatives] believe it was the wrong decision. Politicians have stated their opinions about the decision publicly, and those who believe it was the wrong decision sometimes make harshly critical statements about the Supreme Court and its decision.

Importantly, however, the narrow curbing items contained additional party cues with respect to supporters and opponents of the Court-curbing measures proposed. For *Citizens United*, supporters of curbing were "Democrats and progressives" (rather than "Some people"), while opponents were "Republicans and conservatives" (rather than "Others"). For *Obergefell*, these attributions were reversed. We also slightly edited these narrow curbing items so that they could be included in the control condition as well.[17] Thus, in contrast to the 2016 YGS experiment, we can compare the effect of left–right identity on narrow curbing across the control, no cues, and polarized cues conditions.

[17] For example, in the control condition, the jurisdiction stripping item reads, "The Constitution gives Congress the power to determine the Supreme Court's jurisdiction, that is, the types of issues the Court may and may not decide. Some people argue that Congress should take away the Court's power to decide some controversial issues. Others argue that Congress should not limit the Supreme Court's jurisdiction."

TABLE 6.3 *Partisan reactions to decisions in 2017 QS experiment*

Citizens United* v. *FEC

Prominent Republicans and conservatives have said the following about the decision:

"For too long, some in this country have been deprived of full participation in the political process. With today's monumental decision, the Supreme Court took an important step in the direction of restoring the First Amendment rights of these groups." – Senator McConnell (R, KY)

"I am pleased that the Supreme Court has acted to protect the Constitution's First Amendment rights of free speech and association." – Senator Cornyn (R, TX)

"Today's Supreme Court decision affirms the Bill of Rights and is a victory for liberty and free speech." – Representative King (R, IA)

"Today's decision by the Supreme Court ... serves as an affirmation of the constitutional rights provided to Americans under the first amendment." – Previous Republican National Committee Chairman Steele

Prominent Democrats and progressives have said the following about the decision:

"Terrible decision. One of the most lawless decisions in the history of this country and of the Supreme Court." – Senator Feingold (D, WI)

"Today's decision by the Supreme Court is a triumph for special interest and judicial activism at its worst." – Senator Durbin (D, IL)

"This is a very, very sad day for American democracy and this is a very radical, radical decision that came out of the Supreme Court of the United States – a court that said they respected precedent." – Representative Van Hollen (D, MD)

"With this decision, the Supreme Court has thumbed its nose at precedent, at the Congress, and most importantly, the will of the people." – Representative Eshoo (D, CA)

Obergefell* v. *Hodges

Prominent Democrats and progressives have said the following about the decision:

"Today the Supreme Court fulfilled the words engraved upon its building: 'Equal justice under law.' The decision is a victory for ... all those seeking to live in a nation where every citizen is afforded equal rights." – Senator Sanders (I, VT)

"I enthusiastically applaud the Supreme Court's decision in the case of Obergefell v. Hodges. Now, same-sex couples throughout the country will be guaranteed the recognition and legal protections they so fully deserve." – Representative Schultz (D, FL)

"Today's decision ... is a major victory for equality and an important step toward a fairer and more just society for all Americans." – Governor Nixon (D, MO)

"This ruling represents our country at its best: inclusive, open, and striving towards true equality." – Former Democratic Senator and Secretary of State Clinton

Prominent Republicans and conservatives have said the following about the decision:

(continued)

TABLE 6.3 *(continued)*

"Another example of extreme judicial overreach ... [This] needs to be a decision made by the people through their elected representatives, not by judicial fiat." – Representative King (R, IA)

"Five unelected lawyers overruled 320 million Americans. That's not the way our Constitution operates and it is a sad moment for the court when you have judges seizing authority that does not belong to them." – Senator Cruz (R, TX)

"The Supreme Court is completely out of control, making laws on their own, and has become a public opinion poll instead of a judicial body." – Gov. Jindal (Republican, LA)

"I fundamentally disagree with the court rewriting the law and assaulting [the Constitution]. Our founding fathers did not intend for the judicial branch to legislate from the bench." – Governor Perry (R, TX)

Our key independent variable is again left–right identity, which is the average of partisanship and ideological identification ($r = 0.51$). As in the 2016 YGS, we first recode left–right identity conditional on the direction of ruling so that higher values represent greater identification with groups expected to disagree with the Court's ruling. We again refer to this measure as "policy disagreement."[18]

The 2017 QS also allows for a consideration of the moderating role of "affective polarization" (Iyengar, Sood, and Lelkes 2012), which we operationalized as the absolute difference between each subject's feelings toward the Democrats and the Republicans, measured on one-hundred-one-point feeling thermometers. Thus, the scale ranges from 0 to 100, with higher values indicating more polarized feelings about the two parties.[19]

In all models, we include controls for age, gender, race and ethnicity, educational attainment (operationalized as a set of dummy variables), and

[18] As in the 2016 YGS, we also examined the effect of partisanship separated from ideology, and the results do not change.

[19] This operationalization rests on the assumption that the vast majority of partisan identifiers do not feel much more positive about the out-party than the in-party, but a small percentage of citizens do express these more extreme forms of partisan ambivalence in our sample (Lavine, Johnston, and Steenbergen 2012). Due to this issue, our estimates of the moderating role of affective polarization will be a bit conservative, because a small number of subjects who strongly dislike their own party will receive moderate to high values on the polarization variable. A possible solution would be to code affective polarization as the difference between in- and out-party feelings, but this would remove all independents from the analysis. In the end, we felt that the former approach was the lesser of two evils.

political engagement (based on political interest only; the survey did not include knowledge items). Unfortunately, these data did not include a measure of household income nor one of religiosity. All variables were recoded to range from 0 to 1 prior to analysis.

Policy Disagreement, Polarization, and Court-Curbing

We begin by considering the effect of policy disagreement on support for narrow and broad forms of Court-curbing, conditional on both affective polarization and the party cue treatment conditions. We estimated two regression models for each of the two dependent variables: one for the no party cues condition and one for the polarized party cues condition (we consider the control condition in supplemental analyses below). Each model regresses its respective dependent variable on policy disagreement, affective polarization, the interaction of the two, and our set of controls. The estimates were obtained via ordinary least squares.

The interaction between policy disagreement and affective polarization was statistically significant and substantively meaningful for narrow Court-curbing in both the no cues and the polarized cues conditions. Specifically, higher levels of affective polarization are associated with stronger effects of policy disagreement on support for narrow curbing. In contrast, we find no significant interactions for broadly targeted Court-curbing. For sake of comparison with narrow curbing, however, we will consider the conditional estimates of disagreement on broad curbing in what follows.

The full regression results are shown in Table A6.5. We estimated the conditional effects of policy disagreement, across both affective polarization and the party cues treatment conditions, and plot these results in Figure 6.4. The left panel shows the results for narrow curbing and the right panel shows the results for broad curbing. In each case, the points represent the conditional effect of policy disagreement at three levels of affective polarization (along the x-axis). The solid dots are for the no cues condition and the open circles are for the polarized party cues condition. The extended vertical lines are 95 percent confidence bounds.

First, we again replicate the stark difference between the responsiveness of narrow and broad forms of Court-curbing to disagreement with single Court decisions. For broad curbing, we find significant effects of policy disagreement in the polarized cues condition among citizens with moderate and high levels of affective polarization, but nowhere else. Moreover, none of these estimates for broad curbing are statistically distinguishable from any of the others. They also pale in comparison to the very large, and

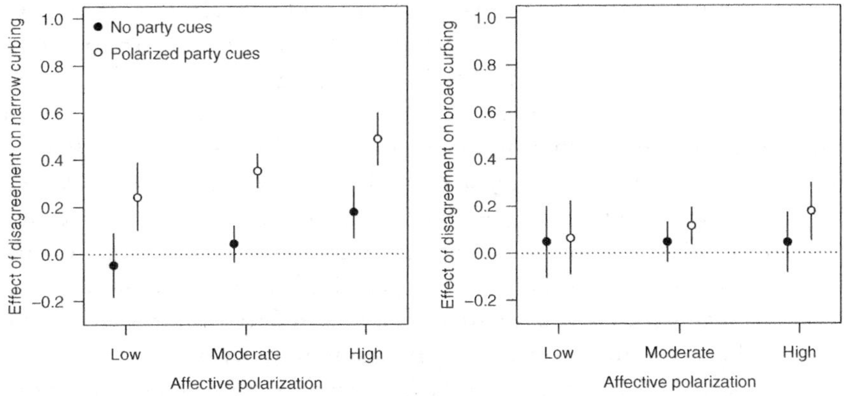

FIGURE 6.4 The effects of specific policy disagreement on support for narrow and broad curbing across polarization conditions and affective polarization, 2017 QS experiment. The points represent the change in support for narrow or broad curbing for a change in specific policy disagreement from minimum to maximum at the 5th, 50th, and 95th percentiles of affective polarization; extended lines are 95 percent confidence bounds; see Tables 3.2 and 3.3 for the items that make up the curbing scales; this figure is based on model estimates in Table A6.5.

highly conditional, effects of policy disagreement on support for narrow forms of curbing. For this latter dependent variable, the effect of policy disagreement on support for curbing increases substantially as a function of *both* party polarization *and* affective polarization. To see the former, compare the effects of disagreement within each category of affective polarization (on the x-axis): in each case, there is a statistically significant increase in the effect of disagreement moving from the no cues to the polarized cues condition. To see the latter, compare the effects of disagreement along the x-axis within each category of party polarization: moving from low to high affective polarization is associated with a large and statistically significant increase in the effect of disagreement. Taken together, there is a very large difference in the role of disagreement comparing unpolarized to polarized environments. When the parties overlap, and citizens have mixed feelings about their opponents, the effect of policy disagreement on narrow Court-curbing is effectively zero. When both affective and party polarization are high, by contrast, the effect of disagreement on curbing is nearly 50 percentage points.[20]

[20] The 2017 QP study also included items measuring preferences on the specific issues involved in the rulings (campaign finance and gay marriage). We ran the policy

This first analysis leads to a few important conclusions. First, we replicate the effect of partisan polarization (relative to no partisan cues) on support for narrow forms of Court-curbing. We also replicate the strong asymmetry in the effect of policy disagreement comparing broad to narrow forms of curbing. While there is a small and significant effect of disagreement on broad curbing in the polarized condition, it is not statistically distinguishable from the no cues condition and only emerges for affectively polarized citizens. While this result must be taken with a grain of salt, it does suggest the potential for polarized party politics to translate disagreement with even a single decision into broader attacks on the Court. This possibility is worthy of attention in future work.

Second, we find a strong role for affective polarization as a moderator of policy disagreement on narrow forms of curbing. The effect of disagreement on support for curbing is much larger for citizens who sharply dislike their political opponents. Indeed, it is important to emphasize again just how large these effect sizes are: among affectively polarized citizens in a polarized environment, the effect of policy disagreement approaches half of the entire scale of support for narrow curbing. There are few (if any) variables in the literature that show effect sizes of this magnitude on curbing-related dependent variables. Even among citizens who are only moderately affectively polarized, polarized party cues produce effect sizes for disagreement that are about one-third of the scale of the dependent variable.

As with the previous study, we think it is worthwhile to take a step back and consider the implications of these models for specific curbing proposals. In this case, we have three distinct narrow curbing policies: stripping the Court's jurisdiction in the relevant issue areas (marriage and campaign finance), overturning the ruling directly, and refusing to comply with the decision. We plot the results for the individual items in Figure 6.5.[21] The

disagreement analyses substituting these issue items for left–right identity and patterns across treatment conditions and dependent variables are the same, though the effect of issue preferences on curbing is less responsive to polarization than political identity, which is to be expected. Nonetheless, the effect of issue-based policy disagreement on support for narrow curbing is substantial and doubles in magnitude moving from the no cues to the polarized cues condition and from low to high affective polarization in the cues condition. When both types of polarization are high, the effect of issue-based policy disagreement on narrow curbing is over 30 percentage points.

21 As in the 2016 YGS, we estimated ordered logistic regressions and we plot the predicted probabilities of support by combining the top categories for each item. For compliance, we combine response categories "not too important" and "not at all important" to indicate support for curbing. For the other two variables, we combine the top three categories.

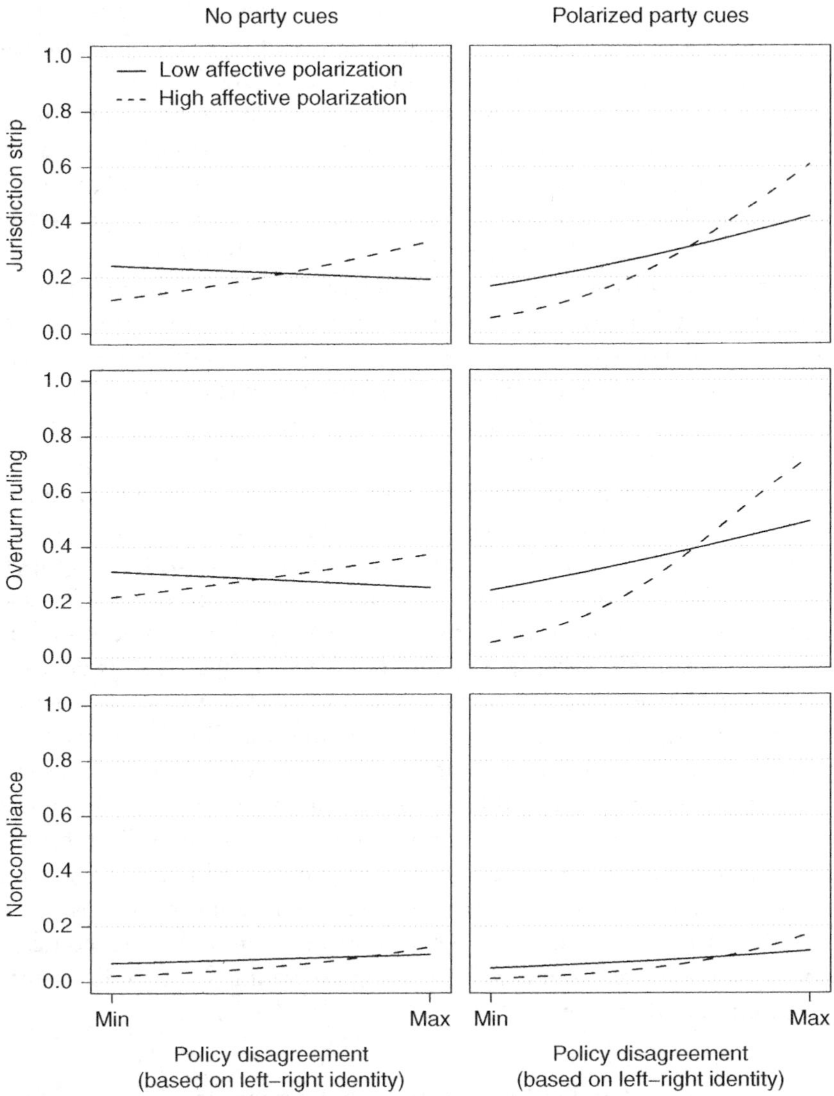

FIGURE 6.5 The predicted probability of support for three forms of narrow curbing across specific policy disagreement, polarization conditions, and affective polarization, 2017 QS experiment. See Table 3.3 for the wording of each item; this figure is based on model estimates in Table A6.6.

left three panels show the results for the no cues condition and the right panels for the polarized cues condition. Each row represents one of the three dependent variables. The y-axes indicate the probability of supporting the respective policy, while the x-axes represent increasing levels of policy disagreement. Solid lines indicate low levels of respondent affective polarization while dashed lines indicate high levels.

Looking first at noncompliance, we see low levels of support in all conditions for all citizens, though about one in five affectively polarized citizens support noncompliance in the polarized cues condition, which is a meaningful percentage. Overall, however, noncompliance appears to be a particularly "difficult" narrow curbing item.[22] Responsiveness to disagreement is much stronger for both overturning the ruling and jurisdiction stripping. Moreover, both items are quite responsive to both forms of polarization. For example, there is effectively no relationship between disagreement and support for either curbing approach among affectively neutral citizens in unpolarized environments (the solid lines in the first two panels of column one). An increase in either affective or party polarization, however, substantially increases the effect of policy disagreement. To see the effect of affective polarization, compare the slopes of the lines within any given panel. To see the effect of party polarization, compare the slopes of the same line-type across panels within a given row. This also implies that one form of polarization can partly offset low levels of the other. For example, when parties are polarized on the issue, even affectively *un*polarized citizens show a substantial increase in support for curbing as a function of disagreement (i.e., the solid lines in the first two panels of the second column). And among polarized citizens in polarized environments, the relationship of policy disagreement to support for curbing is massive: a change from minimum to maximum disagreement is associated with an increase in support for overturning the ruling from 0.06 to 0.72 and is associated with an increase in support for jurisdiction stripping from 0.06 to 0.61. This is striking: in polarized contexts, a *majority* of citizens opposed to a ruling are willing to strip the Court's jurisdiction in that area.

Another Look at Partisan Asymmetries

In our final analysis of the chapter, we substitute the original left–right identity measure for the recoded, disagreement measure, and examine its relationship with support for narrow and broad curbing in the six

[22] However, we did find substantial effects of decision disagreement on support for noncompliance in the 2009 TESS study. Heterogeneity of responsiveness across curbing policies and contexts is an interesting topic for future work.

treatment conditions compared to the control condition. By comparing to a control, in which citizens did not read about *any* issue, we can examine which groups are changing the most, and we can also examine the extent to which partisan polarization over Court decisions – independent of the direction of the decision – may have negative consequences for judicial independence, on average. We estimated a total of twelve regression models: three each (control, liberal decision, conservative decision) for the no cues and polarized party cues conditions, for each of the two dependent variables (narrow and broad curbing). We report the results in Figure 6.6.

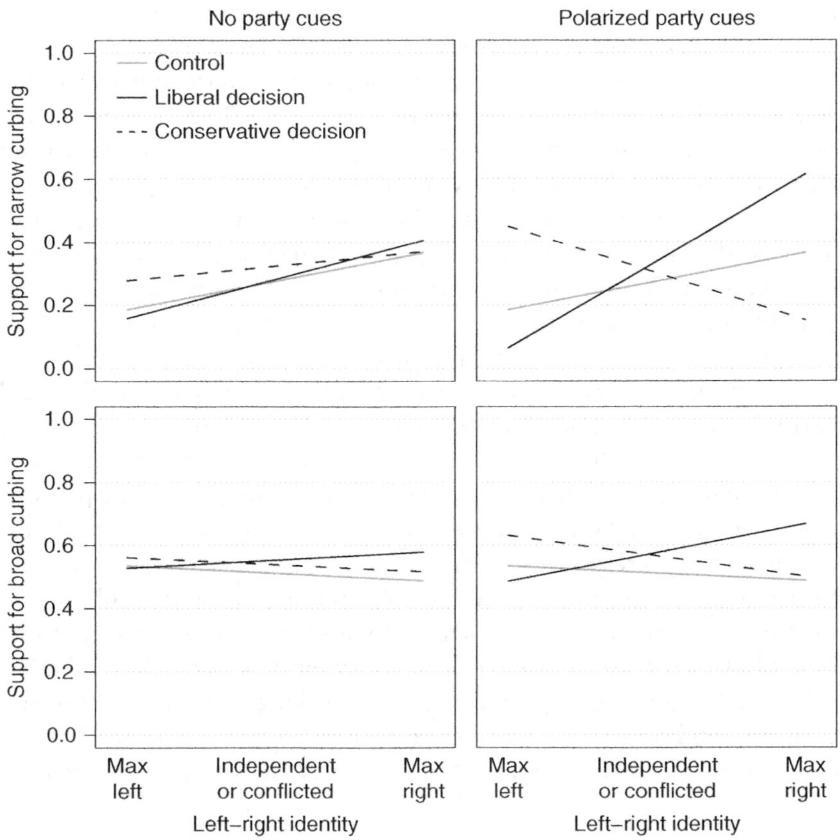

FIGURE 6.6 Predicted support for narrow and broad curbing across left–right identity, decision direction, and polarization conditions, 2017 QS. See Tables 3.2 and 3.3 for the items that make up the curbing scales; this figure is based on model estimates in Tables A6.7 and A6.8.

In each panel, the x-axis ranges from very liberal, strong Democrats to very conservative, strong Republicans, and the y-axis indexes support for narrow (top row) or broad (bottom row) Court-curbing. The grey solid lines are for the control condition, the black solid lines are for the liberal decision condition, and the dashed lines are for the conservative decision condition. To simplify the presentation, we hold affective polarization constant at a moderately high level (its 75th percentile) and focus on changes due to party polarization.[23] Looking first at the top left panel – support for narrow curbing in the no party cues condition – we see little difference between the control and liberal decision conditions. In both these conditions, very conservative, strong Republicans are more supportive of narrow curbing than very liberal, strong Democrats (by eighteen and twenty-five points, respectively), and these differences are statistically significant. This difference is cut in half in the conservative decision condition. If we look closer, we see that this is mostly due to movement among liberal Democrats, who become significantly more supportive of narrow curbing in the conservative decision condition relative to both the control (nine points) and the liberal decision condition (twelve points). Thus, in the absence of party cues, we see a slight asymmetry, such that Democrats are more likely to respond to a disliked decision than Republicans, though Republicans show a higher average level of support for narrow curbing. This is similar to what we saw in the 2016 YGS study.

This asymmetry is erased, however, with the introduction of polarized party cues (top-right panel). In this condition, both liberal Democrats and conservative Republicans become more supportive of narrow curbing, relative to the control, in the face of a disliked decision and strong pressure from in-partisans. Moreover, both partisan groups become *less* supportive of curbing in response to a liked decision and out-partisan attacks on the Court. All changes from the control condition are statistically significant for very liberal, strong Democrats and very conservative, strong Republicans. Moreover, these effects are again substantial. The relationship of left–right identity to support for curbing is 0.55 in the liberal decision condition and –0.30 in the conservative decision condition – a treatment effect of 85 points.[24] Looking at the results another way,

[23] In contrast to the combined analyses, the interaction of affective polarization and left–right identity was only significant for the conservative decision condition with polarized cues, though the coefficients were in the expected direction for all models. The combined analysis is more efficient because it has a larger sample size. We nonetheless examine the interactive models for all conditions to maintain comparability.

[24] And these effects are holding affective polarization at only its 75th percentile.

very liberal, strong Democrats are 38 percentage points more supportive of narrow curbing when exposed to a conservative decision relative to a liberal decision in a polarized environment. Very conservative, strong Republicans, by contrast, are 47 points less supportive. Overall, we find less evidence for an asymmetry in these data relative to the 2016 YGS. Indeed, if anything, right-leaning citizens are more responsive in this study.

The bottom two panels again suggest that broad curbing measures are far less responsive to single-decision disagreement than narrow curbing measures. In the no cues and control conditions, there are no significant relationships between left–right identity and curbing support. Very conservative, strong Republicans, however, are slightly, though not significantly, more supportive of broad curbing measures (by 9 points) comparing the liberal decision condition to the control condition. There is also no significant difference with the conservative condition, however, which complicates the interpretation of this effect. Overall, broad curbing measures are not very responsive to policy disagreement for either right- or left-wing citizens in the absence of party cues.

The results are a bit more interesting in the polarized cues condition. First, for both liberal and conservative decisions, we see a significant and substantively meaningful relationship between left–right identity and support for broad curbing measures. In the former, a change from very liberal, strong Democrat to very conservative, strong Republican is associated with an increase in support for curbing of 18 percentage points. In the conservative decision condition, by contrast, the same change is associated with a drop in support of 13 percentage points. Further, both liberals and conservatives become significantly more supportive of broad curbing measures when exposed to a disliked relative to a liked decision in a highly polarized environment. For very liberal, strong Democrats, support for broad curbing measures increases by 14 percentage points comparing conservative to liberal decisions. For very conservative, strong Republicans, support increases by about 18 percentage points comparing liberal to conservative decisions. These are important effects given that they are driven by only a single decision. Thus, even if narrow curbing is *more* responsive than broad curbing, partisans still update their beliefs about the Court in response to disliked decisions, and these updates contribute to their preferences over reducing the independence of the Court. Moreover, the translation of updated beliefs into broad curbing is facilitated by partisan polarization. We also find an asymmetry for broad curbing, such that citizens become more supportive of broad curbing relative to the control condition when exposed to a disliked decision, but do not become less supportive of broad curbing (again, relative to the control) when exposed to a liked decision. This suggests a negativity, rather than positivity, bias in how citizens respond to the Court's rulings. This is consistent with recent work by Christenson and Glick (2019), who find a negativity bias in the responsiveness of institutional support for the Court to actual decisions during the 2013 term.

Summary of the 2017 QS

In this second experimental study, we examined how citizens respond to a more realistic version of partisan polarization, one in which elite actors harshly criticize the Court and support narrow curbing measures designed to limit the impact of a disliked decision. The results strongly reinforce the conclusions from the 2016 YGS: policy disagreement rooted in left–right identity sharply increases support for narrow forms of Court-curbing and this relationship is significantly stronger in the presence of partisan polarization. We also found support for the moderating role of *affective* polarization in this study. We again find that disagreement is less influential for broad forms of Court-curbing than narrow forms; however, this second study provides evidence that even broad curbing responds meaningfully to single decisions in polarized environments. This study thus replicates the results for broad curbing from the 2009 TESS study, reported in Chapter 5. Indeed, in the polarized cues condition, strong identifiers were ten to twenty points more supportive of broad curbing measures when exposed to disliked decisions. Moreover, the pattern for broad curbing exhibits a negativity (rather than positivity) bias: the Court's institutional integrity is attacked for disliked decisions, but not rewarded for liked ones.

CONCLUSION

The Supreme Court's efficacy rests on its ability to legitimize the policies it creates through its rulings (Choper 1980; Mondak 1994). Citizens must be willing to accept decisions with which they disagree, rather than fight them tooth and nail to limit their impact. When these conditions do not hold, the Court must bend its will to the other branches and to the public to avoid confrontation and achieve acceptable policy outcomes (Carrubba and Zorn 2010; Clark 2011; Vanberg 2001). In this chapter, we have shown that partisan polarization threatens its independence in exactly this way. When citizens strongly dislike members of the other party, and when the parties are sharply divided over a ruling, the legitimizing capacity of the Court is substantially reduced. In such contexts, a surprisingly large number of citizens are willing to support measures that limit the impact of Court decisions, including stripping the Court's jurisdiction in broad and important issue areas, such as marriage and campaign finance. Our first experiment demonstrates that this is more than just coarse partisan cue-taking and has something to do with the nature of polarization itself. Our second experiment demonstrates that heated partisan conflict and discourse may pose a substantial threat to the judiciary. Indeed, in the latter case, support for even broad forms of Court-curbing – e.g., public referenda, Congressional vetoes of Court decisions – responds to disliked decisions.

Mondak (1994, 676) anticipated these results over two decades ago. Summarizing the findings of several studies, he argues that "the experiments show that persons evaluating issues that are of low personal relevance or interest defer heavily to the Supreme Court. Conversely, the impact of the Court's credibility is minimal when policies are of greater personal relevance, because institutional prestige is only one aspect of the evidence evaluated by the decision maker." One way to think about the effects of partisan polarization is in terms of its impact on the perceived relevance of the issue to important social and political identities. When partisans are sharply divided, identity is strengthened (Druckman, Peterson, and Slothuus 2013). This raises the stakes, and the battle takes on symbolic and emotional elements that would be absent if the policy and the decision were considered only on their own terms, independent of their partisan and ideological associations (Mason 2018). When the parties are polarized, every issue seems like a critical front in an ongoing war, and the Court is inevitably caught in the crossfire.

These results suggest that the Court is not nearly as different, in the minds of citizens, as previous work suggests (e.g., Gibson 2007). Indeed, the same dynamics observed in other political contexts, such as Congress (Hetherington and Rudolph 2015) and in debates over public policy (e.g., Druckman, Peterson, and Slothuus 2013; Slothuus and de Vreese 2010), seem to hold in the context of the Supreme Court as well. Until very recently, the received wisdom in the literature on the Court and public opinion was that we need an entirely different model for how citizens respond to Court policymaking. Our results, as well as a growing literature (e.g., Christenson and Glick 2015a; Nicholson and Hansford 2014), suggest this wisdom needs revision. The forces of partisan affect and identity, and the cues handed down by elites, seem to shape Court opinion in ways entirely consistent with standard models of American mass politics that have been so successful in other areas.

This chapter also contributes to an ongoing literature concerned with the negative implications of partisan polarization for democracy. The concern in this literature is that polarization, and the high stakes and low trust of one's opponents it entails, leads to the degeneration of norms of forbearance: the willingness to forego actions that, even when technically allowed by the rules of the game, are nonetheless destructive of the institutions over which each side seeks control (Hetherington and Rudolph 2015; Levitsky and Ziblatt 2018; Svolik 2018). For example, we demonstrate that many citizens are willing to use Congress's power to strip the Court's jurisdiction in important issue areas.

We opened this book with a salient, real-world example: the unwillingness of the Republican-controlled Senate to consider Merrick Garland, even though President Obama had nearly a year remaining in his presidency. How is it that Senate Republicans could accomplish this feat? The answer can be found in the formal models of legislative–judicial interactions discussed in the first chapter of the book: Congressional partisans with an interest in attacking the Court are constrained only by the willingness of those they represent to punish such moves, even when doing so is politically inconvenient – *especially* when doing so is politically inconvenient. Our experiments suggest that partisan polarization sharply reduces citizens' willingness to defend the Court. The Garland case is but one real-world instance of this dynamic.

Yet the impact of citizens' lack of support is often *unseen*, or at least very difficult to observe, because it operates through changes in the Court's decision-making, as the justices anticipate and seek to avoid confrontation with the other branches and with the public (e.g., Carrubba and Zorn 2010; Clark 2011; Epstein, Knight, and Martin 2001; Rosenberg 1992). In this way, partisan polarization constrains the set of viable choices the justices can make and reduces judicial independence. Moreover, as shown in the 2017 QS, sharp polarization, such as that observed during Kavanaugh's confirmation battle, may increase support for broader curbing measures among members of the losing party. This has important implications for the Court in the medium-term future, as left-wing elites begin to call for more extreme measures to dilute the Court's conservative majority. Our results suggest that, within the current polarized context at least, many citizens on the left will be willing to go along with these proposals.

TABLE A6.1 *Models of broadly and narrowly targeted Court-curbing, by polarization conditions, 2016 YGS*

	No cues (narrow)	Unpolarized (narrow)	Polarized (narrow)	No cues (broad)	Unpolarized (broad)	Polarized (broad)
Intercept	0.49 (0.08)	0.34 (0.09)	0.36 (0.10)	0.62 (0.07)	0.55 (0.08)	0.64 (0.09)
Age	−0.08 (0.07)	0.07 (0.07)	−0.05 (0.07)	−0.03 (0.06)	0.16 (0.06)	−0.00 (0.06)
Female	−0.08 (0.03)	−0.01 (0.03)	−0.08 (0.03)	−0.02 (0.03)	0.03 (0.03)	−0.03 (0.03)
Black	−0.01 (0.05)	−0.01 (0.05)	−0.04 (0.05)	0.05 (0.04)	0.01 (0.04)	−0.01 (0.05)
Hispanic	−0.03 (0.04)	0.05 (0.05)	−0.01 (0.05)	0.02 (0.04)	−0.04 (0.05)	0.02 (0.05)
HS degree	−0.11 (0.06)	−0.02 (0.07)	−0.01 (0.08)	−0.06 (0.06)	−0.01 (0.06)	−0.07 (0.07)
Some college	−0.07 (0.07)	−0.03 (0.07)	−0.04 (0.08)	−0.02 (0.06)	−0.03 (0.06)	−0.10 (0.07)
BA degree	−0.05 (0.07)	0.00 (0.07)	−0.06 (0.08)	−0.09 (0.07)	−0.05 (0.07)	−0.10 (0.08)
Post-grad	−0.17 (0.08)	−0.02 (0.09)	−0.07 (0.09)	−0.15 (0.08)	−0.06 (0.08)	−0.15 (0.08)
Income	−0.11 (0.12)	−0.04 (0.13)	−0.05 (0.12)	−0.00 (0.11)	−0.18 (0.12)	−0.03 (0.11)
Engagement	−0.12 (0.05)	−0.10 (0.05)	−0.13 (0.05)	−0.37 (0.05)	−0.27 (0.05)	−0.29 (0.04)
Religiosity	0.04 (0.04)	0.14 (0.04)	0.00 (0.04)	0.02 (0.04)	0.11 (0.04)	0.07 (0.04)
Policy disagreement	0.18 (0.04)	0.21 (0.05)	0.33 (0.05)	0.00 (0.04)	0.02 (0.04)	0.07 (0.04)
R^2	0.15	0.16	0.23	0.27	0.24	0.22
N	353	360	362	353	360	363

Notes: Data are from the 2016 YGS. Entries are ordinary least squares estimates and standard errors (in parentheses). The dependent variables for the "narrow" and "broad" models are, respectively, the narrowly targeted and broadly targeted Court-curbing scales; higher values indicate greater support for Court-curbing. Separate models are estimated for each polarization experimental condition. Policy disagreement, based on the left–right identity measure, is coded relative to the ideological direction of the ruling so that higher values indicate greater disagreement.

TABLE A6.2 *Models of narrowly targeted Court-curbing (item by item), by polarization conditions, 2016 YGS*

	No cues (comply)	Unpolarized (comply)	Polarized (comply)	No cues (final word)	Unpolarized (final word)	Polarized (final word)
Age	−0.77 (0.49)	0.25 (0.48)	−0.66 (0.50)	−0.20 (0.47)	0.47 (0.46)	−0.03 (0.46)
Female	−0.31 (0.22)	0.18 (0.21)	−0.42 (0.22)	−0.54 (0.21)	−0.28 (0.21)	−0.52 (0.21)
Black	0.03 (0.32)	0.15 (0.34)	−0.25 (0.37)	0.02 (0.32)	−0.29 (0.35)	−0.42 (0.36)
Hispanic	−0.13 (0.32)	0.64 (0.37)	−0.81 (0.38)	−0.01 (0.33)	−0.13 (0.37)	0.47 (0.36)
HS degree	−0.88 (0.46)	−0.22 (0.49)	0.49 (0.61)	−0.33 (0.43)	−0.10 (0.48)	−0.05 (0.56)
Some college	−0.59 (0.49)	−0.41 (0.50)	0.17 (0.61)	−0.18 (0.45)	−0.18 (0.48)	−0.26 (0.57)
BA degree	−0.72 (0.53)	−0.29 (0.54)	−0.13 (0.63)	0.21 (0.50)	0.04 (0.52)	−0.17 (0.58)
Post-grad	−1.61 (0.63)	−0.43 (0.62)	−0.08 (0.68)	-0.66 (0.57)	−0.09 (0.59)	−0.39 (0.64)
Income	−0.43 (0.85)	−0.38 (0.96)	−1.56 (0.97)	−0.97 (0.84)	0.11 (0.95)	0.58 (0.83)
Engagement	−0.76 (0.38)	−0.49 (0.36)	−0.74 (0.34)	−0.68 (0.36)	−0.71 (0.35)	−0.83 (0.33)
Religiosity	0.39 (0.30)	0.52 (0.29)	−0.02 (0.30)	0.17 (0.28)	0.99 (0.29)	0.16 (0.30)
Policy disagreement	0.83 (0.33)	1.11 (0.34)	1.46 (0.33)	1.51 (0.32)	1.35 (0.33)	2.50 (0.34)
Pseudo-R^2	0.12	0.09	0.05	0.07	0.05	0.08
N	353	360	361	353	360	361

Notes: Data are from the 2016 YGS. Entries are ordered logit estimates and standard errors (in parentheses). The dependent variables are the individual narrowly targeted Court-curbing items (final word and comply); higher values indicate greater support for Court-curbing. Separate models are estimated for each polarization experimental condition. Policy disagreement, based on the left–right identity measure, is coded relative to the ideological direction of the ruling so that higher values indicate greater disagreement.

TABLE A6.3 *Models of narrowly targeted Court-curbing, by polarization and direction of ruling conditions, 2016 YGS*

	No cues (lib decision)	Unpolarized (lib decision)	Polarized (lib decision)	No cues (con decision)	Unpolarized (con decision)	Polarized (con decision)
Intercept	0.51 (0.12)	0.32 (0.11)	0.43 (0.13)	0.83 (0.11)	0.68 (0.13)	0.73 (0.13)
Age	0.02 (0.09)	0.11 (0.09)	0.06 (0.10)	−0.19 (0.10)	0.00 (0.10)	−0.15 (0.10)
Female	−0.09 (0.04)	−0.05 (0.04)	−0.09 (0.05)	−0.07 (0.04)	0.04 (0.04)	−0.03 (0.04)
Black	0.03 (0.07)	−0.08 (0.08)	−0.03 (0.08)	−0.06 (0.07)	0.07 (0.07)	−0.03 (0.08)
Hispanic	0.03 (0.06)	0.05 (0.07)	−0.06 (0.07)	−0.08 (0.07)	0.08 (0.08)	0.06 (0.07)
HS degree	−0.16 (0.10)	0.05 (0.09)	−0.06 (0.11)	−0.05 (0.09)	−0.16 (0.11)	0.07 (0.12)
Some college	−0.13 (0.10)	0.05 (0.09)	−0.03 (0.11)	−0.02 (0.09)	−0.15 (0.12)	−0.02 (0.12)
BA degree	−0.07 (0.11)	0.16 (0.10)	−0.08 (0.12)	−0.02 (0.10)	−0.21 (0.12)	−0.02 (0.12)
Post-grad	−0.20 (0.12)	0.11 (0.12)	−0.12 (0.13)	−0.15 (0.12)	−0.20 (0.13)	0.01 (0.14)
Income	0.01 (0.16)	−0.14 (0.23)	−0.06 (0.19)	−0.24 (0.18)	−0.05 (0.17)	−0.01 (0.16)
Engagement	−0.21 (0.07)	−0.21 (0.07)	−0.28 (0.07)	−0.00 (0.07)	0.02 (0.07)	0.03 (0.07)
Religiosity	0.10 (0.07)	0.12 (0.06)	−0.03 (0.06)	0.00 (0.06)	0.12 (0.06)	−0.01 (0.07)
Left–right identity	0.15 (0.07)	0.22 (0.07)	0.36 (0.07)	−0.19 (0.07)	−0.16 (0.08)	−0.26 (0.08)
R^2	0.19	0.23	0.30	0.16	0.14	0.18
N	179	177	182	174	183	180

Notes: Data are from the 2016 YGS. Entries are ordinary least squares estimates and standard errors (in parentheses). The dependent variable in each model is the narrowly targeted Court-curbing scale, where higher values indicate greater support for Court-curbing. Separate models are estimated for each polarization by direction of ruling experimental condition. For left–right identity, higher values are more conservative/Republican.

TABLE A6.4 *Models of broadly targeted Court-curbing, by polarization and direction of ruling conditions, 2016 YGS*

	No cues (lib decision)	Unpolarized (lib decision)	Polarized (lib decision)	No cues (con decision)	Unpolarized (con decision)	Polarized (con decision)
Intercept	0.69 (0.11)	0.61 (0.10)	0.58 (0.10)	0.53 (0.10)	0.45 (0.11)	0.61 (0.13)
Age	-0.01 (0.09)	0.12 (0.09)	0.05 (0.08)	-0.08 (0.08)	0.19 (0.09)	-0.09 (0.09)
Female	-0.07 (0.04)	0.01 (0.04)	-0.04 (0.04)	0.06 (0.04)	0.05 (0.04)	0.03 (0.04)
Black	0.08 (0.07)	0.09 (0.07)	0.04 (0.07)	0.07 (0.06)	-0.01 (0.06)	0.05 (0.07)
Hispanic	0.07 (0.06)	-0.05 (0.07)	0.01 (0.06)	-0.01 (0.06)	-0.00 (0.07)	0.06 (0.07)
HS degree	-0.14 (0.10)	-0.02 (0.08)	-0.05 (0.09)	0.00 (0.08)	0.02 (0.10)	-0.06 (0.11)
Some college	-0.03 (0.10)	-0.08 (0.08)	-0.10 (0.09)	-0.03 (0.08)	0.03 (0.10)	-0.09 (0.11)
BA degree	-0.09 (0.11)	-0.07 (0.09)	-0.10 (0.10)	-0.09 (0.09)	0.00 (0.11)	-0.05 (0.12)
Post-grad	-0.08 (0.12)	-0.05 (0.11)	-0.10 (0.10)	-0.23 (0.10)	-0.04 (0.11)	-0.14 (0.13)
Income	-0.21 (0.15)	-0.13 (0.22)	-0.16 (0.15)	0.28 (0.16)	-0.19 (0.15)	0.06 (0.15)
Engagement	-0.41 (0.07)	-0.34 (0.07)	-0.32 (0.05)	-0.31 (0.07)	-0.21 (0.06)	-0.24 (0.06)
Religiosity	-0.02 (0.06)	0.07 (0.06)	0.05 (0.05)	0.00 (0.05)	0.11 (0.05)	-0.06 (0.06)
Left–right identity	0.09 (0.07)	0.08 (0.07)	0.22 (0.06)	0.07 (0.06)	-0.01 (0.07)	0.20 (0.07)
R^2	0.31	0.28	0.35	0.33	0.22	0.21
N	179	177	183	174	183	180

Notes: Data are from the 2016 YGS. Entries are ordinary least squares estimates and standard errors (in parentheses). The dependent variable in each model is the broadly targeted Court-curbing scale, where higher values indicate greater support for Court-curbing. Separate models are estimated for each polarization by direction of ruling experimental conditions. For left–right identity, higher values are more conservative/Republican.

TABLE A6.5 *Models of broadly and narrowly targeted Court-curbing, by polarization conditions, 2017 QS*

	No cues (narrow)	Polarized (narrow)	No cues (broad)	Polarized (broad)
Intercept	0.42 (0.07)	0.17 (0.07)	0.69 (0.07)	0.55 (0.07)
Age	−0.08 (0.05)	0.11 (0.05)	−0.31 (0.05)	−0.38 (0.05)
Female	−0.04 (0.02)	0.01 (0.02)	−0.01 (0.02)	0.01 (0.02)
Black	−0.02 (0.03)	0.02 (0.03)	0.02 (0.03)	0.06 (0.03)
Hispanic	0.00 (0.03)	0.07 (0.03)	0.08 (0.03)	0.05 (0.03)
HS degree	0.05 (0.05)	0.02 (0.06)	−0.03 (0.06)	0.01 (0.06)
Some college	0.03 (0.05)	0.02 (0.05)	−0.06 (0.06)	0.02 (0.06)
BA degree	0.02 (0.05)	−0.00 (0.06)	−0.13 (0.06)	−0.00 (0.06)
Post-grad	0.01 (0.06)	0.01 (0.06)	−0.12 (0.06)	−0.04 (0.06)
Engagement	−0.11 (0.04)	−0.05 (0.04)	0.00 (0.04)	0.10 (0.04)
Policy disagreement	−0.05 (0.07)	0.24 (0.07)	0.05 (0.08)	0.06 (0.08)
Affective polarization	−0.12 (0.06)	−0.15 (0.06)	0.00 (0.07)	−0.02 (0.07)
Policy disagreement × Affective polarization	0.23 (0.11)	0.25 (0.11)	−0.00 (0.12)	0.11 (0.12)
R^2	0.05	0.20	0.10	0.17
N	633	597	633	597

Notes: Data are from the 2017 QS. Entries are ordinary least squares estimates and standard errors (in parentheses). The dependent variables for the "narrow" and "broad" models are, respectively, the narrowly targeted and broadly targeted Court-curbing scales; higher values indicate greater support for Court-curbing. Separate models are estimated for each polarization experimental condition. Policy disagreement, based on the left–right identity measure, is coded relative to the ideological direction of the ruling so that higher values indicate greater disagreement.

TABLE A6.6 *Models of narrowly targeted Court-curbing (item by item), by polarization conditions, 2017 QS*

	No cues (strip)	Polarized (strip)	No cues (final say)	Polarized (final say)	No cues (comply)	Polarized (comply)
Age	−0.58 (0.37)	0.36 (0.37)	−0.64 (0.36)	0.52 (0.37)	−0.50 (0.37)	1.12 (0.38)
Female	−0.33 (0.16)	−0.03 (0.16)	−0.09 (0.15)	0.04 (0.16)	−0.16 (0.16)	0.07 (0.17)
Black	−0.15 (0.23)	−0.06 (0.25)	−0.37 (0.23)	0.16 (0.25)	−0.00 (0.23)	0.20 (0.26)
Hispanic	−0.22 (0.24)	0.62 (0.23)	−0.01 (0.24)	0.35 (0.23)	0.15 (0.24)	0.00 (0.24)
HS degree	0.13 (0.40)	0.31 (0.47)	0.35 (0.40)	−0.19 (0.43)	0.44 (0.41)	0.85 (0.46)
Some college	0.10 (0.39)	0.58 (0.46)	0.13 (0.39)	−0.33 (0.42)	0.39 (0.40)	0.72 (0.46)
BA degree	0.01 (0.40)	0.29 (0.47)	0.23 (0.40)	−0.35 (0.44)	0.21 (0.41)	0.32 (0.47)
Post-grad	−0.10 (0.44)	0.37 (0.49)	0.32 (0.44)	−0.26 (0.45)	−0.10 (0.44)	0.47 (0.48)
Engagement	−1.18 (0.29)	−0.43 (0.29)	−0.49 (0.29)	−0.22 (0.30)	−1.59 (0.30)	−0.91 (0.31)
Policy disagreement	−0.39 (0.55)	1.17 (0.58)	−0.35 (0.54)	0.95 (0.60)	0.34 (0.57)	0.78 (0.61)
Affective polarization	−0.97 (0.49)	−1.42 (0.52)	−0.54 (0.49)	−1.94 (0.55)	−1.31 (0.52)	−1.61 (0.54)
Policy disagreement × Affective polarization	1.80 (0.86)	2.28 (0.92)	1.17 (0.86)	3.07 (0.95)	1.61 (0.90)	2.18 (0.95)
Pseudo-R^2	0.04	0.08	0.03	0.09	0.07	0.09
N	633	597	633	596	633	597

Notes: Data are from the 2017 QS. Entries are ordered logit estimates and standard errors (in parentheses). The dependent variables are the individual narrowly targeted Court-curbing items; higher values indicate greater support for Court-curbing. Separate models are estimated for each polarization experimental condition. Policy disagreement, based on the left–right identity measure, is coded relative to the ideological direction of the ruling so that higher values indicate greater disagreement.

TABLE A6.7 *Models of narrowly targeted Court-curbing, by polarization and direction of ruling conditions, 2017 QS*

	Control (no decision)	No cues (con decision)	Polarized (con decision)	No cues (lib decision)	Polarized (lib decision)
Intercept	0.44 (0.08)	0.27 (0.10)	0.32 (0.10)	0.30 (0.09)	0.08 (0.10)
Age	−0.22 (0.05)	−0.11 (0.07)	0.03 (0.07)	−0.08 (0.06)	0.13 (0.06)
Female	−0.03 (0.02)	−0.00 (0.03)	0.00 (0.03)	−0.06 (0.03)	0.01 (0.03)
Black	−0.02 (0.03)	0.02 (0.04)	0.01 (0.05)	−0.00 (0.04)	0.05 (0.04)
Hispanic	0.03 (0.04)	0.04 (0.04)	0.05 (0.04)	−0.02 (0.04)	0.09 (0.04)
HS degree	−0.01 (0.06)	0.01 (0.08)	0.06 (0.08)	0.03 (0.07)	0.00 (0.08)
Some college	−0.05 (0.06)	0.01 (0.08)	0.03 (0.07)	0.04 (0.07)	0.02 (0.08)
BA degree	−0.06 (0.06)	−0.01 (0.08)	0.06 (0.08)	−0.00 (0.07)	−0.05 (0.08)
Post-grad	−0.05 (0.07)	−0.04 (0.08)	0.03 (0.08)	0.03 (0.07)	0.02 (0.08)
Engagement	−0.17 (0.04)	−0.05 (0.05)	−0.03 (0.05)	−0.16 (0.05)	−0.04 (0.05)
Left–right identity	0.11 (0.09)	0.25 (0.09)	−0.04 (0.11)	0.22 (0.10)	0.40 (0.10)
Affective polarization	−0.02 (0.08)	0.12 (0.08)	0.14 (0.09)	−0.01 (0.08)	−0.07 (0.08)
Left–right identity × Affective polarization	0.10 (0.14)	−0.27 (0.15)	−0.39 (0.17)	0.05 (0.15)	0.21 (0.15)
R^2	0.17	0.05	0.12	0.14	0.33
N	320	312	294	321	303

Notes: Data are from the 2017 QS. Entries are ordinary least squares estimates and standard errors (in parentheses). The dependent variable in each model is the narrowly targeted Court-curbing scale, where higher values indicate greater support for Court-curbing. Separate models are estimated for each polarization by direction of ruling experimental condition. For left–right identity, higher values are more conservative/Republican.

TABLE A6.8 *Models of broadly targeted Court-curbing, by polarization and direction of ruling conditions, 2017 QS*

	Control (no decision)	No cues (con decision)	Polarized (con decision)	No cues (lib decision)	Polarized (lib decision)
Intercept	0.81 (0.11)	0.74 (0.11)	0.73 (0.10)	0.74 (0.10)	0.52 (0.11)
Age	−0.31 (0.07)	−0.30 (0.07)	−0.43 (0.07)	−0.32 (0.07)	−0.34 (0.07)
Female	0.05 (0.03)	0.01 (0.03)	−0.00 (0.03)	−0.02 (0.03)	0.04 (0.03)
Black	0.04 (0.04)	0.00 (0.04)	0.03 (0.05)	0.05 (0.05)	0.08 (0.05)
Hispanic	0.09 (0.05)	0.10 (0.05)	0.06 (0.04)	0.05 (0.05)	0.05 (0.05)
HS degree	−0.10 (0.08)	−0.05 (0.09)	−0.01 (0.08)	−0.04 (0.08)	0.04 (0.09)
Some college	−0.13 (0.08)	−0.06 (0.09)	−0.00 (0.08)	−0.08 (0.08)	0.05 (0.09)
BA degree	−0.24 (0.08)	−0.15 (0.09)	−0.01 (0.08)	−0.12 (0.08)	0.01 (0.09)
Post-grad	−0.25 (0.09)	−0.21 (0.10)	−0.14 (0.08)	−0.05 (0.08)	0.06 (0.10)
Engagement	0.05 (0.06)	0.06 (0.06)	0.13 (0.06)	−0.05 (0.06)	0.08 (0.06)
Left–right identity	−0.09 (0.12)	−0.07 (0.11)	−0.17 (0.11)	−0.02 (0.12)	−0.03 (0.12)
Affective polarization	−0.12 (0.10)	−0.06 (0.09)	−0.02 (0.09)	−0.00 (0.09)	−0.06 (0.09)
Left–right identity × Affective polarization	0.06 (0.18)	0.04 (0.17)	0.05 (0.17)	0.11 (0.17)	0.30 (0.18)
R^2	0.20	0.14	0.24	0.10	0.14
N	320	312	294	321	303

Notes: Data are from the 2017 QS. Entries are ordinary least squares estimates and standard errors (in parentheses). The dependent variable in each model is the broadly targeted Court-curbing scale, where higher values indicate greater support for Court-curbing. Separate models are estimated for each polarization by direction of ruling experimental condition. For left–right identity, higher values are more conservative/Republican.

7

Procedural Perceptions and Motivated Reasoning

It is commonly thought that perceptions of procedural fairness constrain citizens' willingness to attack the Supreme Court in the face of disliked decisions. Extensive and well-known scholarship by Tyler and colleagues has advanced this proposition across various legal and institutional contexts (e.g., Levi, Sacks, and Tyler 2009; Sunshine and Tyler 2003; Tyler 1994, 2006b, 2006a), including the Supreme Court (Tyler and Rasinski 1991). Perceptions that the Court makes decisions in a fair and impartial manner foster a belief that the Court has rightful authority. In turn, citizens accept its decisions as legitimate, even when they disagree with them, and punish attempts at Court-curbing. In this view, the biggest threat to the Court is the increasing politicization of the institution in the media; for example, highly publicized, hyper-partisan nomination, and confirmation battles (Gibson and Caldeira 2009a).

Examples of politicization abound. To take a recent one, Bloomberg published an editorial following the 2018 decision in *Husted* v. *A Philip Randolph Institute*, which concerned purging of voter rolls in Ohio, and was decided in favor of the state's current law. The decision broke clearly along ideological lines, and the headline of the opinion piece was "The Supreme Court Takes a Nakedly Political Turn."[1] Examples of statements in this piece are indeed concerning for Court-watchers: "It would be nice if legal principle had played any role in the decision on either side, but it didn't, not really"; "So the best, albeit unfortunate conclusion is that the justices are just being political"; "Partisanship should not inform statutory

[1] www.bloomberg.com/view/articles/2018–06-11/ohio-voter-registration-case-at-supreme-court-is-pure-politics

interpretation in this way"; "No matter which side you think is correct, the partisan breakdown on a voting rights case is not a great look for the justices." From a process-based perspective, stories like this threaten to unmask the Court's ideological and partisan nature and break the myth of legality (e.g., Baird and Gangl 2006; Hitt and Searles 2018; Johnston and Bartels 2010; Scheb and Lyons 2001; Solberg and Waltenburg 2014; Spill and Oxley 2003; Strother 2017). The long-term implications are a decline in institutional legitimacy.

Yet, in addition to providing process information, articles such as the Bloomberg piece also inform citizens about the *outcome* of the decision – was it congenial to liberal or conservative interests? Did Democrats or Republicans "win" this round? We have presented an array of cross-sectional, panel, and experimental evidence that suggests that citizens are moved powerfully by such information about decision outcomes – that they seek to curb the Court in the face of disliked decisions, and that this is particularly true in the contemporary era of party polarization. Moreover, we presented evidence in Chapter 5 that the effect of outcome information is larger than the effect of procedural information. That is, when a case description includes both outcome and procedural information (as in the Bloomberg article above), it is outcome information that matters most for Court-curbing. Our findings suggest that citizens care more about winning salient partisan and ideological battles than they do about contributing to the legitimacy of the Court, and procedural information may matter less to Court-curbing than previously thought. So, where does this leave process-based theories?

We think the answer rests with contemporary theories of motivated reasoning (Kunda 1990, 1999; Leeper and Slothuus 2014). As described in Chapter 2, political reasoning is driven by an attempt to balance directional and accuracy goals (Lavine, Johnston, and Steenbergen 2012). Directional goals seek a particular conclusion. For example, one may wish to gratify an important social or political identity, conform to the opinion of close others, or reinforce one's prior opinion on a policy issue. Accuracy goals, by contrast, seek the best, or most justifiable, judgment or decision, whatever that may be. Citizens pursue both types of goals. We would like to believe that our political groups and policies are the "best" ones because this promotes cognitive consistency and reflects high social status (Festinger 1957; Tajfel and Turner 1979).[2] At the same time, we also

[2] For recent formal treatments of cognitive consistency motives in political science, see Acharya, Blackwell, and Sen (2018) and Little (2019).

wish to see ourselves as rational people who care about the truth of the matter, and we are often held to account by others (Kunda 1990; Lerner and Tetlock 1999). These latter considerations act as constraints on our ability to believe what we wish, independent of the facts. Considerations of procedural fairness operate as constraints in a like fashion. As the results of previous chapters suggest, citizens often prefer to curb the Court in response to disliked decisions, but they may also be aware that such brazen political attacks are antithetical to the Court's special apolitical role in American politics. Put another way, discontent with the partisan, ideological, or policy implications of a decision is typically an illegitimate basis on which to launch a Court-curbing attack.

For these reasons, we think, it is rare to hear a call for Court-curbing justified in open political terms, as a naked attempt to get the desired outcome. Far from it! As the quotes in Table 6.3 suggest, these types of attacks are almost always justified in terms of some fault in the Court, its processes of decision-making, or the unethical machinations of the *other* political party. In other words, discontent with Court decision-making feeds curbing attempts, but these are rationalized by appealing to supposed deviations of the Court and its justices from widely shared norms of impartiality and legalism – that is, of procedural fairness. The reason for the problematic decision, then, is that justices are "activist," ignored precedent, are "legislating from the bench," and are unduly influenced by pressure groups, citizens, and opposing partisans. Since the Court has betrayed its own principles – and our shared norms regarding the role of the judiciary – curbing actions are not attacks but rather legitimate attempts to right a wrong. The upshot is that perceptions of procedural fairness should be, to a substantial degree, *endogenous* to partisan, ideological, and policy discontent with the Court. When citizens like one or a series of decisions, they bolster these decisions and defend the Court by appealing to the impartiality, fairness, and legalism of the process by which the outcome was reached. Conversely, when citizens disagree with the Court, they build support for curbing attempts by attacking the procedural foundations of the Court's legitimacy.

Is there any existing evidence for this claim? In fact, the general question about the flow of causality surrounding procedural perceptions and institutional loyalty was debated by Gibson (1989, 1991) and Tyler and Rasinski (1991) and also summarized and further examined by Mondak (1993). Tyler and Rasinski argue the conventional wisdom of procedural justice theory – procedural fairness shapes institutional legitimacy. They further argue that legitimacy mediates the impact of procedural justice on acquiescence (or compliance) with the Court's rulings. Gibson argues that procedural perceptions do not influence acquiescence to the Court, and instead, legitimacy (or diffuse support) simultaneously influences both acquiescence and procedural perceptions. In a subsequent analysis of the *Bush* v. *Gore* ruling, Gibson et al. (2003b) provide evidence that the flow of causality runs more from legitimacy to procedural fairness (of the ruling in particular) rather than vice versa. Mondak's (1993) experimental analysis also questions Tyler and Rasinski's claim that procedural justice influences institutional legitimacy, though it does not offer clear evidence for Gibson's argument. Moreover, recent research by Badas (2016), Simon and Scurich (2011), and Strother and Gadarian (2019) provides evidence that agreement and disagreement with Court outcomes can shape perceptions of the Court's decision-making (see also Cann and Yates 2016). Thus, while limited, existing work provides reasons to question the exogeneity of procedural perceptions to both policy discontent and institutional support for the Court.

In line with our theoretical discussions in Chapter 2, we also examine the hypothesis that political engagement will increase directionally motivated reasoning. This expectation is rooted in the idea that engaged citizens have both greater motivation and greater ability to engage in reasoning of this sort (e.g., Huddy, Mason, and Aarøe 2015; Kahan et al. 2012; Slothuus and de Vreese 2010; Taber and Lodge 2006). Engaged citizens have a greater investment in their political identities and more at stake in any given political battle, and their greater knowledge of politics makes it easier to reason a way to their desired conclusions. Further, engaged citizens are more likely to be aware of and endorse norms of a politically independent judiciary. Thus, the engaged should be more likely to recognize that Court-curbing conflicts with broader political values. This should create a stronger motivation to rationalize curbing through attacks on the Court's procedural fairness. In turn, we expect that indicators of political engagement will increase the size of the relationship between disagreement with the Court's decisions and perceptions of procedural fairness and objectivity.

In the present chapter, we test both the unconditional and conditional hypotheses with cross-sectional, panel, and experimental data. Some of these data we have seen in previous chapters, and some are new to this chapter. As in previous chapters, we seek converging evidence across diverse methods. To the extent that our results hold across studies with heterogeneous methodological attributes, confidence in our conclusions will be stronger. In our studies using observational data, we seek evidence for (1) a relationship between general policy disagreement with the Court and its justices and perceptions that the Court and its members are politicized in their decision-making; and (2) a relationship between disagreement with a specific decision – namely, *NFIB* v. *Sebelius* (the ACA/ health care ruling) – and perceptions that the outcome was reached through biased, unfair, and politicized procedures. In our experimental data, we look for evidence of the effect of single decisions by randomly assigning respondents to read about congenial or uncongenial decisions. In these latter studies, the experimental design also allows us to examine how procedural information – information regarding how the justices reached their decision – affects procedural perceptions. If procedural justice theory is right, we should observe strong effects of procedural information on perceptions that the Court in general, and in the specific case, makes decisions in a fair and impartial manner. In contrast, if our theory is right, we should observe a stronger relationship between the ideological direction of the *outcome* and perceptions of procedural fairness.

OBSERVATIONAL DATA

We discuss our results in two sections: observational (including both cross-sectional and panel data) and experimental. We begin with the former, which includes four datasets. Three of these we have used in previous chapters: the 2005 Annenberg Supreme Court survey (2005 ASCS), the 2011 Freedom-Tolerance survey (2011 FTS), and the 2012 American Panel Study (TAPS). We add one new dataset as well: the 2005 Citizenship, Involvement, and Democracy study, which contains a supplemental section – collected and utilized by Gibson and Caldeira (2009a) – concerning the nomination and subsequent confirmation of Samuel Alito to the Supreme Court (2006 Alito). All datasets are summarized in Table 3.1.

We use the 2005 ASCS and the 2011 FTS datasets to examine the hypothesis that perceptions of general policy disagreement with the Court are associated with perceptions that the Court is politicized. For both studies, policy disagreement is measured identically to Chapter 4. In the 2005 ASCS, procedural perceptions are measured with eight items, which formed a reliable scale ($\alpha = 0.74$). These items include perceptions of the extent to which political actors (e.g., interest groups, the President) influence Court decision-making and the general fairness and objectivity of the Court and its justices. We list the items in Table 7.1. For all datasets, we have coded procedural perceptions so that higher values indicate greater negativity. We will thus refer to these scales as "perceptions of politicization" to be clear that higher values indicate perceptions that the Court is politicized rather than fair, objective, and legalistic.

TABLE 7.1 *Items measuring perceptions of politicization in observational studies*

2005 ASCS

"To what extent do you think the current Supreme Court is influenced by ________ when making their decisions – to a great extent, moderate extent, small extent, or not at all?"

- public opinion
- the president
- Congress
- conservative interest groups
- liberal interest groups

Which of the following statements comes closer to your beliefs about the Supreme Court? (1) The Court is fair and objective in its rulings, or (2) The Court is sometimes politically motivated in its rulings

Thinking about the current Supreme Court, please tell me if you strongly agree, somewhat agree, somewhat disagree or strongly disagree with the following statement:

- The decisions of the Supreme Court favor some groups more than others
- The Supreme Court gets too mixed up in politics

2011 *FTS*

"Do you agree strongly, agree, disagree, or disagree strongly?" [Consistent with Gibson and Nelson (2014), "Uncertain/Don't know" coded as middle category]

- The Supreme Court gets too mixed up in politics.
- Supreme Court justices are just like any other politicians; we cannot trust them to decide court cases in a way that is in the best interests of our country.

2006 *Alito*

"If Judge Alito is confirmed, how likely do you think it is that he would ________?"

- Strictly follow the law no matter what people in the country may want
- Try to maintain the appearance of being fair and impartial no matter what the cost
- Be especially concerned about protecting people *without power* from people and groups *with power*
- Stay entirely independent of the president and the government
- Give conservatives/liberals a strong voice in how the constitution is interpreted
- Respect existing Supreme Court decisions by changing the law as little as possible

(continued)

TABLE 7.1 *(continued)*

- Uphold the values of those who wrote our constitution two hundred years ago
- Base his decisions on the fact that he is a Republican
- Base his decisions on the fact that he is a conservative
- Make fair and impartial decisions

TAPS
Pre-decision stem: "How big of a role do you think each of the following will play in the decision of the Court?"

Post-decision stem: "How much of a role did each of the following play in the Supreme Court's decision on health insurance?"

- The personal views of the justices about the health insurance requirement
- The justices' analysis and interpretation of the law
- The views of the average American about the requirement
- The public's likely reaction to the Court's decision
- The justices' liberal or conservative views
- Whether the justice was appointed by a Democratic or Republican president
- President Obama's views on the legal issues

"Please indicate whether you agree with the following." [strongly agree, agree, neither agree nor disagree, disagree, strongly disagree]

- The Supreme Court gets too mixed up in politics.

We are more limited in the 2011 FTS with respect to items measuring perceptions. One item is straightforward, and asks about the extent to which the Court is "too mixed up in politics" (this item is also included in the 2005 ASCS). A second item is arguably also a measure of perceptions that the Court is fair, objective, and apolitical: "Supreme Court justices are just like any other politicians; we cannot trust them to decide court cases in a way that is in the best interests of our country." This item is far from perfect. It is double-barreled, mixes the concept of "trust" with perceptions of politicization, assumes that "trustworthy" implies making decisions that are in the "best interests of our country," and does not clarify what is meant by "best interests." Nonetheless, we think it is serviceable for our purposes, as the focus of the item is on the claim that justices are just like other politicians. It is also correlated with the "mixed up" item to a substantial degree ($r = 0.42$).[3] We thus combined the two into a single scale. In both the

[3] Both items were used as indicators of "institutional legitimacy" by Gibson and Nelson (2015b). Consistent with our argument in Chapters 1 and 2, we contend that perceptions of politicization should be considered distinct from support for Court-curbing.

2005 ASCS and the 2011 FTS, political engagement is measured identically to Chapter 4, and we use the same set of control variables as well.

The 2006 Alito study concerned the nomination and confirmation of Justice Samuel Alito, and we thus focus our analysis on the relationship between perceptions of ideological disagreement with Alito and expectations regarding Alito's decision-making (items for the dependent variable are shown in Table 7.1).[4] Respondents were asked to place both themselves and Alito on a ten-point scale ranging from "extremely liberal" to "extremely conservative." We take the absolute difference between these scales as our measure of perceived policy disagreement. Given that Alito was nominated by a Republican president, we also examine a standard measure of partisanship as a second indicator of disagreement, which ranges from strong Democrat to strong Republican. Procedural perceptions are measured with ten items, which formed a reliable scale, and are listed in Table 7.1 ($\alpha = 0.80$).[5] We measure political engagement with a three-item measure of Court-specific political knowledge.[6] Controls for this study include both standard demographics, religiosity, and four multi-item scales of democratic values, including support for a multiparty system, support for the rule of law, political tolerance, and support for liberty over order.[7]

We take advantage of the panel design from TAPS. These data contain a unique set of items concerning citizens' perceptions of the Court's decision in *NFIB* v. *Sebelius* (i.e., on "Obamacare"). In the May 2012 wave of the study, *prior* to the decision, respondents were asked about their expectations regarding how the justices would go about making the decision in the case. Specifically, they were asked about seven different considerations, which are listed in Table 7.1, and which range from the opinion of President Obama to the justices' analysis and interpretation of the law. In the July 2012 wave of the study, respondents were again asked about these seven considerations, but were now tasked with evaluating how the justices *actually* made the decision in *NFIB* v. *Sebelius*. In both waves, respondents were also given the more standard item asking about

[4] While the 2006 Alito has a panel component, it is not relevant to our analyses (see Gibson and Caldeira 2009a). We analyze the second wave as a cross-sectional dataset (see Table 3.1).

[5] An eleventh item was available, but it was (weakly) negatively correlated with the rest of the scale, and was thus excluded.

[6] The questions include the following: (1) are justices elected or appointed? (2) do they serve for a set number of years, or for life? (3) does the Court have the last say on Constitutional issues?

[7] See Gibson and Caldeira (2009a, 56) for the exact wordings of the items in these scales.

the extent to which the Court is "too mixed up in politics." Since all eight items were asked in both waves, we could calculate a measure we call the "expectations–perceptions gap" in Court politicization. We first combined all eight items within each wave into a single scale with higher values indicating greater perceptions of politicization.[8] We then subtracted each respondent's score in the May wave from their score in the July wave. This final measure represents the difference in each respondent's *expectations* regarding the Court's decision-making in *NFIB* v. *Sebelius* and their perceptions of the Court's *actual* decision-making in that case. Positive values indicate that the Court was more politicized than expected, while negative values indicate the opposite. Since the decision in this case was generally seen as a "win" for President Obama and Democrats, our hypothesis is that conservatives and Republicans will show significant, positive changes from May to July (denigrating the decision), while Democrats will show significant negative changes (bolstering the decision). As in Chapter 5, we use two measures of policy disagreement: health insurance (ACA) preferences and left–right identity. Moreover, we expect this pattern to be stronger for the politically engaged. We measure political engagement in the same way as Chapter 5, and we include all the same controls.

Results

We will consider the results of each study in turn, and we begin with the 2005 ASCS. We estimated two models, one for each measure of general policy disagreement. Each model regressed perceptions of politicization on disagreement, political engagement, the interaction of the two, and our set of control variables. Regression estimates for all models in this chapter are reported in the appendix tables. The interaction is large and statistically significant for our interval measure of disagreement. For our nominal measure, all three interaction terms are in the expected, positive direction, but they only approach statistical significance in each case. We plot the conditional effects for each measure in Figure 7.1. The left panel shows the results for the interval measure. The x-axis represents the respondent's degree of policy disagreement with the Court, and the y-axis represents predicted values of perceptions of politicization. The three lines represent estimates for respondents at low (5th percentile), moderate (50th percentile), and high (95th percentile) levels of political engagement, respectively. The estimates

[8] $\alpha = 0.73$ for the May wave, and $\alpha = 0.69$ for the July wave.

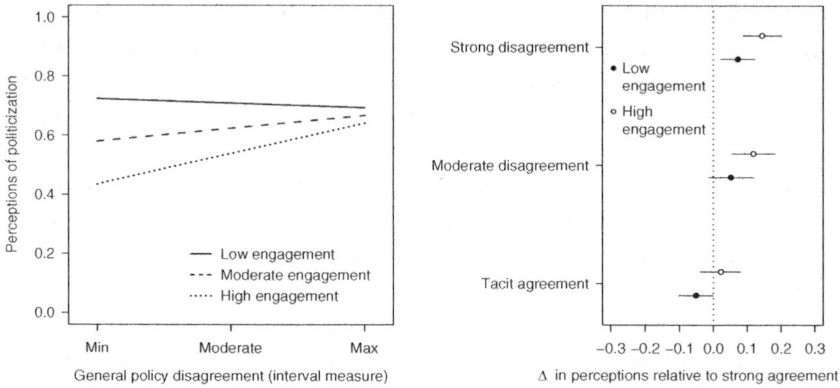

FIGURE 7.1 The effect of general policy disagreement on perceptions of politicization across levels of political engagement, 2005 ASCS. In the left panel, lines represent predicted values of perceptions across general policy disagreement (based on the interval measure); in the right panel, points are estimated effects on perceptions comparing each category of disagreement to "strong agreement"; see Table 7.1 for the items that make up the perceptions scale; extended lines are 95% confidence bounds; this figure is based on model estimates in Table A7.1.

are consistent with theoretical expectations, as well as prior work on motivated reasoning in political psychology. At low levels of engagement, there is no relationship at all between policy disagreement and perceptions. At moderate levels of engagement, however, a change from minimum to maximum disagreement is associated with a statistically significant, 9 percentage point increase in perceptions of politicization. That is, citizens who see themselves as disagreeing with the Court's decision-making are also more likely to think the Court is influenced by external political actors and makes its decisions in a biased and unfair manner. The relationship is even stronger for the highly sophisticated. For these respondents, a change from minimum to maximum entails an increase of over 20 points – or one-fifth of the scale of the dependent variable.

We can also consider the interaction from another perspective: how the effect of political engagement on perceptions of politicization changes across levels of policy disagreement. As previous scholars have argued (e.g., Gibson and Caldeira 2009a), politically knowledgeable and active citizens tend to show higher levels of support for the Supreme Court, including positive perceptions of its decision-making. This is true, on average, in these data as well. Importantly, however, this average effect of engagement is driven primarily by those in policy *agreement* with the

Court. Among those who agree with the Court's ideological direction, there is a large negative effect of political engagement. Indeed, as engagement changes from low to high, perceptions of politicization drop by about 30 percentage points. Among those who strongly disagree with the Court's decision-making, however, the gap between high and low engagement is a mere 5 points. One interpretation of these results is that politically unengaged citizens tend to see the Court as politicized no matter what; among the engaged, however, perceptions of procedural fairness emerge, but *only* when they agree with the Court's policy output. This seems consistent with the notion that politically sophisticated citizens are more capable of constructing arguments in favor of their preferred positions than the unsophisticated – they are better at rationalizing – and that they are more motivated to do so. The important point is that perceptions of politicization are indeed closely tied to perceptions of policy disagreement in the way expected by motivated reasoning theory, and it is the most knowledgeable and active citizens who most readily connect these two sets of perceptions. The results for our second measure are shown in the right panel of Figure 7.1. Here again we see meaningful and significant effects of disagreement with the Court on perceptions of politicization and, for both moderate and strong disagreement, the effect is larger (though not significantly so) for the politically engaged.

The results for the 2011 FTS are shown in Figure 7.2. First, there is a large unconditional effect of our interval-level policy disagreement variable on perceptions of politicization, but no significant interaction. This is reflected in the left panel of Figure 7.2, where the lines for low, moderate, and high engagement are about parallel. A change from minimum to maximum policy disagreement is associated with an increase in perceptions of politicization of about 15 percentage points in each case. We do, however, find a meaningful and significant interaction of our second, nominal measure of disagreement with political engagement. As shown in the right panel of Figure 7.2, engagement substantially increases the effect of seeing the Court as either too liberal or too conservative. Among the highly engaged, for example, a change from "about right" to "too liberal" is associated with an increase in perceptions of politicization of 14 points, while a change to "too conservative" is associated with an increase of 17 points. Thus, while both measures provide support for the motivated reasoning hypothesis, only the second measure provides support for the engagement interaction hypothesis.

We turn now to the results for the 2006 Alito study. In non-interactive models, as expected, both perceived ideological distance from Alito and

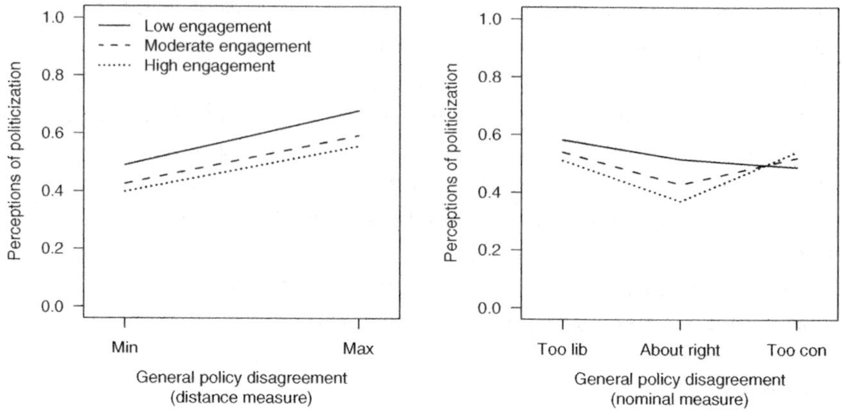

FIGURE 7.2 Perceptions of politicization across general policy disagreement and levels of political engagement, 2011 FTS. See Table 7.1 for the items that make up the perceptions scale; this figure is based on model estimates in Table A7.2.

stronger Democratic partisanship predict higher perceptions of politicization. Those ideologically furthest from Alito are 25 points more pessimistic about his future decision-making than those who see themselves in perfect ideological alignment with the future justice. Similarly, strong Democrats are 13 points more pessimistic than strong Republicans. Importantly, however, both ideological distance and partisanship show significant interactions with political engagement. The conditional marginal effects for each are shown in Figure 7.3. In the left panel, the x-axis represents perceived ideological distance from Alito, and the y-axis represents the predicted value of perceptions of politicization. In the right panel, the x-axis is respondent partisanship, ranging from strong Democrat to strong Republican. The four lines in each panel represent the four possible values of political engagement in this study. Among the unengaged, we find no relationship between ideological or partisan disagreement with Alito and perceptions. However, at all three of the other values of engagement, for both measures of disagreement, there is a positive relationship between ideological distance and perceptions of politicization.[9] Moreover, the relationship increases substantially in magnitude. For the ideological distance measure, at high levels of engagement, a change from min to max is associated with an increase in perceptions of

[9] The marginal effect for partisanship at moderate-low engagement just misses statistical significance. All other conditional marginal effects are significant.

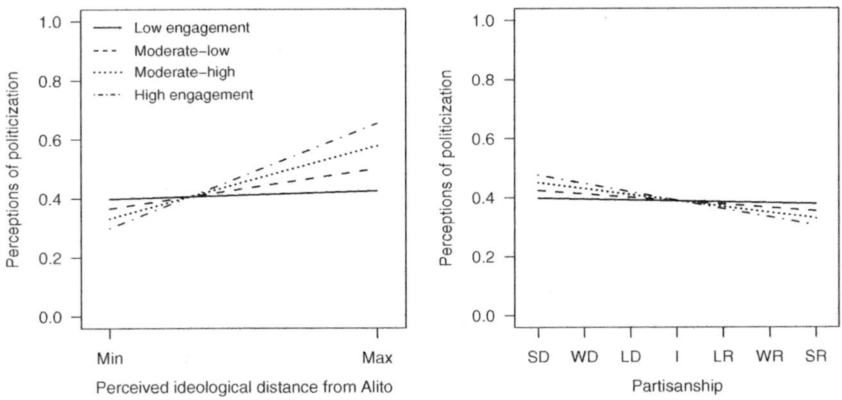

FIGURE 7.3 Perceptions of politicization across ideological distance from Alito, partisanship, and levels of political engagement, 2006 Alito. See Table 7.1 for the items that make up the perceptions scale, which ranges from zero to one; this figure is based on model estimates in Table A7.3.

politicization of 35 percentage points, or over one-third of the scale of the dependent variable.

The results for the TAPS are also consistent with theoretical expectations. The interactions with engagement for health insurance preferences and left–right identity are large and in the theorized direction.[10] The conditional marginal effects are shown in Figure 7.4. The y-axes represent the predicted gap between expectations of the Court's decision-making in *NFIB* v. *Sebelius* and perceptions of the Court's actual decision-making (after the fact). Thus, a predicted value of zero implies no difference, on average, between expectations and perceptions. The solid line shows the results for respondents at low levels of political engagement. For these respondents, across levels of health insurance preferences and political

[10] $p < 0.07$ and $p < 0.01$, respectively. As discussed in Chapter 5, there are differences between the weighted and unweighted regression results for models with engagement interactions using the TAPS panel. The weighted models tend to produce nonsensical results for those at low levels of political engagement. We think this has to with the relatively small number of respondents with low levels of engagement in these data. We thus report the unweighted estimates here. The weighted estimates can be generated using our reproduction materials for Chapter 7. In brief, models with weights predict that, for very unengaged citizens, there is a strong *negative* relationship between policy disagreement and perceptions of politicization (though these conditional effects are not statistically significant). Nonetheless, the significance level for the interactions remains the same and the estimates of the effect of policy preferences and left–right identity for engaged citizens are nearly identical across weighted and unweighted models.

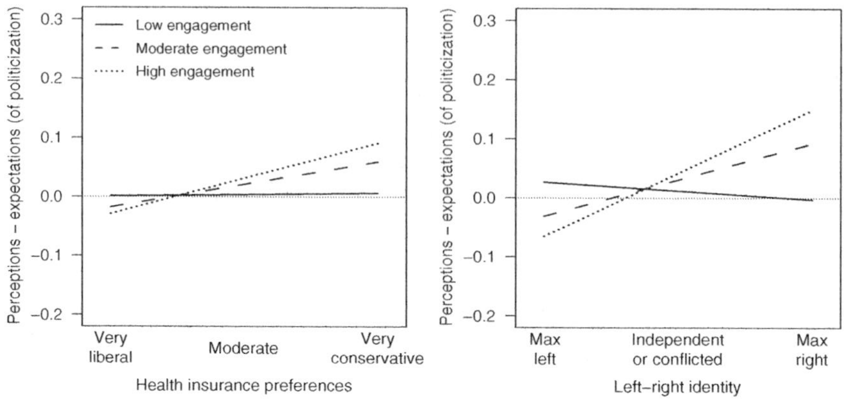

FIGURE 7.4 The expectations–perceptions gap in judgments about the Court's decision process in *NFIB* v. *Sebelius* as a function of health insurance preferences, left–right identity, and political engagement, 2012 TAPS. The y-axis represents the difference between respondents' expectations of how the Court *would* make its decision in *NFIB* (asked prior to the decision) and perceptions of how the Court *did* make the decision (asked after the decision) – positive (negative) values indicate that the Court was more (less) politically influenced than expected; the theoretical range of the scale ranges from −1.0 to 1.0; see Table 7.1 for the items that make up the perceptions scale; this figure is based on model estimates in Table A7.4.

identity, there is no significant difference in expectations and perceptions, on average. At high levels of engagement, by contrast, we find a pattern consistent with directionally motivated reasoning. Specifically, the expectations–perceptions gap for liberal respondents is negative and statistically different from zero (it is negative but statistically insignificant for health insurance preferences). This means that very liberal, strong Democrats' perceptions of the Court's actual decision-making in the *NFIB* case were more positive than their expectations prior to the decision (by 7 percentage points). Among the engaged, conservative Republicans and those with conservative health insurance preferences show the exact opposite pattern, and an even larger change from pre- to post-decision. Indeed, very conservative, strong Republicans' perceptions of the Court's decision-making were 15 percentage points more politicized than their expectations prior to the decision, while those with conservative insurance preferences were nine points more cynical. The pattern for moderately engaged citizens is very similar, though with smaller magnitudes.

Summary of Observational Results

Across four very different studies we have found support for our theoretical expectations. When citizens disagree with the Court – either in general, or with specific cases or justices – they see the Court as more politicized in its decision-making procedures. Moreover, this relationship tends to be stronger among politically engaged citizens. This is consistent with the claim that the engaged are more motivated and able to rationalize their beliefs about the Court by appealing to shared values and norms.

Nonetheless, these results are not dispositive. The biggest threat to inference, in the first three studies at least, is reverse causality: it is possible that citizens who see the Court as politicized are more likely to see themselves as ideologically distant from the Court as well. While we find this theory less plausible than our own, it is consistent with the data. The reverse causality critique seems less applicable to the TAPS study as we examined changes in perceptions of politicization across a short span of time, in response to a single decision, and we held disagreement constant by measuring it prior to the decision. Still, it might be the case that the results are unique to this one decision. As suggested by Christenson and Glick (2015a), Chief Justice Roberts' ruling in this case was widely perceived as "strategic" in the sense of seeking to minimize public backlash. Perhaps the positive gap between perceptions and expectations of politicization among conservatives and Republicans is simply a legitimate response to a surprising case of actual politicized decision-making – that is, they accurately perceived the nature of the decision, and this was particularly true for politically engaged and attentive citizens. This does not, of course, explain the *negative* gap between perceptions and expectations among liberal Democrats for whom a motivated reasoning account fits better. Still, given that the effect for Republicans is quite a bit stronger, it would be useful to find additional evidence for directionally motivated reasoning.

Limitations notwithstanding, and taken together, we think these observational analyses are useful and provide support for our theory. We turn now to a very different methodological approach to exploring these dynamics.

EXPERIMENTAL DATA

The primary problem facing our observational work is reverse causality: perceptions of disagreement may be endogenous to procedural perceptions. Solving this problem requires experimentally manipulating disagreement. Happily, we have two experimental studies available that manipulated this variable, and which also have measures of procedural perceptions: the 2009 TESS, and the 2016 YouGov experiment (2016 YGS). Further, both studies included orthogonal experimental manipulations of procedural information, thus allowing for a direct test of the process-based approach alongside our own. We examine each of these studies in turn.

The 2009 TESS Study

We described the 2009 TESS study in detail in Chapter 5. Recall that we randomly assigned respondents to receive one of two possible treatments that varied information regarding the outcome of a case before the Supreme Court concerning government monitoring of citizens' communications (the exact wording of the treatments can be found in Table 5.1). The outcome was either "liberal" (restricts the government's ability to monitor citizens) or "conservative" (upholds the government's ability to monitor citizens). Recall that a second experimental factor was also included in this study that is directly relevant to the present chapter. Specifically, we randomly assigned respondents to receive procedural information regarding the decision – that is, *how* the decision was made by the justices. In the levels of this factor, we attempted to capture some of the most important considerations identified by previous work as relevant to citizens' judgments about the legitimacy of Court decisions (e.g., Baird and Gangl 2006; Gibson and Caldeira 2009a; Hibbing and Theiss-Morse 1995, 2002). The text of these can be found in Table 5.1 and corresponds with no procedural information (a control condition), counter-majoritarian (emphasizing that the Court struck down Congressional legislation), ideological (use of justices' ideology to decide), bargaining and compromise (justices made deals to come to an agreement), or legalistic (followed the law and precedent). If procedural justice theory is correct in this context, then information regarding the procedures used by the justices to come to a decision should have a large effect on perceptions of the decision's procedural fairness. In contrast, if our theory of directionally motivated reasoning is correct, *outcome* information should have a large effect on procedural perceptions, and this should be particularly true for politically engaged citizens. It is also possible, of course, that both theories contribute important insights, and thus both procedural and outcome information matter.

Unfortunately, these data do not contain a full set of procedural perceptions items. One item, however, may serve our purposes reasonably well. Specifically, respondents were asked the following: "Do you feel that the Court's decision is consistent or inconsistent with the U.S. Constitution?" Response options ranged on a four-point scale from "very consistent" to "very inconsistent." While imperfect, this item indirectly taps procedural perceptions. That is, if the Court's decision-making process is purely legalistic in the sense discussed in Chapter 2, then the decision is consistent with the Constitution almost by definition. The question thus asks whether the Court is doing what it is presumably supposed to do: examining the facts of the case and their relationship to the Constitution and precedent.[11]

We estimated two models in which we regressed this item on each of our two measures of decision disagreement from Chapter 4. The first is based on policy preferences (based on a four-point scale) and is coded to range from strong agreement to strong disagreement. The second is based on left–right identity (average of partisanship and ideology) and is recoded so that higher values indicate political identities expected to disagree with the decision. These data do not have a direct measure of political engagement, so we instead rely on education as an indirect indicator. We constructed a dummy variable coded one for respondents with a bachelor's degree or higher and coded zero for all others. We included both this dummy and its interaction with decision disagreement in the models. We also included dummy variables for our procedural treatments, with the control (no procedural information) as the excluded category. Each dummy thus encodes the mean difference in procedural perceptions between the respective condition and the procedural control condition. Finally, we included the same control variables as in Chapter 5. Since the dependent variable is ordinal, we estimated an ordered logit model.

As expected, we find significant interactions between decision disagreement and political engagement (proxied by education) in both models. Since ordered logit coefficients are difficult to interpret, we converted these into predicted probabilities and plot the results in Figure 7.5. The

[11] One might argue that this question simply taps respondents' preferences over the issue at hand, but this is not quite right. It is possible that one can both dislike a policy *and* agree that the policy is Constitutional. To take a recent example, one may strongly disagree with travel or immigration bans on individuals living in certain parts of the world, but nonetheless believe that the president has the authority to enact such bans. Still, we acknowledge that the item leaves much to be desired.

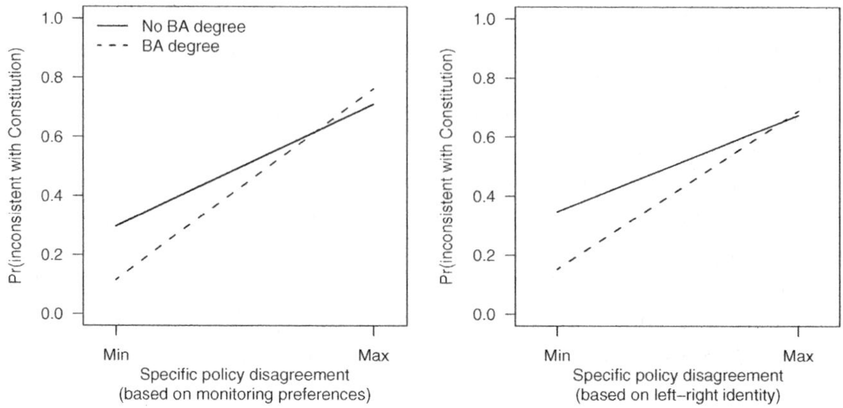

FIGURE 7.5 The probability of stating that the Court's decision is inconsistent with the Constitution across specific policy disagreement and levels of education, 2009 TESS experiment. This figure is based on model estimates in Table A7.5.

x-axes represent degree of disagreement with the Court's decision, while the y-axes represent the probability that the respondent said the decision was "inconsistent" with the Constitution – that is, the probability they gave a response of three or four on the four-point scale. Overall, we see a very large and statistically significant effect of decision disagreement on procedural perceptions, but the effect is also quite a bit larger for respondents with a BA degree relative to those without. For the latter group, a change from low to high policy disagreement is associated with a 41-percentage-point increase in the probability of saying "inconsistent," while for the former group, this increase is 64 points. The estimates are 33 and 54 points, respectively, for the left–right identity measure of disagreement. As with the observational studies, we can also consider the interaction from the perspective of the effect of education at different levels of policy disagreement. We find that education increases perceptions of procedural fairness, but *only* when the individual agrees with the decision. When the individual disagrees, there is no relationship between education and perceptions. Thus, in both cases, we find strong support for the idea that decision disagreement leads to motivated delegitimization of the decision and also strong support for the moderating role of engagement. Importantly, the experimental design ensures that this pattern cannot be attributed to the effect of procedural judgments on disagreement, because disagreement itself was randomly assigned and is thus exogenous by design. All information about this decision, save the outcome, is identical for those randomly assigned to agreement or disagreement.

We find no significant effects of the counter-majoritarian, ideological, or bargaining and compromise procedural conditions, relative to the procedural control condition. In other words, respondents do not seem to base their judgments of procedural justice on information concerning these considerations. We do, however, find that information suggesting a legalistic character to the decision-making process (the last procedural condition) does have a significant effect on procedural perceptions, and in the direction expected by procedural justice theory. Respondents randomly assigned to the legalistic decision condition were over 12 percentage points more likely to say that the decision is consistent with the Constitution than those assigned to the procedural control condition. Thus, while the effect of disagreement with the outcome is quite a bit larger in magnitude, at least one type of procedural information has a substantively important effect on perceptions of procedural fairness, namely, information that the justices engaged primarily in legalistic reasoning. These results are consistent with Baird and Gangl's (2006) prior experimental work using a less representative sample.

The 2016 YGS

For our final analysis of the chapter, we return to the 2016 YGS study discussed in Chapters 5 and 6. Recall that this study includes two separate experiments: the party polarization experiment discussed in the previous chapter and the procedural information experiment discussed in Chapter 5. We focus on the latter here. We randomly assigned respondents to read about one of several liberal or conservative Supreme Court decisions (see Table 5.2). That is, each respondent read about one decision, that decision was either liberal or conservative, and within their respective ideology category, respondents were randomly assigned to one of four possible decisions. In the procedural experiment, they were also randomly assigned to receive one of three treatments concerning the way in which the justices went about making the decision: no procedural information, procedurally positive information, or procedurally negative information. We list the exact wording for each procedural treatment in Table 5.3. Finally, some respondents were randomly assigned to a true control, and received no decision information at all – that is, they simply responded to the dependent variables.

TABLE 7.2 *Items measuring perceptions of politicization in 2016 YGS*

"We would like to know whether you agree or disagree with the following assessments of how the Supreme Court makes decisions." [agree strongly, agree moderately, agree a little, disagree a little, disagree moderately, disagree strongly]

- The Supreme Court makes decisions fairly and objectively
- The Supreme Court's decisions are influenced by partisanship and ideology
- The Supreme Court's decisions are influenced by special interests
- The Supreme Court makes decisions based on legal and constitutional principles

In Chapter 5, our focus was on Court-curbing, but this experiment also included several items tapping procedural perceptions. These are listed in Table 7.2 and formed a reliable scale ($\alpha = 0.72$). As seen, they differ from the item used in the 2009 TESS study in that they tap perceptions of the way the Court goes about making its decisions in general, rather than on the specific case at hand. In turn, this represents a more demanding test of our theory: we examine how information about a single decision affects general perceptions of the Court's procedural fairness. We operationalize disagreement with the Court's decision identically to Chapters 5 and 6, using left–right identity (averaging partisanship and ideology).[12]

We estimated a series of regression models using the same operationalization of political engagement, and including the same set of control variables, as in Chapters 5 and 6. Since policy disagreement with the Court's decision cannot be calculated in the true control condition, we begin by considering the effect of each procedural treatment relative to the true control and ignore (for the moment) our hypotheses concerning disagreement with case outcomes. This allows for a simple test of the hypothesis, derived from procedural justice theory, that positive procedural information should decrease perceptions of politicization and negative procedural information should have the opposite effect. This first regression model includes three dummy variables for the no procedural information, positive information, and negative information conditions, with the true control condition as the excluded baseline.

The results for this model provide only weak support for the process-based approach. Relative to the true control condition, there is indeed

[12] Recall that there are no policy-specific attitudes in these data.

a statistically significant effect of receiving negative procedural information on perceptions of Court politicization. Specifically, respondents assigned to the negative condition were 5 percentage points more negative in their assessments of the Court's general decision procedures than those assigned to the control. This effect is small but meaningful and statistically distinguishable from zero. However, the coefficients for both the no procedural information and the positive information conditions are also positive, indicating that exposure to these conditions also increased perceptions of politicization. Moreover, while not significantly different from zero, these treatment effects are not statistically distinguishable from the negative procedural information condition either. Thus, while we have some evidence that negative information may have a deleterious effect on perceptions of the Court's procedural fairness, this effect cannot be disentangled from that of receiving *any* information about a Court decision, regardless of the nature of the accompanying procedural information. Taken together, these results do not provide much support for the process-based perspective.

We turn now to models that include decision disagreement, and thus exclude the true control condition. We treat the no procedural information condition as the baseline comparison group for the positive and negative procedural treatments. In contrast to our previous studies, we find no support for an interaction between disagreement and political engagement. While the relationship is in the expected direction, it does not attain statistical significance. The unconditional effect of policy disagreement is, however, significant. A change from minimum to maximum is associated with a 5 percentage point increase in perceptions of politicization. Thus, consistent with our theory, respondents randomly assigned to read about a disliked Court decision are significantly more likely to see the Court as politicized as a general matter. As with the 2009 TESS study, we can be confident of the causal role of the decision direction itself, as it was randomly assigned.

Nonetheless, the effect size is much smaller than our estimates from the preceding studies. One reason is that we are examining the effect of only one decision on *general* perceptions. Moreover, we are using a general measure of policy disagreement (left–right identity) rather than an issue-specific measure. Further exploration reveals that this is also due, in part, to the baseline skepticism about the Court's procedures among right-leaning citizens, as well as an asymmetry in how respondents reacted to decisions that were consistent and inconsistent with their partisan and ideological leanings. Specifically, we estimated separate models for liberal and conservative decision conditions and included left–right identity as our key independent variable. Identity was coded so that higher values indicate more right-wing orientations. We thus expect this variable to be positively related to perceptions of politicization in the liberal decision condition and negatively related to perceptions in the conservative condition. Since we are now coding identity in its "raw" form, we can also consider its relationship with perceptions of politicization in the true control condition, in which respondents received no decision information at all. The results are plotted in Figure 7.6.

As the figure demonstrates, there is a positive relationship between left–right identity and perceptions of politicization in the control condition, which implies that conservative Republicans are more skeptical of the Court in 2016, independent of any additional information about decision outcomes. This is consistent with our findings with these data in the previous empirical chapters, which examined support for Court-curbing. Moreover, we find no change (compared to the control) in perceptions of politicization among either liberal Democrats or conservative Republicans in conditions where the decision was *consistent* with

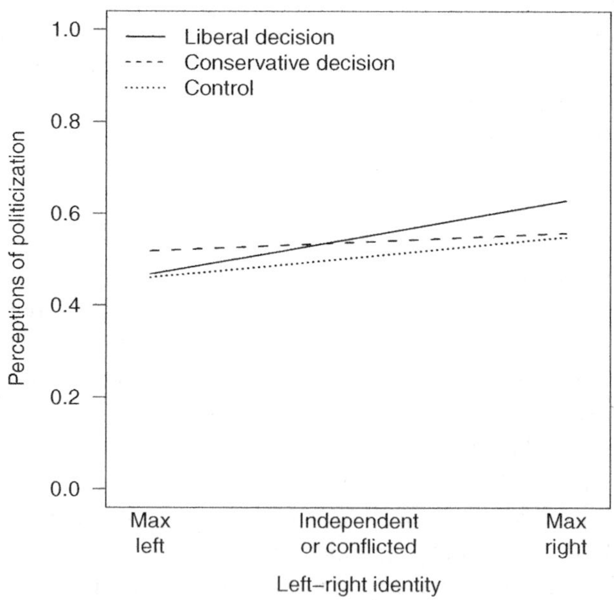

FIGURE 7.6 Perceptions of politicization across left–right identity and the ideological direction of the Court's decision, 2016 YGS experiment. See Table 7.2 for the items that make up the perceptions scale; this figure is based on model estimates in Table A7.6.

their identities. That is, receiving congenial information about a Court decision did not enhance perceptions of the Court's procedural fairness and objectivity. However, we do find increases in perceptions of politicization (relative to the control) among citizens on both the left and right in conditions where the decision was *inconsistent* with their identities. For very liberal, strong Democrats, perceptions of politicization were 6 percentage points higher in the conservative decision condition relative to the control condition (95% CI = [-0.01, 0.12]). For very conservative, strong Republicans, perceptions were 8 points higher in the liberal decision condition than in the control condition (95% CI = [0.01, 0.15]).

Taken together, the results of this second experiment provide qualified support for our theory. First, we find little support for the process-based perspective: the provision of positive and negative procedural information has similar effects on perceptions of politicization. Rather than procedural information affecting perceptions of politicization, this study suggests that simply being exposed to any decision information may reduce perceived fairness. Second, we find a significant increase in perceptions of politicization as a function of partisan and ideological disagreement with the Court's decisions. The effect of decision outcomes on perceptions of politicization was also driven largely by exposure to uncongenial (rather than congenial) decisions. This is itself interesting, as it suggests (contra positivity theory) a negativity (rather than positivity) bias in citizens' reactions to decisions. This finding is again consistent with the work of Christenson and Glick (2019). While the effects are smaller here than in previous studies, it is also important to emphasize that we examined *general* procedural perceptions rather than decision-specific perceptions. This study provides no support, however, for our hypothesis that political engagement moderates the impact of policy disagreement.

CONCLUSIONS

In this chapter we attempted to reconcile the findings of preceding chapters with procedural justice theory. We argued that procedural perceptions do not drive acceptance of decision outcomes (i.e., legitimation). Rather, acceptance of decision outcomes – which is primarily based on policy agreement – drives procedural perceptions. Citizens care primarily about getting the policy outcomes they desire, and they use procedural considerations as a way to bolster liked decisions and denigrate and delegitimize disliked decisions. When the Court issues congenial decisions, citizens extoll the virtues of the process by which the outcome was reached.

Conversely, in the face of uncongenial decisions, they argue that the justices were unduly influenced by outside pressure groups and fell victim to biased and unfair forms of reasoning that ignore law, precedent, and the Constitution. In other words, citizens engage in motivated defense of their position on the outcome by selectively highlighting positive or negative procedural information. In doing so, they construct justifications for engaging in, or defending the Court from, curbing attacks. Moreover, this tendency is often (though not always) stronger among the most politically active and knowledgeable citizens.

Our theory and findings turn procedural justice theory on its head: procedural perceptions are, to a large extent, endogenous rationalizations rather than prime movers. While we find some evidence for the causal importance of procedural information on procedural perceptions, it is quite a bit weaker in its influence, on average, than agreement or disagreement with the decision outcome. Evidence for our conclusions comes from four observational studies – including one panel dataset surrounding a major decision on the Affordable Care Act – and two very different experiments separated by seven years. As in previous chapters, the methodological diversity underpinning our conclusions gives us confidence that we have hit on an important fact about American public opinion of the Supreme Court.

APPENDIX

TABLE A7.1 *Models of perceptions of politicization, 2005 ASCS*

	(1)	(2)
Intercept	0.87 (0.06)	0.73 (0.03)
Age	−0.06 (0.03)	−0.07 (0.02)
Female	0.01 (0.01)	0.03 (0.01)
Black	0.03 (0.03)	0.02 (0.02)
Hispanic	0.02 (0.03)	0.00 (0.02)
Some college	−0.02 (0.02)	−0.03 (0.01)
BA degree	−0.05 (0.02)	−0.06 (0.01)
Post-grad	−0.04 (0.03)	−0.06 (0.02)
Income	−0.05 (0.03)	−0.07 (0.02)
Engagement	−0.43 (0.12)	−0.23 (0.05)
Political trust	−0.11 (0.03)	−0.07 (0.02)
Religiosity	0.02 (0.02)	0.05 (0.02)
Policy disagreement (interval)	−0.07 (0.08)	
Policy disagreement (interval) × Engagement	0.35 (0.18)	
Policy disagreement (nominal)		
Tacit agreement		−0.06 (0.03)
Moderate disagreement		0.04 (0.04)
Strong disagreement		0.06 (0.03)
Policy disagreement (nominal) × Engagement		
Tacit agreement × Engagement		0.11 (0.07)
Moderate disag. × Engagement		0.10 (0.08)
Strong disag. × Engagement		0.11 (0.07)
R^2	0.15	0.16
N	605	1433

Notes: Data are from the 2005 ASCS (see Chapter 3 for descriptions of all datasets). Entries are ordinary least squares estimates and standard errors (in parentheses). The dependent variable is the perceptions of politicization scale (see Table 7.1); higher values indicate greater perceptions of politicization. Post-stratification weights are used in both analyses.

TABLE A7.2 *Models of perceptions of politicization, 2011 FTS*

	(1)	(2)
Intercept	0.81 (0.06)	0.87 (0.06)
Age	−0.01 (0.04)	−0.01 (0.04)
Female	−0.01 (0.02)	−0.01 (0.02)
Black	−0.02 (0.03)	−0.00 (0.04)
Hispanic	0.04 (0.03)	0.02 (0.03)
HS degree	0.00 (0.03)	−0.02 (0.03)
Some college	−0.07 (0.03)	−0.08 (0.03)
BA degree	−0.09 (0.04)	−0.09 (0.04)
Post-grad	−0.08 (0.04)	−0.08 (0.04)
Class	−0.00 (0.02)	0.00 (0.02)
Engagement	−0.14 (0.06)	−0.22 (0.06)
Rule of law	−0.12 (0.06)	−0.13 (0.06)
Liberty over order	−0.14 (0.05)	−0.15 (0.05)
Tolerance	−0.07 (0.04)	−0.07 (0.04)
Religiosity	−0.02 (0.03)	−0.02 (0.03)
Policy disagreement (distance)	0.20 (0.15)	
Policy disagreement (distance) × Engagement	−0.05 (0.19)	
Policy disagreement (nominal)		
Too liberal		0.03 (0.08)
Too conservative		−0.13 (0.07)
Policy disagreement (nominal) × Engagement		
Too lib. × Engagement		0.11 (0.10)
Too con. × Engagement		0.30 (0.10)
R^2	0.20	0.23
N	697	730

Notes: Data are from the 2011 FTS. Entries are ordinary least squares estimates and standard errors (in parentheses). The dependent variable is the perceptions of politicization scale (see Table 7.1); higher values indicate greater perceptions of politicization. Post-stratification weights are used in both analyses.

TABLE A7.3 *Models of perceptions of politicization, 2006 Alito study*

	(1)	(2)
Intercept	0.44 (0.07)	0.46 (0.08)
Age	-0.09 (0.04)	-0.17 (0.04)
Female	0.01 (0.02)	0.02 (0.02)
Black	0.04 (0.03)	0.01 (0.03)
Hispanic	-0.01 (0.05)	0.00 (0.05)
HS degree	-0.02 (0.04)	-0.00 (0.04)
Some college	-0.04 (0.04)	-0.01 (0.04)
BA degree	-0.02 (0.05)	0.00 (0.05)
Post-grad	-0.02 (0.05)	0.03 (0.05)
Income	-0.06 (0.04)	-0.08 (0.04)
Engagement	-0.10 (0.04)	0.08 (0.04)
Religiosity	-0.09 (0.04)	-0.08 (0.04)
Rule of law	0.04 (0.06)	0.06 (0.06)
Support for multiparty system	0.11 (0.08)	0.06 (0.08)
Tolerance	-0.05 (0.04)	-0.06 (0.04)
Liberty over order	-0.01 (0.07)	0.02 (0.07)
Policy disagreement (distance)	0.03 (0.09)	
Policy disagreement (distance) × Engagement	0.33 (0.11)	
Partisanship		-0.02 (0.07)
Partisanship × Engagement		-0.15 (0.08)
R^2	0.25	0.19
N	271	294

Notes: Data are from the 2006 Alito study. Entries are ordinary least squares estimates and standard errors (in parentheses). The dependent variable is the procedural expectations scale (see Table 7.1); higher values indicate expectations in the political direction. For partisanship, higher values are more Republican. Post-stratification weights are used in both analyses.

TABLE A7.4 *Models of procedural expectations–perceptions gap surrounding the* NFIB *(health care) ruling, May and July 2012 waves of TAPS*

	(1)	(2)
Intercept	−0.03 (0.07)	0.03 (0.06)
Age	0.10 (0.04)	0.10 (0.04)
Female	−0.02 (0.01)	−0.02 (0.01)
Black	−0.07 (0.02)	−0.05 (0.02)
Hispanic	0.05 (0.02)	0.05 (0.02)
HS degree	−0.03 (0.04)	−0.02 (0.04)
Some college	−0.04 (0.03)	−0.04 (0.03)
BA degree	−0.05 (0.03)	−0.04 (0.03)
Post-grad	−0.04 (0.04)	−0.04 (0.04)
Income	0.00 (0.03)	−0.00 (0.03)
Engagement	−0.04 (0.06)	−0.12 (0.06)
Rule of law	0.10 (0.04)	0.08 (0.04)
Liberty over order	−0.03 (0.04)	−0.04 (0.03)
Tolerance	−0.03 (0.03)	−0.02 (0.03)
Religiosity	0.02 (0.02)	0.01 (0.02)
Health insurance preferences	−0.02 (0.06)	
Health insurance preferences × Engagement	0.14 (0.08)	
Left–right identity		−0.09 (0.08)
Left–right identity × Engagement		0.30 (0.10)
R^2	0.07	0.08
N	1250	1250

Notes: Data are from the May 2012 and July 2012 waves of TAPS. Entries are ordinary least squares estimates and standard errors (in parentheses). The dependent variable is the expectations-perceptions gap regarding how the Court will rule on *NFIB* (see Table 7.1); positive values indicate that the Court was more politicized than expected.

TABLE A7.5 *Models of perceptions of politicization, 2009 TESS*

	(1)	(2)
Age	0.07 (0.27)	0.18 (0.26)
Female	0.02 (0.12)	0.05 (0.11)
Black	−0.30 (0.22)	−0.16 (0.21)
Hispanic	−0.07 (0.21)	−0.16 (0.21)
BA degree	−1.19 (0.23)	−1.10 (0.27)
Income	−0.28 (0.27)	−0.20 (0.27)
Procedural experimental conditions		
Counter-majoritarian	0.15 (0.19)	−0.04 (0.19)
Ideological	−0.08 (0.18)	−0.17 (0.17)
Politicized	−0.07 (0.18)	−0.12 (0.18)
Legalistic	−0.55 (0.18)	−0.66 (0.18)
Policy disagreement (monitoring preferences)	1.78 (0.21)	
Policy disagreement (mon. pref.) × BA degree	1.46 (0.38)	
Policy disagreement (left–right identity)		1.38 (0.28)
Policy disagreement (l-r ident.) × BA degree		1.16 (0.46)
Pseudo-R^2	0.08	0.04
N	1042	1046

Notes: Data are from the 2009 TESS study. Entries are ordered logit estimates and standard errors (in parentheses). The dependent variable is the perception of whether the ruling was consistent with the Constitution; higher values indicate more politicized perceptions (inconsistent with Constitution).

TABLE A7.6 *Models of perceptions of politicization, 2016 YGS*

	All conditions	All decision conditions	Liberal decisions	Conservative decisions	Control
Intercept	0.45 (0.03)	0.48 (0.04)	0.41 (0.05)	0.55 (0.05)	0.42 (0.06)
Age	0.06 (0.03)	0.09 (0.03)	0.10 (0.04)	0.07 (0.04)	−0.07 (0.06)
Female	−0.02 (0.01)	−0.02 (0.01)	−0.01 (0.02)	−0.03 (0.02)	0.02 (0.03)
Black	−0.05 (0.02)	−0.05 (0.02)	0.02 (0.03)	−0.08 (0.03)	−0.01 (0.05)
Hispanic	−0.01 (0.02)	−0.02 (0.02)	−0.04 (0.03)	0.01 (0.03)	0.07 (0.06)
HS degree	0.01 (0.02)	−0.00 (0.03)	0.00 (0.04)	−0.00 (0.04)	0.02 (0.05)
Some college	0.00 (0.03)	−0.02 (0.03)	−0.00 (0.05)	−0.03 (0.04)	0.06 (0.06)
BA degree	−0.01 (0.03)	−0.01 (0.03)	−0.01 (0.05)	−0.01 (0.04)	−0.06 (0.06)
Post-grad	0.01 (0.03)	−0.01 (0.03)	−0.02 (0.05)	0.02 (0.05)	0.08 (0.07)
Income	0.03 (0.05)	0.06 (0.06)	0.14 (0.08)	−0.06 (0.08)	−0.12 (0.16)
Religiosity	0.06 (0.02)	0.06 (0.02)	0.04 (0.03)	0.04 (0.03)	−0.01 (0.04)
Engagement	0.04 (0.02)	0.02 (0.02)	0.01 (0.03)	0.04 (0.03)	0.14 (0.05)
No process info	0.03 (0.02)				
Negative process info	0.05 (0.02)	0.01 (0.01)	0.02 (0.02)	−0.00 (0.02)	
Positive process info	0.02 (0.02)	−0.02 (0.01)	−0.02 (0.02)	−0.01 (0.02)	
Policy disagreement		0.05 (0.02)			
Left–right identity			0.16 (0.03)	0.04 (0.03)	0.09 (0.05)
R^2	0.04	0.06	0.11	0.07	0.12
N	1250	1071	542	529	179

Notes: Data are from the 2016 YGS. Entries are ordinary least squares estimates and standard errors (in parentheses). The dependent variable is the scale of perceptions of politicization (see Table 7.2); higher values indicate more politicized perceptions. "Policy disagreement" is left–right identity coded relative to the direction of the ruling, where higher values indicate greater disagreement with the ruling. For "left–right identity," higher values are more conservative/Republican (see text for details). Fixed effects for the rulings are specified in models 2–4 but not reported in this table.

8

Reconsidering the Public Foundations of Judicial Independence

In this book we have sought to shed light on when and why citizens support measures to curb the Supreme Court. We situated our work in the context of two overarching frameworks – policy versus process-based accounts of Court-curbing – that often make competing predictions. The process-based approach emphasizes the "wide and deep reservoir of goodwill" that the Court enjoys in the public mind. In this view, citizens see the Court as procedurally just and fulfilling a unique and important role in the American political system. In turn, they defend the institution from politically motivated attacks by elite actors. The policy-based approach, by contrast, argues that citizens are only weakly principled and care most about getting policy, partisan, and ideological victories – especially in times of sharp polarization – even if this means subverting the power and independence of the Court. The outcome of this debate is critical to our understanding of the Court's legitimacy in the mass public and its power vis-à-vis the other institutions of American government.

On the one hand, citizens can serve as "guardians of judicial independence" by punishing elite actors for subverting the Court's power in the political system. In this way, the public can be an important source of capital for the Court – a credible threat – as it engages strategically with other institutions. On the other hand, the public can operate as a *constraint* on judicial power, by tolerating or actively supporting elite efforts to attack the Court and its decisions. Anticipating lack of public support, the justices may adjust their decision-making to stay within the bounds of public opinion and the preferences of the legislature and executive. The Court's policymaking discretion is thus directly related to its degree of institutional support among citizens. We return to these big picture themes later in this chapter, but we first offer a broad summary of our primary conclusions and contributions to the literature.

SUMMARY OF PRIMARY CONTRIBUTIONS

Conceptual Contributions

We believe our book makes two significant conceptual contributions to the literature on public attitudes toward courts. First, we have sought to distinguish the concepts of diffuse support, legitimacy, and institutional loyalty from both support for court-curbing and procedural perceptions of judicial decision-making. Past work has often conflated these in practice. For example, a common approach is to create a "diffuse support" scale that averages opposition to curbing (e.g., doing away with the Court) with procedural perceptions (e.g., the Court is too mixed up in politics).[1] Regardless of one's preferred theoretical approach, we think it is critical to distinguish support for or opposition to Court-curbing from procedural perceptions. From the process-based perspective, these perceptions are an important influence on willingness to curb, while from the policy-based perspective they are an endogenous rationalization. In both cases, these are distinct concepts that occupy different places in models of public opinion. By keeping the two separate, we can test competing predictions arising from different theories (as we do, for example, in Chapter 7).

Importantly, we also argue for a clear conceptual and operational distinction between "opposition to Court-curbing" and "institutional legitimacy." This point is worth emphasizing. The Court is "legitimate" if people believe it has rightful authority to render rulings for the polity. For this reason, citizens who see the Court as legitimate will tend to oppose Court-curbing. But people may also oppose curbing simply because it produces congenial policy outputs. As we have argued, observational equivalence plagues attempts at inferring legitimacy based on support for or opposition to Court-curbing. This point is particularly important given that the Court may behave strategically to stay within the bounds of public opinion. Specifically, if the Court knows that it lacks public support it may change its behavior to avoid curbing attacks (Clark 2011). There is thus an equilibrium in which many citizens see the Court

[1] As we discussed in Chapters 1 and 2, these scales have also used "trust." But the point we are making here relates specifically to procedural perceptions.

as far from legitimate yet still oppose Court-curbing because they largely get what they want in terms of policy outcomes. This implies that legitimacy cannot be measured directly on surveys by asking about Court-curbing because we cannot know whether opposition to curbing is *instrumental* (the Court is delivering congenial outputs) or *principled* (the Court is perceived to have rightful authority). A corollary to this is that institutional legitimacy is not a dependent variable to be included in regression models but must be inferred from behavior in situations where respecting the Court's authority requires foregone political benefits. Perceived legitimacy is like political tolerance in this respect: it can only be observed under pressure. In practice, this means that legitimacy is put to its strongest test by comparing support for Court-curbing between citizens who differ only in terms of whether they are policy "winners" or "losers" (Gibson 2015).

An empirical focus on Court-curbing (as opposed to the more abstract notion of legitimacy) is also useful because it cuts to the heart of questions that motivate the literature in the first place: to what extent is the public willing to defend the Court's power and independence in the political system? When people support attacks on the Court, they are sending a signal that they want to rein in the Court to better reflect majoritarian preferences – they want more democratic accountability. When they oppose such attacks, they are expressing a preference for a robust, independent role for the Court so that it can act as a constraint on other institutions of government. Our focus on this concept also allows us to connect the literature on public opinion more clearly to literatures on judicial decision-making and strategic interaction among the branches.

Our second conceptual contribution is to make the crucial distinction between *narrowly targeted* and *broadly targeted* Court-curbing. Narrow curbing is a circumscribed attack on the Court's authority in the context of a specific ruling or policy area. Broad curbing, by contrast, is an attempt to alter the institution more fundamentally and reduce its independence from majoritarian institutions. While this distinction is often implicit in the literature (e.g., decision acceptance versus opposition to fundamental changes to the Court), we make it a core feature of a unified theoretical framework. We also make a distinction between two forms of policy disagreement: general policy disagreement (disagreement with the broad ideological or partisan direction of the Court) and specific policy disagreement (disagreement with specific rulings or policies). These conceptual distinctions have important implications for our theory, as we hypothesize that general policy disagreement will have a greater impact on broad curbing compared to specific policy disagreement, and specific policy disagreement will have a greater impact on support for narrow relative to broad curbing.

A Reservoir of Goodwill?

Scholars and political commentators often repeat a conventional wisdom that the Court enjoys a deep reservoir of goodwill from the public at large. In Chapter 3, we took a deep dive into baseline public support for the Court looking at various facets of evaluation, including approval, confidence, trust, procedural perceptions, and support for broad and narrow Court-curbing. This was a descriptive analysis of aggregate opinion which provided a setup for our more systematic analyses in subsequent chapters. One robust conclusion is that the reservoir of goodwill among the public is not as deep and wide as many seem to think. That is, even if we assume that every person who opposes Court-curbing does so because they see the Court as legitimate (a tenuous assumption for the reasons previously discussed), the public's degree of loyalty to the Court is not as strong as commonly believed.

We reported declining support for the Court over the last two decades in terms of approval, confidence, and measures of broad Court-curbing. Supreme Court approval currently hovers around just 50 percent. The percentage having "a great deal" or "quite a lot" of confidence in the Court has declined to under 40 percent in recent years; the same levels apply to satisfaction with the direction of the Court's policymaking. On procedural perceptions, a significant share of the public sees the Court in political terms. There is certainly not broad-based subscription to a "myth of legality" – citizens realize that justices rely on politics and ideology when making decisions – though we also show that citizens believe that law matters in Court decisions. In this sense, citizens subscribe to a hybrid model: justices make decisions on the basis of both law and politics.

We also found interesting differences in levels of support among Court-curbing options. We found striking levels of enthusiasm for majoritarian control over the Court, such as public referenda on Court decisions and retention elections for justices. While certain measures of broad curbing receive only minority support, we found it surprising that opposition to some of the "hardest" items, like "doing away with the Court" or "issues reduced," is only 50–60 percent in recent years. For narrow curbing, baseline opposition to giving the Court the last word on constitutional issues was quite high (but lower when compared to Congress), while support for noncompliance and jurisdiction stripping were typically lower. There is perhaps an irony in these patterns: the public often shows higher baseline support for what are typically seen as more extreme forms of curbing (e.g., support for retention elections versus support for noncompliance with single decisions).

In sum, the Court's level of baseline support is not critically low, but neither is it "wide and deep." This is important because the baseline numbers represent the most optimistic portrait of the public's institutional loyalty, as well as a "cushion" the Court can count on if it makes unpopular decisions (Gibson and Nelson 2015b). As we have argued and shown, many citizens oppose curbing simply because they agree (or don't strongly disagree) with the Court's current output, but they readily flip to support when it suits their political goals. This suggests that the Court is more vulnerable to serious attacks on its institutional integrity than previously thought.

The Impact of Policy Disagreement on Support for Court-Curbing

Across several empirical studies using diverse research designs, we found a robust effect of policy disagreement on support for Court-curbing. There were a couple of exceptions, of course, but we are confident in our primary substantive takeaway that policy disagreement is a primary basis for Court-curbing. Simply put, when citizens disagree with the Court's policymaking they are quite likely to attack the Court's independence and power. This conclusion challenges process-based conventional wisdom and supports other recent empirical work (e.g., Christenson and Glick 2015a; Nicholson and Hansford 2014).

Our theory and empirics also highlight differences in the effects of different types of policy disagreement. In Chapter 4, we demonstrated that general policy disagreement has a strong impact on support for broadly targeted Court-curbing. This conclusion is supported by reanalysis of several existing national surveys containing multiple measures of disagreement and a diverse array of broad curbing items. Indeed, our comparative analysis of support for various curbing measures is, to our knowledge, a first in the literature. Moreover, we found that disagreement is typically just as strong a predictor of Court-curbing as many of the "usual suspects" highlighted by the literature, including democratic values and political engagement. This is consistent with our framework which argues that citizens are only weakly principled and that sophisticated citizens engage in motivated reasoning to justify their attacks on the Court.

In Chapter 5 we turned to disagreement with single Court decisions. As hypothesized, we found that specific disagreement has a much stronger impact on support for narrow curbing than broad curbing. This makes sense: if disagreement is circumscribed, use a scalpel rather than an axe. Importantly, however, specific disagreement does have a small, but substantively meaningful, impact on support for broad curbing. Specifically, we found evidence for increases in support for broad curbing as a function of single disliked decisions in both experimental data and panel data surrounding major Court rulings. As we have argued, a single decision provides (noisy) information about the general ideological tenor of the Court and policy-concerned citizens will thus update their perceptions to some degree. This likely accounts for the modest, but significant, effects found in several of our studies. This suggests that a *string* of disliked decisions can have large effects on support for broad curbing – a conclusion that is consistent with the results from Chapter 4.

At a more abstract level, our results suggest that perceived Court legitimacy in the mass public is lower than previously thought. As argued in Chapters 1 and 2, legitimacy can only be observed when citizens are put to the test – when political expediency conflicts with institutional loyalty. This is exactly the situation we have examined in our book and we find that citizens are often quite willing to curb the Court. Importantly, we found no evidence that the impact of disagreement is tempered by political engagement. Indeed, the only interaction we found was a *positive* one: engaged citizens in the 2016 YGS are *more* likely to support narrow curbing than the unengaged (see Chapter 6). The lack of a negative interaction with engagement is important because it is the politically active who are most likely to hold their representatives accountable (or not) at the voting booth. It is these citizens who create the incentives for politicians to attack or respect the Court.

Given our findings, we might think of the Court's authority as politicized in the public in the sense that people grant the institution authority when it delivers congenial rulings but seek to rein in its power in the face of uncongenial rulings. This is a far cry from perceived legitimacy as we understand it. Nonetheless, we encourage future work to calibrate more precisely the degree of legitimacy the Court enjoys by expanding our analysis. We think it would be especially useful to explore more deeply the specific types of curbing policies that are most popular in the public or that are most susceptible to elite influence. Where is the Court most vulnerable?

The Impact of Process on Support for Court-Curbing

While our book puts forward a comprehensive theoretical framework concerning the role of policy disagreement, we also unify the claims of much previous literature within a broad process-based approach focused on democratic values, procedural perceptions, and political engagement. And ultimately, we present one of the most comprehensive empirical examinations of the process-based approach in the context of the US Supreme Court. While our results often conflict with the claims of previous work in this tradition, we also find substantial evidence for the importance of political engagement, democratic values, and (to a lesser extent) some forms of procedural information in shaping support for and opposition to Court-curbing.

For instance, we consistently find that political knowledge and engagement reduce baseline support for Court-curbing. This is consistent with positivity theory, which argues that exposure to the Court fosters a perception that it is different from the other institutions in American government, especially Congress (e.g., Gibson and Caldeira 2009a; Gibson, Lodge, and Woodson 2014). And indeed, the engaged are generally less likely to report politicized perceptions of judicial decision-making. Again, however, we find no evidence that engagement tempers the effect of policy disagreement on support for Court-curbing. This is less consistent with positivity theory, which claims that exposure to the legitimizing symbols of the Court offsets discontent with its rulings. Thus, despite lower baseline levels of support for Court-curbing, the engaged are just as *responsive* to policy discontent. Moreover, in Chapter 7, we found evidence that political engagement often moderates the effect of policy disagreement on perceptions of politicization. That is, engaged citizens are especially likely to engage in motivated delegitimization of judicial decision-making, which is consistent with other work on motivated reasoning in political science.

Our analyses in Chapter 4 strongly support the claim that endorsement of democratic values – such as support for the rule of law and minority political rights – reduces enthusiasm for Court-curbing. These variables consistently matter in prior research and our results are consistent with these studies. However, we think our work also raises an important point that is not always fully appreciated in the literature. Specifically, the distribution of these values in the public is highly skewed: most people endorse them and very few people fully reject them. Analyses that examine only "min to max" effects of values overstate their practical importance because very few people fall at the minimum. While it is true that people who reject democratic values are quite hostile to the Court, such people are rare. The flip side of this fact is that democratic values provide only weak protection for the Court. Consistent with a long-standing literature on political tolerance, far more people endorse these values in the abstract than abide them in practice. Indeed, when we examine the practical effects of values on Court-curbing, we find that policy disagreement has similarly sized effects.

Given that both values and policy disagreement matter, we think there is a lot more work to be done at the intersection of these two sets of variables. In particular, we think future research could more systematically explore situations where core values are clearly in conflict with policy-related motives. As discussed in Chapter 2, one possibility is that citizens often fail to appreciate the relevance of their values in specific contexts, such as Supreme Court decisions. Another possibility is that they simply care more about getting policy victories, especially when politics is polarized. Our data cannot clearly adjudicate these two claims. When there is a clear conflict, are people willing to forego narrow political gain to uphold their core democratic values? At what point do citizens "sell out" their principles? To what extent do values and policy disagreement *interact* with one another?

We also think that moving the literature on values forward will require greater attention to conceptualization and measurement. At present, there is only weak theory connecting core values to institutional support for courts. What is the conceptual space of democratic values and, within this space, which are most important to understanding public opinion of the judiciary (and why)? The current literature tends to work with a grab bag of vaguely defined constructs with relatively poor measurement properties. And the subset of values used often changes from one application to the next. We need to start with better theory concerning how (and which) values matter and then develop better measures.

Perhaps our most significant challenge to the literature concerns the impact of procedural aspects of the decision process on support for Court-curbing. Procedural justice theory argues that compliance and institutional loyalty arise from perceptions that the process is fair. People are willing to abide even disliked decisions so long as rulings are reached in a way that is procedurally legitimate. Past work has *measured* procedural perceptions and estimated their effects on legitimacy using primarily cross-sectional data, which raises questions of causal ordering. In our experimental studies in Chapter 5, we directly explored the causal impact of procedural factors on support for Court-curbing. First, in two survey experiments we randomly assigned subjects to positive versus negative procedural conditions. With one exception (a small effect of strict legalism on opposition to curbing), these procedural characteristics had null effects. Our evidence is consistent that policy disagreement more strongly influences support for Court-curbing than the nature of the decision process.

Second, in Chapter 7, we found experimentally that procedural perceptions are *endogenous* to policy disagreement. That is, when citizens dislike a decision, they delegitimize it by attacking the process by which it was reached. We argue that citizens are primarily motivated by securing the policy outcomes they desire. Rather than a genuine cause of support for the Court, procedural perceptions are used to bolster congenial decisions and undermine uncongenial ones. People tend to praise the process by which the outcome was reached when they agree with the policy but criticize procedures when they disagree. Thus, citizens defend their stands on judicial outcomes by selectively emphasizing positive or negative procedural information. In doing so, they construct justifications for engaging in, or defending the Court from, curbing attacks. Taken together, these experimental results strongly question the claim that procedural perceptions are a prime mover of attacks on the Court.

Polarization and Court-Curbing

In Chapter 6, we examined whether partisan polarization amplifies the effect of policy disagreement on support for both narrow and broad Court-curbing. Judgments about Court-curbing do not happen in a political vacuum, as the introductory paragraphs in Chapter 1 make clear. Elected officials representing the major parties criticize and praise Court rulings and citizens are generally susceptible to partisan cues. Importantly, research in political psychology suggests that party polarization at both the elite and mass levels increases the power of mass partisanship at the expense of other considerations. In Chapter 6, we showed that the Court is not exceptional in this respect. Contrary to previous claims, our results indicate that partisan polarization reduces the Court's legitimizing capacity. Specifically, the effect of policy disagreement is much stronger under polarized than unpolarized conditions and when elite partisans directly support Court-curbing actions. We thus expect that the Court will be increasingly caught in the crossfire between polarized partisans. Conservatives want to capitalize on finally achieving a reliable conservative majority on the Court, while liberals fear that crucial progressive gains attained since the start of the New Deal era are at serious risk of being rolled back. Every future appointment on the Court will be a hard-fought battle and the future of the Court will depend crucially on election outcomes – which party wins the White House and controls the Senate.

The consequences of polarization could become even more pronounced if the current Court generates an onslaught of conservative rulings, which could trigger the kinds of threats to the Court's power and independence discussed in the opening pages of Chapter 1 and increase the constituency for such proposals. This scenario could become even more tense if Democrats gain control of both chambers of Congress and the White House. Though the pre-Kavanaugh Court had also been polarized, it had retained at least one swing justice which moderated the Court's outputs – delivering a mix of victories for liberal and conservative causes alike, meaning that one side could not be angry for long. That has changed now that Justice Kavanaugh has replaced Justice Kennedy, the last of the swing justices. For the current Court, all eyes will be on Chief Justice Roberts, whom liberals hope will fill the "swing vote void" and whom conservatives hope will stay true to the conservative cause.

Our polarization results argue strongly against the notion of "Supreme Court exceptionalism." The political force of partisan identity, combined with cues delivered by elected officials, influence public judgments of the Supreme Court in a manner resembling dominant models of American political behavior. While received wisdom casts the public as guardians of judicial independence, our results suggest that partisan polarization reduces citizens' willingness to defend the Court. Rather than serving as guardians, many citizens, in the face of disagreeable rulings, seem perfectly willing to rein in the Court to better reflect their own preferences.

Public Opinion and Judicial Independence

Many argue that the judiciary is the weakest branch in the sense that the Supreme Court has limited powers of implementation and enforcement. This implies that judicial efficacy rests on the willingness of other actors in the executive and legislative branches not only to respect but in many cases actively promote the Court's decisions, even when they disagree with its rulings. Moreover, Congress has substantial power to threaten the Court's longer-term institutional integrity as a means of bringing the justices to heel. Legislators can strip the Court's jurisdiction, change its composition, and restrict its budget through the standard legislative process. It can also make more fundamental changes through Constitutional amendments that alter the interinstitutional balance of power (e.g., restrictions on tenure, getting rid of the Court altogether). While some of the latter moves may have seemed far-fetched even two years ago, they are now openly discussed among influential voices in American politics.

Whatever one's opinion on these issues, the relative weakness of the Court's formal power raises important questions concerning judicial independence. Can the Court exert influence on American politics if it is beholden to actors with often-conflicting interests? It would seem, at least initially, that the Court can only set policy at points agreeable to these actors – that is a far cry from textbook ascriptions of judicial power to the Court. Yet a venerable line of theorizing suggests that independence is possible because there may be substantial costs to policymakers for curbing the Court. In this view, electorally minded political actors refrain from attacking the Court's decisions and institutional integrity because they fear the repercussions of such actions in the voting booth. As Vanberg (2015, 177) explains,

> If the integrity of the judiciary and respect for its decisions are values that a sufficient number of citizens are willing to defend by withdrawing support from policy makers who attack judicial independence, policy makers are likely to conclude that disciplining the court or resisting unwelcome decisions is not worth the potential costs of a public backlash. Public support provides a shield for judicial independence.

The stronger the public's dedication to such values, the stronger the Court's bargaining position. As Justice Elena Kagan puts it, "Every single one of us needs to realize how precious the court's legitimacy is. You know we don't have an army. We don't have any money. The only way we can get people to do what we think they should do is because people respect us."[2]

A direct implication of our results, then, is that the Court has less independence – and thus less power and influence – than it would in a world where citizens were more principled and the received wisdom on public opinion of the judiciary was closer to the mark. Core values, procedural considerations, and exposure to the legitimizing symbols of the Court are only weak constraints on citizens' willingness to curb the Court in the face of policy-related disagreement. Support for broad Court-curbing measures responds meaningfully to sustained policy disagreement with the Court and, to some degree at least, to single salient decisions.

[2] https://apnews.com/5de5bcd5a4744eacae624c703b62664e

Support for noncompliance, legislative attacks, and removal of the Court's jurisdiction increase substantially as a function of disliked decisions. Further, our experiments in Chapter 6 suggest that partisan polarization in American politics – at both the elite and mass levels – directly threatens judicial independence because it reduces citizens' willingness to sanction in-party elites for attacks on the Court. Indeed, when elites back Court-curbing attempts, partisans often follow their lead. Thus, the level of *evinced* respect for the Court and its justices is less than Justice Kagan and others may desire. In turn, formal models suggest the Court must strategically alter its decision-making to stay within the bounds of public opinion and elite preferences. In this sense, the public constrains, rather than expands, the discretion of the Supreme Court in American politics.

POTENTIAL CRITICISMS AND FUTURE DIRECTIONS

In these final sections of the book, we consider possible responses to our policy-based theory and its implications for the public foundations of judicial independence and power. We consider how these responses might alter our conclusions, as well as the broader insights – and opportunities for future research – that these critical treatments generate.

Is Our Study an Outlier?

Our conclusions regarding citizens' willingness to curb the Court conflict with the most influential narrative of the last thirty years of public opinion research on this topic (e.g., Caldeira and Gibson 1992; Gibson and Caldeira 2009a; Gibson, Caldeira, and Baird 1998; Gibson and Nelson 2015b; Tyler and Rasinski 1991). For example, Gibson (2007, 532) argues that

> the U.S. Supreme Court is widely supported by the American people, and that support has little to do with ideology or partisanship. Instead, loyalty toward the institution is grounded in broader commitments to democratic institutions and processes, and more generally in knowledge of the role of the judiciary in the American democratic system ... it appears that the Supreme Court has sufficient institutional legitimacy to be able to continue to perform its assigned role within the American democratic scheme, even within the context of deep substantive divisions within the American mass public.

Similarly, Gibson and Nelson (2015b, 173) conclude that "the legitimacy of the Supreme Court is not much dependent upon the Court making decisions that are pleasing to the American people." In a similar vein, emphasizing process-related factors, Tyler and Rasinski (1991, 626) argue, "The conclusion ... is that procedural justice strongly influences institutional legitimacy and, through it, the acceptance of institutional decisions ... The influence of procedural justice is particularly striking because agreement or disagreement with Supreme Court decisions has little influence on legitimacy." And Peter Irons, while acknowledging that motivated reasoning about Court decisions is common among "cynics" like himself, argues that

> what matters is whether the public continues to believe the court has the authority to make decisions – and whether those decisions are obeyed by both the debate's winners and losers. In this regard, with the notable exception of calls to resist court orders in school desegregation cases in the 1950s and 1960s ... the legitimacy of the institution has never been seriously at risk.[3]

As we noted in Chapter 1, this seems to be the dominant perception among the intelligentsia, to the point that current debates revolve around whether the public affords the Court *more* legitimacy than it deserves.

In turn, the reader may view our findings with some skepticism, as they cut against the prevailing wisdom. Is our work an outlier? We do not think so. We believe our findings are consistent with a broader literature on the Supreme Court within political science and with an emerging line of empirical research that also questions this narrative, even as we extend this work and unify it within a general theoretical framework. For example, our findings are consistent with prior research that documents an important relationship between Court decision-making and aggregate confidence in the Court. As the Court gets further away from aggregate public opinion, the public's confidence in the Court declines (Durr, Martin, and Wolbrecht 2000). Confidence also appears to respond directly to opinion on salient cases (e.g., flag burning and abortion; see Grosskopf and Mondak 1998). As other researchers have pointed out, however, this work relies on measures that only loosely approximate our key construct of interest: support for Court-curbing. Confidence may be closer to "specific support" or performance evaluations than institutional loyalty.[4] Our results are thus complementary to research on confidence, as

[3] He goes on to argue that it is process-related factors – not partisan conflict over issues – that is the real potential threat to the Court's power: "in the wake of the nakedly partisan outcome of Justice Kavanaugh's confirmation, and Trump's relentless and insulting attacks on 'so-called' judges whose decisions he decries, it cannot be said with certainty that the federal courts will weather this Category 5 pounding." www.nbcnews.com/think/opinion/has-supreme-court-lost-its-legitimacy-ncna966211.

[4] See also Benesh (2006) for a study of confidence in state courts.

we clearly demonstrate, across a wide range of tests, that citizen support for Court-curbing also responds strongly to policy disagreement.

Our findings are also consistent with previous empirical work on Court decision-making. As discussed in Chapter 1, Clark (2009, 2011) has made a strong theoretical and empirical case that the introduction of Court-curbing legislation is driven to a substantial extent by public preferences and that the Court alters its decision-making when it senses discontent within the mass public. More specifically, Clark (2011, 132) finds that the ideological motivation of Court-curbing legislation introduced and sponsored by members of Congress is associated with the ideological leaning of the aggregate public. For example, as the public becomes more liberal in the aggregate, liberal legislators are more likely than conservative ones to sponsor Court-curbing bills. Thus, legislators appear to be responding to significant demand for Court-curbing within the public. At the very least, they seem to believe that the public will not *punish* Court-curbing attempts and use these as an opportunity for position-taking on salient issues.

The association between public mood and Court-curbing is reflected in strategic decision-making by the justices. Clark (2011, 221) finds that justices vote more consistently with the ideological direction of Congress when they observe a high volume of Court-curbing legislation (a signal of public discontent). Moreover, he finds a direct effect of aggregate public ideology on Court decision-making: as the public becomes more liberal, the justices vote more liberally, on average. Such a pattern is consistent with the idea that the Court adjusts its decision-making to avoid public discontent, because it is worried about its institutional integrity, which suggests that the public constrains judicial independence.[5] Such strategic responsiveness to public opinion seems *inconsistent* with the idea that public support for the Court is rooted solely in process-based factors. Clark does not, however, provide any direct evidence for the claim that citizens seek to curb the Court in response to ideological drift or disliked

[5] The relationship between Court decision-making and public mood is also consistent with other explanations (Erikson, Mackuen, and Stimson 2002; McGuire and Stimson 2004; Mishler and Sheehan 1993; Stimson, Mackuen, and Erikson 1995). For example, it is possible that the justices and the public are responding to similar societal forces, or that public opinion operates primarily through the nomination of justices via the president (e.g., Norpoth and Segal 1994; Segal and Spaeth 2002). There is evidence, however, that there is a real influence of public opinion on the Court's decision-making that is due to strategic concerns with protecting its institutional integrity (e.g., Casillas, Enns, and Wohlfarth 2011; Hall 2014; Mishler and Sheehan 1996).

decisions. Our book thus provides a valuable empirical complement by demonstrating that demand for Court-curbing does indeed increase as a function of policy-related discontent. Moreover, we extend this work to show that partisan polarization strengthens the dynamic.

Our findings are also consistent with an emerging line of work in the public opinion literature. In a methodologically innovative study, Christenson and Glick (2015a) surveyed a set of respondents before and directly after the Affordable Care Act decision in *NFIB* v. *Sebelius*. They found that respondents' perceptions of their ideological distance from the Court changed because of the decision and that this change in perceptions was associated with changes in institutional support for the Court. Specifically, those who saw themselves as further from the Court after the decision also afforded the Court lower levels of support, while those who found themselves closer to the Court after *NFIB* showed higher levels of institutional loyalty. The authors also embedded an ingenious quasi-experiment: a substantial portion of their respondents received the second wave after a CBS report was released which argued that Chief Justice Roberts had strategically altered his decision (in favor of the individual mandate) as a ploy to protect the Court's legitimacy. Christenson and Glick find that this treatment exacerbated the negative effect of ideological distance on institutional support.

This moderating role of the "Roberts flip" treatment seems, at first, consistent with a process-based approach: negative procedural perceptions hurt the Court's legitimacy, at least among those who see the Court as ideologically distant. Interestingly, however, the treatment also increased the *positive* effect of ideological *proximity*. Among respondents who saw themselves as closer to the Court after *NFIB*, information about Roberts' strategic flip *enhanced* institutional support for the Court. This latter finding is inconsistent with the process-based approach: why would perceptions of politicization increase institutional loyalty? Indeed, Christenson and Glick (2015a) note that the finding was surprising.

By contrast, we think this pattern fits perfectly within our theoretical framework. Looking at the actual treatment materials for the pseudo-experiment (see the authors' supplemental online appendix), they do not simply provide information about Roberts' strategic calculations; they also provide clear partisan and ideological cues and suggest that the decision is highly consequential for partisan and ideological interests in American politics. In other words, the treatment is quite similar (in practice) to our own polarization treatments in Chapter 6.[6] The upshot is that the process-based perspective only explains half of the results from this treatment: citizens who disagreed with the decision became more negative toward the Court when receiving information about non-legalistic decision-making. Process-based theories *cannot* explain why citizens who agreed with the decision showed higher levels of institutional support when learning about the Court's politicization. We think a better interpretation is offered by our theory: the effects of policy agreement and disagreement on, respectively, opposition to and support for Court-curbing increase as a function of perceived partisan and ideological polarization over an issue. Our theory predicts both sides of Christenson and Glick's (2015a) asymmetry.

Clark and Kastellec (2015) also find results consistent with our framework. Specifically, they examine support for two broad curbing measures: restriction on life tenure for the justices and giving Congress and the President the power to reverse Supreme Court decisions on constitutional questions. Their experiment varied the source of support for these proposals: "some people," "some Democrats," or "some Republicans." Among Democratic and Republican identifiers, they find meaningful changes in support for these policies as a function of the source cues with which they are associated. For example, while there is broad support for restricting life tenure, this support drops significantly among partisans who learn that the policy is supported by the opposing party. We see this dynamic as generally consistent with the idea that citizens will oppose broad curbing measures when they perceive that the Court's partisan and ideological direction is consistent with their own. Just as citizens use partisan cues to figure out the ideological implications of complex public policy proposals (e.g., Cohen 2003; Druckman, Peterson, and Slothuus 2013), they may use these cues to determine whether the Court is congenial or uncongenial to their political interests.

In another recent article, Nicholson and Hansford (2014) examine support for narrow Court-curbing in the guise of policy acceptance (akin to support for judicial supremacy): should a specific decision be accepted as the final word on the matter or should there be an effort to challenge and change the decision? Respondents in this study read about

[6] Consider a few examples: "Chief Justice John Roberts initially sided with the Supreme Court's four conservative justices to strike down the heart of President Obama's health care reform law, the Affordable Care Act, but later changed his position and formed an alliance with liberals," "Roberts then withstood a month-long, desperate campaign to bring him back to his original position," and "Leading politicians, including the President himself, had expressed confidence the mandate would be upheld."

a recent Court decision on one of several issues (e.g., gun control). They were assigned to one of three conditions which varied the description of the decision.[7] In the first, they simply read that the "Supreme Court" made the decision, while in the other two the key passage read that a "Democratic-appointed majority" or "Republican-appointed majority" made the decision. A few important findings emerge from this paper that seem consistent with our broader theoretical framework. First, partisanship strongly interacts with the ideological direction of the decision to shape policy acceptance – Republicans are less willing to accept liberal decisions and Democrats are less willing to accept conservative ones. This again suggests that the Court has limited legitimizing capacity. Further, the presence of party cues associated with the Court majority increases the size of the policy disagreement effect in at least some cases. Third, the partisan gap in policy acceptance is larger on "hot-button" issues (e.g., gun control) than less salient ones (e.g., juvenile sentencing). The authors interpret this as a moderating effect of "polarization." Overall, then, these results fit nicely with our general theoretical framework: support for narrow Court-curbing responds very strongly to single decisions and this support is amplified by both partisan cues and partisan polarization. The empirical work in our book significantly extends this important article in three separate experiments, examining a broader range of narrow curbing measures (compliance, jurisdiction stripping), providing explicit comparisons to broad curbing, and examining the moderating role of partisan polarization explicitly.[8]

In sum, while our theory and empirical findings conflict with the received wisdom in the public opinion literature (Gibson and Caldeira 2009a; Gibson and Nelson 2015b), we believe they are quite consistent with a broader literature in political science (e.g., Choper 1980; Clark 2011; Grosskopf and Mondak 1998) and with an emerging set of studies that challenge the process-based approach using unique observational and experimental designs (e.g., Bartels and Johnston 2013; Christenson and

[7] There were several additional conditions in this experiment, but these are not relevant to the current discussion.

[8] Nicholson and Hansford (2014) interpret the differences they find across the two sets of issues as a polarization effect, but their operationalization of polarization is confounded with all other differences that exist between these sets of issues. In contrast, we operationalize partisan polarization directly as the distance between party elites combined with intra-party homogeneity and vary polarization levels *within* issue conditions. We further extend the polarization hypothesis by examining the moderating effect of affective polarization among citizens.

Glick 2015a; Clark and Kastellec 2015; Nicholson and Hansford 2014). In a recent talk, Chief Justice Roberts argued that the "judicial branch is – how it must be – very different [from the political branches]." But the Supreme Court just isn't that different in the mind of the average citizen – it is a political institution, and the models and concepts that serve political behavior scholars well in other areas (e.g., Druckman, Peterson, and Slothuus 2013) are powerful in the context of the Supreme Court as well.

Support for Court-Curbing on Surveys Is Cheap Talk

Another concern is that we rely on survey responses to tap support for Court-curbing. Should we take such self-reports seriously? Would citizens who claim to support major changes to the Court in the abstract follow through if such proposals found footing in Congress? An alternative perspective is that survey respondents use Court-curbing items as a low-cost opportunity to express an attitude toward the Court and its decisions, but they are not serious about the actions implied by the items. In a real-world scenario, where the cost to the Court is real, these same citizens would back down and support the Court. If this perspective is correct, Court-curbing items are better understood as indicators of "specific support" or "performance satisfaction." This idea is related to "expressive" survey responding or "partisan cheerleading." For example, Bullock et al. (2015) find that gaps in factual beliefs (e.g., the unemployment rate) between Democrats and Republicans are reduced when partisans are paid for correct answers. One interpretation is that many citizens know the correct answers to such questions, but since partisan cheerleading is costless, they use factual questions as opportunities to express their opinions about the parties and their leaders.[9] Once one raises the opportunity cost of expressive responding, partisan divergence is substantially reduced. We think this argument needs to be taken seriously, and we agree that additional work exploring behavioral measures, as supplements to surveys, would be useful. At the same time, we do not think our reliance on surveys is problematic for our conclusions.

First, this critique rests on the idea that while survey responses are costless, real-world support for Court-curbing would be costly. We are skeptical that this is true, because what matters is the individual's *marginal* effect on outcomes. In an electoral context, for example, one's

[9] Other interpretations are also possible. For example, payments for correct answers may motivate a more intensive canvassing of long-term memory and thus a higher probability of generating the correct answer.

probability of being decisive is very small, and this creates strong incentives for expressive voting (Brennan and Lomasky 1993; Caplan 2007; Schuessler 2000). Moreover, in the real world, social pressures to conform to the party line are likely to be *stronger*, not weaker (e.g., Sinclair 2012). We tried to create such pressures in our Chapter 6 polarization experiments, but these treatments are inevitably somewhat artificial and cannot perfectly recreate the intensity of partisan battles where close friends and associates, and elected representatives of one's own party, are standing together against an equally united partisan out-group. Such strong pressures for conformity may outweigh any slight increase in instrumental motivations generated by the real-world context.

Second, survey responses can matter independently of what they imply about voting behavior or other forms of participation. Public surveys shape the media narrative and help to inform people about what their fellow partisans and other citizens believe (Mutz 1998). Such beliefs can be quite influential in shaping opinion on important issues (e.g., Johnston and Ballard 2016). Further, to the extent that elites monitor public opinion to get a sense of where their constituents stand on key issues, public opinion surveys can shape position-taking and policymaking among elected representatives and judges (e.g., Clark 2011).

Finally, citizens respond in predictable ways to variation in the content of the Court-curbing items across contexts, which seems inconsistent with the idea that they are misreporting their true opinions. Frivolous respondents should largely ignore policy content and take advantage of all opportunities to express their negative attitudes toward the Court's decision. Instead, items we have labeled "broadly targeted" curbing proposals respond strongly to perceived policy drift but only weakly to individual decisions. Narrowly targeted items, by contrast, respond very strongly to disagreement with single decisions. We think our theory better accounts for the pattern of responses observed.

We agree that exploration of behavioral indicators of support for Court-curbing is a worthwhile pursuit moving forward, but surveys are still a useful method for studying this topic and survey responses can have a meaningful impact on politics in their own right.

Division and Polarization Protect the Court from Curbing Attempts

We argue that the deep political divisions characterizing contemporary American politics are a threat to judicial independence. However, an alternative argument is that such divisions – both in the public and on the Court itself – mitigate the threat from Court-curbing and allow the justices to rule based on their own preferences. For example, Gibson and Nelson (2015b, 173) argue that

> the Court as currently configured is unlikely to consistently disappoint either the left or the right . . . . Perhaps a court closely divided on ideology cannot produce the consistent decisional fuel needed to ignite a threat to the institution's legitimacy . . . . An ideologically divided court is able to please both liberals and conservatives with its decisions and therefore decisional displeasure does not build to the point of igniting challenges to the institution's legitimacy.

Indeed, as we have shown in previous work (Bartels and Johnston 2013), even during the more center-right Rehnquist and Roberts Court eras, the Court was quite balanced in the ideological direction of its decisions and actually leaned more in the *liberal* direction in its most salient rulings (i.e., those that receive substantial media coverage). That "liberal lean" in highly salient rulings continues into the present, as we discussed in Chapter 5. Thus, both the left and the right are confronted with decisions that disappoint, and both receive decisions that gratify their partisan proclivities. For neither group, perhaps, does the Court drift far enough from their policy preferences to spark a serious push for fundamental changes to the institution. We think this argument ultimately fails, but it is useful to consider why.

First, even if we accept the core of the argument, the Court is only sheltered so long as the justices are relatively evenly divided by partisanship and ideology. If the Court were to drift too far to either the left or the right for a sustained period, this perspective implies that there *would* be sufficient "decisional displeasure" to spark challenges to its institutional integrity. Indeed, this is what we see in patterns of support for Court-curbing as a function of *perceived* policy distance from the Court (Chapter 4). We also see this dynamic in contemporary American politics; for example, in the willingness of Republicans to countenance conservative Senators' intransigence on the nomination of Merrick Garland or in calls for broad Court-curbing among the left in reaction to the Court's rightward shift after two consecutive Trump appointments.

However, Gibson and Nelson (2015b) suggest a "new math" of institutional loyalty: that the justices, even in cases of ideological drift, can rely on substantial baseline levels of institutional support as protection. That is, even if they disappoint a large percentage of ideologues on the left or right at a given point in time, there will still be only a minority of citizens willing to attack the Court, because moderate citizens (and some ideologues) oppose drastic changes to the institution (see also Graham and Svolik 2018 for a related discussion). But when we look across Court-curbing proposals, this is not always the case. For example, while baseline levels of support for "doing away with the Court" are indeed low, substantial support can be found for narrow curbing measures, such as legislative overrides, constitutional amendments, and jurisdiction stripping, all of which undermine the Court's ability to set policy at its ideal point (see Chapter 6; see also Nicholson and Hansford 2014). Moreover, even fundamental changes to the institution often garner substantial baseline levels of support. For example, citizens seem quite supportive of proposals to restrict tenure or add majoritarian veto points, such as public referenda on decisions, direct Congressional overrides of constitutional interpretation, or retention elections for justices (see Chapter 3; see also Clark and Kastellec 2015). In such cases, a large swing in institutional support due to ideological drift could be exactly the spark needed to generate calls for major changes to the Court, some of which may already be quite popular, even among moderates.

A more significant problem with this argument is that it treats judicial decision-making as exogenous to public opinion and thus conflates lack of observed Court-curbing with judicial independence. But *why* does the Court seem to consistently disappoint both the left and the right, and why is this particularly true on salient decisions (Bartels and Johnston 2013)? Why, for example, did Chief Justice Roberts "flip" on *NFIB v. Sebelius*? One answer is that the justices are making concessions to the public will to maintain their support, avoid direct confrontations, and mitigate calls for Court-curbing. In other words, the Court often pleases both liberals and conservatives for strategic reasons. In turn, lack of widespread public support for fundamental changes to the Court does not imply high levels of legitimacy, institutional loyalty, or a "deep reservoir of goodwill." On the contrary – it is exactly because citizens are willing to curb the Court as a function of policy disagreement that the justices avoid drifting too far from public opinion. We see this pattern in the history of Court-curbing legislation in Congress: when the Court strays too far from the public mood – such as in the New Deal era – ideologically motivated Court-curbing attacks increase, and the Court shifts back toward the public's preferences (Clark 2011).

This point is worth emphasizing: a Court that seeks to please both sides to maintain its support is a *constrained* Court, not a strongly independent one. Given strategic decision-making by the justices, we should thus think of the public's willingness to curb as latent, in V.O. Key's (1961) sense: dormant, but capable of being activated by the right set of conditions. This is indeed what we have shown in our experimental findings: elite cues to attack or defend the Court powerfully shape mass partisans' orientation toward the justices and their decisions. But this fact means that "legitimacy" cannot be defined as *levels* of current opposition to Court-curbing – we must observe the dynamics to see how loyal citizens really are. The quiescent waters of aggregate opinion may belie a more antagonistic orientation toward the Court's role in American politics. The justices understand this and seek to avoid deviating too far from the public on important issues. In turn, it is possible for two seemingly contradictory claims to be simultaneously true: first, that most citizens oppose fundamental changes to the Court and, second, that most citizens afford the Court moderate to low levels of legitimacy. Opposition to Court-curbing is not principled but strategic, and the Court is giving citizens enough of what they want, on average, to avoid major confrontations.

Finally, even if partisan divisions on and off the Court protect the justices from fundamental changes, and from congressional or presidential attacks on individual decisions, narrow curbing can occur at a local level where the Court may be less protected by political polarization. The country may be sharply divided in the aggregate, but there are plenty of places where opinion is more homogenous. If the Court's efficacy rests largely on parity among competing political groups, then it is quite vulnerable to localized curbing. The obvious example is Southern communities' (lack of) response to the *Brown* v. *Board of Education*[10] decisions and widespread intransigence on school desegregation. Local noncompliance has also been severe for the Court's orders in decisions involving religious practices in public schools (e.g., McGuire 2009). As Choper (1980, 152) reports, for example, only a subset of Tennessee school districts changed their policy on school prayer in response to the ruling in *Abington School District* v. *Schempp*,[11] and even those who did evinced only partial and limited forms of compliance,[12] which, according to Katz (1965, 407), "should serve to dispel the notion that society automatically responds to the will of the Supreme Court." Discussing the response to the decision in

[10] 347 U.S. 483 (1954); see also *Brown II* (349 U.S. 294, 1955) and *Cooper* v. *Aaron* (358 U.S. 1, 1958).

[11] 374 U.S. 203 (1963)

[12] For example, some districts made participation voluntary or left the decision up to the teacher.

McCollum v. *Board of Education*,[13] which restricted religious instruction on public school property, Patric (1957, 464) concludes:

> [I]n some instances reaction was felt the day after the Court ruled. In others, the ruling seemed simply to be ignored. If any single generalization can be made from this discussion, it is that the impact nationwide of a Supreme Court decision is by no means uniform. The various patterns of compliance adopted in the local situations where the decision was sought to be enforced indicate that there is considerable latitude of modes of compliance with a decision of the highest court of the land.

Beyond noncompliance, the Supreme Court's (lack of) legitimizing capacity has implications for the strength and nature of legislative challenges that will be leveled against the Court's decisions over time, and thus the ability of the justices to secure a preferred policy outcome over the long run. Abortion is a particularly good example. Here, many states have seen concerted, and often quite successful, legislative efforts to make abortion more difficult, despite the constitutional rights outlined in *Roe* v. *Wade*. As suggested by Franklin and Kosaki (1989), rather than legitimizing a given position, the Court may simply force the issue's salience, leading to enduring divisions within the public (see also Zilis 2015).

The broader point is that the efficacy of the Court (and courts generally) often rests on local support in communities that may be both relatively homogenous in their values and hostile to the Court's decision. It is probably too much to expect local representatives to stand athwart a united constituency supporting curbing attacks. Indeed, such representatives are unlikely to be long for the political world. In focusing attention primarily on broad forms of Court-curbing that require the participation of federal institutions, Gibson and Nelson (2015b) may miss a great deal of what is important in the implementation problem (e.g., Vanberg 2001). In the case of local compliance to Court decisions, and other forms of narrow Court-curbing, it makes a big difference whether we are living in a world where citizens see the Court as legitimate or one where institutional support is fickle and driven by policy agreement.

Politicization of the Court Has Driven a Decline in Legitimacy

We have argued that citizens care primarily about policy victories and little about procedural factors. They focus on decision outcomes, not the process

[13] 333 U.S. 203 (1948)

by which the decisions were generated. But perhaps a revised version of the process-based approach can explain our findings. In this version, citizens in *contemporary politics* focus only on outcomes – and are thus unresponsive to procedural factors – but this is because judicial decision-making has become more politicized over time. Perhaps the justices themselves are to blame for citizens' lack of institutional loyalty. Eric Posner[14] points to a keynote address from newly appointed justice Brett Kavanaugh (2017, 1909–10): "When we watch a Notre Dame-Michigan game, we do not ask whether the referees are Irish fans or Wolverine fans. Yet when we watch the Supreme Court, too many Americans think the decision is pre-baked based on the party of the President who appointed the Justices or the policy preferences of the Justices." As Epstein and Posner (2018) suggest, this is perhaps understandable, because the correlation between party of appointing president and the decisions justices make on close cases has increased drastically in recent decades. They argue that this increase in seemingly preordained outcomes is the primary threat to the Court's independence:

> In the past 10 years, however, justices have hardly ever voted against the ideology of the president who appointed them. Only Justice Kennedy, named to the court by Ronald Reagan, did so with any regularity. That is why with his replacement on the court an [sic] ideologically committed Republican justice, it will become impossible to regard the court as anything but a partisan institution .... For the first time in living memory, the court will be seen by the public as a party-dominated institution, one whose votes on controversial issues are essentially determined by the party affiliation of recent presidents .... Frustrated with the Supreme Court's opposition to the New Deal, President Franklin Roosevelt tried to pack the court – that is, add more justices. Although the plan died in Congress, the court also backed down from its confrontation with the president. Both Roosevelt and the court were badly damaged by the clash. Today we see similar attacks on the judiciary in Hungary, Poland and other illiberal democracies. Assaults on judicial independence are made easier when the public comes to view the judiciary as a political body. This risk, and not just the identity of the next justice, should be at the center of public attention.

Gibson and Caldeira (2009a) make a similar argument in their work on the Alito nomination in the mid-2000s. They argue that while the Court's legitimacy does not suffer from partisan or ideological disagreement directly, it may be harmed by protracted, divisive nomination contests that paint the Court in nakedly partisan terms.

[14] http://ericposner.com/yet-when-we-watch-the-supreme-court-too-many-americans-think-the-decision-is-pre-baked-based-on-the-party-of-the-president-who-appointed-the-justices/

Woodson (2015) suggests an interesting modification to the standard process-based approach that is consistent with this idea. In this version, politicized decision-making does not lead directly to calls for Court-curbing as in, say, Tyler and Rasinski (1991). That is, citizens do not unconditionally attack the Court because it is a politicized institution. Rather, politicized decision-making *creates the conditions* necessary for the policy-based model we present in the book. Perceptions of politically motivated decision-making force citizens to think strategically about the Court (see also Bartels and Johnston 2012; Woodson 2018, 2019). In turn, they give and withhold support for the justices based on their perceptions of the partisan and ideological content of their decisions. Once the Court is politicized, citizens treat it as a political institution. Perhaps the best model is one that synthesizes the process- and policy-based models.

We think this is a reasonable perspective that should be taken seriously. However, we also suggest caution in adopting this interpretation of our results. First, it treats the public's procedural perceptions as exogenous but, as we have shown, they are strongly influenced by agreement and disagreement with the Court's decision-making. Second, and perhaps more importantly, we need to consider carefully the reasons for Court politicization and their relationship to public opinion. Specifically, we should not assume that judicial partisan polarization is exogenous to citizens' perceptions and preferences, and we should ask *why* the Court is more partisan than in the past. What has facilitated the appointment of loyal partisans to the high bench? Is this simply an instance of elected officials ignoring the public's desire for a "neutral, impartial judiciary that decides cases based on settled principles without regard to policy preferences or political allegiances or which party is on which side in a particular case" (Kavanaugh 2017, 1909)? We think our theory offers an alternative – and to our mind, more plausible – answer: the *demand* for judicial appointments that ignore partisanship and ideology just isn't that strong as a general matter (Bartels and Johnston 2012), and it has been steadily decreasing as partisan polarization has increased since the 1970s.

In our view, partisan judicial appointments are serving a similar function as Court-curbing legislation in Congress (Clark 2011) – they allow elected officials to take positions on important issues in a high-profile manner. As congressional and mass-level polarization has increased, the incentive to use the appointment process to score partisan points has grown. As Epstein and Posner (2018) suggest, "President Trump was always going to pick a conservative for the Supreme Court. The only question has been whether to replace Justice Anthony Kennedy with a 'business conservative' or a 'religious conservative.' No one seriously thought that he would consider a moderate, a liberal or an ideologically ambiguous replacement." This is true, and the reason is that the demand for such appointments within the Republican party is weak. Indeed, in recent work, Sen (2017) shows that citizens rely primarily on the partisan leanings of a Court nominee in making judgments about that nominee – including whether that nominee is qualified – and this is particularly true for politically sophisticated individuals. In other words, the most politically active citizens, those most likely to hold their representatives accountable at the voting booth, are *least* likely to demand a nonpartisan process focused on legal qualifications. Thus, understanding the demand side of judicial appointments and decision-making is critical to making sense of changes in the Court's composition and degree of partisan polarization. If citizens are unwilling to punish their representatives for partisan appointments – indeed, if they prefer such appointments – then we should expect an increasingly partisan Court.

Importantly, however, we think there is room for both the policy- and process-based perspectives to matter. We might think of these as reinforcing dynamics – as a positive feedback loop – driving continued politicization of the judiciary (Bartels and Johnston 2012). Citizens are already weakly principled, and partisan polarization reduces principled decision-making even further. In turn, the Court becomes more partisan in practice, which simply reinforces citizens' incentives to treat the Court as a political institution (Woodson 2015), which further polarizes the Court, and so on. Moreover, even if our policy-based perspective captures an important part of American public opinion, it clearly does not explain everything. The behavior of at least some portion of citizens is well described by the process-based approach. The dynamics set in motion by the remainder of the public – namely, an increasingly politicized Court – may thus harm the legitimacy of the Court in the eyes of process-concerned citizens. This again suggests a positive, rather than negative, feedback process. We think these more nuanced interactions between policy and process concerns offer exciting opportunities for future research on this topic.

Recapitulating the Exhaustible Capital Framework

In seminal contributions, Choper (1980) and Mondak (1992, 1994) advance a theoretical framework in which the Supreme Court has a store of institutional (or political) capital that it uses strategically in the pursuit of public acceptance of its decisions. In this view, the Court builds a fund of institutional support through pleasing decisions which it then spends down when it needs to make counter-majoritarian rulings. Each displeasing decision depletes accumulated capital until, finally exhausted, the public favors fundamental changes to the institution to bring the justices to heel. Recognizing this, the Court manages its capital carefully and avoids accumulating too much "debt" in the public mind. For example, Choper (1980, 139) argues that

> the federal judiciary's ability to persuade the populace and public leaders that it is right and they are wrong is determined by the number and frequency of its attempts to do so .... At some point ... the Court's continued antimajoritarian rulings will tip the balance of credit accumulation and expenditures and animate a public sentiment that it has but a gossamer claim to legitimacy in a democratic society.

Similarly, Mondak (1992, 458) argues that "these dynamics form a systemic view of legitimacy: If institutional approval can be used to confer policy legitimacy, and if in conferring policy legitimacy institutional support is expended, then institutional legitimacy functions as a political currency; public support allows the 'purchase' of some increment of policy approval."

There are thus similarities between this work and our own. Both emphasize the importance of policy disagreement to Court-curbing; both predict that sustained ideological drift from voters generates attacks on the Court; and both expect that the justices make strategic choices to protect the Court's independence. To what extent is our approach simply a recapitulation of the exhaustible capital framework? While there is clearly overlap in the implications of this work and our own, we believe the two approaches are distinct, make different predictions, and have different implications. Most importantly, our framework rejects the importance of "stores of institutional capital" that can be used to legitimize decisions. Citizens may "talk the talk" of institutional loyalty, but this is strategic and will be abandoned when politically expedient. This implies three important points.

First, while both frameworks suggest that long-term ideological drift will produce challenges to the Court's integrity, we argue that this is *not* due to depleted institutional capital but to citizens' updated beliefs about the Court's general ideological orientation in relation to their own. This may seem like a subtle distinction – and the two frameworks may often be observationally equivalent – but it generates competing predictions in certain circumstances. For example, in our framework citizens are likely to respond to changes in the Court's composition, not just in its decision-making, because composition has implications for the expected stream of future decisions. That is, citizens update their beliefs about the Court's general ideological tenor based on retirements and appointments. Thus, the Court need not deplete a store of goodwill through decision-making before attacks commence. We see this dynamic at work, for example, in recent calls from the left for Court-curbing in response to two Trump appointments. One might respond, however, that the *expectation* of a series of disagreeable decisions depletes *expected future* capital and this is sufficient to elicit preemptive curbing attacks. In this case, however, the two frameworks seem observationally equivalent because, in both cases, citizens simply care about ideological congruence over the long-run. We thus prefer the more parsimonious theory that does not require the additional, and somewhat amorphous, notion of institutional capital.

A more important difference between the theories concerns the treatment of narrow Court-curbing and policy legitimacy (Mondak 1992). In this domain, the capital hypothesis has similar implications to the process-based approach: so long as the Court has not expended its store of goodwill – which should be rare, given strategic decision-making – it has substantial capacity to legitimize its decisions, even for citizens who strongly disagree with them. This implies a small relationship between indicators of policy disagreement and support for noncompliance, jurisdiction stripping, and legislative overrides. Our framework, on the other hand, expects that disagreeable decisions provoke substantial efforts at resisting the implications of those decisions, even among citizens who generally support the Court and reject more fundamental changes. Citizens are apt to support attempts by elected officials and their appointees to subvert the Court's authority, and they justify this resistance by attacking the *Court's* procedural propriety. When it comes to policy legitimacy and narrow curbing, we think the evidence presented thus far better supports the policy-based than the exhaustible capital framework. The Court's legitimizing capacity has been substantially overstated.

Finally, we think our framework is better equipped to deal with the importance of both partisan polarization and of elites in shaping public support for narrow Court-curbing. The exhaustible capital framework, as articulated in previous work, makes no explicit claims regarding either of these factors, despite their centrality in the mass politics literature (e.g., Druckman, Peterson, and Slothuus 2013; Zaller 1992). The effects of polarization and elite cues on Court-curbing could perhaps be accommodated in this framework by assuming that they increase the perceived importance of a given decision, and thus the marginal impact of that decision on capital stores. Choper (1980, 139), for example, argues that depletion of capital occurs as a function of the "felt importance of the policies." But this move decreases the theoretical power of the concept of institutional capital. Indeed, its value is that it motivates citizens to resist curbing – even when it *meaningfully* hurts their narrow partisan interests – and thus to bring the legislature and executive to heel. But if citizens only cede the Court authority on issues of low importance, and if they abandon the Court in the face of substantial partisan pressure, then it is not clear that the institutional capital concept is doing any real theoretical work. Again, it is more parsimonious to assume that citizens are primarily motivated by policy, partisan, and ideological concerns, and pay only lip-service to Court legitimacy.

Nonetheless, we think there is value in the exhaustible capital approach and there is room in the final accounting for both. For example, Mondak (1994) shows that policy agreement strongly influences policy acceptance, but so does the Court's prior institutional legitimacy. Similarly, our framework does not explain why there are differences in baseline support for different forms of narrow Court-curbing (e.g., noncompliance versus legislative overrides) and why a meaningful percentage of citizens resist curbing, even under pressure. We think it would be worthwhile for future research to pursue the similarities and differences between these two approaches in greater detail. Are there contexts in which they make clearly distinct predictions? Can we directly measure accumulated institutional capital and estimate its restraining influence on narrow curbing under pressure? For whom does each framework best describe political behavior? Is there a hybrid approach that is better than either framework in isolation?

Judicial Independence Rests with Elites, Not Citizens

The standard motivation for exploring public opinion of courts is that citizens are the guardians of judicial independence. As Gibson and Nelson (2015b, 162) state,

> If legitimacy is … fragile, then a wise and prudent Court would shift from emphasizing the "minority rights" half of its democratic assignment to becoming more of an agent of "majority rule" …. If so, the "countermajoritarian dilemma"

is truly a profound dilemma. If legitimacy cannot protect the institution when it makes unpopular decisions, then the Court's previous independence may be precarious.

Yet perhaps this line of work has overemphasized the importance of public opinion for the Court's efficacy. That is, perhaps the Court retains a substantial degree of independence, but citizens are less important to this than we thought. Indeed, at least three strains of research suggest that it is political *elites* and elite institutions, not citizens, who provide the foundation for institutional stability in American politics.

The first emerges directly from research on courts. As explained by Vanberg (2015), a robust literature considers the range of benefits that elites often obtain from maintaining an independent judicial branch (e.g., Dahl 1957; Gillman 2002; Ramseyer 1994; Rogers 2001; Whittington 2005). For example, independent courts may serve as a clearinghouse for information about policy, allow elites to avoid blame for difficult policy choices (by passing the buck to judges), or frustrate policy moves by actors in other parties, institutions, or at other levels of government (e.g., state versus federal). In all cases, the idea is that while elites sometimes prefer an independent judiciary and sometimes prefer a docile one, attacking the Court's integrity is an all or none affair. Even small acts of subversion can lead to tit-for-tat battles with other parties that threaten the long-term integrity of the Court. To the extent that elites often benefit from an independent judiciary, it may serve their long-term interests to forego the smaller, immediate benefits to Court-curbing (including gratifying public opinion).

Second, the institutional barriers to Court-curbing may provide the Court with greater leeway to pursue its ideal points. This is clearest in the case of broad forms of curbing which often require changes to the Constitution to enact, and thus the support of two-thirds of both houses of Congress along with three-quarters of the states. In many cases, at least, the Court may feel secure less from the public's institutional loyalty than from the sheer difficulty of successfully passing major curbing legislation. As Choper (1980, 55) suggests,

> [Fundamental changes call] for one or the other of the elected branches to act affirmatively, and usually the concurrence of both departments is required. Moreover, all the dominant forces of inertia – of maintenance of the status quo, of inaction due to the frequent absence of cohesive majorities and to the fragmentation of power – that are present in the national political process work to safeguard the Court.

Even narrow forms of Court-curbing – such as legislative overrides – face challenges due to institutional factors. As Carrubba and Zorn (2010, 813) argue, for example, the Court has substantial discretion to set policy when its ideal point falls between those of the House and Senate, because any move in either direction would make one chamber worse off. In this case, Congress cannot agree on which direction to move and the Court benefits by obtaining its most-preferred policy. A related example is that many constituencies are quite diverse, especially in the Senate, and this reduces the payoff to Court-curbing among elected representatives in Congress.

The third strain emerges from work on political tolerance. As we reviewed in Chapter 2, classic work on tolerance suggests that citizens are only weakly principled in the sense that they are often willing to restrict the political rights of strongly disliked groups (e.g., Prothro and Grigg 1960; Sullivan, Piereson, and Marcus 1982). This work raises questions quite like the ones we confront here: if citizens are willing to sacrifice democratic values for narrow partisan gain, who or what sustains American democracy over the long run? In the face of these empirical results, some theorists have turned to elite-driven explanations. As McClosky (1964, 374) famously argued, "The evidence suggests that it is the articulate classes rather than the public who serve as the major repositories of the public conscience and as the carriers of the Creed. Responsibility for keeping the system going, hence, falls heavily upon them."[15] Consistent with this claim, we have found in previous work that while "legal elites"[16] also engage in directionally motivated reasoning about Court decisions, they are almost universally opposed to broad forms of Court-curbing (Bartels, Johnston, and Mark 2015). Recent work makes similar claims in the context of democratic backsliding. As Levitsky and Ziblatt (2018, 20) argue, "Although mass responses to extremist appeals matter, what matters more is whether political elites, and especially parties, serve as filters. Put simply, political parties are democracy's gatekeepers."

[15] As McCloskey explains (1964, 361), this argument was made previously by V.O. Key (1961). Summarizing, the former writes, "V.O. Key, going a step further, suggests that the viability of a democracy may depend less upon popular opinion than upon the activities and values of an 'aristocratic' strain whose members are set off from the mass by their political influence, their attention to public affairs, and their active role as society's policy makers."

[16] "Legal elites" were defined as lawyers practicing before the US Courts of Appeals.

The importance of elites is reinforced by our empirical findings. As we demonstrated in Chapter 6, partisan elites have substantial influence on citizens' willingness to engage in Court-curbing. Our second experiment, for example, showed that attaching elite party cues to curbing proposals, in the context of a hyper-partisan environment, greatly increases the demand for curbing among those who disagree with the Court's decision. These findings are consistent with the broader literature on elite cue-taking for courts (e.g., Clark and Kastellec 2015; Nicholson and Hansford 2014) and in American public opinion more generally (e.g., Bisgaard and Slothuus 2018; Cohen 2003; Druckman, Peterson, and Slothuus 2013; Lenz 2012). The upshot is that citizens use elites to guide their decisions about what types of attitudes and behavior toward the Court are acceptable. If elites find it in their interest to protect the Court's integrity for reasons independent of public opinion (e.g., Vanberg 2015) and send strong cues that curbing is unacceptable behavior in our democracy, many fewer citizens will be motivated to attack the Court. Conversely, if elites turn against the Court, citizens are quite likely to follow. Choper (1980, 154) makes a similar argument: "the strong inference remains that the heights to which popular sentiments rise are strongly influenced by how the 'political stratum' handles the issue; that even in regard to such highly sensitive matters as school segregation, political enforcement and opinion leadership are important factors in shaping public attitudes and fostering compliance." He provides an illuminating example in the geographical variation of compliance with the school prayer decision in *Abington School District* v. *Schempp*. As he explains (Choper 1980, 152), compliance with the decision was largely dependent on the opinion of the attorneys general (AG) in each state: compliance was consistent in places where the AG supported the Court's decision and nearly non-existent in places where the AG opposed the decision.

Thus, from this perspective, the Court achieves independence in American politics, to the extent it does, not because citizens restrain the worst impulses of short-sighted elites, but because elites temper the "heights to which popular sentiments rise," and mitigate – or simply ignore – the latent tendency of citizens to support Court-curbing in response to disliked decisions. Of course, as Choper (1980, 153) also notes, it is critical not to overestimate the willingness of elites to stand against a united public – strong selection pressures would make quick work of such individuals. However principled elites may be, unprincipled *citizens* still leave the Court in a far weaker position than it would otherwise be. Nonetheless, our results do suggest that the literature may need to adjust its view of the relative importance of citizens – compared to elites, institutions, and the status quo – in fostering judicial independence. While much work sees principled citizens constraining policy-minded elites, our work suggests the converse may be just as, or more, important to the judiciary.

Beyond the Supreme Court

Finally, our book focuses only on the Supreme Court, which decides about eighty cases per year – most of the judicial work in the country occurs in other venues. It is thus critical to study public support for court-curbing more broadly (see Cann and Yates 2008, 2016). We expect our theoretical framework will be useful to scholars interested in studying lower courts and may be especially useful for studying legislative–judicial interactions at the state level. Indeed, in recent years there have been several curbing attacks on state supreme courts that seem to fit our expected patterns well. In Pennsylvania, for example, the state supreme court overruled the Republican-controlled state legislature and redrew the state's congressional map. In response, Republican legislators pushed for impeachment of the judges who voted in favor of the redrawn districts. The Brennan Center for Justice found fifty-one court-curbing bills across sixteen states in 2018 alone, and this appears to be part of an ongoing trend.[17] This is exactly what we would expect if partisan polarization fosters court-curbing. And to the extent that the factors identified by process-based theorists matter to some extent – and some of our results suggest they do – then state courts are likely to be more vulnerable to polarized politics than the Supreme Court. That is, norms against attacking lower courts may be weaker than for the Supreme Court. Courts at the state level may also be more vulnerable because the mechanisms of curbing are more varied. For example, in North Carolina in 2018, citizens considered (but ultimately rejected) a ballot measure to change the North Carolina constitution which would take the power to fill inter-election judicial vacancies from the governor and move to a more complicated, multi-stage process involving all three branches and with substantial power vested in the legislature.

[17] www.brennancenter.org/analysis/legislative-assaults-state-courts-2018. We thank Arvind Krishnamurthy for pointing us to these data.

Moving forward, this is perhaps one of the most important areas for future research on law and society. We think our book provides a guiding theoretical and conceptual framework for a deeper exploration of court-curbing at all levels, in America and other countries around the world.

References

Abramowitz, Alan. 2010. *The Disappearing Center: Engaged Citizens, Polarization, and American Democracy*. New Haven, CT: Yale University Press.

Abramowitz, Alan I., and Kyle L. Saunders. 2008. "Is Polarization a Myth?" *Journal of Politics* 70(2): 542–55.

Acharya, Avidit, Matthew Blackwell, and Maya Sen. 2018. "Explaining Preferences from Behavior: A Cognitive Dissonance Approach." *Journal of Politics* 80(2): 400–11.

Achen, Christopher H. 1975. "Mass Political Attitudes and the Survey Response." *American Political Science Review* 69(4): 1218–31.

Achen, Christopher H., and Larry M. Bartels. 2016. *Democracy for Realists: Why Elections Do Not Produce Responsive Government*. Princeton, NJ: Princeton University Press.

Ansolabehere, Stephen, Jonathan Rodden, and James M. Snyder. 2008. "The Strength of Issues: Using Multiple Measures to Gauge Preference Stability, Ideological Constraint, and Issue Voting." *American Political Science Review* 102(2): 215–32.

Armaly, Miles T. 2018. "Extra-Judicial Actor Induced Change in Supreme Court Legitimacy." *Political Research Quarterly* 71(3): 600–13.

Badas, Alex. 2016. "The Public's Motivated Response to Supreme Court Decision-Making." *Justice System Journal* 37(4): 318–30.

Baddeley, Michelle. 2018. *Copycats and Contrarians: Why We Follow Others ... and When We Don't*. New Haven, CT: Yale University Press.

Baird, Vanessa A., and Amy Gangl. 2006. "Shattering the Myth of Legality: The Impact of the Media's Framing of Supreme Court Procedures on Perceptions of Fairness." *Political Psychology* 27(4): 597–614.

Bartels, Brandon L. 2015. "The Sources and Consequences of Polarization in the U.S. Supreme Court." In *American Gridlock: The Sources, Character, and Impact of Political Polarization*, ed. James A. Thurber and Antoine Yoshinaka. New York, NY: Cambridge University Press.

Bartels, Brandon L., and Christopher D. Johnston. 2012. "Political Justice? Perceptions of Politicization and Public Preferences toward the Supreme Court Appointment Process." *Public Opinion Quarterly* 76(1): 105–16.

2013. "On the Ideological Foundations of Supreme Court Legitimacy in the American Public." *American Journal of Political Science* 57(1): 184–99.

Bartels, Brandon L., Christopher D. Johnston, and Alyx Mark. 2015. "Lawyers' Perceptions of the U.S. Supreme Court: Is the Court a 'Political' Institution?" *Law & Society Review* 49(3): 761–94.

Bartels, Brandon L., and Diana C. Mutz. 2009. "Explaining Processes of Institutional Opinion Leadership." *The Journal of Politics* 71(1): 249–61.

Baumeister, Roy F., Ellen Bratslavsky, Catrin Finkenauer, and Kathleen D. Vohs. 2001. "Bad Is Stronger than Good." *Review of General Psychology* 5(4): 323–70.

Benesh, Sara C. 2006. "Understanding Public Confidence in American Courts." *Journal of Politics* 68(3): 697–707.

Bisgaard, Martin, and Rune Slothuus. 2018. "Partisan Elites as Culprits? How Party Cues Shape Partisan Perceptual Gaps." *American Journal of Political Science* 62(2): 456–69.

Braman, Eileen. 2006. "Reasoning on the Threshold: Testing the Separability of Preferences in Legal Decision Making." *The Journal of Politics* 68(2): 308–21.

2009. *Law, Politics, and Perception: How Policy Preferences Influence Legal Reasoning*. Charlottesville, VA: University of Virginia Press.

Braman, Eileen, and Thomas E. Nelson. 2007. "Mechanism of Motivated Reasoning? Analogical Perception in Discrimination Disputes." *American Journal of Political Science* 51(4): 940–56.

Brandt, Mark J. et al. 2014. "The Ideological-Conflict Hypothesis: Intolerance among Both Liberals and Conservatives." *Current Directions in Psychological Science* 23(1): 27–34.

Brennan, Geoffrey, and Loren Lomasky. 1993. *Democracy and Decision: The Pure Theory of Electoral Preference*. New York, NY: Cambridge University Press.

Bullock, John G., Alan S. Gerber, Seth J. Hill, and Gregory A. Huber. 2015. "Partisan Bias in Factual Beliefs about Politics." *Quarterly Journal of Political Science* 10: 519–78.

Bybee, Keith J. 2010. *All Judges Are Political – Except When They Are Not: Acceptable Hypocrisies and the Rule of Law*. Stanford, CA: Stanford University Press.

Caldeira, Gregory A., and James L. Gibson. 1992. "The Etiology of Public Support for the Supreme Court." *American Journal of Political Science* 36(3): 635–64.

Cann, Damon M., and Jeff Yates. 2008. "Homegrown Institutional Legitimacy: Assessing Citizens' Diffuse Support for State Courts." *American Politics Research* 36(2): 297–329.

2016. *These Estimable Courts: Understanding Public Perceptions of State Judicial Institutions and Legal Policy-Making*. New York, NY: Oxford University Press.

Caplan, Bryan. 2007. *The Myth of the Rational Voter: Why Democracies Choose Bad Policies*. Princeton, NJ: Princeton University Press.

Carmines, Edward G., and James A. Stimson. 1980. "The Two Faces of Issue Voting." *American Political Science Review* 74(1): 78–91.

Carpini, Michael X. Delli, and Scott Keeter. 1996. *What Americans Know about Politics and Why It Matters*. New Haven, CT: Yale University Press.

Carrubba, Clifford J. 2009. "A Model of the Endogenous Development of Judicial Institutions in Federal and International Systems." *Journal of Politics* 71(1): 55–69.

Carrubba, Clifford J., and Christopher Zorn. 2010. "Executive Discretion, Judicial Decision Making, and Separation of Powers in the United States." *The Journal of Politics* 72(3): 812–24.

Casey, Gregory. 1974. "The Supreme Court and Myth: An Empirical Investigation." *Law & Society Review* 8(3): 385–420.

Casillas, Christopher J., Peter K. Enns, and Patrick C. Wohlfarth. 2011. "How Public Opinion Constrains the U.S. Supreme Court." *American Journal of Political Science* 55(1): 74–88.

Choper, Jesse H. 1980. *Judicial Review and the National Political Process: A Functional Reconsideration of the Role of the Supreme Court*. Chicago, IL: University of Chicago Press.

Christenson, Dino P., and David M. Glick. 2015a. "Chief Justice Roberts's Health Care Decision Disrobed: The Microfoundations of the Supreme Court's Legitimacy." *American Journal of Political Science* 59(2): 403–18.

2015b. "Issue-Specific Opinion Change: The Supreme Court and Health Care Reform." *Public Opinion Quarterly* 79(4): 881–905.

2019. "Reassessing the Supreme Court: How Decisions and Negativity Bias Affect Legitimacy." *Political Research Quarterly* 72(3): 637–52.

Cizmar, Anne M. et al. 2004. "Authoritarianism and American Political Behavior from 1952 to 2008." *Political Research Quarterly* 67(1): 71–83.

Clark, Tom S. 2009. "The Separation of Powers, Court Curbing, and Judicial Legitimacy." *American Journal of Political Science* 53(4): 971–89.

2011. *The Limits of Judicial Independence*. New York, NY: Cambridge University Press.

Clark, Tom S., and Jonathan P. Kastellec. 2015. "Source Cues and Public Support for the Supreme Court." *American Politics Research* 43(3): 504–35.

Clawson, Rosalee A., Elizabeth R. Kegler, and Eric N. Waltenburg. 2001. "The Legitimacy-Conferring Authority of the U.S. Supreme Court: An Experimental Design." *American Politics Research* 29(6): 566–91.

2003. "Supreme Court Legitimacy and Group-Centric Forces: Black Support for Capital Punishment and Affirmative Action." *Political Behavior* 25(4): 289–311.

Clawson, Rosalee A., and Eric N. Waltenburg. 2009. *Legacy and Legitimacy: Black Americans and the Supreme Court*. Philadelphia, PA: Temple University Press.

Cohen, Geoffrey L. 2003. "Party over Policy: The Dominating Impact of Group Influence on Political Beliefs." *Journal of Personality and Social Psychology* 85(5): 808–22.

Converse, Phillip E. 1964. "The Nature of Belief Systems in Mass Publics." In *Ideology and Discontent*, ed. David E. Apter. New York, NY: Free Press of Glencoe.

Crawford, Jarret T., and Jane M. Pilanski. 2014. "Political Intolerance, Right and Left." *Political Psychology* 35(6): 841–51.

Dahl, Robert A. 1957. "Decision-Making in a Democracy: The Supreme Court as a National Policy-Maker." *Journal of Public Law* 6(2): 279–95.

Ditto, Peter H., and David F. Lopez. 1992. "Motivated Skepticism: Use of Differential Decision Criteria for Preferred and Nonpreferred Conclusions." *Journal of Personality and Social Psychology* 63(4): 568–84.

Doty, Richard M., Bill E. Peterson, and David G. Winter. 1991. "Threat and Authoritarianism in the United States, 1978–1987." *Journal of Personality and Social Psychology* 61(4): 629–40.

Druckman, James N., Erik Peterson, and Rune Slothuus. 2013. "How Elite Partisan Polarization Affects Public Opinion Formation." *American Political Science Review* 107(1): 57–79.

Durr, Robert H., Andrew D. Martin, and Christina Wolbrecht. 2000. "Ideological Divergence and Public Support for the Supreme Court." *American Journal of Political Science* 44(4): 768–76.

Easton, David. 1965. *A Systems Analysis of Political Life*. New York, NY: John Wiley.

Epstein, Lee, and Jack Knight. 1998. *The Choices Justices Make*. Washington, DC: CQ Press.

Epstein, Lee, Jack Knight, and Andrew D. Martin. 2001. "The Supreme Court as a Strategic National Policymaker." *Emory Law Journal* 50(2): 583–611.

Epstein, Lee, and Eric Posner. 2018. "If the Supreme Court Is Nakedly Political, Can It Be Just?" *The New York Times*. www.nytimes.com/2018/07/09/opinion/supreme-court-nominee-trump.html (December 13, 2018).

Epstein, Lee, and Jeffrey A. Segal. 2000. "Measuring Issue Salience." *American Journal of Political Science* 44(1): 66–83.

Erikson, Robert S., Michael B. Mackuen, and James A. Stimson. 2002. *The Macro Polity*. New York, NY: Cambridge University Press.

Farganis, Dion. 2012. "Do Reasons Matter? The Impact of Opinion Content on Supreme Court Legitimacy." *Political Research Quarterly* 65(1): 206–16.

Feldman, Stanley. 1988. "Structure and Consistency in Public Opinion: The Role of Core Beliefs and Values." *American Journal of Political Science* 32(2): 416–40.

Feldman, Stanley, and Christopher Johnston. 2014. "Understanding the Determinants of Political Ideology: Implications of Structural Complexity." *Political Psychology* 35(3): 337–58.

Feldman, Stanley, and Karen Stenner. 1997. "Perceived Threat and Authoritarianism." *Political Psychology* 18(4): 741–70.

Festinger, Leon. 1957. *A Theory of Cognitive Dissonance*. Stanford, CA: Stanford University Press.

Fiorina, Morris P. 1981. *Retrospective Voting in American National Elections*. New Haven, CT: Yale University Press.

Fiorina, Morris P., Samuel J. Abrams, and Jeremy C. Pope. 2006. *Culture War? The Myth of a Polarized America*. 2nd ed. New York, NY: Pearson Longman.

Flynn, D. J., Brendan Nyhan, and Jason Reifler. 2017. "The Nature and Origins of Misperceptions: Understanding False and Unsupported Beliefs about Politics." *Political Psychology* 38(S1): 127–50.

Fontana, David, and Donald Braman. 2012. "Judicial Backlash or Just Backlash? Evidence from a National Experiment." *Columbia Law Review* 112(4): 731–99.

Franklin, Charles H., and Liane C. Kosaki. 1989. "Republican Schoolmaster: The U.S. Supreme Court, Public Opinion, and Abortion." *American Political Science Review* 83(3): 751–71.

Friedman, Barry. 1998. "The History of the Countermajoritarian Difficulty, Part One: The Road to Judicial Supremacy." *NYU Law Review* 73(2): 333–433.

2005. "The Myths of Marbury." In *Arguing Marbury v. Madison*, ed. Mark Tushnet. Stanford, CA: Stanford University Press.

2009. *The Will of the People: How Public Opinion Has Influenced the Supreme Court and Shaped the Meaning of the Constitution*. New York, NY: Farrar, Straus and Giroux.

Friedman, Barry, and Erin F. Delaney. 2011. "Becoming Supreme: The Federal Foundation of Judicial Supremacy." *Columbia Law Review* 111(6): 1137–93.

Gibler, Douglas M., and Kirk A. Randazzo. 2011. "Testing the Effects of Independent Judiciaries on the Likelihood of Democratic Backsliding." *American Journal of Political Science* 55(3): 696–709.

Gibson, James L. 1989. "Understandings of Justice: Institutional Legitimacy, Procedural Justice, and Political Tolerance." *Law & Society Review* 23(3): 469–96.

1991. "Institutional Legitimacy, Procedural Justice, and Compliance with Supreme Court Decisions: A Question of Causality." *Law & Society Review* 25(3): 631–36.

1998. "A Sober Second Thought: An Experiment in Persuading Russians to Tolerate." *American Journal of Political Science* 42(3): 819–50.

2006. "Do Strong Group Identities Fuel Intolerance? Evidence from the South African Case." *Political Psychology* 27(5): 665–705.

Gibson, James L. 2007. "The Legitimacy of the U.S. Supreme Court in a Polarized Polity." *Journal of Empirical Legal Studies* 4(3): 507–38.

2011. "A Note of Caution about the Meaning of 'The Supreme Court Can Usually Be Trusted ...'" *Law & Courts: Newsletter of the Law & Courts Section of the American Political Science Association* 21(3): 10–16.

2015. "Legitimacy Is for Losers: The Interconnections of Institutional Legitimacy, Performance Evaluations, and the Symbols of Judicial Authority." In *Motivating Cooperation and Compliance with Authority: The Role of Institutional Trust*, eds. Brian H Bornstein and Alan J Tomkins.

Gibson, James L., and Gregory A. Caldeira. 2009a. *Citizens, Courts, and Confirmations: Positivity Theory and the Judgments of the American People*. Princeton, NJ: Princeton University Press.

2009b. "Confirmation Politics and the Legitimacy of the U.S. Supreme Court: Institutional Loyalty, Positivity Bias, and the Alito Nomination." *American Journal of Political Science* 53(1): 139–55.

2009c. "Knowing the Supreme Court? A Reconsideration of Public Ignorance of the High Court." *The Journal of Politics* 71(2): 429–41.

2011. "Has Legal Realism Damaged the Legitimacy of the U.S. Supreme Court?" *Law & Society Review* 45(1): 195–219.

Gibson, James L., Gregory A. Caldeira, and Vanessa A. Baird. 1998. "On the Legitimacy of National High Courts." *American Political Science Review* 92(2): 343–58.

Gibson, James L., Gregory A. Caldeira, and Lester Kenyatta Spence. 2002. "The Role of Theory in Experimental Design: Experiments Without Randomization." *Political Analysis* 10(4): 362–75.

2003a. "Measuring Attitudes toward the United States Supreme Court." *American Journal of Political Science* 47(2): 354–67.

2003b. "The Supreme Court and the US Presidential Election of 2000: Wounds, Self-Inflicted or Otherwise?" *British Journal of Political Science* 33(4): 535–56.

2005. "Why Do People Accept Public Policies They Oppose? Testing Legitimacy Theory with a Survey-Based Experiment." *Political Research Quarterly* 58(2): 187–201.

Gibson, James L., Milton Lodge, and Benjamin Woodson. 2014. "Losing, but Accepting: Legitimacy, Positivity Theory, and the Symbols of Judicial Authority." *Law & Society Review* 48(4): 837–66.

Gibson, James L., and Michael J. Nelson. 2014. "The Legitimacy of the US Supreme Court: Conventional Wisdoms and Recent Challenges Thereto." *Annual Review of Law and Social Science* 10(1): 201–19.

Gibson, James L., and Michael J. Nelson. 2015a. "Can the U.S. Supreme Court Have Too Much Legitimacy?" In *Making Law and Courts Research Relevant: The Normative Implications of Empirical Research*, ed. Brandon L. Bartels and Chris W. Bonneau. New York, NY: Routledge.

Gibson, James L., and Michael J. Nelson. 2015b. "Is the U.S. Supreme Court's Legitimacy Grounded in Performance Satisfaction and Ideology?" *American Journal of Political Science* 59(1): 162–74.

Gibson, James L., and Michael J. Nelson. 2016. "Change in Institutional Support for the US Supreme Court: Is the Court's Legitimacy Imperiled by the Decisions It Makes?" *Public.Opinion Quarterly* 80(3): 622–41.

2017. "Reconsidering Positivity Theory: What Roles Do Politicization, Ideological Disagreement, and Legal Realism Play in Shaping U.S. Supreme Court Legitimacy?" *Journal of Empirical Legal Studies* 14(3): 592–617.

Gibson, James L., Miguel M. Pereira, and Jeffrey Ziegler. 2017. "Updating Supreme Court Legitimacy: Testing the 'Rule, Learn, Update' Model of Political Communication." *American Politics Research* 45(6): 980–1002.

Gigerenzer, Gerd, and Daniel G. Goldstein. 1999. "Betting on One Good Reason: The Take the Best Heuristic." In *Simple Heuristics That Make Us Smart*, ed. Gigerenzer, Gerd and Peter M. Todd. New York, NY: Oxford University Press.

Gillman, Howard. 2002. "How Political Parties Can Use the Courts to Advance Their Agendas: Federal Courts in the United States, 1875–1891." *American Political Science Review* 96(3): 511–24.

Goren, Paul. 2005. "Party Identification and Core Political Values." *American Journal of Political Science* 49(4): 881–96.

2013. *On Voter Competence*. New York, NY: Oxford University Press.

Goren, Paul, Christopher M. Federico, and Miki Caul Kittilson. 2009. "Source Cues, Partisan Identities, and Political Value Expression." *American Journal of Political Science* 53(4): 805–20.

Graham, Matthew, and Milan W. Svolik. 2018. "Democracy in America? Partisanship, Polarization, and the Robustness of Support for Democracy in the United States." *Working Paper*.

Groenendyk, Eric. 2013. *Competing Motives in the Partisan Mind: How Loyalty and Responsiveness Shape Party Identification and Democracy*. New York, NY: Oxford University Press.

Grosskopf, Anke, and Jeffery J. Mondak. 1998. "Do Attitudes toward Specific Supreme Court Decisions Matter? The Impact of Webster and Texas v. Johnson on Public Confidence in the Supreme Court." *Political Research Quarterly* 51(3): 633–54.

Haidt, Jonathan. 2001. "The Emotional Dog and Its Rational Tail: A Social Intuitionist Approach to Moral Judgment." *Psychological Review* 108(4): 814–34.

2012. *The Righteous Mind: Why Good People Are Divided by Politics and Religion*. New York, NY: Vintage.

Hall, Matthew E. K. 2011. *The Nature of Supreme Court Power*. New York, NY: Cambridge University Press.

Hall, Matthew E. K. 2014. "The Semiconstrained Court: Public Opinion, the Separation of Powers, and the U.S. Supreme Court's Fear of Nonimplementation." *American Journal of Political Science* 58(2): 352–66.

Hanmer, Michael J., and Ozan Kerem Kalkan. 2013. "Behind the Curve: Clarifying the Best Approach to Calculating Predicted Probabilities and Marginal Effects from Limited Dependent Variable Models." *American Journal of Political Science* 57(1): 263–77.

Heider, Fritz. 1958. *The Psychology of Interpersonal Relations*. New York, NY: Wiley.

Hetherington, Marc J., and Thomas J. Rudolph. 2015. *Why Washington Won't Work: Polarization, Political Trust, and the Governing Crisis*. Chicago, IL: University of Chicago Press.

Hetherington, Marc J., and Joseph L. Smith. 2007. "Issue Preferences and Evaluations of the U.S. Supreme Court." *Public Opinion Quarterly* 71(1): 40–66.

Hetherington, Marc J., and Elizabeth Suhay. 2011. "Authoritarianism, Threat, and Americans' Support for the War on Terror." *American Journal of Political Science* 55(3): 546–60.

Hetherington, Marc J., and Jonathan D. Weiler. 2009. *Authoritarianism and Polarization in American Politics*. New York, NY: Cambridge University Press.

Hibbing, John R., and Elizabeth Theiss-Morse. 1995. *Congress as Public Enemy: Public Attitudes Toward American Political Institutions*. New York, NY: Cambridge University Press.

2001. "Process Preferences and American Politics: What the People Want Government to Be." *American Political Science Review* 95(1): 145–53.

2002. *Stealth Democracy: Americans' Beliefs about How Government Should Work*. New York, NY: Cambridge University Press.

Higgins, E. Tory. 1996. "Knowledge Activation: Accessibility, Applicability, and Salience." In *Social Psychology: Handbook of Basic Principles*, ed. E. Tory Higgins and Arie W. Kruglanski. New York, NY: Guilford Press.

Hill, Seth J. 2017. "Learning Together Slowly: Bayesian Learning about Political Facts." *The Journal of Politics* 79(4): 1403–18.

Hill, Seth J., and Chris Tausanovitch. 2015. "A Disconnect in Representation? Comparison of Trends in Congressional and Public Polarization." *The Journal of Politics* 77(4): 1058–75.

Hitt, Matthew P., and Kathleen Searles. 2018. "Media Coverage and Public Approval of the U.S. Supreme Court." *Political Communication* 35(4): 566–86.

Hoekstra, Valerie J. 2000. "The Supreme Court and Local Public Opinion." *American Political Science Review* 94(1): 89–100.

2003. *Public Reaction to Supreme Court Decisions*. New York, NY: Cambridge University Press.

Hoekstra, Valerie J., and Jeffrey A. Segal. 1996. "The Shepherding of Local Public Opinion: The Supreme Court and Lamb's Chapel." *The Journal of Politics* 58(4): 1079–1102.

Huckfeldt, Robert, Jeffrey Levine, William Morgan, and John Sprague. 1999. "Accessibility and the Political Utility of Partisan and Ideological Orientations." *American Journal of Political Science* 43(3): 888–911.

Huddy, Leonie, Lilliana Mason, and Lene Aarøe. 2015. "Expressive Partisanship: Campaign Involvement, Political Emotion, and Partisan Identity." *American Political Science Review* 109(1): 1–17.

Iyengar, Shanto, and Kyu S. Hahn. 2009. "Red Media, Blue Media: Evidence of Ideological Selectivity in Media Use." *Journal of Communication* 59(1): 19–39.

Iyengar, Shanto, and Adam Simon. 1993. "News Coverage of the Gulf Crisis and Public Opinion: A Study of Agenda-Setting, Priming, and Framing." *Communication Research* 20(3): 365–83.

Iyengar, Shanto, Gaurav Sood, and Yphtach Lelkes. 2012. "Affect, Not Ideology: A Social Identity Perspective on Polarization." *Public Opinion Quarterly* 76(3): 405–31.

Iyengar, Shanto, and Sean J. Westwood. 2015. "Fear and Loathing across Party Lines: New Evidence on Group Polarization." *American Journal of Political Science* 59(3): 690–707.

Johnston, Christopher D., and Andrew O. Ballard. 2016. "Economists and Public Opinion: Expert Consensus and Economic Policy Judgments." *Journal of Politics* 78(2): 443–56.

Johnston, Christopher D., and Brandon L. Bartels. 2010. "Sensationalism and Sobriety: Differential Media Exposure and Attitudes toward American Courts." *Public Opinion Quarterly* 74(2): 260–85.

Johnston, Christopher D., D. Sunshine Hillygus, and Brandon L. Bartels. 2014. "Ideology, the Affordable Care Act Ruling, and Supreme Court Legitimacy." *Public Opinion Quarterly* 78(4): 963–73.

Johnston, Christopher D., Howard G. Lavine, and Christopher M. Federico. 2017. *Open Versus Closed: Personality, Identity, and the Politics of Redistribution*. New York, NY: Cambridge University Press.

Johnston, Christopher D., and Julie Wronski. 2015. "Personality Dispositions and Political Preferences Across Hard and Easy Issues." *Political Psychology* 36(1): 35–53.

Jost, John T., Jack Glaser, Arie W. Kruglanski, and Frank J. Sulloway. 2003. "Political Conservatism as Motivated Social Cognition." *Psychological Bulletin* 129(3): 339–75.

Jost, John T., Chadly Stern, Nicholas O. Rule, and Joanna Sterling. 2017. "The Politics of Fear: Is There an Ideological Asymmetry in Existential Motivation?" *Social Cognition* 35(4): 324–53.

Kahan, Dan M. et al. 2012. "The Polarizing Impact of Science Literacy and Numeracy on Perceived Climate Change Risks." *Nature Climate Change* 2: 732–35.

2015. "Climate-Science Communication and the Measurement Problem." *Advances in Political Psychology* 36(S1): 1–43.

Kahan, Dan M., Hank Jenkins-Smith, and Donald Braman. 2011. "Cultural Cognition of Scientific Consensus." *Journal of Risk Research* 14(2): 147–74.

Kahan, Dan M., Ellen Peters, Erica Cantrell Dawson, and Paul Slovic. 2017. "Motivated Numeracy and Enlightened Self-Government." *Behavioural Public Policy* 1(1): 54–86.

Kam, Cindy D. 2007. "When Duty Calls, Do Citizens Answer?" *The Journal of Politics* 69(1): 17–29.

Katz, Ellis. 1965. "Patterns of Compliance with the Schempp Decision." *Journal of Public Law* 14(2): 396–408.

Kavanaugh, Brett M. 2017. "Keynote Address: Two Challenges for the Judge as Umpire: Statutory Ambiguity and Constitutional Exceptions." *Notre Dame Law Review* 92(5): 1907–19.

Key, Jr., V. O. 1961. *Public Opinion and American Democracy*. New York, NY: Alfred A. Knopf.

Kinder, Donald R., and Nathan P. Kalmoe. 2017. *Neither Liberal nor Conservative: Ideological Innocence in the American Public*. Chicago, IL: University of Chicago Press.

Klar, Samara. 2014. "Partisanship in a Social Setting." *American Journal of Political Science* 58(3): 687–704.

Klar, Samara, and Yanna Krupnikov. 2016. *Independent Politics: How American Disdain for Parties Leads to Political Inaction*. New York, NY: Cambridge University Press.

Kramer, Larry D. 2001. "Foreword: We the Court." *Harvard Law Review* 115(1): 5–169.

2004. *The People Themselves: Popular Constitutionalism and Judicial Review*. New York, NY: Oxford University Press.

Krehbiel, Keith. 1998. *Pivotal Politics: A Theory of U.S. Lawmaking*. Chicago, IL: University of Chicago Press.

Kritzer, Herbert M. 2001. "The Impact of Bush v. Gore on Public Perceptions and Knowledge of Supreme Court." *Judicature* 85(1): 32–38.

Kruglanski, Arie W. 1989. "The Psychology of Being 'Right': The Problem of Accuracy in Social Perception and Cognition." *Psychological Bulletin* 106(3): 395–409.

Kunda, Ziva. 1990. "The Case for Motivated Reasoning." *Psychological Bulletin* 108(3): 480–98.

1999. *Social Cognition: Making Sense of People*. Cambridge, MA: MIT Press.

Lakoff, George. 2016. *Moral Politics: How Liberals and Conservatives Think, Third Edition*. Chicago, IL: University of Chicago Press.

Landau, Mark J. et al. 2004. "Deliver Us from Evil: The Effects of Mortality Salience and Reminders of 9/11 on Support for President George W. Bush." *Personality and Social Psychology Bulletin* 30(9): 1136–50.

Lavine, Howard G., Christopher D. Johnston, and Marco R. Steenbergen. 2012. *The Ambivalent Partisan: How Critical Loyalty Promotes Democracy*. New York, NY: Oxford University Press.

Layman, Geoffrey. 2001. *The Great Divide: Religious and Cultural Conflict in American Party Politics*. New York, NY: Columbia University Press.

Leeper, Thomas J., and Rune Slothuus. 2014. "Political Parties, Motivated Reasoning, and Public Opinion Formation." *Political Psychology* 35(S1): 129–56.

Lelkes, Yphtach. 2016. "Mass Polarization: Manifestations and Measurements." *Public Opinion Quarterly* 80(S1): 392–410.

Lelkes, Yphtach, and Sean J. Westwood. 2017. "The Limits of Partisan Prejudice." *The Journal of Politics* 79(2): 485–501.

Lenz, Gabriel S. 2012. *Follow the Leader? How Voters Respond to Politicians' Policies and Performance*. Chicago, IL: University of Chicago Press.

Lerner, Jennifer S., and Philip E. Tetlock. 1999. "Accounting for the Effects of Accountability." *Psychological Bulletin* 125(2): 255–75.

Levendusky, Matthew. 2009. *The Partisan Sort: How Liberals Became Democrats and Conservatives Became Republicans*. Chicago, IL: University of Chicago Press.

Levi, Margaret, Audrey Sacks, and Tom Tyler. 2009. "Conceptualizing Legitimacy, Measuring Legitimating Beliefs." *American Behavioral Scientist* 53(3): 354–75.

Levitsky, Steven, and Daniel Ziblatt. 2018. *How Democracies Die*. New York, NY: Crown Publishing.

Little, Andrew T. 2019. "The Distortion of Related Beliefs." *American Journal of Political Science* 63(3): 675–89.

Lodge, Milton, and Charles S. Taber. 2013. *The Rationalizing Voter*. New York, NY: Cambridge University Press.

Lopez, Jesse, and D. Sunshine Hillygus. 2018. "Why So Serious?: Survey Trolls and Misinformation." *Working Paper*.

Malhotra, Neil, and Stephen A. Jessee. 2014. "Ideological Proximity and Support for The Supreme Court." *Political Behavior* 36(4): 817–46.

Marcus, George E., John L. Sullivan, Elizabeth Theiss-Morse, and Sandra L. Wood. 1995. *With Malice Toward Some: How People Make Civil Liberties Judgments*. New York, NY: Cambridge University Press.

Mark, Alyx, and Michael A. Zilis. 2018. "The Conditional Effectiveness of Legislative Threats: How Court Curbing Alters the Behavior of (Some) Supreme Court Justices." *Political Research Quarterly*: (Forthcoming).

Marshall, Thomas R. 1989. *Public Opinion and the Supreme Court*. Boston, MA: Unwin Hyman.

2008. *Public Opinion and the Rehnquist Court*. Albany, NY: State University of New York Press.

Mason, Lilliana. 2015. "'I Disrespectfully Agree': The Differential Effects of Partisan Sorting on Social and Issue Polarization." *American Journal of Political Science* 59(1): 128–45.

2018. *Uncivil Agreement: How Politics Became Our Identity*. Chicago, IL: University of Chicago Press.

McCarty, Nolan, Keith T. Poole, and Howard Rosenthal. 2006. *Polarized America: The Dance of Ideology and Unequal Riches*. Cambridge, MA: MIT Press.

McClosky, Herbert. 1964. "Consensus and Ideology in American Politics." *American Political Science Review* 58(2): 361–82.

McGuire, Kevin T. 2009. "Public Schools, Religious Establishments, and the U.S. Supreme Court: An Examination of Policy Compliance." *American Politics Research* 37(1): 50–74.

McGuire, Kevin T., and James A. Stimson. 2004. "The Least Dangerous Branch Revisited: New Evidence on Supreme Court Responsiveness to Public Preferences." *Journal of Politics* 66(4): 1018–35.

Merolla, Jennifer L., and Elizabeth J. Zechmeister. 2009. "Terrorist Threat, Leadership, and the Vote: Evidence from Three Experiments." *Political Behavior* 31(4): 575.

Mishler, William, and Reginald S. Sheehan. 1993. "The Supreme Court as a Countermajoritarian Institution? The Impact of Public Opinion on Supreme Court Decisions." *American Political Science Review* 87(1): 87–101.

1996. "Public Opinion, the Attitudinal Model, and Supreme Court Decision Making: A Micro-Analytic Perspective." *The Journal of Politics* 58(1): 169–200.

Mondak, Jeffery J. 1990. "Perceived Legitimacy of Supreme Court Decisions: Three Functions of Source Credibility." *Political Behavior* 12(4): 363–84.

1991. "Substantive and Procedural Aspects of Supreme Court Decisions as Determinants of Institutional Approval." *American Politics Quarterly* 19(2): 174–88.

1992. "Institutional Legitimacy, Policy Legitimacy, and the Supreme Court." *American Politics Quarterly* 20(4): 457–77.

1993. "Institutional Legitimacy and Procedural Justice: Reexamining the Question of Causality." *Law & Society Review* 27(3): 599–608.

1994. "Policy Legitimacy and the Supreme Court: The Sources and Contexts of Legitimation." *Political Research Quarterly* 47(3): 675–92.

Mondak, Jeffery J., and Shannon Ishiyama Smithey. 1997. "The Dynamics of Public Support for the Supreme Court." *Journal of Politics* 59(4): 1114–42.

Morton, Rebecca B., and Kenneth C. Williams. 2010. *Experimental Political Science and the Study of Causality: From Nature to the Lab*. New York, NY: Cambridge University Press.

Murphy, Walter F. 1962. *Congress and the Court*. Chicago, IL: University of Chicago Press.

Murphy, Walter F., and Joseph Tanenhaus. 1968. "Public Opinion and the United States Supreme Court: Mapping of Some Prerequisites for Court Legitimation of Regime Changes." *Law & Society Review* 2(3): 357–84.

Mutz, Diana C. 1998. *Impersonal Influence: How Perceptions of Mass Collectives Affect Political Attitudes*. New York, NY: Cambridge University Press.

2006. *Hearing the Other Side: Deliberative Versus Participatory Democracy*. New York, NY: Cambridge University Press.

Nagel, Jack H. 1975. *The Descriptive Analysis of Power*. New Haven, CT: Yale University Press.

Nagel, Stuart S. 1965. "Court-Curbing Periods in American History." *Vanderbilt Law Review* 18(3): 925–44.

Nelson, Michael J., and James L. Gibson. 2017. "Testing Spatial Models of Politics: The Perils of Subtraction-Based Measures of Subjective Ideological Proximity." *Working Paper*.

Nelson, Michael J., and Steven S. Smith. 2015. "Change and Stability in the U.S. Supreme Court's Legitimacy." *Unpublished Manuscript*.

Nelson, Michael J., and Alicia Uribe-McGuire. 2017. "Opportunity and Overrides: The Effect of Institutional Public Support on Congressional Overrides of Supreme Court Decisions." *Political Research Quarterly* 70(3): 632–43.

Nelson, Thomas E., Rosalee A. Clawson, and Zoe M. Oxley. 1997. "Media Framing of a Civil Liberties Conflict and Its Effect on Tolerance." *American Political Science Review* 91(3): 567–83.

Nicholson, Stephen P., and Thomas G. Hansford. 2014. "Partisans in Robes: Party Cues and Public Acceptance of Supreme Court Decisions." *American Journal of Political Science* 58(3): 620–36.

Nicholson, Stephen P., and Robert M. Howard. 2003. "Framing Support for the Supreme Court in the Aftermath of Bush v. Gore." *Journal of Politics* 65(3): 676–95.

Norpoth, Helmut, and Jeffrey A. Segal. 1994. "Popular Influence on Supreme Court Decisions." *American Political Science Review* 88(3): 711–16.

Patric, Gordon. 1957. "The Impact of a Court Decision: Aftermath of the McCollum Case." *Journal of Public Law* 6(2): 455–64.

Peffley, Mark, Marc L. Hutchison, and Michal Shamir. 2015. "The Impact of Persistent Terrorism on Political Tolerance: Israel, 1980 to 2011." *American Political Science Review* 109(4): 817–32.

Peffley, Mark, Pia Knigge, and Jon Hurwitz. 2001. "A Multiple Values Model of Political Tolerance." *Political Research Quarterly* 54(2): 379–406.

Petersen, Michael, Rune Slothuus, Rune Stubager, and Lise Togeby. 2011. "Freedom for All? The Strength and Limits of Political Tolerance." *British Journal of Political Science* 41(3): 581–97.

Pritchett, C. Herman. 1961. *Congress versus the Supreme Court, 1957–1960*. Minneapolis, MN: University of Minnesota Press.

Prothro, James W., and Charles M. Grigg. 1960. "Fundamental Principles of Democracy: Bases of Agreement and Disagreement." *The Journal of Politics* 22(2): 276–94.

Ramirez, Mark D. 2008. "Procedural Perceptions and Support for the U.S. Supreme Court." *Political Psychology* 29(5): 675–98.

Ramseyer, J. Mark. 1994. "The Puzzling (In)Dependence of Courts: A Comparative Approach." *The Journal of Legal Studies* 23(2): 721–47.

Roccas, Sonia, Lilach Sagiv, Shalom H. Schwartz, and Ariel Knafo. 2002. "The Big Five Personality Factors and Personal Values." *Personality and Social Psychology Bulletin* 28(6): 789–801.

Rogers, James R. 2001. "Information and Judicial Review: A Signaling Game of Legislative-Judicial Interaction." *American Journal of Political Science* 45(1): 84–99.

Rosenberg, Gerald N. 1992. "Judicial Independence and the Reality of Political Power." *The Review of Politics* 54(03): 369–98.

Salamone, Michael F. 2014. "Judicial Consensus and Public Opinion: Conditional Response to Supreme Court Majority Size." *Political Research Quarterly* 67(2): 320–34.

2018. *Perceptions of a Polarized Court: How Division among Justices Shapes the Supreme Court's Public Image*. Philadelphia, PA: Temple University Press.

Scheb, John M., and William Lyons. 2000. "The Myth of Legality and Public Evaluation of the Supreme Court." *Social Science Quarterly* 81(4): 928–40.

2001. "Judicial Behavior and Public Opinion: Popular Expectations Regarding the Factors That Influence Supreme Court Decisions." *Political Behavior* 23(2): 181–94.

Schuessler, Alexander A. 2000. *A Logic of Expressive Choice*. Princeton, NJ: Princeton University Press.

Segal, Jeffrey A., and Harold J. Spaeth. 2002. *The Supreme Court and the Attitudinal Model Revisited*. New York, NY: Cambridge University Press.

Segal, Jeffrey A., Chad Westerland, and Stefanie A. Lindquist. 2011. "Congress, the Supreme Court, and Judicial Review: Testing a Constitutional Separation of Powers Model." *American Journal of Political Science* 55(1): 89–104.

Sen, Maya. 2017. "How Political Signals Affect Public Support for Judicial Nominations." *Political Research Quarterly* 70(2): 374–93.

Simon, Dan, and Nicholas Scurich. 2011. "Lay Judgments of Judicial Decision Making." *Journal of Empirical Legal Studies* 8(4): 709–27.

Sinclair, Betsy. 2012. *The Social Citizen: Peer Networks and Political Behavior*. Chicago, IL: University of Chicago Press.

Singer, Matthew. 2018. "Delegating Away Democracy: How Good Representation and Policy Successes Can Undermine Democratic Legitimacy." *Comparative Political Studies* 51(13): 1754–88.

Slotnick, Elliot E., and Jennifer A. Segal. 1998. *Television News and the Supreme Court: All the News That's Fit to Air?* New York, NY: Cambridge University Press.

Slothuus, Rune, and Claes H. de Vreese. 2010. "Political Parties, Motivated Reasoning, and Issue Framing Effects." *The Journal of Politics* 72(3): 630–45.

Solberg, Rorie Spill, and Eric N. Waltenburg. 2014. *The Media, the Court, and the Misrepresentation: The New Myth of the Court*. New York, NY: Routledge.

Spill, Rorie L., and Zoe M. Oxley. 2003. "Philosopher Kings or Political Actors? How the Media Portray the Supreme Court." *Judicature* 87(1): 22–29.

Staton, Jeffrey K. 2010. *Judicial Power and Strategic Communication in Mexico*. New York, NY: Cambridge University Press.

Stephenson, Matthew C. 2004. "Court of Public Opinion: Government Accountability and Judicial Independence." *Journal of Law, Economics, & Organization* 20(2): 379–99.

Stimson, James A., Michael B. Mackuen, and Robert S. Erikson. 1995. "Dynamic Representation." *American Political Science Review* 89(3): 543–65.

Stouffer, Samuel Andrew. 1955. *Communism, Conformity, and Civil Liberties: A Cross-Section of the Nation Speaks Its Mind*. New York, NY: Doubleday.

Stoutenborough, James W., Donald P. Haider-Markel, and Mahalley D. Allen. 2006. "Reassessing the Impact of Supreme Court Decisions on Public Opinion: Gay Civil Rights Cases." *Political Research Quarterly* 59(3): 419–33.

Strother, Logan. 2017. "How Expected Political and Legal Impact Drive Media Coverage of Supreme Court Cases." *Political Communication* 34(4): 571–89.

Strother, Logan, and Shana Gadarian. 2019. "The Supreme Court in a Polarized Era: Is Legitimacy at Risk?" *Working Paper*.

Stumpf, Harry P. 1965. "Congressional Response to Supreme Court Rulings: The Interaction of Law and Politics." *Journal of Public Law* 14(2): 377–95.

Sullivan, John L., James Piereson, and George E. Marcus. 1982. *Political Tolerance and American Democracy*. Chicago, IL: University of Chicago Press.

Sunshine, Jason, and Tom R. Tyler. 2003. "The Role of Procedural Justice and Legitimacy in Shaping Public Support for Policing." *Law & Society Review* 37(3): 513–48.

Svolik, Milan W. 2018. "When Polarization Trumps Civic Virtue: Partisan Conflict and the Subversion of Democracy by Incumbents." *Working Paper*.

Taber, Charles S., and Milton Lodge. 2006. "Motivated Skepticism in the Evaluation of Political Beliefs." *American Journal of Political Science* 50(3): 755–69.

Tajfel, Henri, and John Turner. 1979. "An Integrative Theory of Intergroup Conflict." In *The Social Psychology of Intergroup Relations*, ed. William G. Austin and Stephen Worchel. Monterey, CA: Wadsworth.

Tesler, Michael. 2015. "Priming Predispositions and Changing Policy Positions: An Account of When Mass Opinion Is Primed or Changed." *American Journal of Political Science* 59(4): 806–24.

Treanor, William Michael. 2005. "Judicial Review before 'Marbury.'" *Stanford Law Review* 58(2): 455–562.

Treier, Shawn, and D. Sunshine Hillygus. 2009. "The Nature of Political Ideology in the Contemporary Electorate." *Public Opinion Quarterly* 73(4): 679–703.

Tsebelis, George. 2002. *Veto Players: How Political Institutions Work*. Princeton, NJ: Princeton University Press.

Tushnet, Mark. 1999. *Taking the Constitution Away from the Courts*. Princeton, NJ: Princeton University Press.

Tyler, Tom R. 1994. "Governing amid Diversity: The Effect of Fair Decisionmaking Procedures on the Legitimacy of Government." *Law & Society Review* 28(4): 809–32.

2006a. "Psychological Perspectives on Legitimacy and Legitimation." *Annual Review of Psychology* 57(1): 375–400.

2006b. *Why People Obey the Law*. Princeton, NJ: Princeton University Press.

Tyler, Tom R., and Kenneth Rasinski. 1991. "Procedural Justice, Institutional Legitimacy, and the Acceptance of Unpopular U.S. Supreme Court Decisions: A Reply to Gibson." *Law & Society Review* 25(3): 621–30.

Uhlmann, Eric Luis, T. Andrew Poehlman, and John A. Bargh. 2009. "American Moral Exceptionalism." In *Social and Psychological Bases of Ideology and System Justification*, eds. Aaron C. Kay, John T. Jost, and Hulda Thorisdottir. New York, NY: Oxford University Press.

Vanberg, Georg. 2001. "Legislative-Judicial Relations: A Game-Theoretic Approach to Constitutional Review." *American Journal of Political Science* 45(2): 346–61.

2005. *The Politics of Constitutional Review in Germany*. New York, NY: Cambridge University Press.

2015. "Constitutional Courts in Comparative Perspective: A Theoretical Assessment." *Annual Review of Political Science* 18(1): 167–85.

Vasilopoulos, Pavlos, George E. Marcus, and Martial Foucault. 2018. "Emotional Responses to the Charlie Hebdo Attacks: Addressing the Authoritarianism Puzzle." *Political Psychology* 39(3): 557–75.

Webster, Donna M., Linda Richter, and Arie W. Kruglanski. 1996. "On Leaping to Conclusions When Feeling Tired: Mental Fatigue Effects on Impressional Primacy." *Journal of Experimental Social Psychology* 32(2): 181–95.

Webster, Steven W., and Alan I. Abramowitz. 2017. "The Ideological Foundations of Affective Polarization in the U.S. Electorate." *American Politics Research* 45(4): 621–47.

Whittington, Keith E. 2005. "'Interpose Your Friendly Hand': Political Supports for the Exercise of Judicial Review by the United States Supreme Court." *American Political Science Review* 99(4): 583–96.

2007. *Political Foundations of Judicial Supremacy: The Presidency, the Supreme Court, and Constitutional Leadership in U.S. History*. Princeton, NJ: Princeton University Press.

Woodson, Benjamin. 2015. "Politicization and the Two Modes of Evaluating Judicial Decisions." *Journal of Law and Courts* 3(2): 193–221.

2018. "The Dynamics of Legitimacy Change for the U.S. Supreme Court." *Justice System Journal* 39(1): 75–94.

2019. "The Causes of the Legitimacy-Conferring and Republican Schoolmaster Capabilities of Courts." *Journal of Law and Courts* 7(2): 281–303.

Zaller, John, and Stanley Feldman. 1992. "A Simple Theory of the Survey Response: Answering Questions versus Revealing Preferences." *American Journal of Political Science* 36(3): 579–616.

Zaller, John R. 1992. *The Nature and Origins of Mass Opinion*. New York, NY: Cambridge University Press.

Zilis, Michael A. 2015. *The Limits of Legitimacy: Dissenting Opinions, Media Coverage, and Public Responses to Supreme Court Decisions*. Ann Arbor, MI: University of Michigan Press.

2018. "Minority Groups and Judicial Legitimacy: Group Affect and the Incentives for Judicial Responsiveness." *Political Research Quarterly* 71(2): 270–83.

Zink, James R., James F. Spriggs, and John T. Scott. 2009. "Courting the Public: The Influence of Decision Attributes on Individuals' Views of Court Opinions." *Journal of Politics* 71(3): 909–25.

Index